HOMES, CITIES AND NEIGHBOURHOODS

Homes, Cities and Neighbourhoods

Planning and the Residential Landscapes of Modern Britain

BARRY GOODCHILD
Sheffield Hallam University, UK

ASHGATE

Published by
Ashgate Publishing Limited
Gower House
Croft Road
Aldershot
Hampshire GU11 3HR
England

Ashgate Publishing Company
Suite 420
101 Cherry Street
Burlington, VT 05401-4405
USA

Ashgate website: http://www.ashgate.com

British Library Cataloguing in Publication Data
Goodchild, Barry
  Homes, cities and neighbourhoods : planning and the
  residential landscapes of modern Britain
  1. City planning - Great Britain - History 2. Housing
  policy - Great Britain - History 3. Neighbourhood - Great
  Britain - History 4. Urban landscape architecture - Great
  Britain - History
  I. Title
  307.1'216

Library of Congress Cataloging-in-Publication Data
Goodchild, Barry.
  Homes, cities and neighbourhoods : planning and the residential landscapes of modern
  Britain / by Barry Goodchild.
      p. cm.
  Includes bibliographical references and index.
  ISBN 978-0-7546-7125-1
  1. City planning--Great Britain--History. 2. Housing policy--Great Britain--History. 3.
  Neighborhoods--Great Britain--History. 4. Urban landscape architecture--Great Britain--
  History. I. Title.

  HT169.G7G64 2008
  307.1'2160941--dc22

                                                                              2008013458

ISBN 978-0-7546-7125-1

Mixed Sources
Product group from well-managed
forests and other controlled sources
www.fsc.org Cert no. SGS-COC-2482
© 1996 Forest Stewardship Council

Printed and bound in Great Britain by
TJ International Ltd, Padstow, Cornwall

Contents

List of Tables

List of Plates

Preface

I have written this book out of a long-standing interest in the subject and an awareness of the limitations of a typical academic article. The contents are a product of reflection over many years of research, reading, teaching and discussions with many different people. However, the text itself is mostly a product of writing and rewriting from the summer of 2006 onwards. Huw Thomas, Jim Kemeny, Aimee Ambrose, Paul Hickman, Alan Murie and Chris Couch read earlier drafts at successive stages of completion. I am grateful for their comments.

The material provides an account to December 2007. The account is about Britain as a whole with selective international comparisons. In practice, the weight of available information favours England rather than Wales or Scotland.

PART A
Introduction

Chapter 1

The Aims and Scope

Let us imagine a typical urban area in Britain. This urban area is an imaginary place, but one that includes a cross-section of the conditions and types of neighbourhood found in all British cities. It has neighbourhoods of high housing demand and a vibrant city centre. Equally, it has zones of industrial dereliction, depressed house prices and social deprivation. Likewise, this urban area possesses a full range of house types. It possesses nineteenth-century terraces and tenements, low density residential suburbs of varied dates, inner city flats that were built by the local council and privately developed city centre flats.

What are the processes that have created the residential landscapes of this urban area? How can one classify the main periods in their formation? What are the distinctive processes at work at present compared to say 40 or 50 years ago? What has been the role of planning? What is its likely, continuing role? What are the main contemporary planning issues? What are the lessons for practitioners and those interested in practice?

Such are the questions that concern this study. Though the account includes many examples, the aim is not to provide a detailed account of a specific place or city. Instead the aim is to draw out general tendencies and issues in the history of planning and urban development. Likewise, the aim is not to provide specific recommendations or examples of good practice, but to draw out the broad lessons. Put slightly differently, the aim is to provide a contemporary history of urban planning through a focus on housing. A contemporary history is one that goes beyond narratives and chronology to look at contemporary issues and the dynamics of change.

A contemporary history of residential landscapes focuses on housing as 'urbanism'. This does not mean 'new urbanism', which is a prescriptive method of urban design and is only a small part of the subject matter. Instead, the focus is on urbanism understood as a hybrid field of study between urban design, urban geography and urban planning. Housing as urbanism is concerned with living conditions, with the physical form of housing, with the management of urban growth and sometimes with the management of urban decline.

The Aims

A brief review of the existing literature allows the aims to be stated in more detail as follows.

In Relation to Planning

Providing a new account and a new history of urban planning is the first aim. Planning and housing are mutually interdependent. Planning in the sense of a future-oriented style of intervention, helps determine the form of housing and the future of residential areas. Conversely, public concerns about affordable good quality housing help determine planning policy. Planning involves an assessment of future demands and needs in relation to urban development. In relation to land take and overall costs, housing and its related infrastructure provide the main components of such assessments.

The close links between housing and planning do not mean an untroubled relationship. From the first planning legislation, the Housing, Town Planning, Etc. Act, 1909 to the present, the relationship has been characterised by conflicts about policy aims and priorities. Housing and planning have evolved together in response to external political and economic changes, but not in a coherent, co-ordinated way. Each decade has had its orthodoxy, each has had its voices of dissent and each has typically been characterised by a multitude of reports and policy recommendations that impinge on both housing and planning in different ways.

A series of reports illustrate the range of sometimes conflicting policy issues that have affected planning and housing.

- The report of the Urban Task Force *Towards an Urban Renaissance* has promoted urban design in planning, that is to say planning as place making rather than an exercise in land use allocation and has, in this context, placed more emphasis on high density new build, on urban intensification and the renewal of run down neighbourhoods (UTC 1999).
- The *Sustainable Communities* policy plan has argued for integrated planning and housing policies that might facilitate a combination of house building in growth areas and neighbourhood renewal in regions in decline. Again the implication is that planning should conceive of housing in terms of places rather than the simple allocation of land use (ODPM 2003b).
- Finally the Barker Review (2004) of house prices and affordability, a recent policy statement *Homes for the Future* (DCLG 2007c) and a further review of house building delivery by Calcutt (2007) have reasserted the significance of earlier twentieth-century concerns with house completion numbers and the quality of new housing.

The reports mostly deal with England. Since the devolution of powers in 1999, policy and policy debates in Scotland and Wales have largely run in parallel, but with increasing differences in detail. The issues raised in the various reports are, in any case, not unique to Britain. They are likely to arise in any relatively wealthy country characterised by a popular commitment to housing as a focus for consumption; by increasing, but uneven pressure pressures on land resources and property markets; and by an increased concern with environmental protection in all its forms.

Put slightly differently, planning for housing in Britain offers a case study of the issues that arise in planning for sustainable development. Current understandings of sustainable development date from *Our Common Future* by the World Commission on Environment and Development (1987) and the subsequent international policy commitments made at the United Nations Earth Summit of 1992. Sustainable development is an international concept, one that has received numerous and repeated references at virtually all levels of planning from the local to the global.

Yet concepts of sustainable development are also contested. Cautious, pragmatic definitions are mostly about balancing different aspects of policy. The British government's definition of 'sustainable communities' refers, for example, to the need to 'balance and integrate the social, economic and environmental components' of community life.[1] In contrast, other definitions adopt a market-critical, green perspective. Sustainable development means, in this context, a process of developing land, cities and communities in a way that protects biodiversity, promotes human health and minimises the use of finite resources. A recent report, *The Urban Environment* by the Royal Commission on Environmental Pollution (2007), implicitly adopts such a green perspective.

Moreover, the green movement possesses another related division. On one hand, eco-centric or deep green positions treat lifestyle changes as essential to sustainable development. For example, they would argue that affluent individuals and families should minimise the level of winter heating in the home and reduce the level of personal travelling by car and aeroplane. On the other, techno-centric or light green positions assume a continuation of existing lifestyles and attempt to work out technological solutions, including solutions based on redesigning and re-equipping the built environment.

In Britain, the relationship between housing and planning has largely been examined through different specialised accounts. Various examples can be cited – the role of the statutory town planning system (Gallent and Tewdr-Jones 2007); the design of the external environment in housing (Carmona 2001; Edwards 1981); and finally the process of land development (Adam and Watkins 2002, Golland and Blake, eds., 2004). All these different accounts need to be brought together, updated and related to concepts of neighbourhood and community, as is explicit in the Sustainable Communities policy plan. In addition, the various specialist accounts need to be discussed in the context of general studies of planning theory and the history of planning. *Planning and Urban Change* by Ward (2004) is the best-known, recently published history of planning in Britain. Its housing content consists of a series of fragments – the early, pre-1919 garden city movement, the post1945 neighbourhood and the redevelopment projects of the 1950s and 1960s.

Conceptualising the history of planning means in turn seeking a balance between optimism and pessimism, modernism and postmodernism. One obvious trap is to fall into the overoptimistic, grand narratives of progress that were commonplace in the 1950s and 1960s and have been criticised by Sandercock (1998) amongst others. These were histories that saw planning and allied forms of urban design as means of promoting modernity in the built environment and progress in urban management. Examples include Ashworth's *The Genesis of Modern British Town Planning* (1954), for many years, considered the definitive history of the subject; *Public Authority Housing* by Cleeve Barr (1958); and *Homes, Towns and Traffic* by Tetlow and Goss (1965). An extract from the latter summarises the assumptions of this type of optimistic account. 'No one', declared Tetlow and Goss (ibid., 19), 'should doubt the need for a more scientific basis and greater technical competence in reshaping our habitat.' The other, opposing trap is to adopt an exclusive concern with postmodern styles of planning, understood as a pluralist reaction against the modern. Postmodernism, though important, is one, but not the only interpretation of the contemporary world. Instead, a contemporary history must attempt to understand contemporary processes of change whilst simultaneously revealing aspects of continuity with the past.

In Relation to Housing Studies

The second, but no less important aim is to update and extend the history of housing, including relevant aspects of social history. Burnett's *A Social History of Housing*, first published in 1978 and then in a second edition in 1986, continues to provide the most widely cited example of a history of house building and design. Much of its content concerns the nineteenth century, however and the narrative stops in the early 1980s. In any case, updating the history of housing involves more than merely inserting the events of the past few years. Updating also requires a shift in emphasis towards the neighbourhood and, in addition, towards urban design, as is recognised in recent policy shifts represented by the Urban Renaissance policy agenda and the Sustainable Communities policy plan.

Otherwise, housing history and more generally housing studies are either about housing policy, tenure and management or about specific types of housing or episodes in the history of design. The latter, more specific accounts are numerous and diverse. Sim (1993) has covered the history of design in social housing, including contemporary issues but stops towards the end of the 1980s. Rodger (1989) has summarised the origins of nineteenth-century house types, without following subsequent twentieth-century attitudes and policies towards these house types. Swenarton (1981) has examined in detail the rationale for the Homes for Heroes building programme that started in 1919 and the design of the estates and houses built as part of the programme. Others have examined the history of particular house types notably the high rise flat (Sutcliffe, ed., 1974; Glendinning and Muthesius 1994), the bungalow (King 1984) and the English terrace (Muthesius 1982). The history of housing design and house types is, of course, not the same as the history of the urban landscape or of urban development. These are histories of elements and have to be synthesised and brought together.

Housing and the Environment: A New Agenda by Bhatti et al. (1994) is an exception in housing studies. It deals with sustainable development and advocates a new approach to housing policy concerned with 'futurity' (the principle of sustainable development), 'environment' (environmental impact), equity (countering environmental poverty) and 'participation' (involving people in decision-making). *Housing and the Environment* is not a systematic analysis of sustainable development, however in relation to housing and it does not provide analysis of the role of planning as a distinctive form of decision-making. A similar omission applies to the present author's similarly named *Housing and the Urban Environment* (Goodchild 1997). This latter provides an analysis of different aspects of housing quality, the regulation of housing and planning. It does not analyse the characteristics of the planning process and, in addition, does not attempt to chart processes of change, as is the aim of the present study.

A later article by Brown and Bhatti (2003) reflects on the subsequent experience of 'housing and the environment'. The authors note that interest in the environment amongst housing practitioners grew in the 1990s, but that this was not reflected in the growth of relevant theory. As an academic field, housing studies has mostly arisen from the practical concerns of teaching professional housing management or from undertaking contract research. The focus has been on a succession of substantive social problems (homelessness, poor condition, affordability, low demand) or implementation issues (finance, costs and administrative coordination). The assumption has been that somehow sustainability could be incorporated into these conventional housing issues.

Recent research into the use of the home has filled in some of the gaps. It is possible to show, for example, that domestic energy consumption depends on a mutually supportive, three-way interaction between daily routines, a largely taken-for-granted technological infrastructure such as washing machines and showers and dominant cultural conceptions of comfort, cleanliness and convenience (Shove 2003; Owens and Driffill 2006). From at least the middle of the nineteenth century, modernity in housing design and in domestic equipment has been about a search for more space, more privacy, more convenience and more control over room temperatures and this has led to a constant ratcheting up of domestic energy consumption in a way that is difficult to reverse.

Even so, theorising about housing and the environment is not straightforward. In part, as Bhatti (1994, 27-30) has implicitly recognised, the problem is that theorising about housing and the environment requires an exceptionally broad view. The home, for example, is a passive container. It is impossible to construct a history of the home, without invoking changes in culture, changes in the role of women, changes in domestic technology, changes in architecture, changes in the wider urban landscape, changes in housing policy and so on.

More importantly still, theorising remains hindered by disjunctures in practice. The relation between housing and the environment is not harmonious. As stated in the title of a recent report, much of the debate is about *Reducing the environmental impact of housing* (Palmer et al. 2006). The same issue arises in the teaching of town planning to housing students or practitioners. It is easy to see planning as merely an external bureaucratic constraint on development projects and as otherwise largely irrelevant. The tension is deeper than this. The tension is between different aims of planning and, more generally, between housing and environmental policy.

Looking at housing within a specific social scientific disciplinary focus, such as sociology or economics offers a more theoretically informed and less isolated understanding than a practice or policy based account, as Kemeny (1992) in particular has argued. Though housing is important in its own right, it is also important as a means of illuminating broader social processes. Looking at housing from the perspective of planning, including planning theory, itself offers a disciplinary perspective that can illustrate broader processes whilst also dealing with the conflicting economic, social and environmental pressures. Planning, in this context, may be understood as a method of allocating scarce resources – a method that stands in contrast to but also complements the market. Town planning is a specific case of planning, dealing with the allocation of land and property resources, but is not the only case.

Planning theory is, in the most general terms, an exercise in conceptualising the link between knowledge and organised action (Friedmann and Hudson 1974). It is more a theory of the application of knowledge rather than a typical social theory that deals, for example, with the structure of society. Care must, nevertheless, be exercised in tying theory to practice in a way that avoids excessive abstraction. For this reason, theory is best regarded as growing out of history and out of interpretations of practice, including interpretations of the development process, rather than *vice versa*. In contemporary Britain and most other economically advanced countries, planning theory is a means of reflecting on the formulation and application of policies to places and spaces. It covers both procedural (decision-making, administrative and legal) and substantial (spatial and design oriented) issues (Yiftachel 2001). It is therefore particularly well suited to reflecting on processes of urban regeneration and urban development.

A Summary of the Contents

The history of planning and housing can be summarised as follows. In relation to planning, the movement is from a concern with blueprints, with the replacement of the industrial city in its totality and with standardised solutions to a process more concerned with urban improvement, with cultural and social diversity and with market trends. The movement is also one, over the past 20 years, of a search for a new direction in planning, largely based on concepts of environmental sustainability and the compact city. In relation to housing policy, the movement is from a conception of the home as an object, measured in terms of standards and building programmes to the home as part of a neighbourhood.

In part, the forces for historical change are internal to the style of intervention. For example, a housing policy geared up to production and replacement and little else, as was the emphasis from about 1920 to 1970, was always likely to run into problems, given the cost and limited scale of house building in relation to the existing stock. Likewise, modern town planning policy, especially the plans and policies prepared during the 1940s assumed a degree of certainty that was impossible to sustain in practice.

In addition, housing, planning and the process of urban development have changed in response to broader forces. Some of these forces concern the economy (for example the decline of manufacturing) or technology (the growth of the motor car). Others are environmental and social and refer to the impact of affluence and of ethnic and economic divisions. Another, less obvious change concerns the changing security concerns of the state. For example, mass war, such as practiced in the early and mid twentieth century, promoted collective state solutions in a way that has not always persisted in peacetime.

At the same time various continuities are apparent – for example, the existence of a mixed public/ private process of urban development, albeit with a period of publicly-led development in the immediate aftermath of World Wars I and II; the persistence of concerns with environmental health and well-being in various forms, from overcrowding and lack of light before 1914 to contemporary concerns with traffic, noise and antisocial behaviour; and, finally, the persistence of social and neighbourhood inequalities.

Introduction and Structure

There are four main sections, Parts A, B, C and D, comprising in turn the introduction (A), the main body of the narrative (Parts B and C) and the conclusions (D).

Part B *Planning, markets and the industrial city, 1900-1980* proceeds from the material qualities of the residential landscape to a consideration of the idea of planning and finally to an analysis of the impact of planning on the built environment. Part B comprises more than a simple linear chronology. It comprises instead a series of comings and goings, of repeated contrasts and continuities between the past and the present. Compared to a typical planning history, the main difference is a focus on an object, the residential landscape as well as a series of proposals and ideas.

In contrast, Part C *New Forms of Modernity, 1980 Onwards* is organised around themes rather than a chronology. It is about an era that, in relation to planning and urban design, starts with a reaction to the modernism of the twentieth century. It is, in addition, about an era in which governments have sought a more realistic, less ambitious model of intervention. As part of this more realistic model, planning has become one element in a continuing process of change, rather than the key driver. Planning is no longer, if it ever was, an exercise in 'shaping' the future, as Ward (2004, 1) has stated.

The main themes in Part C are the urban landscape as the product of a continuing process of development (Chapter 6: *Quantity and Quality in Housing Development*), as an imaginary object, expressed in urban design and related proposals (Chapter 7: *Urban Design and the Environment*) and as a social object closely tied to systems of social status, lifestyle and the provision of services (Chapter 8: *Neighbourhoods of Choice and Constraint*). These three themes originate in part in poststructural social philosophy and in a similar threefold distinction of types of discourse – the 'real', the 'imaginary' and the 'symbolic'. However, poststructuralism cannot be accepted uncritically or in its entirety. It has to be applied in a way that makes sense in terms of planning practice. The logic of poststructural theory, together with other interpretations of the present is discussed in Chapter 5: *(Re)tracing the Context*.

The history of planning and housing in the twentieth century is characterised by a further distinction – between the era that Hobsbawm (1994) calls the short twentieth century, that is to say the era of mass wars, mass production and clearly defined political ideologies and the chronological twentieth century that lasts from 1990 to 2000. The end of the short twentieth century is arbitrary and open to interpretation, but was largely complete in relation to housing and planning by the 1980s. The start of the short twentieth century is clearer. It starts in 1914 with the outbreak of World War I.

Taking all this into consideration, the history of housing and planning can be divided into three main periods, as shown in Table 1.1. The columns refer to the historical period. These comprise in succession, the early modern and modern eras, both of which are included in Part B and the contemporary era that comprises Part C.

The rows refer to the context of planning, the modalities of planning and the generic landscapes that are produced in each era. The context of planning concerns the social, economic and spatial structure of cities. The modalities of planning refer to the methods of planning and to their theoretical and professional assumptions. A 'generic' landscape is either the typical urban landscapes that are repeated throughout Britain or those landscapes that somehow typify the political ideas and debates of the period in which they are constructed. Generic landscapes define the landscape of the ordinary, as opposed to landscapes of architectural and historical value. The notion of a generic landscape is derived from Clay (1994) who used this as a device for mapping out significant places in a visual analysis of the contemporary city in the US.

The table itself anticipates much of the detail of the text. It risks over-simplification and is confined to the simplest, most easily classifiable aspects of the narrative. It is, nevertheless, included as point of clarification.

Chapter by Chapter Summary

To summarise the contents in more detail: Chapter 2 *Mass Housing* charts the transition from the early modern to the modern era. It starts with the surveys that sought to define the characteristics of the industrial city and, as an extension of this, with an analysis of the main pre-1919 house types. It goes on to document the emergence of the council estate after 1918 and the establishment, therein, of model floor plans and standards. The period after about 1925 is different. This is a period characterised by a rapid expansion in the rate of private house building completions, the creation of the modern suburb and the creation of a consumer culture based on the individual home.

Chapter 3 *Two Types of Planning* analyses the policies and plans established during World War II and implemented for some years afterwards. Theories of central or social planning originated as a method of rational policy making in the 1930s and 1940s at a time of economic instability and political discord. These theories continue to summarise the advantages and disadvantages of planning as a method of resource allocation and politics and continue, in this context, to provide a definition of planning. The subsequent history of policy

Table 1.1   Periodising planning and housing development in Britain

	Aspects of practice →	Early modern	Modern (or orthodox modern or Fordist)	Contemporary (Post-, hypermodern or post-Fordist)
	Apogee →	1900–1914 (though with roots in the nineteenth century)	1920–40 (as an *avant garde* movement) 1920–80 (as mass housing)	1960–80 (as part of the counter-culture) 1980–to date (as the conventional wisdom)
Context	Dominant economic activities	Manufacturing and mining	Manufacturing	Service industries and information
	Main social distinctions	Class	Class	Identity and lifestyle
	Urban form	Concentric rings and sectors: close knit and dense; centres linked to another as conurbations	Concentric rings and sectors: increasingly spread out	Dispersal, partial re-urbanisation
The modalities of planning	Methods of social improvement	Physical upgrading Selective slum clearance, suburban construction	Physical upgrading Mass housing: mass slum clearance	Neighbourhood renewal Comprehensive area-based programmes
	Theory of intervention	Pragmatic civics: (Geddes)	Central planning versus piecemeal regulation Blueprints planning Land use transport systems approaches	Collaborative and partnership planning Planning for diversity
	Main themes in professional discussions	Health, beauty, convenience:	Technical standards Housing form and density	Participation Market impacts such as high house prices; environmental impacts
Generic landscapes	Privately developed	Bye-law streets of terraces (England) or tenements (Scotland) Suburban villas	Ribbon development The 'new' suburban England of the 1930s and 1950s	City-centre mixed use Gentrification Gated communities High density/low rise
	Social housing	The co-partnership garden city estate Inner city blocks and tenements	Homes for Heroes estates New towns High rise	Mixed tenure estates

implementation, from 1945 to about 1970s, is, in part, a dismal story of increasing constraints on the design of new council houses, the abandonment of previous ideals of high quality, social balanced estates and the use of a crude, insensitive and bureaucratic system of slum clearance and redevelopment. The history of housing and planning is less dismal, however, if the experience in Britain is compared to that in the US or France. Post-war development in Britain lacked extensive areas of very low density suburban and exurban housing such as was the experience in the US. Compared to France, housing development involved the development of a significantly higher proportion of houses with gardens and a lower proportion of flats, including high-rise flats.

Chapter 4 *Searching for an Alternative* documents the various ideas and proposals that accompanied the end of the era of modern town planning in the 1960s and 1970s. The ideas involve, in part, the emergence of new utopian visions that gave a positive emphasis to disorder and flexibility. They involved in addition the emergence of new process-oriented theories of planning that rejected a reliance on design-oriented blueprints. Finally, they involved the application of class-based, Marxist theories that sought to define the role of planning and of social housing in the maintenance of the status quo, that is to say the maintenance of capitalism. With the benefit of hindsight, these latter theories are also important in defining the distinction between housing policy in the short twentieth century, to use Hobsbawm's term and that from the 1970s onwards. The class-based theories assume the main social problem to be the generally low standards of working-class housing and urban amenities. From the 1970s onwards, the main social problem became one of marginalised communities and neighbourhoods.

Chapter 5 *(Re)tracing the Context* opens Part C and explains the changing context of planning in the 1980s and 1990s. Three themes and interpretations are apparent: postmodernism, hypermodernism and post-Fordism. Postmodernism provides a methodology, largely concerned with discourse and draws attention to the significance of performativity and difference. Hypermodern theories start with processes of flexible consumption and the individual. They focus on increased choice and the management of risk. Post-Fordism is about flexible production, increased competition and increased inequalities. It corresponds to a tendency towards a two-pronged, twin-track urban policy framework with separate strands for the well-housed majority and a poorly housed, excluded minority. Taken together, processes of flexible consumption and production also have implications for the style of public intervention. They imply flexible, transversal practice alongside conventional bureaucratic structures.

Chapter 6 *Quantity and Quality in Housing Development* is about house building and its regulation. The chapter starts with the issue of high house prices, housing shortages and the role of the planning system. More dwellings need to be built and more land allocated for housing within the planning system, as is the view of the present government and most housing pressure groups. Yet, for various reasons, such as the sheer scale of housing shortages and the existence of locational factors, increased house building is unlikely to have much impact on affordability over, say a five-year period. Various alternatives to the conventional developer's home are available, but these are also likely to have a limited impact. Short-life

(30 years or less) prefabricated housing does not offer a viable way forward for a combination of legal and quality reasons. Self-build gives users more influence in design and development, but is only feasible for a minority of individuals and families. The chapter goes on to examine issues relating to the reform of planning practice and the quality of new housing in the context of increased market differentiation, an increased concern with adaptability and flexibility in use and an increased concern with the reduction of carbon emissions.

Chapter 7 *Urban Design and the Environment* examines, in detail, contemporary interpretations and applications of the ideal planned city. At a strategic level, a long-standing distinction remains between urban dispersal and compaction. The former advocates the opening up of existing cities with the creation of parks, urban farms and green infrastructure. The latter favours a combination of higher densities and a continuous built-up area. The compact city serves to protect the countryside, but is only likely to reduce the use of private transport if combined with investment in public transport. A core policy assumption of the compact city, that densities should increase, has now reached its limits in most of England in terms of what is likely to prove acceptable in family houses. The compact city also leads on to a series of other detailed prescriptions for mixed land uses, social mixing and the shared use of residential streets. Each of these prescriptions has a role in promoting liveable urban environments. Finally, from a different perspective, developers have started to propose and build gated communities, surrounded by walls. These are deeply controversial. Their detractors say gated communities cause social separation. Their supporters say that they do the reverse. The best planning response is a degree of pragmatism, determining the exact implications in a specific locality.

Chapter 8 *Neighbourhoods of Choice and Constraint* examines the characteristics of the neighbourhood and the policies appropriate for neighbourhoods in different market conditions. Various types of neighbourhood group exist – based respectively on personal contact, on the management and defence of local spaces and, finally, on shared interests in relation to public authorities. The latter type of group is central to local democracy and to the preparation and implementation of public policies. Policies for the neighbourhood are, in part, dependant on market conditions. In low demand neighbourhoods, the main question has been how to improve the environment, to adapt the housing stock and to assess the case for demolition. Elsewhere, in suburban and high inner city areas, the key questions are about coping with the consequences of gentrification and increased housing need whilst also improving deprived estates and neighbourhoods. Whatever the market condition, improving deprived neighbourhoods raises questions about how to tackle crime and the fear of crime. Various models are available, but their relevance to any particular requires a combination of research and consultation.

Finally, Chapter 9 *Looking Back and Looking Forward* comprises the conclusions. In relation to 'looking back', the trend in physical quality is of a steady and continuing improvement, albeit with a significant minority of people living in poor conditions. The assessment of neighbourhood quality is more difficult, however, as this has only recently been measured in official statistics and the measures themselves have subjective aspects. In relation to the future, the main scenarios can best be imagined through relating economic, social and environmental priorities to different levels of economic growth. It remains uncertain whether greater land availability alone will encourage sufficient house building to meet current targets and needs. More attention needs to be paid to promoting the role of social housing, to reducing the burden of planning agreements on private developers and to giving local authorities a more positive role in land development. The compact city, amended to incorporate notions of carbon zero housing and green corridors, offers a possible definition of the spatial characteristics of the future city, but needs to be applied flexibly in way that recognises uncertainty, the diversity of social demands and the need to maintain and upgrade existing neighbourhoods.

Note

1   Taken from the UK government's website on sustainable development, consulted July 2007 at http://www.sustainable-development.gov.uk/advice/local/index.htm.

Visual Images, their Uses and Limitations

Plate 1   Thumbnail images of the housing stock

There are innumerable examples of architectural and planning textbooks that routinely use photographs and drawings as illustrations, especially as a means of illustrating the technical details of a project or as a guide to design. In a contemporary history of housing, the role of images is more limited. One use as a guide to classification. The English House Condition Survey, for example, uses a series of photographs to classify the housing stock into a typology of different dwelling forms (houses, terraces, high rise etc.) of different eras (DoE, 1993, p. 16). Plate 1 adopts a similar approach, albeit one that is simplified and also includes examples from Scotland.

A classification of building types provides the raw material of a history of housing as a concrete object. Each house type has its own history (Goodchild 2007, 16–27). The housing stock is simultaneously mundane and diverse in its appearance. Indeed, the housing stock is so diverse in appearance that it denies the possibility of capture in a single glance or single picture.

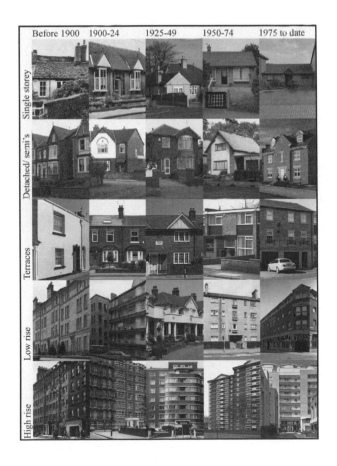

Plate 2   Homes as consumer objects

Images of individual dwellings are also a reminder that the home is a consumer object. The non-plan theorists of the 1960s and postmodern architecture in the 1970s realised this clearly. They appealed to the logic of private builders and the advertising industry. They also drew on the type of housing that was being completed at the time, as is illustrated by these dormer bungalows, that is to say a two storey house with second floor set into the roof space. Bungalows, whether of the dormer or conventional one-storey type, typify twentieth-century suburbia. They met consumer aspirations, but also encouraged urban dispersal and increased car dependency.

Plate 3   Continuity and change

Since the time of the 1960s bungalows, the density of new housing has increased. City centre high rise has become commonplace (3a). Elsewhere developers are required to build on previously used, or brownfield sites, including as shown here a former coal mine (3b). Urban dispersal continues, however. At the same time, developers frequently mimic the historical styles of the past because this gives a sense of permanence and respectability (3c). Even if the aim is to innovate in design, as in the case of these low energy eco-homes, the geometry of architecture leads to familiar shapes in low rise houses, especially terraces (3d).

Plate 4   Mass housing

Residential landscapes are based, in part, on the repetition of building types and styles and to an extent on the standardisation of product. Repetition and standardisation are associated, moreover, not just with social housing (4a) and self-consciously designed modern architecture (4b), but with private housing (4c and 4d), even in some types of self-built housing (4c). Repetition and standardisation, imply mass housing, a loss of individuality and the loss of a sense of place. This is the logic of the large-scale 'mass housing' schemes of the early and mid twentieth century, to some extent mitigated by a greater emphasis on consumer choice in recent house building. Yet the implications are more nuanced than the term 'mass housing' might suggest. Repetition can be used as a conscious element in design to promote a visual rhythm. The scale of repetition, can in any case, be masked by greenery. Likewise, standardisation can be countered by piecemeal modifications to the fabric in low rise housing and by personalisation whereby the occupants stamp their own identity through gardening, do-it-yourself work and home decorations.

Plate 5   Likes and dislikes in the landscapes

Consideration of the dwelling as objects in a landscape has limitations. It distances
the viewer from the object and so downplays the feel of a place. Attitudes towards
housing and the landscape can be tested through asking people to say what
they think of photographs or even giving them a camera and asking them to
photograph what is significant in a town or city or neighbourhood. The results,
illustrated from a study of a renewal area in the North of England, typically
suggest a liking for local landmarks and often for what might otherwise be
considered 'ordinary' street scenes (5a). Greenery is also often liked. However,
residents invariably dislike litter, rubbish, poor maintenance and signs of
vandalism (5b).

Plate 6   Anxiety and impersonality

The intrusion of large structures such as electricity pylons (6a), the noise and pollution of traffic (6b), the fortress-like appearance of some crime prevention measures (6c) and the large scale of residential and other blocks (6d) can also accentuate a sense of anxiety and impersonality in the landscape. More generally, the pace of change and the disappearance of traditional landscapes triggers the formation of community groups eager to defend and improve their locality.

Plate 7   Visions and marketing

Drawings have slightly different characteristics to photographs. Some are made for purely technical purposes. Others, made at the design stage, are intended to draw in the viewer and to make him or her believe that investment in this or that scheme is worthwhile. As such, drawings change the role of the architect or other professional designer from a technician to a marketing agent and, in the most extreme cases, a purveyor of dreams. The downside for architect is that he or she is also likely to become a scapegoat if reality fails to meet the vision. The promotional material for the Homes for Heroes programme, started immediately World War I, provides an example. The drawing (7a), published in *The Builder* (8 October 1920), portrays local authority housing as a hope for the future. A slightly later advertisement for private housing, as published in the *Illustrated Carpenter and Builder* (7 March 1930), offers a similar sunlit future (7b). Current marketing exercises appear less distinctive, perhaps because we are so close to them in time (7c). However, they also imply the existence of a better life.

Plate 8   Decline and abandonment

Physical alterations that arise over time, including decay, also promote changes in meaning. The outcome, most common in the North of England pre-1919 privately-owned stock, is abandonment and almost certain demolition (8a and b). Houses that were once built for wealthy or respectable individuals and families slide down the social scale as they gradually become obsolete. Similar processes are at work in social housing. The Flowers estate in Sheffield, a prestige estate before 1919 and photographed in 2004, provides an example (8c). However, the local authority and former local authority stock also contains examples, for example, high rise, that have been demolished long before their normal life expectancy (8d).

Plate 9   Stability and upgrading

Decay is not inevitable. Houses may be upgraded as relative wealthy individuals and families search for a convenient and attractive place to live, within easy travelling distance of their work. This is the process of gentrification, as illustrated by a street scene from south London (9a). Elsewhere, the relative social status of neighbourhoods is often stable over many years, so long as owners are prepared to invest in repairs and modernisation. Hampstead Garden Suburb provides an example of an estate that has been valued from the date of completion (9b). Together with other similar estates, garden cities and garden suburbs have become an icon of successful planning and urban design. The 'Bevan houses', inspired by the policies of the first post1945 Labour government provide another example (9c). They typify the taken for granted character of much of the housing stock, including much of the stock built by local authorities.

As a result of changes since completion, residential landscapes are generally double coded. They include references both to the initial client groups for which the scheme was built and their current role within the housing market.

The Limits

For some critics, the use of visual material has gone too far in modern culture. Harvey (1989, 359), for example, has, in particular, called for 'a counter-attack of narrative against the image, ethics against aesthetics'. The counter view is that the human eye has its own conscience and its own way of making judgements (Sennett 1990). Visual images do not have to be mere exercises in aesthetics and they do not necessarily imply a superficial level of analysis. Image and narrative are best considered as complementary rather than as contradictory. The rest of this book comprises a written text. The reader is advised, wherever possible, to visualise the implications.

PART B
Planning, Markets and the Industrial City

Chapter 2

Mass Housing

Landscapes and planning go together because both deal with spaces and places. They also demand, in general terms, a historical method of exposition. Exactly how is such an analysis to be undertaken?

One approach, generally called morphological analysis, treats planning as an exercise in regulation, with the built environment being determined partly by the interaction between regulation and developers and, in addition, by a piecemeal and generally slow process of modification to existing design models and an existing urban landscape. As promoted by Conzen (1981), morphological analysis is about the cumulative impact of 'additive' processes, as in suburban extensions and a series of 'transformative' processes such as 'repletion' (the increase of land coverage and/or the height of buildings in existing plots) and the replacement of old building forms by new ones. Morphological analysis also encompasses what might be called pre-development issues such as the pattern of land boundaries, the attitudes of landowners to the sale of their property and the considerations of builders as to what types of scheme might be most profitable and easy to sell. Particularly if development is a protracted process or is delayed, the plans for an area would change over time as builders responded to changing land values and changing patterns of demand (Whitehand and Carr 1999).

Morphological analysis, of the type promoted by Conzen and others, works well with private housing development during the nineteenth and early twentieth centuries, certainly until the 1930s and arguably into the 1960s. Private house builders comprised a huge number of independently minded, but conservative firms and individual entrepreneurs. The design of private housing was a vernacular architecture, influenced by tradition, previous examples and close contact with investors and consumers. Hence it is possible to analyse both housing design and the resulting spatial patterns as the cumulative result of a large number of pragmatic development decisions.

Some types of pre-1919 social housing are an exception. Social housing agencies, of which there were many variations, were more likely to develop innovative, 'model' estates. The garden city estates, mostly developed by co-operative housing societies, in particular offered a break with the past.

However, the scale of social house building was miniscule. In total, taking all types of social housing agency into account, it was almost certainly less than one per cent of the housing stock that existed in 1914, just before the outbreak of World War I (Clarke 1920, 99: RCHS, 1917, 392; Calvert Spensley, 1918). In any case, social housing agencies did not necessarily seek to innovate in design. For example, the illustrations contained in accounts by Thompson (1903) or Cornes

(1905) suggest that at the start of the twentieth century, most local authorities followed the vernacular house types of private developers.

Surveys, By-laws and Model Housing

Morphological analysis is also appropriate to the pre-1919 era because it corresponds closely to the views of contemporaries. The Report of a Royal Commission on Housing in Scotland (1917, 40) provides an example. The report used urban landscapes as an educational device to introduce the reader to social and economic issues.

> In dealing with the problem of urban housing, it will be best to proceed from the more concrete to the more general and abstract questions. If we begin with the actual physical conditions, external and internal, of the houses of a typical ... town, ... we shall then be able better to deal with the economic and ethical factors of domestic life in a modern city.

The approach of the Royal Commission was typical of its time. Even in 1900 or 1917 at the time of the publication of the Royal Commission's report, the big industrial city was a novelty for influential public opinion. The survey remained a key method of research and social criticism. It was central to official enquiries, such as that undertaken by the Board of Trade (1908) into 'working-class rents, housing and retail prices'. It was central to privately funded exercises that sought to document the reality of life amongst the poor. Charles Booth's study of working-class life in London, undertaken between 1886 and 1903, was the first and most exhaustive of the privately funded studies. Last, but not least in relation to planning theory, the survey was central to the philosophy of 'civics', developed by Patrick Geddes. Public intervention had to be preceded, Geddes (1968, 393) emphasised, by a comprehensive survey, a 'concrete study of cities as we find them, or rather as we see them grow'.

The survey method as advocated by Geddes had idealistic, even utopian elements. For Geddes, civic and regional surveys were an educational device, a means of bringing communities together and a means of highlighting the relation between cities and their environment (Abrams 1968, 116–21). They also served a political purpose. They were 'correctives of predatory imperialism' and a counter to the over-powerful 'Absolute State' (Branford and Geddes 1917, 32).

Otherwise and this was more typical of practice, the survey was part of the technology of government. For governments to act they had to understood what they were dealing with. In the context of the predominantly hands-off, laissez-faire policy assumptions of the time, governments also had to be persuaded of the necessity of acting at all.

House Types and Land Development

The survey method, in turn a implied a specific way of looking at cities, not just in terms of its physical form or morphology but in terms of a classification of types, of similarities and differences. The assumptions of the Royal Commission on Housing in Scotland are again instructive. The Royal Commission identified the tenement and its associated system of land development as the main distinguishing feature of housing in Scotland. The tenement gave Scottish cities a distinctive character compared to the two-storey terraces of England and Wales. It also involved a distinctive process of land development.

Tenements and terraces   However, for most of those who gave evidence to the Royal Commission, tenements were more a problem than an asset. Tenements were trying for the very young, for the aged and for women. They were more dangerous in case of fire. The stairs were nearly always dirty and often insanitary. They were more difficult to police. In hot weather, their occupants could not obtain 'the relief of a stroll in their own garden'. They necessitated the provision of far more public open space than cottages. Moreover, even in the most modern tenements the problem of providing open space for children's play had not been fully solved (RCHS 1917, 60–70). More than all this, however, tenements provided smaller accommodation than two-storey houses and in doing this increased levels of overcrowding. In 1901, according to the census of that year, 50 per cent of the Scottish population lived in dwellings comprising one or two rooms, compared to an equivalent proportion in England and Wales of only 8 per cent (Board of Trade, 1908, 259).

Tenements did not reflect consumer wishes. Instead, they had grown owing to a particular and persistent system of land development that involved a combination of high land prices and high residential densities and that was reinforced by a regulatory framework that tolerated high densities. The relationship between the tenement system and high land values was reciprocal and self-reinforcing and was, in the words of the Royal Commission (1917, 347) 'one of the few questions in regard to which the Commission met with almost unanimous opinion'.

The Royal Commission looked at the English tradition of two-storey houses as 'normal', as compared to the peculiarities of the Scottish tenement. If the Royal Commission had looked at other European countries, it might have come to different conclusions. In the industrialist countries of northern Europe, the English practice of building two-storey terraces was the oddity rather than the Scottish practice of four-storey tenements.

Continental visitors noted the distinctiveness of English housing and, like the Scottish Royal Commission, pointed to the expectations of owners as a crucial variable. For instance, in 1904, the German architect Hermann Muthesius (1979, 73) wrote of housing in England, 'There are no property dealers who grow rich on land on which humanity needs to live'.

The absence of land speculation in England, argued Muthesius, had reduced housing costs and enabled most people to occupy their own separate dwelling unit, usually a terraced house. Later, writing in the late 1940s, the Danish architect,

Rasmussen (1947; 1969) told a similar story. Rasmussen (1969, 114) argued that nineteenth-century London was a uniquely prosperous commercial city where the property owner could afford to wait for a return on his investment and where it was possible to build as far as one wished. As a result,

> speculators thought in terms of building speculation rather than land speculation. ... The money was used to produce something (*i.e. – not tied up in land*) and the investor was not interested in building as many houses as possible on a plot but only in building houses as attractive as possible. (Italics added.)

London and other British cities, including those in Scotland, were distinct in one way. In many countries of continental Europe, suburban growth was hindered by a fragmented pattern of agricultural land ownership and not simply by high land values or land speculation. In contrast, in Britain, agricultural land ownership had generally been consolidated through enclosures and other means into relatively large units that could be sold off piecemeal as a development sites (Conzen 1981, 115). Indeed, rural field boundaries remain incorporated into the urban fabric through breaks between one set of street patterns and others.

On the other hand and more importantly, foreign assessments of housing in Britain were generally more appreciative of housing standards than British accounts. Much depended on the type of housing. Suburban middle-class development tended to pay more attention to the niceties of layout and generally included a larger area devoted to private gardens and public space, for example through the use of tree planting in the road. Suburban middle-class architecture in the form of large terraces, semis and detached dwellings also enabled more individual variations and more privacy within the home. However, few British observers in 1900 or 1910 would have accepted Rasmussen's comment that, in relation to working-class housing in England, 'the investor was not interested in building as many houses as possible'. Typical working-class housing comprised and where it has not been demolished it still comprises long terraces of narrow fronted houses, often with corner shops or public houses at the end, that are laid out in the most cost-effective, land-intensive way possible.

In any case, complaints existed about high urban land values and land price inflation in England, just as much as in Scotland or elsewhere in Europe. This was the essence of the pre-1914 political campaigns of the Liberal Party. For example, the most substantial housing report of the Liberal government was that of the Land Enquiry Committee (1914). Simply entitled *The Land*, the Report assumed that high land values were the main economic cause of housing shortages and overcrowding.

Regional types in England   While the dwellings of England consisted mostly of two-storey terraces, the housing stock was not uniform. The Board of Trade survey published in 1908 shows, in particular, significant differences in housing provision within London, between central and suburban areas and between London and the rest of the country. In addition, significant differences existed elsewhere, in provincial cities and regions. Different regions and sometimes each city within a region had its own models and standard types.

In central London, a combination of a large residential population and extensive commercial pressures had raised ground rents far beyond the level at which a working-class household could afford a self-contained cottage. The result was that families lived in smaller accommodation, in more overcrowded conditions and at higher residential densities than elsewhere. Here the Board of Trade (1908, 8–9) identified two main house types, large old dwellings which had been subdivided into smaller units and purpose built flats in a multi-storey block provided by a large institutional landlord such as an Industrial Dwellings Company (a semi-private, semi-philanthropic housing agency), a charitable housing association or the London County Council. The individual flats in the block dwellings were self contained and generally contained an internal toilet, whereas those in the large old dwellings shared facilities.

The block dwellings had generally been developed in the context of piecemeal demolition and slum clearance projects. They were not of universally good quality. Booth (1903, 167) makes reference to blocks which, according to his witnesses, were, 'a scandal and a disgrace', 'block dwellings are better than slums – but that is all'. 'The worst of them have dark stairs, without gates, of which sleeping places are made.'

In the more recently completed suburbs and with the exception of the model estates designed and developed by London County Council, working-class housing was relatively uniform in character. It mostly comprised self-contained family accommodation of five or six habitable rooms in the form of terraces, with a scullery (food preparation area) on the ground floor, this latter usually sited in a back extension along with the toilet (accessible only from the outside) and coal shed. The main exception was a trend towards the provision of low cost cottage flats, each flat having a ground floor access point. Many working-class households took in a lodger to help pay the rent. Cottage flats offered a more elegant and private solution to the high rent of conventional terraced family houses and were, according to Booth (1903, 177–8), the most fashionable type of accommodation for young working-class families in London.

Elsewhere, in the South and East of England, in Wales and, to a lesser extent in the West Midlands, the most common house type was again the narrow-fronted terrace as found in the London suburbs. The dwellings would vary slightly by size, by whether the back extension comprised one or two storeys and by the presence or absence of bay windows. External decoration also varied greatly in detail, style and the level of workmanship. (See Muthesius 1982.) Other than in the more expensive and larger middle-class home, run with the help of a servant, the basic arrangement remained the same, however.

The back addition terrace was sufficiently widespread to have become a national house type by the time of World War I. In the North of England the back addition terrace remained less common, however and of more recent origin. It was occupied 'even when of very plain exterior only by the better class of artisans' (ibid., xvii).

In the North of England, a variety of other generally smaller and more basic house types existed, including some such as the Sunderland one-storey terrace and the Sheffield attic terrace that were confined to one town only. By 1900, three main regional building types were apparent as follows: in Lancashire, the small two up, two down terrace with no back extension; in the former West Riding of Yorkshire, the back-to-back joined together like Siamese twins at the back and therefore without a back window or backyard; and finally, in the North East, small two and three cottage flats, called 'Tyneside flats' or 'back-wing flats' to use Conzen's term (1981, 102).

The regional house-types of the North of England puzzled later historians and geographers, with some emphasising general cultural explanations (Beresford 1971) and others such as Daunton (1983) looking for material explanations in local variations in landholding arrangements or living standards. Landholding was not a relevant consideration. The pattern of different systems, such as leasehold and freehold, did not correlate well with the pattern of house types. In relation to living standards, The Board of Trade's enquiry was specifically established to examine local variations in working-class wages and rents and, if these had had any effect on local house styles, one might safely assume that the effect would have been noted in the report. No such effect is noted. In its case studies, the report did nevertheless make repeated reference to an evolution in style amongst local builders, sometimes linked explicitly to changes in the local byelaws. The implication, therefore, is that local variations were caused by the practices and attitudes of the local building industry, probably influenced by the expectations of local property investors as to what constituted a sound investment and, in addition, by a process of interaction between local building practices and the local building regulation.

'Nothing Gained by Overcrowding!'

For contemporary critics, including the advocates of town planning, nineteenth-century house types did little other than provide a bare acceptable minimum. Raymond Unwin, architect of Letchworth Garden City and Hampstead Garden Suburb was influential in working out an alternative. In *Cottage Plans and Common Sense* Unwin (1902, 3) argued that while the building by-laws had had beneficial public health consequences, they had also allowed 'long projections running out behind, which effectually shade the rooms from such sunshine as they might otherwise get' (ibid., 5). They had allowed backyards which are always 'dreary ... shut in with walls and outbuildings', backyards which offered a 'ghastly prospect' for millions of working women (ibid., 4).

The implication was clear. The back-addition would have to go and more space would have to be provided around the home. Unwin put the case for more space and lower densities in more detail in *Nothing Gained by Overcrowding!* (1912). The subtitle *How the Garden City type of development may benefit both owner and occupier* summarised the argument and also showed how recently developed garden city schemes had started to offer an alternative. Lower density and specifically a maximum of 12 dwellings per hectare (30dph) benefited the occupier because, so long as the building by-laws were relaxed for lower density development, as there were under the planning provisions of the Housing, Town Planning Etc. Act, 1909, sufficient savings could be made in the development of roads, to ensure that the average price of land was reduced. Lower density also benefited the owner because it involved more land being taken for development.

Unwin's argument is hardly convincing in term of its economic logic. The additional profit which owners were supposed to gain from lower densities was dependent on each possessing an infinite amount of land. In addition, from the viewpoint of future residents, garden city development was more expensive. The price of land in the lower density scheme may have been lower but, as the details of *Nothing Gained from Overcrowding* showed, the total cost of land and road per house was more. Moreover, in relation to garden city estates as developed, building costs were also raised by detailed innovations in design such as the breaking up of long monotonous rows of terraces and a preference for broad fronted rather than narrow dwellings. Aldridge (1915, 350–51) estimated that these latter innovations alone added between £23 and £28 to the cost of a cottage, (between about 10 per cent and 15 per cent of the building cost), depending on whether the building by-laws could be relaxed to reduce road length and width. The provision of community facilities such as a meeting room and playing fields were a further expense.

The justification for a radical reduction in densities was also not universally accepted. There was still a degree of uncertainty as to the extent to which private developers and local authorities should take up the model of low density garden city estates. In 1914, the *Town Planning Review* contained a lengthy debate as to how best to promote public health, whether through a combination of reduced overcrowding (a reduction in the occupancy of rooms within the house) and a better diet or alternatively through a reduction of residential densities. The critics suggested that a general improvement of living conditions in cities would eventually improve the health of children and that a general improvement in living standards could only result from a piecemeal adaptation of existing house types and standards. High-density terraces would suffice and were more practical and economic than the type of housing built in garden cities (Edwards 1913).

The supporters of the garden cities responded that these had manifestly lower mortality rates, including lower infant mortality rates and that this was attributable to their lower densities and proximity to the countryside (Reade 1913, 247). Such arguments forgot that the residents of garden city estates were probably better off than average. More than this, however, the supporters of garden cities argued that public expectations had started to change. Henry Vivian (1912, 497), Director of the Co-partners Tenants Ltd, the main commercial investor, reported that, 'the standard, both of demand and supply has been raised, and if some estate developers still proceed on the old lines, they apologise and make excuses'. Similarly, the Report of the Land Enquiry Committee (1914, 117) noted that 'the educational work of housing reformers, and the example set by garden suburbs in various parts of the country, have quickened a desire for houses with more breathing space around them'.

The Legacy

The pre-1919 housing stock influenced housing policy and housing markets throughout the twentieth century. It continues, moreover, to represent a significant, albeit gradually declining proportion of all dwellings. It accounted for about 21 per cent of the English housing stock in 2001 (OPDM 2003a, 10), 20 per cent of the Scottish housing stock in 2002 (Communities Scotland 2002, Table 2.1) and 36 per cent of the Welsh housing stock in 1996.[1] As might be expected the proportion is highest in those towns and cities where industrial and mining activity was concentrated before 1919.

The survival of large numbers of pre-1919 dwellings was probably not expected in the early and mid twentieth century. The garden city was taken up in the mass housing programmes after 1919 and this, in turn, redefined much of the pre-1919 working-class housing stock as obsolete. From the 1920s to at least the 1960s other visions of the planned modern city had the same effect. However, recent assessments have been more favourable, almost certainly inspired by an awareness of the limitations of the supposedly superior twentieth-century dwelling types and layouts.

Demolition and downward filtering   To explain the shifting assessments in more detail, the work of Pevsner (1969, 270) provides a good example of the attitudes of the architectural establishment in the middle of the twentieth century. Pevsner was the author of detailed guides to the architecture of English counties and cities. Yet of nineteenth-century residential areas, the guides say little. As he wrote of South Lancashire, the period in the 50 years before 1919 was merely one when 'the slums and dreary streets of brick cottages were growing apace'. In relation to ordinary English domestic architecture, the period from about 1850 to 1914 was one that could be almost entirely ignored.

The reference to slums implies demolition. By the 1940s, the most radical advocates of housing reform, such as Bowley (1945, 191), were calling for a 'general replacement policy' that would bring all working-class housing up to the accepted modern standard and would facilitate extensive rebuilding. Many terraces and older tenements, albeit the older, smaller dwellings were indeed demolished. In England, back to back terraces were generally the first to go, followed by through terraces in the 1960s and 1970s.

The scale of demolition was huge, though less so in London and the South of England. According to figures collated by Yelling (2000, 234), in the period between 1955 and 1985, the programme involved the demolition or closure (a legal preliminary to demolition) of 1.48 million homes in England and Wales alone, displacing more than 3.66 million people. In South Yorkshire, for example, which may be taken as representative of an older industrial region, 20 per cent of the 1955 housing stock was demolished during the period from 1955 to 1985. In contrast, towns and villages in rural areas and in South East England largely escaped extensive demolition. Likewise, the impact on Greater London was less than the national average. Here about 6 per cent of the 1955 stock was demolished (ibid., 241).

There was an exception, at least for a time. Evaluations of the leafy Edwardian suburb were more favourable. For example, J.M. Richards, one time editor of the *Architectural Review* and leading advocate of modern architecture, explained in detail how pre-1919 middle-class suburbs and the mass suburbs of the 1920s and 1930s both satisfied a desire for individual control. The suburb had, for its residents, two desirable attractions: 'a sense of belonging to a fairly sympathetic world and an opportunity for making out of that world something personal to themselves' (Richards, 1973, 38–9).

At the same time, the process of suburban development triggered a process of downward filtering of previous middle-class homes into what was later called the inner city. In 1936, for example, H.J. Ginns, writing in the *Illustrated Carpenter and Builder* (25 September 1936) stated 'In and around our larger towns there are scores of houses built from 30 to 60 years ago, which are standing empty because they are too big for modern needs'. These empty properties, it was suggested, offered a suitable opportunity for subdivision and conversion into flats. The older middle-class suburbs retained an attractive and sometimes romantic green image, but they too were obsolete unless modernised. Many of the homes have subsequently been subdivided into flats or, if located near to the city centre, converted into commercial property, with their back gardens redeveloped and front gardens turned into parking areas.

Reassessments of pre-1919 housing   The subsequent failures of mass slum clearance eventually led to a re-evaluation of pre-1919 house types, the working-class stock included. In England, from about the 1970s onwards, the terraced house started to become valued as a practical, traditional English solution to housing problems. Taylor (1973, 62), a persistent critic of the high rise solutions of the 1960s, commented, for example,

> the byelaw house was a *reductio ad minimum* of the traditional two storey cottage of English villages. .... Unfashionable as the byelaw suburbs may have been, and fiercely criticised since as 'monotonous sprawl', they nonetheless permitted a development of family life, in the privacy of backyards and back gardens ....

The publication of *The English Terraced House* by Muthesius (1982) provided a more considered, more architectural re-evaluation. Muthesius argued that architects had previously not looked at smaller nineteenth houses and had overlooked their rich local variety, particularly the variety of bricks and other materials used in the façade (ibid., ix–x).

The re-evaluation has continued to the present, with more attention being paid to the layout details of Victorian and Edwardian terraces. The Commission for Architecture and the Built Environment (CABE) is probably the most influential single source of expert advice and information on quality in relation to architecture and urban design. It was established by government in 1999 to provide an authoritative source of advice in England and Wales. For CABE (2005b, 15) 'The layouts of terraced properties present many positive qualities, including definition of public and private realm, densities that support the provision of services within walking distance, connected street layouts and strong urban form and character'.

However, the architectural reassessment is only half the story. The market status of pre-1919 house types is more mixed than the favourable architectural reviews would suggest. In inner London terraces generally provide the only widely available alternative to flats. Larger, often early nineteenth-century terraces have provided the dominant house type for gentrification in Islington and parts of Hackney. Most of these properties would have been built for middle-class families only to have filtered down the housing market and then gentrified from the 1960s onwards. In addition, smaller, two and three bedroom nineteenth-century terraces have provided less expensive owner-occupied accommodation that appeals to first time buyers or to minority groups as for example in parts of Tottenham, Brent and Clapham (Hamnett 2003, 2422).

In contrast, in the Midlands and the North of England, pre-1919 terraces occupy a more down-market role in the housing market. The stock was subject to improvement programmes in the 1970s and 1980s, but the quality of the work varied from property to property and from area to area. In many cases, improvement involved the installation of an internal bathroom and an improved kitchen and little else. The terraces gained flat roof back extensions and flat-roofed loft extensions, but little that might prolong the life of the structure or improve the local environment. In addition, improvement was in a housing market context that has varied and that, in some areas, has discouraged further investment.

The smaller terraces remain in a relatively poor state of repair. They also tend to be located in neighbourhoods affected by the environmental problems of urban deprivation – for example the poor maintenance of public spaces, vandalism and graffiti (ODPM 2003a, 7). Their overall appearance is, according to the critics, drab and 'monolithic' (Gibb and Kearns 2001, 20). Others point to the high maintenance and heating costs of the pre-1914 terraces, their poor energy efficiency and their apparent failure to meet current consumer expectations.[2]

As a result, in the past decade, the older terraces and especially the small working-class terraces on the Midlands and North of England have again been subject to proposals for mass demolition or more rarely, as in an experimental example in Salford, to proposals for radical remodelling, with two units being knocked into one and with the creation of integral car parking and communal areas. Radical remodelling has the advantage of incorporating the embodied energy in the built environment (RCEP 2007, 101). It has fewer adverse environmental consequences than redevelopment. In terms of the social impact, however, radical remodelling is little different from demolition. The initial population would have to move out and the dwellings purchased *en masse*.

Whether either demolition or radical remodelling or an alternative policy of piecemeal improvement is justified is, of course, another question and one that requires a consideration of the public sector costs, the housing market and social effects and the attitudes of residents. Even down-market housing has a useful function – in providing starter homes for young adults and less expensive housing for lower income groups. The small terraces of the Midlands and the North of

England have, in particular, enabled Asian families to settle and acquire property, without facing extensive competition from the white population (Peach 1996).

In Scotland, the rehabilitation of the older housing stock started at about the same time, in the early 1970s, using a different and more ambitious approach. Especially in Glasgow and the west of Scotland, where the housing market was generally weaker, rehabilitation required the collective improvement, usually undertaken by small housing association established for this particular purpose. These housing associations repaired the common elements in the blocks, amalgamated small, one and two room units and rehoused displaced residents. Elsewhere, in Edinburgh and Aberdeen, local authorities used a combination of common repairs grants and enforcement notices to encourage and require private owners to undertake improvement (Robertson and Bailey 1996). In contrast, the improvement of the small terraces in England was more easily suited to voluntary improvements undertaken by individual owners, if necessary with grant aid.

At the same time, the abandonment of clearance in Scotland corresponded to a radical re-assessment of the tenement as a potentially modern house type. *The Tenement* by Worsdall (1979) was one indication of a changed attitude. *The Tenement* offered a detailed analysis of the construction of the tenements in Glasgow and the lifestyles with which they were associated. It also contained a lament for the subsequent twentieth-century estates that were 'with justification' said to 'dehumanise their occupants and also to magnify social problems' (ibid., 12). Soon afterwards, the continuing suitability of tenements as a form of housing was demonstrated by a series of surveys undertaken by the former National Building Agency (1981), showing that the residents of inner city tenement neighbourhoods were more satisfied with their accommodation than the residents of newer and more modern suburban houses. Later still, the architectural quality of the remaining tenements became appreciated as central to the identity and distinctiveness of Scottish cities. (See, for example, Reed 1999, 127.)

The result is an almost complete reversal of attitudes from the beginning to the end of the twentieth century. For the Royal Commission of 1917 tenements were a problem, almost a national disgrace. For influential public opinion in Scotland since the 1970s, in contrast, tenements are a matter of pride and deserve retention and conservation. It should be remembered, however, that in both England and Scotland, the worst examples of pre-1919 housing have disappeared, demolished.

Homes for Heroes

The outbreak in 1914 of World War I meant a cessation of almost all house building. In addition, and this was probably more significant, the sheer disorder and bloodshed of the war amounted to a break with the past and this was represented over and over again by subsequent references to 'pre-war' and 'post-war' situations. The Homes for Heroes building programme that emerged in 1918 and 1919 at the end of the war was likewise a major break with the past. It marked the arrival of both the national state as the lead actor in the provision of working-class housing and led, in addition, to the creation of the council estate as a ubiquitous feature of the urban landscape.

Dissatisfaction with the rate of house building before 1914 would have probably caused political pressures for an expanded house building programme irrespective of the outbreak of hostilities in 1914 (Wilding 1972, 3–17). Even so, the war transformed the scale and form of the programme. The scale of the programme was much larger. In addition, the sheer scale and urgency of action meant a reliance on local authorities rather than the public utility societies of the type that had pioneered low-density garden city estates before 1914. Local authorities provided a comprehensive coverage of the country; they often possessed skilled administrative staff; they had a reliable income from levying rates and they possessed a better record in providing homes for less affluent families (Malpass, 2000a). According to Bowley (1945, 23) local authorities contributed 170,090 dwellings to the Homes for Heroes programme. Public utility societies, in contrast, only contributed 4,545 dwellings.

The Homes for Heroes programme did not constitute part of a national programme for social reconstruction along the lines of that pursued after World War II. Most historians agree that the threat of mass industrial action was a key consideration. Fear of industrial action, together with unsettling example of political instability in Germany and Russia led the government to start a national house building programme as a short-term measure to deal with a particular crisis (Orbach 1977; Swenarton 1981).

Town Planning as Mass Housing

Given its likely scale, the Homes for Heroes programme represented a new principle of town planning as mass housing. Such a description deserves comment. The contemporary advocates of town planning in Britain would have almost certainly argued that town planning was more than housing writ large. It was about town centres, open spaces, the improvement of transport and the management of urban growth.

In addition, Conservative and market-oriented supporters of town planning for example Horsfall (1905) and Nettlefold (1908) tended to avoid any explicit discussion of the design of new working-class housing for the simple reason that they wanted to avoid the direct provision of houses by local authorities, especially subsidised provision. Either, they preferred the regulation of housing conditions, as was the assumption of the Housing, Town Planning Etc Act, 1909. Or they preferred a relatively narrow exercise in civic improvements, similar to but more modest than the parallel City Beautiful movement in the US. The city beautiful favoured architecture over social policy and it appealed to some architect planners in Britain. For Triggs (1909, 5), for example, town planning was no more than 'preserving spots of beauty, providing wider streets, ... open squares and places, with more sculpture and fountains and more tree-planting'.

Even so, the design of model working-class housing was sufficiently important to be extensively debated within the emergent planning profession. In particular, the main planning journals, the *Town Planning Review*, edited at Liverpool

University from 1910 onwards and *Garden Cities and Town Planning*, the main journal of the Garden Cities and Town Planning Association, included numerous articles on the subject immediately before, during and after World War I. The principles of residential layout were, moreover, the main theme in Unwin's *Town Planning in Practice*, arguably the most influential town planning textbook in the pre-1914 era. Unwin later became Chief Architect to the Ministry of Health at the time of the Homes for Heroes programme, so providing a personal link to the early debates in town planning.

Simplification and standardisation   In relation the standards of equipment and the floor plan, the general direction of professional discussions, in architecture and building as well as town planning, was from the specific and experimental to the general. Housing experts tried out different model homes in the various garden city and garden suburb estates and in the housing exhibitions that accompanied them. These specific initiatives were subject to professional criticism and debate and eventually consolidated and simplified in the model floor plans of the Tudor Walters Report (Local Government Board 1918) whose recommendations in turn framed the Homes for Heroes programme.

In relation to the aesthetics of housing, the direction was towards simplicity of form and the avoidance of decoration. Garden city design had rested on the use of 'street pictures' intended to give each street a distinct identity. Unwin explained the rationale in *Town Planning in Practice* (1909). Even where it is not possible to avoid much repetition of semi-detached or detached houses, the use of a street picture should be so arranged as to give a sense of grouping (ibid., 350). Conversely, if the buildings were diverse, the creation of a street picture would provide a sense of cohesion (ibid., 363). A variety of devices was to be used: culs-de-sac, as well as through streets; quadrangles of dwellings built around a green lawn and modelled on the courtyards of the colleges at Oxford and Cambridge; steeply pitched roofs; the breaking up of straight building lines by set-backs; and the breaking up of straight rooflines by dormers, gables and projecting wings. Hampstead Garden Suburb and Letchworth Garden City provide examples of all these devices.

Garden city schemes were not universally admired in the professional journals, however. Conventional standards of architectural good taste favoured simplicity without the devices that Unwin used to make garden city streets look interesting. When the journal *The Builder* (5 July 1905) reviewed the *Cheap Cottages Exhibition* held at Letchworth, it complained of a 'striving after the artificial picturesque' which was 'a weakness of a considerable proportion' of the exhibits. The criticism was aimed, in part, at the superficial decoration that Unwin condemned. But it was additionally aimed at the devices which Unwin and other garden city architects had used to construct a street picture, namely 'the constant employment of very high pitched roofs' and the use 'high-pitched gablets and dormers'. A 'plain, square-lined' cottage was to be preferred.

The criticisms of *The Builder* anticipated the logic of the Homes for Heroes programme. Homes for Heroes housing sometimes retained the principle of breaks in the building and roofline of terraces. The use of such variations was not universal, however and where applied, they were not as prominent as Unwin had proposed. As a further economy measure, roof heights were lower, this being the result of slate rather tile as a roof material. Lower roofs, in turn, eliminated another method that Unwin had used to promote a street picture. The council house became, in the words of its critics, 'a brick box with a slate roof'. Private builders also used slate, but they retained decorative detail such as bay windows and half-timbered gables.

Not all this was necessarily in accordance with popular tastes. Writing as a former regional housing inspector for the Ministry, Sayle (1924, 156) noted that 'architects and housing experts' found the more ornate, older privately developed houses 'infinitely less attractive', than the new council houses. In contrast, as Sayle noted, it was 'at least an open question' whether many of the tenants agreed. However, Sayle's comments are no more than a brief aside, suggesting that the external appearance was less important than the facilities available in the property and the rent.

At the same time and more importantly, The Homes for Heroes programme redefined the logic of policy as one of mass production. Writing in the *Town Planning Review*, Adshead (1916, 246) argued that not only the details, but also the general layout and design of the dwelling should be standardised on the grounds of efficiency. The experience of World War I strengthened such views as it showed the superiority of mass production in the manufacture of weapons and motor vehicles.

The Tudor Walters Committee did not go as far as to endorse a policy of outright standardisation. Despite a concern with economy and despite in addition the inclusion of a range of 'type' floor plans, the report only advocated the standardisation of elements such as doors and windows rather than the house as a whole. The report expressed scepticism whether full standardisation would generate any significant benefits and it warned against monotony, if standardisation were undertaken on a large scale.

In practice, however, the centralisation of the building programme and the desire for quick results diminished the opportunity for variety. The Ministry's increasing insistence on detailed administrative controls had a similar effect. Sayle (1924, 143–4) noted that while, in 1919, practice was relatively flexible,

> As time went on and prices rose ... the policy of the Ministry became less favourable to variations from the ... type, for which the numerous 'type-plans,' 'type-specifications,' 'type contracts' and 'type bills of quantities,' prepared by the Ministry's own staff could be utilised, thus saving both time and money.

In any case, a degree of standardisation would have been inevitable. Standardisation had been growing in privately developed terraced homes as builders searched for the most cost-effective materials (Muthesius 1982). For example, the railways had enabled the transportation of building materials in a way that had been previously impossible. In the Homes for Heroes programme, a combination of bureaucratic control and social idealism took standardisation to a new extreme.

The dependence of standardisation on bureaucracy went almost unrecognised at the time. It is, nevertheless, significant in the light of the attempt by later historians, notably by Tafuri (1976), to explain the history of twentieth-century urban design as the adoption of modern industrial methods of production. Tafuri notes, in particular, how modern architecture focused on the principle of an individual cell that could be produced *ad infinitum*. Though Tafuri did not use the word, this was architecture and planning as 'Fordism' – meaning the industrial production of standardised dwellings, much in the same way as the factories of Henry Ford mass-produced a limited range of cars.

Modern architecture, as this developed on the European continent in the 1920s, also glorified mass production in a way that supports the Fordist thesis. Le Corbusier's *Vers une architecture* published in 1923, for example, contains numerous photographs of cars, includes a chapter devoted to car design and it proposes a prototype mass produced house called a 'Citrohan', which is a pun on the car-maker 'Citroën'. *Vers une architecture*, translated as *Towards a New Architecture*, was first published in English in 1927.[3] Thereafter it became a principal reference book for aspiring modern architects. *Vers une architecture* was an exercise in propaganda, however. It was worlds away from the practicalities of house building, with its reliance on small firms and individual artisans.

Standardisation in the Homes for Heroes programme differed from modern architecture in another way. Modern architecture envisaged using industrial production methods to promote innovation. In contrast, the architectural and planning discourse in Britain always referred to the house types of the past, either to country cottages, as in the design of the garden cities or to Georgian terraces and town houses, as was the preferred model for the critics of the garden city movement. Even though architects in Britain might sometimes used the words 'modern housing' or 'modern architecture', they did not yet mean the creation of any general break with the past. The intended break was more specific and mostly concerned a desire to avoid the faults, as they were seen, of the nineteenth-century city.

The methodology of design and social reform was the same in Scotland, as in England. The method remained one of modernising previous models, notably the tenement, rather than inventing completely new one. As recommended by the Royal Commission on Housing in Scotland, tenements were, in the future, to be limited to three storeys; no single end apartments (one room flats) were to be allowed; no internal layout was to be allowed if, as a consequence, individual flats were built back-to-back; and finally the size and spacing of individual blocks was to be controlled more carefully.

The specification of a standard   The standardisation of housing design implied the specification of a model layout and model standards. The internal layout and equipment standards of the house were the main issue. In 1919, the typical working-class arrangement was for the coal fire in the kitchen to act as the common source for cooking food, warmth and hot water. Another room, located close to the kitchen, was the scullery. This was where food would be prepared, plates cleaned, and where, in addition, the bath would be located, usually in a form that could be moved when not in use. There was no separate bathroom. Another living area, sometimes constituted as a separate room, the parlour, was available for visitors, for special occasions and for activities that could be undertaken away from children and kitchen work. The parlour constituted a relatively public zone of the interior, facing the street. (See *The Builder*, 3 January 1919.)

This was the usual pattern for the respectable working-class living in a cottage or larger terrace in England. For poor families fewer rooms would be available. In Scotland in particular, one room tenement accommodation was common, without a separate bedroom. In a property with a limited number of rooms, a corner or side of the living room might be designated as a parlour. Otherwise, the public zone of the house, to the extent that this existed at all, would be located outside, in the street or in nearby bars and alehouses.

By about 1910, the typical new middle-class home involved significantly higher standards. On the ground floor, it comprised a parlour and separate kitchen that was itself sometimes provided with a gas cooker and washbasin. On the second floor, it possessed a bathroom with a supply of running hot water and a fitted bath and a separate toilet compartment (Muthesius 1982, 90). The middle-class house provided an apparently practical ideal for the organised housing pressure groups. It was obviously easier to run than a more basic working-class home. It also incorporated notions of the home as a place of privacy, as for example in demands for a private bathroom and, in addition, notions of the home as a base for children's study and socialising with others, as in demands for a parlour or second living room.

Women's groups were particularly prominent in the housing campaigns of the time. The suffragette movement and its campaign for equal rights had made women's groups more militant. Yet the home was still regarded as the women's domain and this was explicitly accepted by the Ministry during World War I through the establishment of a subcommittee to represent the woman's viewpoint in the specification of standards. The subsequent reports provided a systematic, arguably the first systematic account of the requirements of a working-class home in relation to both housework and comfort (Ministry of Reconstruction 1918; 1919).

The Tudor Walters report assessed and drew all the previous advice together. The report accepted, with qualifications, the case for a separate scullery, kitchen and parlour on the ground floor. In common with the view of nearly all housing experts, the report also favoured wide-fronted houses for public health reasons, as opposed to the narrow fronted homes used by private developers. Wide fronted houses let in more sunlight and daylight to their ground floor rooms. In relation to the bathroom, the Tudor Walters Committee accepted that previous arrangements 'can no longer be regarded as entirely satisfactory'. It did not go so far, however, as the women's groups in stating that a separate bathroom was a necessity. For reasons of economy and practicalities, the bath would sometimes have to be placed in the scullery.

The Tudor Walters model layouts have an overall area, exclusive of storage, of between 1055 (98.01m^2) and 1080 sq ft (100.33m^2) for parlour houses and between 855 (79.4m^2) and 900 sq. ft (83.6m^2) for non-parlour types. These were large homes in comparison to typical pre-1919 working-class practice. In practice, however, the smaller models tended to predominate in the Homes for Heroes programme (Swenarton 1981, 160). Dwellings built under subsequent legislation in the 1920s and 1930s tended to have lower standards still.

Subsequent accounts by a committee of technical experts, the Dudley Committee (MH 1944) and by Cleeve Barr (1958, 54–6) confirm the absence of a parlour in most council houses built before 1939. For example, the Dudley Committee indicates a variation in floor space between 'roughly 750 and 850 sq. ft' (69.7 and 79m^2) (MH 1944, 13). Cleeve Barr (op. cit.) makes explicit the additional point that most lacked a hot water system. The bath had to be filled manually and was located downstairs in a two-storey house, with all the inconvenience that this caused to the downstairs layout and lifestyles. The slum clearance flats developed in the 1930s had the lowest standards of all. Some even had shared kitchen sinks and baths in cubicles sited off a corridor serving several dwelling units (Cleeve Barr 1958, 56).

The external spacing and density standards of the Homes for Heroes programme were less contentious. The cottages built in the Homes for Heroes programme stood in a street layout where external spacing standards conformed to the precepts of the garden city movement, that is to say, a maximum density of 12 dwellings to the acre, about 30 to the hectare and a minimum distance between facing walls of 70 feet, about 21 metres. This latter was justified as the minimum necessary to admit sunlight, given the particular conditions at Letchworth garden city in midwinter. The logic is unconvincing. Midwinter is the least sunny time of the year, in Letchworth as elsewhere in Britain. However, the justification for the 70 foot/21 metre rule in the usual absence of winter sunshine was not discussed.

The garden city architects knew that their standards were arbitrary. Elsewhere, in *Town Planning in Practice*, in apparent contradiction to the thesis that density ought to be controlled, Unwin (1909, 319–20) admitted, 'It is not possible to fix any absolute limit for the number of houses per acre which can be regarded as a maximum compatible with health and comfort'. The garden city movement wanted to provoke a break with the past and was largely indifferent to the details. In the context of a depressed land market, they were also specifying standards that did not generate substantial cost penalties. Between 1914 and 1920, the cost of land hardly increased while the cost of building roads and sewers tripled – a pattern which inevitably favoured the garden city method of development which sought to economise on roads by using more land (Swenarton 1981, 143).

In the longer term, the internal standards that were controversial and too demanding in 1919 proved durable. Tudor Walters defined the minimum requirements for a family home in a way that persisted long after the report itself was mostly forgotten. The desire for a second living room or parlour became gradually less prevalent, probably because life styles became more informal. However, the floor space of the Tudor Walters model layout standards corresponded almost exactly to the recommendations of the Dudley (MH 1944) and Parker Morris (MHLG 1961) reports, both of which recommended a minimum of 900 sq. ft (83.6m^2). Even in the early 1990s, housing associations were building family homes within the floor space range of Tudor Walters (Karn and Sheridan 1994). Subsequent standards have not greatly changed.

In contrast, the external standards eventually became viewed as arbitrary and obsolete. They influenced suburban layout throughout the interwar period and persisted in a different context into the 1970s. The 70 ft/21 metre rule proved a useful rule of thumb in the regulation of suburban development as it prevented overlooking and so promoted privacy and, in addition, provided sufficient space around the home for car parking. The rationale for the standards shifted, though the standard itself remained the same (Woodford et al. 1976, 55). Indeed the 21 metre rule is still applied by local authorities in England and Wales as a means of regulating infill and small scale extensions in suburban areas. The rule became too difficult to apply in new housing in the context of increased land costs. It was also criticised, notably in the Essex Design Guide, on the grounds of promoting monotony in estate layout and producing open townscapes that could not easily fit into the more enclosed spaces of older settlements. (See County Council of Essex 1973.)

Standardisation, Individualism and the State

The aesthetics of mass housing had implications for politics and in particular for the role of the state. Publicly subsidised house building (other than slum clearance schemes) had always been opposed by pressure groups representing private landlords and more generally by those who favoured laissez-faire and the market. By the time of World War I, aesthetic objections were also put forward. Mass, publicly funded housing programmes implied the end of individuality, the end of diversity and the end of traditional townscapes, or so it was widely believed. They also marked the end of small-scale, co-operative housing reform and the triumph of a more centralised approach.

Standardisation and socialism   The tone of much of the subsequent debate was set by the architectural and planning theorists associated with the critics of picturesque garden city. Adshead (1916) argued that the nineteenth-century view of progress through individual labour was now obsolete. The future lay in industrial organisation. As a result, the standard cottage 'will not be the home of an individual, of an anarchist; but the home of a member of a certain class of the community, of a communist' (ibid., 246). Adshead was an exception, however, in arguing for standardisation and the end of individuality as desirable. Most references were critical. In December 1917, for example, The London *Evening Standard* argued against standardisation on the grounds that the 'result will be the Prussianisation of the country and the destruction of the local character of districts'.

The reference to 'Prussianisation' is ironic given that a similar debate occurred in Germany in the 1930s in which right-wing critics accused public sector housing schemes of ruining the German landscape. (See Miller Lane 1968, 166.) The point is the association between mass house building and the imposition of something alien on the traditional landscape. Soon afterwards, *The Builder* (4 January 1918,

2) developed the same criticism as part of a campaign against subsidies for council housing. The problem lay not in design *per se*, but in

> the erection in a hurry of a large number of small buildings through the medium of State-aided schemes. If we take things quietly and temperately, removing obstacles to private enterprise, we are far more likely to obtain ..., variety and character.

The association between standardisation and public sector intervention was, moreover, sufficiently widespread in other aspects of politics for the Fabian society, a political group within the Labour Party, to publish a paper on the subject. The author, W.A. Robson (1926, 4), admitted that 'the spectre of monotony' was a 'brooding apprehension' amongst many who might otherwise support socialist policies. 'The old objection to the 'dull uniformity' of Socialism which has always seemed so absurd to the Socialists, nevertheless constantly reappears'.

Robson's principal answer was that socialism would promote diversity. 'The ideal Society would be one in which the marriage of individual capacity and environmental opportunity yielded an infinite diversity of life where to-day squalor, monotony, flatness, and stultification hold sway.' Standardisation was 'neither good nor bad' (ibid., 7). Standardisation of legal and political rights was, nevertheless, a precondition of democracy. Standardisation of material condition was an essential characteristic of equality. Standardisation in industry promoted economic efficiency. The point to be avoided was 'the constant repetition of thoughts, sayings and actions'. Such repetition produced the 'standardisation of life' and this was 'antithetic to the highest activities of mankind' (ibid., 11–12).

> The problem which confronts a community at any given time is, therefore, not whether it should standardise the life of its members in every possible respect, or attempts conversely, to maintain a complete diversity; but to what extent, in what measure, how, why and when it should resist or promote measures tending towards uniformity. That is the crux of the whole matter; and a question which may often present very great difficulty.

Standardisation in housing design may be analysed in similar terms. Standardisation was the inevitable result of attempts to build better quality housing, according to a socially accepted minimum and, in addition, according to a defined cost. As such, standardisation in housing could be held to promote both social equality and a greater diversity in individual life. The members of a family living in a three bedroom cottage were much more likely to enjoy a healthy and rewarding life than those living in an overcrowded slum.

Likewise, the pragmatic questions listed by Robson 'to what extent, in what measures' did indeed present great difficulties. If the standard were too modest, the houses would not meet the expectation of pressure groups for something better and could also be accused of stigmatising working-class people as undeserving, as was a charge made by the Labour opposition housing spokesman, John Wheatley, when faced with a reduction in standards in 1923 (Goodchild 1997, 97).

Conversely, if the standard of the Homes for Heroes houses were too ambitious, the rents of the houses on completion were likely to be too high in relation to that prevailing in working-class districts and were likely to generate complaints for this reason. After about 1922, such complaints were commonplace (Sayle 1924, 163). Complaints about high rents were, moreover, widespread, despite a tendency for the completed dwellings to house relatively prosperous families.

While socialists such as Robson sometimes admitted that standardisation and monotony might be a potential problem, they did not examine ways in which trends towards standardisation might be minimised. The dominant socialist tradition in Britain was Fabianism and this assumed that standardisation was inevitable. Yet, the position of Conservative critics was little different. Though they might object to the principle of standardisation, they did little in power to counter its effects. Indeed, Conservative governments often imposed standards on local authorities as a means of preventing what they regarded as the misuse of public funds – for example, in the development of large, well-equipped dwellings. New council housing was standardised, irrespective of the party in power.

The end of co-partnership societies   The Homes for Heroes programme used garden city design principles and layouts. The garden city movement was more than this, however. It was an exercise in communitarian reform, a means to promote public enterprise and service through what Howard (1898/1985, 68) called the 'pro-municipal' work of philanthropic, charitable and responsible financial institutions. It used, moreover, co-partnership and other types of small, locally-controlled housing societies as a vehicle for promoting such pro-municipal work.

Co-partnership housing originated in the general co-operative movement in the 1880s. It involved a combination of renting and collective ownership and had advantages, according to its supporters, of giving residents both a stake in the prosperity of a neighbourhood and a say in its self-government. Bournville, whose development started in 1900, was the first scheme that combined the principles of open garden city layouts with co-partnership housing (RCHS 1917, 269). Other schemes followed, notable examples being suburban schemes at Ealing in West London and Wavertree in Liverpool and an embryonic new town at Letchworth in Hertfordshire.

However, even with some public assistance, the garden cities made relatively slow progress and tended to house better-off workers and their families. Co-partnership housing was more expensive than conventional renting because it involved tenants acquiring a share in the housing society. In addition, some garden city projects, notably Letchworth turned to the development of homes for individual ownership (Purdom: 1913, 76). From 1919 onwards, a combination of the relatively poor terms of financial assistance, high building costs and rent controls almost wholly prevented their continued expansion. A number of new public utility societies were formed after 1919, but few were of the pre-war type. They were mostly either employers' societies or societies to meet the needs of the middle class (Purdom 1922, 167).

There were exceptions. Sayle (1924, 94–6) cites the example of an 'excellent small society' which built three 'bungalows', (i.e. three single-storey blocks) each divided into six one- or two-roomed units, at Malvern in Worcestershire. The society was started by members of the Malvern branch of the National Council of Women and after much delay, mainly caused by disputes with the Ministry of Health, it was completed in May 1922. As documented by Sayle, it is apparent that small housing societies went through the same administrative processes that led to standardisation in local authority hosuing. However, the Malvern experiment was not typical. Sayle (ibid.) states that

> The success of this scheme is all the more creditable to its promoters because, generally speaking, the only Public Utility Societies whose schemes matured and flourished were those with a big individual capitalist or company behind them … the circumstances of the time proved fatal to genuine co-operative effort.

Even the co-partnership societies, established before 1914, struggled to survive in subsequent decades. Houses were sold into conventional home ownership. In some cases, as at Ealing and Wavertree, the remaining assets were acquired by outside commercial interests and managed on commercial lines (Birchall 1995).[4] Some of the early societies have survived to the present, albeit in a modified form. Bournville Village Trust is the best documented example (Groves et al. 2003). In general, however, Sayle is right. After 1919, the times became inconducive to small scale, co-operative effort.

Split Patterns of Housing Provision

The Homes for Heroes programme was discontinued in 1921, just as it was beginning to result in the completion of relatively large numbers of dwellings. The peak year for completions was 1922, when 80,000 were completed. Thereafter completions gradually declined and ceased completely in 1929 (Bowley 1945, 271). The programme ended partly because of the high expense to the Treasury of an open-ended building subsidy, but mostly owing to changed political priorities.

A Conservative government initiated a second experiment in subsidised house building in 1923, with the subsidy fixed at a flat rate and open to all types of builder, not just local authorities. Conservative policy was to limit the building of council houses through requiring, as a condition of financial assistance, that local authorities demonstrate the inability of private builders to meet local needs. A Labour government withdrew this latter condition in the Housing Act 1924 in an attempt to re-establish local authorities as major housing providers. General house building subsidies then persisted in various forms until 1933, after which time policy changed to support new housing in connection to slum clearance.

The Scale of House Building

In a context where all parties recognised the continuing significance of housing shortages, the withdrawal of general building subsidies indicates the main success and the main defining feature of housing provision in the 1920s and 1930s. After about 1925, private house building entered a new long-term cycle, based on building for sale, as opposed for rent. The cycle itself lasted until the end of the 1960s, if the intermission of World War II and the licencing restrictions of the 1940s are omitted. Even before World War II, however, the numbers built were substantial and impressive by both previous and subsequent British standards.

By September 1934, the housing stock had increased by 31 per cent compared to 1919. By March 1939, the housing stock had increased substantially again, by 47 per cent compared to 1919 (Bowley 1945, 274). It was not until another thirty years later, in the 1960s, that annual completions exceeded those of the peak years in the mid 1930s and this was only with the help of a non-traditional building programme led by local authorities. By the 1960s, however, the housing stock had increased in size and the proportional increase was less.

Even in the period from 1919 to 1934, covering the Homes for Heroes programme and the second experiment in subsidised house building, private builders were the main providers. Figures collated by Bowley (1945, 52) suggest that local authorities provided 31 per cent of the total built, with private builders providing the rest.

Public utility societies do not figure as a separate category in Bowley's statistics, almost certainly because the numbers were too small. Relevant figures, available from the Report of the Pole Committee established in 1942, suggest that, in the period from 1919 to 1940, public utility societies and housing associations (as public utility societies were redefined under the Housing Act, 1935) completed about one per cent of all dwellings (CHAC 1944).

In part, house building increased rapidly because the new houses were obviously superior to most of those built before 1919. The new homes had electric lighting, a purpose-built kitchen, bathroom and internal toilet and, as a result, were more easily managed. For the most prosperous households, the new homes were also better adapted to the ownership of a car. In addition, they possessed lower density, garden city and garden suburban surroundings and were located away from the grime and dirt of industrial cities.

The economic context was also favourable, once the building industry recovered from the disruption of World War I. Living standards increased for those in work and an increasing amount of building land was freed by the growth of bus routes, increasing car ownership amongst the middle classes and, around London, by improvements to the passenger rail and underground network. The sites, moreover, were generally available for development at relatively low prices. The agricultural industry was depressed – so farmers were generally willing to sell. In addition, unlike the post-1945 years, there were no effective planning controls.

Especially in the booming London suburbs, a distinct house building industry started to emerge, integrating the processes of marketing, development, construction and personal finance. Some companies, such as Costain, George

Wimpey and especially New Ideal Homesteads the largest company of all, undertook projects of literally hundreds and occasionally thousands of properties. The development by New Ideal Homestead of the Falconwood Park Estate in the London Borough of Bexley, for example, involved the construction of more than 2000 houses in the early 1930s, from about 1932 to 1934.[5]

Outside the special circumstances of Greater London, house building mostly remained the preserve of small firms and individuals. Little capital or specialist expertise was required to set up a construction company or for an existing company to undertake the combined process of land acquisition, development and construction. As a result, once the general economic conditions became favourable, firms came forward to satisfy the demand. The Pole Committee noted, 'a great part of the expansion of the industry was represented by an increase in the number of small firms' (CHAC 1944, 12)

The 'New' Suburbia

The scale of house building meant the creation of a new urban landscape and this effect was magnified by an unprecedented development of roads, shops and especially around London, new factories. In 1933, the novelist and playwright, J.B. Priestley travelled by bus, train and tram around England. His account, published as *English Journey*, showed not two principal types of landscape – urban and rural – as had been the theme in virtually all pre-1919 accounts, including the proposals of Howard for garden cities. Instead, Priestley shows three types of landscape, or he put it three types of England: the 'Old England' of colleges, cathedrals and countryside; the nineteenth-century England of industrial towns and cities, now in decay; and the 'New England' of suburbia and Americanised culture, based on films and mass consumption.

Change was not confined to towns and cities in England, however. Even in Glasgow, one of the most depressed cities in the 1920s and 1930s, small builders constructed neat, rendered bungalows along the radial routes so creating the typical ribbon development of the time (McKean 1999, 136).

Landscapes and house types   The suburbia of the 1920s and 1930s looked different from earlier, Edwardian and Victorian suburbia. The landscape was increasingly viewed from the road, from a car or a bus, rather than a train or tram. As a result, accounts emphasised a landscape of petrol filling stations, parades of shops and occasional cinemas and of how, in addition, suburban growth caused congestion and screened views of countryside from the road. In *English Journey*, for example, Priestley combined reflections on the 'New England' with complaints about being stuck in the fog on the Great North Road.

In addition, the new housing was itself distinct. The new suburbia was more widely spread, more 'sporadic' in the words of its critics than its Victorian and Edwardian middle-class predecessors. It was also intended for a less opulent clientele. Suburbia had become mass housing.

Yet the suburban ideal remained essentially an ideal of individualism, privacy and domesticity. Suburbia was created through the demand of individuals and their families and it was promoted as such. Suburbia, represented as J.M. Richards (1973, 93–4) later stated, a means of creating a private world. The suburb comprised 'castles on the ground' as opposed to the 'castles in the air' of utopian town planning.

Adapting suburbia to mass housing meant the repetition of basic housing forms, notably the semi. In many estates, however, especially in the smaller projects outside Greater London, standardisation was mitigated by the involvement of different builders on different plots. Each builder would use slightly different materials – for example tiles rather than slate for the roof or more or less rendering to the external walls or slightly different detailed features such as porches and weather protection (Whitehand and Carr 1999, 490–94). Builders would also allow individual touches in variations of decorative details or the door or window fittings and would permit designs to change over time, if economies were apparent and advantages existed for the consumer.[6]

In the most affluent areas, mostly in the Home Counties, individual variations went further. A new type of low-density suburbia emerged based on a combination of rail commuting and the use of the motor car. Individual properties were built along country lanes or developers laid out plots for low-density individual development, surrounded by woods and countryside. Edwards (1981, 139) cites Tewin Wood in Hertfordshire as an example.

An affordable version of individual plot development also grew up, notably along the Sussex coast and in Essex. Here, working-class Londoners purchased small agricultural plots and built a wood and asbestos shed or chalet, if only as a temporary holiday retreat and therefore with only a dirt road access and without mains services of gas, electricity, drainage and clean running water. The plot lands, as they were called, expressed a widespread working-class desire for property, even for a tiny plot. Like other forms of suburbia, they also expressed a search, perhaps a futile search for, in the words of Hardy and Ward (1984), 'arcadia', that is to say a rural idyll where they could live a more natural life freed from the pressures of the city.

The development of bungalows came to represent in the most concrete terms the new, increasingly dispersed style of development. The plot lands generally comprised self-built bungalows of diverse shapes and details and this interest in self-build was supported by the development of what would now be called 'kit' housing capable of erection by the future occupier. However, more importantly in terms of the scale of development, the bungalow was also taken up by private house builders and architects as part of their repertoire of house types.

Many were clearly luxury dwellings of their time, though others offered simpler and smaller accommodation and fell within the criteria for the subsidies available for the construction of small dwellings under the 1923 and 1924 Housing Acts. In the ten years after the World War I, the leading building and architectural journals all published articles with examples of innovative bungalow designs, including hybrids between cottages and bungalows.

These same articles also discussed the relative merits and disadvantages of bungalow compared to two-storey houses. They disagreed about whether the bungalow was more or less expensive to build than an equivalent-sized two-storey house. Much, it would appear, depended on the detailed floor plan and specifications. Where the occupier was satisfied with inexpensive materials such as asbestos roof tiles or reduced foundations or timber rather than brick walls, bungalows could be cheaper (*The Builder*, 6 October 1922). Otherwise, bungalows were likely to be slightly more expensive than a two-storey house of a similar size. They required more land, they required more extensive foundations and they involved a greater volume of roofing.

For these latter reasons, and with the exception of some seaside areas, cost-conscious speculative house builders avoided the use of bungalows. Most privately developed bungalows were once-off designs. Council and public utility society bungalows were more likely to be based on standard designs, but were only used as specialised accommodation for the elderly.

All agreed, however that the bungalows offered a more convenient and flexible internal layout, with no stairs and that, in addition, it appealed to contemporary consumer tastes. One anonymous architect, writing in *The Builder* (6 October 1922, 501) stated, for example, that the bungalow appealed to a contemporary desire for 'a simplification of the forms and ceremonies of living'. Their main disadvantage, according to contemporary reports, was to reduce the separation of living and sleeping spaces within the home and therefore to muddy the distinction between private and more public areas, suitable for receiving visitors. At the lower end of the housing market, bungalows were also smaller than most types of two-storey house.

In other English-speaking countries, notably in the US and Australia, bungalows became popular at about the same time for similar reasons. In the US bungalows became the staple of working-class and lower middle-class housing in what is now regarded as the inner ring of suburban development. Bungalows were so common that the Chicago School geographer Burgess (1925) cited these as typical of the outer commuters' zone of housing. In Australia, with its even more plentiful supply of land, the single-storey house represented the twentieth-century dwelling *par excellence*, accounting for the vast majority of dwellings built from the 1920s until the 1970s.

In this context, King (1984) suggests that the bungalow was the first manifestation in domestic architecture of a global economy and global exchange of information. The finance for constructing the bungalow derived from the international economy and from Britain's privileged place within that economy. Likewise, the word itself 'bungalow' derived from Britain's colonial experience in India.

A simpler explanation is that the parallel growth of bungalows in Britain, Australia and the US was caused by similarities in the standard of living, in lifestyles and in consumer preferences. King (1984, 159) suggests that the publication of pattern books of bungalow floor plans in the United States, especially in California, in the decade before the 1914 influenced development in Britain. American bungalow pattern books were available in Britain, as King demonstrates. They were, however, rarely if ever cited in the housing and building journals. Architects and builders looked to pre-1914 examples of single-storey dwellings, including rural examples that had little obvious connection either to

Indian colonial housing or to US models. Architects and builders were also aware that the term itself 'bungalow' had Indian origins, but again Indian architectural examples were not cited. Moreover, in contrast to practice in Australia, the specifically Indian feature of a 'veranda' as a shaded sitting out area was poorly adapted to the cool British climate and was seldom used.

The use of bungalows apart, a degree of continuity existed in the internal layout of small family homes. The smaller semis of the 1920s and 1930s were closely related to the three bedroom pre-1919 narrow fronted terraces, at least to the larger pre-1919 terraces. The typical semi was itself narrow fronted, as this provided a mean of economising on street carriageway. It possessed a ground floor comprising two living rooms, a parlour (now also called a sitting room) at the front and a living/dining room at the back adjacent to the kitchen which itself took the form of small back extension. Continuity of floor plan with older terraces is probably the main reason for the popularity of semis amongst builders and the customers. Elsewhere in Europe semis were relatively uncommon.

The arrangement between the parlour at the front and the living room at the back, in turn, allowed a distinction in use between a public side of the home, which was open to visitors and a private zone at the back (Ramsey 1939). The typical kitchen in a middle-class semi was too small to accommodate even a small breakfast table. It was no more than a 'machine for preparing meals' as the architect Gibberd said with apparent approval (*Illustrated Carpenter and Builder*, 5 August 1932). As a result the living room would remain, as before 1919, the main place for meals.

Meeting conflicting requirements   The style and appearance of the home was important to house purchasers and was recognised as such by developers. As Edwards (1981, 128) notes, if the suburban house 'was to be effective as a status-symbol, it had to be built in a recognisable style'. A variety of styles were available – the 'cottage' style of the early garden city and most commonly used for bungalows, the highly popular 'mock-Tudor', with black and white timbers and leaded lights and finally, in the 1930s, the 'modern' or 'modernistic' style (with streamlined, linked bay windows, a smooth rendered wall usually painted in white and sometimes a flat roof). Some builders offered a choice of style using the same floor plan. Various types of neo-Classical were another possibility, though in smaller dwellings these suffered from too close a similarity to council housing. Neo-classical styles also favoured sash windows that had become generally unpopular (*Illustrated Carpenter and Builder*, 19 May 1939, 1310).

Self-consciously modern design offered an additional though less common style. At first, in the 1920s, house buyers would have only obtained a modern-looking house if they had consciously wanted something different and could have afforded an architect. Even then they might have had to face the hostility of the local planning authority. Aesthetic control on the details could be applied by local authorities even if the use of planning controls to stop construction was limited by the likely compensation payments.

The technical durability of the modern style was a further constraint, at least in its pure 'ultramodern' variant and was widely criticised in the specialist journals.

Ultramodern architecture used flat roofs that were expensive to build and had a greater risk of water penetration. It used extensive window areas that suffered from the heat in the summer and from the cold on sunless days. It also used a white painted, smooth cement render that quickly became dirty in industrial areas and that weathered poorly.

Yet, in another sense of the word, that of being up-to-date, all the various styles were modern. The industrial city of the nineteenth and early twentieth century was dirty and dark. The interior of the houses were similar. They generally possessed poor standards of natural light and typically used a combination of deep curtains and dark paintwork. The suburban houses built in the 1920s and 1930s were brighter and more colourful. Under the heading of 'Polychrome in the Ascendant', one contributor to the *Illustrated Carpenter and Builder* (12 July 1929) praised 'cubist architecture' for drawing attention to the role of strong colours. A few years later, the same journal reported, 'architects today seemed to be taking more interest in colour than ever before' (9 August 1935).

Domestic life had moved into the sun and the sun itself had become a recurrent theme in the architectural drawings and internal decorations of the time, on the front gate, on lamps and on the fireplace (Oliver et al. 1981, 184). Domestic life had moved into the sun, not so much through the careful design of wide-fronted houses as continued to be the practice in council housing. It moved into the sun, more as a matter as style, as lifestyle and as visual style.

Though they would not have used such words, developers provided dwellings that were simultaneously 'elaborate and mean' (Edwards 1981, 128). For marketing reasons, they wished to appeal to a common denominator in taste, to a sense of style and, generally though less so in the case of the modernist housing, to an established, romantic, leafy image of suburbia. Equally, they generally had to ensure that their product was relatively cheap and this became an ever more pressing concern once in the 1930s developers turned increasingly to housing skilled working-class families and not just the middle class. A desire to reduce cost in turn meant a preference for simple dwelling forms, repetition, the use of inexpensive materials and, in London where land prices were higher, the development of schemes at the maximum density of 12 to the acre (30 to the hectare) (or slightly more if the builder believed that this was possible).

Driving down costs gave rise, in turn, to charges of poor quality 'jerry building'. The private builders paid too much attention to the superficialities of style, rather than the soundness of construction, it was argued. They also sought to speed up the rate of house production through piecework payments, that is payments by what is completed rather than the time spent on the job. In doing all this, moreover, they used untrained men.

The charge of jerry building was difficult to prove or disprove, as judgements about building standards always have a subjective element and often can only be determined through close inspection of the work itself, during the construction process. Moreover both the criticism of jerry building and its denial came mostly from sources that had an interest in the subject. The charge came from architects who disliked private housing for aesthetic reasons, from the advocates of council housing and from the supporters of the building trade unions that generally disliked the piecework method of payment. The denial came from the building industry and those associated with the building societies.

In the long term, the criticisms proved to be misguided. The durability and repairs record of the privately built interwar stock has generally been as good as any other period. The stock has not produced a higher incidence of maintenance problems than would be expected of any housing of its age. Indeed, the maintenance costs have generally been less than post1945 council housing. (See, for example, DoE 1993.) The main problem has been the relatively poor thermal characteristics, compared to later dwellings (DCLG 2007, 31).

In the 1930s, however, and for many years thereafter the criticisms of jerry building were credible. House purchasers lacked any form of universal industry guarantees or insurance, such as was eventually established by the National House Building Council. This latter, initially known as the National House Builders Registration Council (NHBRC), was established in 1937 by a trade organisation, the National Federation of Building Trade Employers. However, industry take-up was slow. Even as late as 1963, the NHBRC could claim to cover only some 26 per cent of new homes. Moreover, the scope of the protection remained inadequate in the view of the critics, including the national press (Competition Commission 1991, 5–7).

The housing boom of the 1920s and 1930s coincided with the disappearance of local design differences in private housing, despite the continued dominance of small local builders. Most likely, local variations disappeared once builders adopted the models available in the national trade journals such as the *Illustrated Carpenter and Builder* and consumer journals such as *Ideal Homes* and the annual *Ideal Homes Exhibition*. The former offered a method whereby small builders could advertise their design needs to each other and receive advice, including model internal plans. The latter, *Ideal Homes* and the *Ideal Homes Exhibition* were, as the reference to 'ideal' suggests, a means of defining aspirations at the upper end of the housing market, but they also offered model floor plans and elevations.

Ideal Homes was promoted predominantly for a female readership. The advertising material prepared by the larger house builders sometimes emphasised the same theme. The advertisements of New Ideal Homestead stated, for example, that their homes were 'designed by a woman for the woman'. [7] Nevertheless, the suburban home also appealed to men. J. M. Richards' later account of suburbia, initially published in 1946, repeatedly used the term 'him' and 'he' when explaining its popularity. In the face of global uncertainties, including the threat of war, suburbia represented a 'real world' where 'he', the suburban dweller could feel at home and 'cultivate his garden'.

Suburbia as a cultural discourse   Given the estimate by Bowley (1945, 274) of a 47 per cent increase in the housing stock between 1919 and 1939, the scale of urban growth must have been substantial. Since the new housing was of significantly lower density than the old, and given the growth of the associated paraphernalia of suburbia – shopping parades, new roads, petrol filling stations, new factories etc. – the built-up area of British cities increased by at least half, probably by about 60 per cent.

Most obviously large-scale suburban growth was a threat for those who wished to protect the countryside. The title of *England and the Octopus*, by Williams-Ellis (1928) summarises the fear. Suburbia was the octopus with its arms engulfing its prey – the English countryside.

The bungalow, much more than two-storey houses, was a particular villain owing to its novelty and horizontal lines and tendency to consume more land (Abercrombie 1939). Suburbia was 'bungaloid' growth (Williams-Ellis 1928, 141) – a type of infectious rash spreading over the skin of the countryside.

Yet suburbia understood as mass housing was also unavoidable. It could not be condemned without also condemning to the vast number of people who aspired to this new style of life. For this reason, the critique of suburbia was often little more than an exercise in snobbery. It was an attack on the supposedly bad taste of the masses. The fault of bungalows, for Clough Ellis, for example, was their 'gratuitously flashy or exotic appearance' (ibid., 142), whatever this was.

Not all assessments of suburbia were negative. J.B. Priestley argued that it would be unwise to come to a hasty judgement, whether for good or bad. The 'New England' of suburbia, though standardised, had a sense of popular appeal and dynamism that, in different ways, both old England and nineteenth-century England lacked. This New England was 'essentially democratic'. Access to suburbia needed money, but not much money. It was a 'large-scale mass-production job, with cut prices'. 'In this new England, for the first time in history, Jack and Jill [i.e. common people] are nearly as good as their master.' More people, including more working-class people, were enjoying a decent standard of living and were starting to create their own culture, albeit one that, for Priestley, was over-influenced by American examples.

England still had no city worthy of its citizens, in Priestley's view. The strengths of suburbia did not preclude a case for better planning. Yet suburban growth at least meant that the British city had escaped the physical straightjacket of the nineteenth century.

Social Segregation and Slum Clearance

Though Priestley did not say so, the distinction between the old England, largely developed in the nineteenth-century and the new twentieth-century suburban England implied new and more extensive forms of social segregation. There is some uncertainty about whether the nineteenth-century city was more segregated than its predecessors. The middle classes remained in social contact with working-class and poorer families in their role as employers of servants. Some servants would live in the same house as their employers. Others would live nearby and walk to their employer's home. It was, as a result, in the interests of middle-class families not to move too far away from working-class streets. In contrast, the development of labour-saving houses enabled the middle classes to live amongst themselves in separate suburbs (Mann 1965, 83–4).

Increased spatial separation of different classes was also a separation of people living in owner-occupied and council housing. At first, on completion in the early 1920s, Homes for Heroes estates generally contained a mixture of skilled working-class families and others headed by men in clerical and managerial occupations. Some Homes for Heroes estates retained their social distinctiveness as a home to a predominantly skilled working-class and middle-class population. Roehampton in south London is an example (Bayliss 2001). Elsewhere better-off residents gradually moved out, especially in the context of the slum clearance drives of the 1930s.[8]

The rehousing of people from slums was a particular factor in changing the social composition of council estates. Slum clearance involved the rehousing, in the words of White (1950, 18–19), of 'a large number of families living in poverty, a high proportion of people needing help of one kind or another, and more than their proportion of problem families'. The slum clearance drives of the 1930s differed in another way from the Homes for Heroes programme. The tenants had to move, whether they wished to or not. Slum clearance was a compulsory rather than a voluntary exercise, the disruption of which caused objections from local residents, as White (ibid.) also noted.

Increases in rent level, consequent of rehousing, were the main complaint amongst those rehoused. The increases were so severe that, in at least one case in Stockton-on-Tees, documented by M'Gonigle (1933), rehousing increased death rates. In the face of higher rents, poorer families economised by reducing their diet to the point that this started to affect their health and that of their children. Housing policy remained constrained, as before 1919, by problems of poverty.

The experience of slum clearance was hardly an advertisement for further intervention along the same lines. Yet there was virtually no dissent amongst influential public opinion. Slum clearance was inevitable and desirable in the long term.

Slum clearance procedures were simplified under the Housing Act, 1930. Local authorities were no longer required to pay compensation on the full value of unfit property (Jarmain 1948, 121). They were given, moreover, more attractive financial subsidies to encourage the construction of replacement houses. Both government and local authorities indicated their desire to undertake slum clearance on a large scale. Initial plans, made by local authorities in 1933, envisaged the demolition of 266,000 houses (English et al. 1976, 22).

Given the existence of overcrowding and shared dwellings (more than one household in the same house) the number of replacement houses was likely to exceed the number of cleared properties. As a result, the initial impact of slum clearance was to promote further suburban expansion rather than redevelopment in the form of flats. From 1937 to 1939 flats only represented about one-eighth of all dwellings in tenders approved by the Ministry of Health. The vast majority of these would have been walk-up flats of up to five storeys. Even so, though relatively few in number, the existence of flatted estates again suggested that council housing was set apart and distinctive. A split housing policy implied a polarised pattern of housing provision and ultimately increased social segregation.

Notes

1   The figure is taken from a summary of the energy conservation characteristics of the housing stock, consulted May 2006 at the DEFRA website http://www.defra.gov.uk/ Environment/energy/research/domestic/index.htm.

2   Innovacion Limited and Ove Arup & Partners Ltd (2006) *The North's Residential Offer: Policy and Investment Review Phase I Report*, available at the website of the Northern Way, consulted June 2007 at http://www.thenorthernway.co.uk/downloaddoc. asp?id=260&page=207&skin=0.

3   The first English edition was translated from the thirteenth French edition with an introduction by Frederick Etchells, as indicated by the on-line public access catalogue of Cambridge University available July 2005 at http://ul-newton.lib.cam.ac.uk/cgi-bin/ Pwebrecon.cgi?DB=local&PAGE=First.

4   Local histories of Ealing (Brentham) and Wavetree co-parternship schemes are available on the web, consulted January 2008 at http://www.brentham.com/index.html; and http://www.liverpool.ndo.co.uk/wgs/page5.html.

5   Ideal Homes: suburbia in focus website consulted August 2003 at http://www.ideal-homes.org.uk/bexley/danson-estate.html.

6   *The Working-class Owner-occupied House of the 1930s Modern History*: MLitt: Oxford Thesis by M. Crisp, 1998 consulted May 2004 at http://www.pre-war-housing.org.uk/. The most relevant section is Chapter 5, 'Building the New Homes' at http://www.pre-war-housing.org.uk/chapter5buildingthenewhomesthehousethespeculativedeveloperbuilt. htm.

7   *Ideal Homes, Suburbia in Focus*, consulted August 2003 at http://www.ideal-homes. org.uk/index1a.html.

8   Data and interpretation offered in *The Birth of the Council Tenants Movement*, available May 2004 at http://freespace.virgin.net/labwise.history6/1934.html.

Chapter 3

Two Types of Planning

In terms of housing policy, the impact of World War II was similar to that of World War I. Again an era of private house building was replaced by an era from 1945 to the 1950s where council house building predominated. In terms of town planning, however, the difference in practice was substantial. By the 1940s, town planning offered a comprehensive vision, or what later critics (Hall et al. 1973, 45; Taylor 1998, 3–19) would call a comprehensive 'blueprint,' of the future. Small-scale blueprint plans had existed since at least the first exercises in planned estate development, before 1919. Indeed, as a method of design, blueprints have a much longer history. In contrast, the preparation of a comprehensive blueprint of a large city had seldom, if ever been attempted before.

The Ups-and-Downs of National Planning

Though this was seldom stated explicitly, the credibility of any comprehensive blueprint presupposed a programme of social and economic intervention of sufficient power to fix urban development into a specific pattern. The plans presupposed, to use the discourse of the 1930s, the emergence of a new form of 'national planning' that ran in parallel with and strengthened town planning as an exercise in design and regulation.

Yet the significance of concepts of national planning has seldom been fully recognised in histories of town planning or housing. With some exceptions, notably Hebbert (1983), the typical history of planning focuses on the Barlow Report, that is to say the Royal Commission on the Distribution of the Industrial Population (1940) and identifies this report as evidence of a new and more ambitious approach to town planning. The Barlow report is indeed important, but it is arguable whether the Barlow report would ever have been commissioned without the prior existence of a movement for national planning.

In the early 1970s, a US planning theorist, Friedmann, called the debate between the national planning movement in Britain and its opponents the 'great debate', meaning a debate that, though rooted in a specific historic period in the 1930s and 1940s, set the context for justifications and critiques of planning thereafter (Friedmann and Hudson, 1974). Another 30 years after Friedmann's comments, the 'great debate' still serves to clarify the main definitions of and rationales for planning. The term itself 'great debate' is a dramatic device and is almost certainly more of significance from the perspective of hindsight rather than in terms of the party politics of the time. The term also does not necessarily mean that the protagonists faced each other in a debating chamber or through contributing opposing articles to a journal. Whether the protagonists did explicitly confront each other is a matter for a more detailed study of the history of ideas. For the most part, they did not. The claims and counter claims were indirect.

The Logic: Planning as a Method of Government

The context for national planning was a declining lack of confidence in liberal capitalism, associated with mass unemployment in the 1930s and the apparent economic advance of totalitarian dictatorships, such as Nazi Germany and the Soviet Union. The origins of national planning were therefore not specific to Britain or to any other single country. They lay in a more general sense of malaise. In the US, for example, calls for national planning became fashionable in the 1930s in the form of the 'New Deal', itself mostly intended to tackle unemployment and regional economic depression (Friedmann 1987, 106–7).

In Britain, the idea of national planning was closely associated with a pressure group 'Political and Economic Planning' (PEP), established in 1931.[1] National planning, as the aims of PEP suggested, was a new approach to government, based on a belief in the value of science and common sense in resolving common problems. Planning, so conceived, transcended party-political differences in an effort to tackle problems and reconstruct society. However, support for planning was not merely confined to the members of one or two pressure groups. In a history of Britain in the 1930s, Muggeridge (1940, 264–5), noted how, alongside a renewed interest in science and social interest, 'plans were in the air'. Similar sentiments were also noted in building and architectural journals that otherwise had little interest in political ideas. In 1933, an editorial in *The Illustrated Carpenter and Builder* (19 May) noted, 'Among the followers of all parties and of none, there are numbers of people who hold that the planning of national activities is a necessity'.

National planning in the sense promoted by PEP meant, as was later explained by its leading theorist, the German refugee and sociologist Karl Mannheim (1971, 193) 'foresight deliberately applied to human affairs so that the social process is no longer merely the product of conflict and competition'. Planning was therefore distinct from both conventional politics with its reliance on conflict and distinct, in addition, from the market economy with its dependence on competition. Unlike politics, planning sought to identify solutions based on social science and an understanding of social and economic trends. It sought to reduce the ideological content of policy, so making policy more rational in relation to its likely effects. Unlike the market, planning involved a long-term view and one based on a consideration of a variety of factors rather than just price. Planning involved 'substantial rationality', that is to say the ability to synthesise a strategic perspective rather than the narrower 'functional' rationality associated with bureaucracies and private firms (1971, 52–8).

Planning, so conceived, was inevitable, as its absence would lead to social chaos and economic breakdown or so Mannheim argued. It amounted to a style of government that liberal democracies such as Britain would have to adopt.

Without democratic planning, events would lead to the emergence of totalitarian planning such as existed elsewhere in Europe. The planned society was therefore a stage in the evolution of Western society. The planned society was, moreover, a centralised society. Planning was about the regulation of social change as a unity from 'certain central positions' (ibid., 193). Central planning had to rely on a strong bureaucracy and this would override local interests and variations in the implementation of national policies.

National planning is open as to the extent to which it relied on the public ownership of the means of production. Mannheim (1971, 293–306), for example, discussed at length the potential of indirect controls or 'field structures', to use Mannheim's term, for example through legal and administrative regulation and, in addition, through changing the situation in which individuals find themselves.

The reference to indirect controls corresponds, moreover, broadly to the view of PEP and to centre-left and centre-right political opinion throughout the 1930s (Marwick 1964). Planning was an intelligent means whereby the national state would tackle problems. It accepted the case for greater public intervention in social and economic life, whilst also accepting the essential soundness of established society. Problems could still be tackled through persuasion and through generating a consensus. Even before the outbreak of World War II, the discourse of planning was as a form of social and economic 'reconstruction' and not as a form of redevelopment or revolution. The main priority was to save the economy from collapse, as appeared possible for a time in the 1930s and to tackle other immediate problems.

In contrast, others supported national planning as a more decisive break with the past and, as part of this, advocated a self-consciously socialist project modelled on the Soviet experience. For example, in *Plan or no Plan*, Wootton (1934, 8) commended the experience of economic planning in the Soviet Russia as an alternative that, despite its limitations and ambiguities, was 'by unanimous consent' not capitalism. For later generations, references to Soviet planning appeared ludicrous and dangerous. In the 1930s, however, during the Great Depression, Soviet practice looked more attractive, especially as its inefficiency and routine cruelty was not yet fully understood or appreciated.

The Application

For town planning, the regional dimension of national planning was especially important. The 1930s was a period not just of high levels of unemployment but of marked regional variations, between the depressed North of England, Scotland and Wales and a relatively prosperous London and the South East. The depressed industrial regions and the prosperous Home Counties both had an interest in economic planning at a national level. The depressed industrial regions could gain some of the affluence that had previously been denied. Conversely, the prosperous Home Counties could avoid the pressure of population growth and the loss of countryside through continued house building. National planning was a prerequisite therefore of any attempt to plan the distribution of the industrial population and this was emphasised in the Barlow Report, in 1940.

A planned building programme   Planning in relation to house building offered another means of stabilising the economy and one that also impinged on the older and more limited practice of town planning. Public investment in housing, as in other fields, could be used, so the advocates of planning argued, to maintain full employment during periods of economic depression. Conversely, during times when further expansion threatened the capacity of the building industry, national planning would mean exercising restraints over 'non-essential' house building (meaning house building for those who were already well housed) as well as other types of non-essential building.

Nye Bevan, the Minister for Housing in the 1945 Labour government, put the argument as follows. Faced with demands from the Conservative opposition to expand private house building, Bevan argued that the house-building programme had to be planned.

> if we are to have any correspondence between the size of the building force on the sites and the actual provision of the material coming forward to the sites from the industries, there must be some planning. If we are to plan, we have to plan instruments and the speculative housebuilder, by his very nature, is not a planable instrument. (Quoted by Foot 1973, 73)

Most of the civil servants and most of the housing experts at the Ministry likewise accepted the case for economic coordination. Whatever the long-term prospects for private enterprise, a point on which most experts were optimistic, the amount of building work would have to be controlled for at least a short-term period. Otherwise, building costs and prices would experience rapid inflation much as had accompanied the Homes for Heroes programme.

A national, centrally controlled building programme, in turn, encouraged proposals to establish a national housing agency that would work alongside or replace local authorities. Bevan, however, considered local authorities were sufficiently 'planable' and above all were more democratic than a national organisation (Foot 1973, 72). In any case, local authorities already possessed the relevant experience, given their work in the 1920s and 1930s and were, therefore, well suited to the purpose (Malpass 2003b). The main exception concerned the development and management of the new towns intended to rehouse people leaving the big cities, especially London. These became the responsibility of centrally controlled corporations.

Compensation and betterment   The planned post-war house building programme necessarily involved the acquisition of development sites, including expensive urban sites. In this context, the idea of national planning was relevant to what was then known as the 'compensation and betterment' problem. This was the tendency for private landowners to ask for large sums of money as compensation for compulsory purchase or for the refusal of planning permission whilst refusing to make any contribution for any enhancement in land values caused by public action. Without resolving the compensation and betterment problem, an effective planning system simply was not possible. Local authorities would grant planning permission merely for fear of the financial consequences of refusal.

The Town and Country Planning Act 1932 and its predecessors had specified a series of cases, mostly covering detailed layout, where compensation would not be payable. These were treated as an exception rather than as a general legal principle, however. If a local authority refused to allow housing on a greenfield site, for example, compensation was most likely due. Local authorities could and often commonly did attempt to delay compensation payments through a legal technicality whereby they resolved to prepare a planning scheme on an interim basis only. However, delaying payment offered no long-term solution.

An expert committee, called the Uthwatt Committee (Ministry of Works and Planning 1942).was established to review the subject in 1941. In the context of previous problems, as well in the context of the Barlow Report and its emphasis on the planned location of industry, the Uthwatt committee wanted a new approach. Planning now had 'a meaning not attached to it in any legislation nor until recently in the minds of the public' (ibid., 12) 'The advance towards a new conception of planning under positive central control marks a turning point'. Henceforth, 'private and local initiative must be subject to State control' (ibid., 10–11).

'Positive central control', to use the words of Uthwatt, meant that land values were created by the community rather than the individual and this in turn reversed the previous rationale that favoured compensation but not betterment. Exactly because, land values were created by the community, the individual owner could generally expect no compensation if, for some reason, the community wished to acquire land or curtail property rights. Absence of compensation was to be the rule, rather than the exception.

The logic of central planning, the report noted, was the nationalisation of land, as was then advocated by the Labour Party. Full land nationalisation was too contentious for an official committee, however. Instead, the report recommended a combination of the nationalisation of the development rights of landowners; the public purchase of development land at more favourable terms than before; and the imposition of an annual betterment levy on all land.

The Town and Country Planning Act, 1947 followed the principles of the Uthwatt report, while differing on many of the details. The Act abolished the previous requirement for compensation on refusal of planning permission. It also provided powers to ensure that sites would be made available as and when desired, with compensation payable at existing use value, rather than market values. Private transactions were expected to take place at the same level. Developers were required to pay to a central agency, the Central Land Board, an amount representing the difference between existing use value and the value after development. The difference, in effect, amounted to a 100 per cent betterment tax on the development value of land. Where owners did sell at a price higher than existing use values, the Central Land Board was entitled to undertake compulsory purchase (Cullingworth 1980, 14).

The Ambiguities and Limitations

The growth of public intervention in the period from 1940 to 1947 was so marked as to constitute in the words of one contemporary 'the culmination of a planning revolution' (Fogarty 1948, 22). Revolutions, even of the modest type associated with housing and planning, are not always what they seem, however. They are seldom reversible in the sense of allowing a complete return to the past. Events always move on. However, they may prove unsustainable and, in the case of national planning did prove unsustainable, so triggering further change.

Critiques of social technocracy   The context, in the midst of World War II, was itself a reason why proposals for national planning might not last or at least might have gone too far. Many historians have noted how the second world war promoted radical change, even more so than the first. In the context of the war, the Coalition government commissioned numerous reports and studies about how to plan for peacetime and these encouraged a popular mood for radical change of a type that, in turn, encouraged the election of the Labour government in 1945. On other hand, of course, once the specific and unusual historical conditions of total war had disappeared and once, in addition, the victory euphoria of 1945 had subsided, the enthusiasm for national planning was also likely to disappear or weaken (Calder 1968; Reade 1987; Titmus 1958).

In any case, a popular mood for radical change was not universal in Britain. The reforms introduced by the Labour government in the late 1940s included some concrete measures of great electoral popularity. The establishment of the National Health Service is the obvious example. Planning was not like this. It was an abstract activity and one that evoked fears of bureaucracy, standardisation and the loss of individuality.

Fears of bureaucracy and standardisation were commonplace in Britain in the 1920s and 1930s. Robson's Fabian Pamphlet, published in 1926, provides an example. The novel *Brave New World*, by Aldous Huxley, first published in 1932, provides another, albeit one that is mostly about the de-individualising impact of biological rather than social engineering. Brave New World was set in the distant future in 'AF 632', that is to say 632 years after Ford initiated production-line motor manufacturing. It was a world of extreme uniformity in which Fordist techniques are treated as a quasi-religion. People are manufactured in breeding chambers according to predefined standards and criteria and then trained in a way to promote conformity of behaviour.

Even during the war, the supporters of central planning noted an ambiguity in popular attitudes towards peacetime reconstruction. Cole (1943, 1–2) noted for example: 'People might talk one minute about the new world they wished to see, and the next about how nice it will be to get back to their old jobs and their old homes, or to something as like them as can be managed.'

The war was fought to defend democracy and freedom. Democracy and freedom in turn implied a degree of scepticism towards the centralised arrangements of national planning. The political case for national planning remained contentious throughout the 1940s for exactly this reason. Mannheim

(1971, 338) complained, for example, of the 'theory, current in England, that democracy and planning are mutually exclusive'.

The reference to 'current in England' suggests that the distrust of central planning was confined to Britain. The distrust was perhaps more marked in Britain than other European countries, though it is difficult to establish this with any degree of certainty. It is, nevertheless, possible to find examples of a similar distrust elsewhere, notably in Germany in the pre- and post-Hitler eras. In particular, critiques of planning were developed after 1945 by members of the Frankfurt school of social philosophy, a Marxist-oriented group of social philosophers who were as equally opposed to Soviet-style communism as to Western capitalism. Adorno (1967) argued that social planning as presented by Mannheim was a superficial, elitist and ultimately authoritarian exercise in managing and suppressing social contradictions 'without penetrating to the foundations of society'. In a similar vein, Marcuse (1964) railed against a rationally organised 'one dimensional' society on the grounds that this prevented fundamental change and restricted human imagination.

The Frankfurt School critique remains significant in raising issues about the relationship between technology, social progress and individual freedom. Often without explicit recognition, the critique re-enters planning theory in the 1990s in attempts, for example by Healey (1992) to work out the basis for an alternative, more democratic and humanistic planning practice. The key idea is drawn from a later Frankfurt philosopher, Habermas (1971), who argued that modernisation in Western society is characterised by the growth of communicative rationality, rationality based on debate, and not simply by the growth of technical rationality, as Marcuse had supposed. Base planning decisions on this notion of communicative rationality, therefore and it will have the potential for democratic change. The limitations of communicative planning remain much the same as noted by Adorno of central planning. It is often not so much the definition of rationality that is significant, but who gains and who loses.

However, considered as a critique of the operation of central planning, the Frankfurt School critique missed the point. The critique assumes a degree of perfection in planning and a degree of control that is probably not achievable in a modern society and certainly not achieved in Britain in the 1940s.

In principle, World War II provided apparently ideal conditions for experiments in economic planning, or so one might think. The existence of severe labour shortages and all kinds of materials led to the introduction of controls over virtually all aspects of economy, including the location of industry. The war effort also created a political consensus about production aims that would have hardly been possible in peacetime. Yet, even in such circumstances, economic planning did not go so far as to specify a comprehensive range of production targets. It was solely concerned with the production of armaments, especially the production of aircraft. No attempt was made to specify the inputs to aircraft production and the main producing firms engaged in extensive sub-contracting (Hare 1983, 221–2).

The practice of the Labour government elected in 1945 comprised a similar mix of direct interventions and regulation. Although Labour introduced an extensive range of nationalisations, including the Bank of England, the coal mining industry, the railway industry and development rights in land, it left the bulk of manufacturing industry and services in private ownership. Labour sought to manage rather than plan the economy and it avoided the use of investment or production targets such as characterised Soviet-style five year plans.

The building industry provides an example. The Labour government made no attempt to nationalise the construction industry. House building companies, once they had recovered from the effects of the war, merely turned from the development of homes for sale to undertaking contract work for local authorities. Most of the council houses built after 1945 were built by private contractors rather than the direct labour force of the local authority (Malpass 2003a). Some companies did particularly well. George Wimpey, for example, prospered through the use of a patented construction method, called 'no-fines' concrete, that avoided post-war shortages of bricks and bricklayers.

In practice, economic planning under the post-war Labour government became a means of coping with a succession of individual problems (Sabatino 1956, 34). The so-called 'planned' house building programme provides an example. No national building targets were specified and production was constantly hindered by shortages, the 'brick crisis of 1946, the cement crisis of 1947, the fuel and power crisis of 1947, the timber bottleneck and the balance of payments crisis of 1949' (ibid., 36).

There was a further problem. The 1947 Town and Country Planning Act required owners to sell at existing use values. This had removed the incentive for owners to sell and threatened to bring the property market to a halt. Some slowing down in land sales had been expected by Ministry officials, but not to the extent that proved to be the case.

The shortfall in development sites did not cause immediate problems in the 1940s. Reconstruction in Britain largely depended on development by public agencies, notably by local authorities. Land shortages were likely to cause problems in the future, however (Cullingworth 1980, 31). They also encouraged speculative land purchases and a series of deliberate attempts on the part of private land owners to find a way around the anti-speculation provisions of the 1947 Act.

In defence of economic liberalism   The problems encountered by the Labour government, and they were not simply confined to house building and planning, would lead eventually to the re-election of a Conservative government in 1951 and to a retreat from the most overtly collectivist, socialist aspects of post-war planning and housing policy. In the meantime, proposals for central planning generated a backlash amongst the defenders of economic liberalism. In particular, Hayek (1944, 32–41) who was the most influential critic, argued that the very complexity of modern societies precluded national planning and required, instead, the use of competitive markets. Hayek, like Mannheim, adopted an evolutionary view of history, but it was one that saw evolution arising from impersonal, competitive pressures rather than from any self-conscious, collective exercise in moulding the future of society. Competition rather than planning offered economic stability and a means of increasing national wealth.

The argument rested on the methods of economic coordination. Central coordination was likely to prove inflexible and limited in its potential application. Decentralised coordination, in contrast, was a contradiction of terms, if this simply meant allowing producers to operate without some economic discipline.

The price mechanism had proved an effective way of indicating the economic benefit of different goods and services and of introducing such discipline. However, Hayek (ibid., 36–37) added

> The important point is that the price system will fulfil this function [of coordination] only if competition prevails, that is, if the individual producer has to adapt himself to price changes and cannot control them. Or in other words if he has to cater for the needs and purse of the consumer. The more complicated the whole, the more dependent we become on that division of knowledge between individuals whose separate efforts are co-ordinated by the mechanism of the price system.

Competition was additionally important because it provided a spur to innovation. Standardisation and planning might lead to a short-term reduction in production costs, but in the long term the quality of the product would suffer and become less friendly to consumers. Competition was the only way in which something better might develop (ibid., 38). Planning was, therefore, only justified in circumstances where the usual rules of competition did not apply. Planning was, moreover, only justified for specific and limited aims, rather to achieve a general social transformation, as its advocates such as Mannheim wished.

Town planning was an exception, justified in a way national planning was not (ibid., 35). 'It is, for example, a commonplace that many of the problems created by modern towns, like many other problems caused by close contiguity in space are not adequately solved by competition.'

In principle, such problems might be solved in a purely market-based economy by aggrieved parties claiming damages through the legal system. However, the large number of land use changes and property developments would soon overwhelm the courts. Developers would face uncertainties and the pace of development would suffer. Thus, the 'general formulas of private property of freedom of contract do not provide an immediate answer to the complex problems which city life raises' (Hayek 1960, 241; Sorensen and Day 1981, 392). Some superior authority or some superior land owner is required to resolve potential conflicts more quickly than can be achieved through civil law procedures. Local authorities, through their regulatory and inspection responsibilities, could fulfil the functions of such an authority or superior. Town planning was, in other words, justified on grounds of economic efficiency compared to the alternatives. Without some form of town planning, urban life and more generally the conditions for market-based urban growth would break down or, at least become increasingly expensive to maintain.

In addition, Hayek recognised the existence of poor quality structures and a lack of sanitary facilities as potential justifications for intervention and so admitted the case for slum clearance as well as improvement policies to prevent dwellings decaying to the point that clearance becomes necessary. Planning could further be justified to provide 'public utilities' (Hayek 1944, 35) and to protect and enhance 'the streets and the public amenities which are essential to city life' (Hayek 1960, 349). The scope of town planning encompassed therefore programmes in infrastructure investment and redevelopment and was not confined purely to the control of development. As a result, there is scope in the context of Hayek's principles for debate about how much public intervention is justified.

Nevertheless, there is a marked difference between Hayek's position and that of the advocates of national planning. Hayek (1944, 40) argued that it was simply not possible to reconcile all the different aims represented by different pressure groups. National planning was being advocated by those who wished to preserve the countryside, by those who wished to clear out the slums and those who wished to build roads in the countryside. Once national planning was implemented, the previously concealed tensions would become apparent. Where public policy aims did diverge, Hayek (1944, 31) argued, the sole aim should be to promote competition.

Hayek's position was narrower and harsher than is understood by any concept of market failure that involves environmental and social considerations. For Hayek, for example, slum clearance was only justified for its neighbourhood effects, not as a means of helping residents. The logic was undemocratic. Whatever the views of the electorate of public opinion, the promotion of efficiency and competition would have priority.

Hayek's position was also out of line with that of Conservative governments in power in Britain in the 1950s and 1960s. Politics in the 1950s returned to the consensual, common-sense, middle of the road urged by PEP and other planning pressure groups twenty years earlier. Harold Macmillan, Conservative Minister of Housing from 1951 to 1954 and Prime Minister between 1957 and 1963 had, in particular, been a prominent supporter of national planning in the 1930s. Hayek's position was instead closer to the rationale of the New Right Conservative governments of the 1980s, during the period of Office of Margaret Thatcher and these explicitly sought to reject the post-1945 consensus.

The Continuing Relevance

Of the various contributors to the great debate, Hayek has proved the most widely quoted and discussed. This is not surprising given the popularity of neoliberal ideas since about 1980. For town planning and for related public interventions in urban development, however, it was not just Hayek's attack on central planning that was significant. Equally significant was the way in which Hayek recognised that the problems of pollution and the problems of city life are an exception where limited public intervention is justified. In doing this, Hayek showed the likely resilience of town planning in the face of attacks from the supporters of markets and private property and outlined a pattern of argument that is recurrent amongst neoliberal economic theory (Lai 2002). Hayek's observations about the economic necessity of some limited form of town planning helps explain, for example, why Margaret Thatcher's government did not undo planning control, other than in a few specially designed 'Enterprise Zones'. The detractors of planning can argue, in any specific case, that environmental problems and related urban problems are unimportant or exaggerated. They cannot easily argue that the market offers a way of resolving such problems

Planning as an ideal type   There is another, more easily overlooked and more theoretical legacy. The great debate also established a different way of looking at planning – as an exercise in political economy and as part of this an exercise in the allocation of resources. Town planning, according to this definition is merely a particular and more specialised form of resource allocation, one that deals with land, property and public infrastructure. Mannheim's definition of planning as an alternative to conflict and competition is the relevant starting point. Planning is more than a mere series of public interventions. Instead, it offers a distinct way of organising and supplementing the market and a means in addition of leading, as well as following the policies of the state.

Providing more detail on the characteristics of the planning process requires a brief detour into studies of national planning. The subsequent experience in the 1950s and 1960s in the communist countries of eastern Europe provides the clearest examples of economic planning. The experience in France at about the same time is also relevant to understanding the political aspects. Both in eastern Europe and in France governments were more committed to the pursuit of a national plan, compared to Britain.

There is a risk of misunderstanding in all this. Economic planning in post-war communist countries is an example of practice that subsequent generations of professional town planners would generally like to forget. Central planning, as practised in the former communist-controlled countries of eastern Europe, failed to generate wealth as quickly as in mixed and market-based economies. It also had a poor record of environmental protection. Nevertheless, economic planning in the 1950s and 1960s helps define the characteristics of planning as an ideal type, in other words as a relatively simple idea without the clutter and historical baggage of statutory planning systems. Ideal, in the context of an ideal type, does not mean desirable. It means instead a type of practice that is defined in terms of a general idea and a series of characteristics rather than one.

These ideal type characteristics are summarised in Table 3.2, with the addition of a row dealing with housing criteria.

Planning enables governments to supplement or replace price indicators through taking a long term view of trends. It works through statistical reports, analyses and projections that are mostly concerned with physical variables, for example, the numbers of dwellings built and expected to be built rather than their price. Assessments of housing rest on the measurement of need, for example projections of future household numbers and the number of substandard dwellings in need of replacement or improvement. 'Need' in a centrally planned system refers to the whole population, not just the needs of these who cannot afford a decent home.

In addition, though this goes beyond the scope of the table, planning has specific advantages in public policy. It provides a means of incorporating social and environmental criteria into the process of economic development in a way

Table 3.2   A comparison of information flows in the market and in planning

Characteristics	Market	Planning
Major information types	Offers and counter-offers: advertising: order: confirmation: contract modification of contract: payment for fulfilment of contract	Statistical reports: plan proposals and counter proposals: plan-bargaining, critique of the plan proposal instruction or recommendation to those implementing the plan
Character of reflection (*i.e. the relation between knowledge and action*)	The information directly reflects the real action	The information reflects the real action perhaps through several transmissions
Time lag between anterior information and real action (*this latter including development*)	Preceding it only slightly, almost simultaneous	Preceding it by considerable time (1–5–14–20 years)
Role of memory	Small: short-time horizon	Large: long-time horizon
Measure (*criteria for action*)	Price information has the outstanding role	Variables measured in both physical and value terms: the former have the outstanding role
Relevant housing criteria	*Prices, pattern of demand*	*Needs, standards*
Is the flow of goods accompanied by money flow?	Yes	No
Vertical versus horizontal flow of information	Both, but the horizontal flows are dominant	Both, but the vertical flows are dominant

Source: Kornai 1971, 336. Italics added.

that a purely market-based approach would automatically ignore. Need is itself a social rather than market-based criterion. Planning does not, however, guarantee that social and environmental factors are considered. Command and control planning of the former Soviet block countries was, for example, notorious for neglecting these. Much depends on the political context to determine which policy aims have priority.

At the same time, planning is a top-down exercise that is relatively remote from the pattern of costs and the wishes of consumers and works best in conditions of scarcity, that is to say where demand exceeds supply. Planning is less able to determine patterns of consumption when there is a surplus of goods on the market. In such circumstances, consumers have more choice and more bargaining power.

The relation between supply and demand is also relevant to the extent to which spatial planning can control the pattern of urban development. Planning is less able to direct the pattern of urban development at times and places of weak housing demand and less able to direct commercial and industrial development than housing (Bramley and Kirk 2005). Local authorities are eager to attract commercial and industrial development. As a result sites are more plentiful and developers can choose where to go. Partly for this reason, conventional forms of town planning are also poorly adapted to dealing with the problems that arise from urban decline (Shankland et al. 1977, 161; URBED 2005, ix–x).

Given the pattern of advantages and limitations, no sensible government would wish to rely wholly either on the market or on planning. Some combination of modes of action is necessary. To give a housing example, a reliance on physical measures such as demographic projections and the number of house completions of need can give a distorted picture of housing trends. House price indicators also have to be considered, as for example is stressed in the Barker Review (2004). Conversely, as has been a criticism of Barker, it is impossible to allow a purely market-oriented approach to housing land release if a government wishes to influence long-term patterns of urban development. (House of Commons 2005a, paras 17–23).

The cost of planning is also relevant. Hayek justified town planning as being efficient and speedier than the resolution of disputes by the courts. Developers would almost certainly comment that planning can itself delay development and impose costs and would argue for speedier decisions. Governments have often agreed with developers (even though the appeals system that is under government control is also slow). The promotion of performance and value for money has become a significant theme in planning policy in England since about 2000, excessively so in the view of critics (Kitchen 2007, 183–4).

Considered as an exercise in resource allocation, planning also has political characteristics that may be summarised as an ideal type. The experience of national economic planning in France in the 1960s provides an example. Once established and institutionalised, planning has, in principle, the potential to transform politics. 'The plan', in the words of an account by Cohen (1969, 159) centralises both political time and space. It pulls a vast range of decisions into a single framework and insists that they be decided simultaneously. The politics of frequent, individual and partial decisions becomes a politics of simultaneous, interrelated and long term decisions – The politics [of the plan] are comprehensive, simultaneous and explicit.

Planning, as the quotation suggests, has advantages in ensuring that a variety of different factors are considered together. In doing this, moreover, planning offers a means of resolving conflicting values and requirements. At the same time, the ideal type characteristics of planning as politics become muddied. Pressure groups do not want to work within the fixed parameters of a plan, especially if they believe that this does not correspond to their interests.

Cohen's account of economic planning stresses the opposition of established industrial interests to any proposal that might undermine or limit their activities. In relation to housing, the risk is for investment to be dominated by the logic of economic production and concerned only with the most basic standards. For critics of centrally planned urban development in France, this is exactly what happened in the 1960s (Castells and Godard 1974). Similar issues of poor quality, mass produced dwellings also arose in Britain in council housing in the 1950s and 1960s, though here land shortages were probably the more important constraint.

Finally, even if broad aims can be agreed, implementation cannot be taken for granted. Central planning depends on the effective coordination of different bureaucracies to ensure that no specific agency goes off track. Co-ordination was not of significant concern whilst town planning remained fixed on blueprints of urban growth, as was the case in the 1940s and 1950s in Britain. The blueprint generated its own coordinating logic. Coordination has, however, become increasingly critical in the context of efforts, from the 1960s and 1970s onwards, to pursue more flexible, collaborative styles of intervention and, in particular, in the context of policies to direct public resources into deprived neighbourhoods (Stewart 1999).

All this is to anticipate the subsequent history of urban development and of planning in the latter half of the twentieth century, whilst also showing that the great debate continues to provide a point of reference. The most enduring lesson is simply that concepts of planning as an exercise in political economy provide both a simple means of understanding the concept of planning and a means, in addition, of understanding why planning in practice is so slippery and difficult to define.

Planning and social democracy   The experience of central planning in the former Soviet Union raised, from the outset, a basic question about whether planning is compatible with democracy and individual freedom. The subsequent development of postmodern ideas is a further challenge. The conventional postmodern position is, in part, like that of Hayek. It is to argue that comprehensive planning is impossible, if not downright dangerous in undermining democracy and that, in any case, a consensus is impossible. Sandercock (1998, 57–84), whose writings may be taken as representative, seeks, for example, to distance planning from any form of knowledge that claims to be comprehensive and objective. Knowledge must instead be considered plural and relative. It must be generated 'through dialogue', 'from experience' and from the local and the particular.

In addition, postmodernism suggests that market forces contribute to pluralism. A notable example comprises the way in which, in many different countries, specialist ethnic shops and businesses have opened in ethnic neighbourhoods (Fainstein 2001; Sandercock 2003, 132–4). One wonders whether these would have opened if shopping provision had been strictly controlled. The housing market provides another example. It is unlikely that ethnic groups would have been able to adapt the existing stock to their own cultural requirements if they had rented from a social housing agency, with the strict management regulations generally in force. New arrivals might not have been able to find any home, without the availability of private rented homes.

Yet market forces also have limits. They can only provide decent homes if the occupants can afford the rent or the mortgage repayment. And this is the point. For those who wish to retain a commitment to social justice and to the maintenance of minimum living standards, a total rejection of the welfare state and of modern planning leads to a logical impasse.

The question is to find some way of specifying the logic of a democratic style of planning that might meet the objections of postmodernism. In *Freedom under Planning* (1945) Wootton developed such an argument, one that also offers an alternative to Mannheim's heavy reliance on scientific notions of rationality. *Freedom under Planning* is also a significant variation compared to Wootton's earlier work *Plan or no Plan* with its apparently uncritical references to Soviet practice.

The argument may be summarised as follows: Even if there were no common objectives in the complex societies of the twentieth century, there remained points of common agreement – for example of the need to eradicate mass unemployment, to improve standards of education or to make the best use of resources. The task of planning was to 'discover' these points of agreement amongst different viewpoints (ibid., 136).

People are likely to accept the desirability and broad direction of policies and plans, even if they do not agree with all the detail. Moreover, it is active citizens, in disagreeing with aspects of the plan or in opposition to aspects of its implementation, who are likely to provide the most effective guarantors of democracy. The likely persistence of disputes after the establishment of a planning system is itself evidence that planning is compatible with democracy. Conversely, the existence of debates and conflicts about the aims and direction of planning is not evidence of failure.

A degree of caution was necessary, however, to counter the risks of over-centralisation and of unaccountable officials. 'Every extension of government activity ... needs ... a corresponding growth of small local organs', Wootton (1945, 156) commented. Concepts of civic activity needed to be revived, including the role of voluntary organisations.

Wootton's defence of planning does not end debates about the role and organisation of planning, about how to resolve disputes between local and national priorities if these conflict with one another or about the relative efficiency of private and public intervention. Wootton's defence of planning is, nevertheless, sufficient to show that planning, including central planning is itself consistent with social democracy and pluralism, if accompanied by an admission of political debate and dissent as healthy and if accompanied, in addition by an effort to involve voluntary and other local groups.

The 'great debate' remains relevant in another way. The movement for central planning established a concern with managing the future and though the methods of management were criticised by Hayek, the basic assumption – the orientation towards the future – has remained a more or less constant feature of economic policy thereafter. In town planning, the promise of future management was initially ignored. Ashworth (1954, 236–7), at the time the leading historian of town planning suggested 'the unique contribution of town and country planning may be overlooked by concentrating on 'planning' in general'. However, from the 1960s onwards, researchers and scientists in a diverse range of disciplines started to investigate the future of cities, as well as in the 1970s the future of the whole globe. In terms of the history of ideas, such a future orientation can be traced back to the advocates of central planning in the 1930s and 1940s and this is their continuing contribution.

Defining the Modern City

World War II was the single greatest disaster to affect European cities in the twentieth century. In most countries in western Europe, the initial emphasis was on reconstruction pure and simple, largely on the basis of pre-existing layouts and building practice (Grebler 1956). The scale of physical destruction in continental Europe was often greater than in Britain and this physical destruction was matched by disruption in the systems of public administration. In Britain, in contrast, the institutional structures of the national state survived the war intact and emerged with probably greater confidence than before. Encouraged in part by the vogue for central planning, governments were able to prepare for peacetime reconstruction and, as part of this, they sought to lay down a long term view for urban development from the outset.

The policies and plans had two main aspects. At a strategic level, planners and architects were able to reflect on the previous experience of house building and redevelopment and the various models that had been offered as an alternative. These models enabled a view of urban development from above, in terms of general physical planning principles. At a more detailed level, consumer surveys, as well as reviews of housing standards and design enabled a view from below in terms of consumers' views and the local environment.

A View from Above: Blueprints for Urban Growth

In relation to the preparation of models for the future, the garden city movement was especially influential. In 1918 the Garden Cities and Town Planning

Association, at the time the only pressure group interested in long term, strategic town planning, established a new internal committee, the New Towns Group and called on the government to develop 100 new towns as part of its building programme. The garden city was now conceived as a free-standing new town rather than as before 1914 as a low density residential area. It was also conceived as a spatial object, as a blueprint, rather than as a distinctive method of voluntary and co-operative urban development. The idea was to show how the garden city could itself define the aims of town planning. As Purdom (1921, 10) noted in *Town Theory and Practice* 'a multitude of town plans, guided by no purpose or by an inadequate or mean purpose, would be worse than no plans at all'.

Clarifying the aims of town planning was not a simple exercise, however. So long as town planning had been concerned, as it had before 1914, with not-for-profit exercises in housing development, it could succeed in obtaining support from all sections of influential public opinion, with the exception of those working-class groups who argued for council housing. Consideration of comprehensive planning, and ultimately consideration as part of this, the ideal city, in contrast, encountered a new constellation of viewpoints, interests and social ideals. Later, F.J. Osborn (1945, 201–2), at that time the leading spokesman for the garden cities movement described the 1920s and 1930s as 'the period of confusion' in which the followers of Howard had been under attack from all sides.

The impact of modern architecture   The confusion, or to be more accurate the lack of an agreed view, derived, in part, from the repetition of the garden city by local authorities and private house builders. Critics looked at the new suburbs of the 1920s and 1930s, sometimes advertised as being designed and constructed on garden city lines, and suggested that this was the inevitable outcome of the garden city movement. More than this, however, confusion, as seen by the garden city movement, arose from the multiplicity of different models available for planning the future city, apart from that of the free-standing garden city.

The influence of the modern movement in architecture was a particular threat to the garden city movement as it encouraged a search for innovation in housing design. Innovation was, moreover, especially important in the context of mass slum clearance projects. Virtually every pressure group and many planning experts, other than the Town and Country Planning Association (the successor body to the Garden Cities Association), considered low density solutions were impractical and, in the view of some, undesirable on social grounds. As Abercrombie (1935, 203) explained, oblivious to the likely stigmatising effects after completion, 'the inhabitants of the slums represent a quite distinct class ..., possessed of small means or aptitude for garden suburb conditions'. Equally, however, few people wished to repeat even in a modernised form the terraces and tenements that had been demolished.

The modern movement offered a theoretical solution to the problems of mass redevelopment in the form of Le Corbusier's *City of Tomorrow* and *Radiant City* both of which included proposals for what might be termed a vertical garden city. Based on the development of high flats, Le Corbusier's models suggested that it might be possible to bring more light and air into high-density slums, whilst avoiding or at least reducing large-scale population dispersal.

The modern movement also offered a few practical examples. By 1939, local authorities had already completed a few schemes that had been influenced by innovations in workers' housing in continental Europe and that, by virtue of the use of white, cement rendered exteriors, looked radically different from older blocks of tenement housing, as indeed was the intention. Modern flats were to replace Victorian tenements and were to give high density living a more attractive image (Ravetz 1974). The St Andrews Street project in Liverpool, Ossulston Street near to St Pancras in London and Quarry Hill flats in Leeds provide examples.

Later, from the 1960s onwards, the St Andrews Project and Quarry Hill flats encountered a series of technical and social problems. The flats in St Andrews street became known locally as the Bull Ring and after a period during which they became notorious for its drug problems were converted into student housing in 1998/99. (Information provided by Linda Sheridan.) Quarry Hill flats, after becoming one of the more notorious and undesirable estates in Leeds, were eventually demolished in the 1970s largely owing to the use of structural methods that raised modernisation and repair work beyond a reasonable cost. In the 1940s, however, these schemes were still new and still regarded as examples of progressive architecture at its best.

Modern flats, above all high rise, were the most obvious and visible contribution of modern architecture. They were symptomatic of an approach that defined the future of towns in terms of models. Most subsequent historians and critics of town planning have similarly interpreted modern architecture in terms of buildings and new urban design models. They have looked at Le Corbusier's proposals, in particular and seen little more than a monumental exercise in geometrical logic with little practical sense. Jacobs (1964, 33) suggested that the Le Corbusier's ideal city was 'like a wonderful mechanical toy' that said 'nothing but lies' about how cities work. Sandercock (1998, 24), citing B. Hooper (1995), has provided a feminist variant, suggesting that these ideal cities were no more than 'a poem of male desire' that prioritised the straight line over the 'chaotic sensings and respondings of body, the realm of female'.

This latter feminist criticism is nonsense. To take Le Corbusier's *Unité d'Habitation* completed in 1952 in Marseille as an example. Otherwise known as a prototype for the Radiant City, the *Unité d'Habitation* housed 900 people in 337 flats of varied internal floor plans and sizes. The block is equipped with a range of communal facilities, including a crèche, a rooftop paddling pool, gymnasium and running track, whilst the flats are equipped with a fitted kitchen and, in some cases, flexible partition walls. The scheme could be accused of assuming the existence of a conventional nuclear family in which women undertook the house work and child rearing. But so did virtually all housing built at this time in Europe and North America. The scheme was not even based on the total primacy of the straight line, as least no more than is convenient in the design of the spaces in and around a house. The roof, in particular, contains organic-looking sculptural features. In any case, rectangular rooms and rectangular dwellings and flats are easier to build and better suited to accommodating furniture than circular or irregularly shaped rooms.[2]

Questions remain, however, about the broader logic of Le Corbusier's project. The essence of the modern movement was its focus on modernity and, by implication, its focus on time. Le Corbusier sought to destroy the cities of the past because they were old and obsolete. Modern housing and modern cities were not simply intended to work efficiently. They were intended to look modern. As Sennett (1990, 173) suggests, 'Le Corbusier hoped to erect a new awareness of time, the sense of *now*' (italics in the original). In doing this, moreover, Le Corbusier paid little attention to what existed previously and sought, instead, wholesale changes in the name of efficiency and progress. The *Plan Voisin*, named after its commercial sponsor, a motor car manufacturer and published in 1925, was an extreme example. It sought to rebuild the historic centre of Paris in favour of roads, parks and tower blocks of 60 storeys.

Promoting a sense of time is an issue where, as Sennett (ibid.) also notes, the theories of modernism have to be answered in their own terms. Aspects of the survey before plan approach of Geddes offered a possible alternative. The survey had an educational purpose in seeking to promote a better public understanding of urban development and city life and this was expressed through 'city pageants' (what would now be called street festivals), city exhibitions and cultural centres.

Otherwise, satisfactory methods of marking time through design only emerged later, in the aftermath of the modern movement and in the aftermath of blueprint planning. Lynch and Hack (1989, 174) provide, for example, a series of practical ideas about how a sense of time might be accentuated – contrasting old and new buildings and old and new districts; remodelling old buildings and converting them to new uses; choosing materials that weather handsomely; the incorporation of trees and shrubs that will mature, grow and in the long term decay and that will also mark the passage of seasons; and, finally, promoting events and anniversaries that provide a sense of occasion to public space.

Elsewhere, Lynch (1972) argued that the passing and rhythms of time are central to the experience of living in a city. As a result, a successful exercise in planning is one that 'celebrates and enlarges the present while making connections with past and future'. Such temporal diversity and temporal linkage was outside the discourse of blueprint planning as this operated in the 1930s and 1940s.

The models applied   The advisory plans for the County of London Plan, (Forshaw and Abercrombie 1943), for Greater London (Abercrombie 1945) and for the Clyde Valley Plan (Abercrombie and Matthew 1949) showed how the models might be applied. London and the Clyde Valley, more particularly in the latter case the city of Glasgow, possessed the most serious and complex housing problems in Britain. If plans could be prepared for these two cities, they could be prepared almost anywhere.

The plans had, as their major theme, the promotion of better living conditions through planned decentralisation, the reduction of residential densities in the inner area and the establishment of open space and green space networks. The cities were conceived as comprising a series of rings around a core, with each ring being defined by a combination of residential density, the location of industry and the use of land for open space and recreation.

In the case of the plans for London, five rings were identified, along with a core. The core and the two innermost zones constituted the pre-1919 neighbourhoods for which a substantial reduction in population was recommended. Around this older area was a suburban ring largely developed since 1919, for which the plans recommended no major change apart from limited peripheral expansion. The average residential density in the suburban zones was about 50 persons to the acre (or 10dpa or 25dph) and this was accepted as the maximum for the future (Abercrombie 1945, 34).[3] Outside the suburban ring was a wide green belt, where building was prohibited. Finally, outside the green belt, new development in expanded or new towns was assumed to be at a still lower density.

The main policy decision was to determine how far to go in reducing inner area densities. The County of London Plan stated that a maximum density of 100 persons to the acre (20 dpa or about 50 dph) would have been preferable. At this level and assuming the usual generous external spacing standards of the time, all families with children would have been able to live in houses with gardens if they wished, given the mixed development of low rise (three storeys) and high rise (eight storeys) flats. A standard of 136 persons per acre (28 ppa or 69 dph) was more practical for redevelopment areas, with higher densities still in the West End and adjoining residential areas that were not to be redeveloped.

The density policies represented a compromise between reality and the ideal and also between the supporters of the modern movement, nearly all of whom favoured high density flatted estates and older, more established garden city movement. Osborn (1945, 202), the main defender of the garden city movement complained about 'continental technicians', meaning the modern architects who ignored the English tradition of houses with gardens. However, Osborn also accepted the plan as the 'first fully-worked-out "Garden City" plan for a great metropolis'. The basic principles of the plans were accepted by London County Council in 1945 and formed the basis of the development plans prepared under the Town and Country Planning Act, 1947.

Elsewhere in England, new towns were deemed unnecessary and previous trends of suburban expansion were expected to continue, albeit with local 'overspill' schemes where one council would build in the area of an adjoining authority. Overall policy for densities was set by the Ministry of Health in its housing manuals and these again envisaged a pattern of concentric zones with the higher density areas closer to the centre. The density levels were for overall calculation only and covered extensive areas – so encouraging flexibility in detailed application and the mixed development of flats and houses (MH 1944).

The Clyde Valley Plan (Abercrombie and Matthew 1949) dealt with a smaller conurbation than Greater London, but one with more intense overcrowding, where densities were higher and where, in addition, outward expansion was constrained by surrounding hills. Three maximum residential density zones were recommended for the city of Glasgow, at 120 persons to the acre (296 pph or about 59 dph), 90 persons to the acre (216 pph or 43 dph) and 60 persons to the acre (148 pph or 39 dph), with similar but lower density zones for other towns within the regions.[4] Given the obsolete character of tenements, the plan assumed, in addition, that all or possibly nearly all the existing nineteenth-century housing stock would be replaced.

The Clyde Valley Plan differed from the plans for London on numerous points. The outer suburbs were to be developed to a higher density; the green belt was more like a green backcloth to a dispersed conurbation than a distinct ring; above all, the plan promoted the almost complete replacement of nineteenth century and older areas rather than as in London a selective programme of slum clearance and expansion.

In addition, the Clyde Valley plan differed from the plans for London in that the main proposals were opposed by the main local authority. Glasgow Corporation had already prepared its own plan, the so-called Bruce Plan, that proposed building at uniformly high densities to the city boundaries, without regard to any possible green belt designations and involving the redevelopment of every area of the city over a period of 50 years, including the redevelopment of existing suburban housing estates to a higher density. The Clyde Valley Plan's proposal to move population away from Glasgow was not in the city corporation's interest. In any case, the city faced immediate problems of rehousing that required the identification of development sites.

The long term effects of the plans for London and the Clyde Valley have been mixed. The plans combined a mixture of radical remodelling of the older urban fabric in a way that would horrify contemporary conservationists, with a conservative respect for the overall pattern of urban development. They failed to anticipate the scale of social change in the 1950s and 1960s and failed in particular to anticipate the scale of population change – for example, higher than expected population growth in South East England, combined with private sector decentralisation from London and most other English cities and, in the case of the Clyde Valley, long-term, progressive economic and population decline. The plans also failed to find a lasting solution to polarised views about future densities and future housing forms. In both Greater London and the Clyde Valley region debates about densities continued for many years afterwards.

As statements of the ideal city, the plans and especially the plans for London were more influential. The London Plans in particular brought together various proposals, including proposals for garden cities, in an imaginary urban landscape that could be adapted to changing conditions and that became widely accepted as defining the planned English city (Mort 2004). The redevelopment of older housing was part of this vision, but now looks dated. The County of London Plan, for example, contains images of high density redevelopment of a type that looks like the prototype for estates completed in the late 1950s and 1960s. Other aspects of the proposed urban landscape, notably the green belt and the system of interconnected open spaces, have, in contrast, persisted as influential spatial concepts to the present.

A View from Below: Housing Preferences and Standards

The preparation of large-scale regional plans proceeded in tandem with the specification of standards and other detailed matters in housing design and in addition with the provision of guidance on the respective merits of flats and houses. The basic choices would have been familiar to architects and housing experts in 1919. The method of making the choice was different, however, and involved the use of consumer surveys. A large scale housing survey undertaken in 1941 and 1942 by what would now be called a market research company 'Mass Observation' (1943, 46) provides the best example. The name of the survey company summarises the main assumptions. Mass consumer surveys would provide an informed basis for public planning. They would give a view from below, complementing the abstract calculations of the advisory plans.

Domestic technology and women   The Mass Observation survey compared the views of people living in council and garden city estates, including in the case of council estates, people living in three- and four-storey flats and it also undertook a comparison of the views of these residents with those who lived in older property built before 1919. In doing this, the survey provides the first reliable and representative assessment of consumer reaction to the homes built in the twentieth century. Admittedly, the survey had limitations. The number of owner-occupiers was under-represented, as the report itself acknowledges (ibid., 175). It was an English rather than Scottish survey and does not help clarify whether Scottish housing expectations were as distinctive as sometimes claimed. Nevertheless, the survey provides information about attitudes towards the home that is simply unavailable from other sources.

The survey is significant, moreover, as not just the first effort to record the views of a representative national sample of consumers, but the last. No similar survey was attempted again and, from the 1960s onwards, it would have been almost impossible to undertake a similar survey. The diversity of the housing stock and the diversity of residents preclude any such global overview of housing expectations. Recent consumer surveys in design examine either recently completed housing or particular types of housing or, as in the large national surveys such as the Survey of English Housing and English House Condition Survey that look at overall housing satisfaction rather than the details of design.

For those interviewed, all of whom were women, the general urban environment was an important influence on whether they liked their home. Old housing areas, the report (ibid., xxi) noted, were 'often actively disliked'. Nevertheless, the main issue was whether modern fittings and equipment were provided in the home – above all a properly equipped kitchen, an internal toilet and bathroom. The report of survey (Mass Observation 1943, xi) states:

> Convenience of the home generally, particularly in relation to rearing children, plays an important part in deciding home satisfaction, and the newer types of home seem to be better planned in this respect. Labour saving devices are much appreciated, and are constantly asked for if absent.

For the women respondents to the Mass Observation survey, it was the contrast between the old, pre-1919 and the newer homes that provided the main influence on their judgements. The respondents wanted to get rid of the old and generally did not mind living in a flat if this was the only way of obtaining a new home. They found flats 'convenient and labour-saving to run' (ibid., 58). To this extent much of the contemporary architectural and planning debate – notably about flats versus houses – was irrelevant. The housing crisis remained a shortage of accommodation built and designed to modern standards and available at a price or rent which working-class people could afford.

Even so, flats did not represent a long term, popular ideal for respondents to the Mass Observation survey. 'For every one person who said that she would like to live in a flat, ten would like to live in a small house or bungalow.' Most people lived in flats because they had no choice. 'If people could, without having long journeys to work, live in a house of their own, the majority would infinitely prefer it' (ibid., ix).

The language of the Mass Observation report, notably the discussion of labour saving devices, deserves attention. It suggests that the women interviewed accepted traditional assumptions about their role in the home. They would remain responsible for housework and child rearing and would continue to spend most of their time running the home. Improved domestic technology and improved housing design, as offered in modern homes, were likely therefore to save time on specific tasks, to reduce the amount of physical hard work and to raise standards and expectations of 'good' housekeeping, without necessarily reducing the overall amount of time spent by housewives in homework. Other available evidence also suggests that most women retained a traditional view of their role and that the time spent on housework increased in the 1940s and 1950s. In the late 1950s, for example, the time spent on housework, as defined by the housewives, reached an average of about 58 hours per week, according to the estimate of Ravetz (1995, 222–3) who cites Gershuny (1983, 145–56).

Some qualifications are necessary. The evidence on the exact hours spent in housework is fragmentary and subject to uncertainties as to how the respondents to surveys define housework and, in particular, whether this includes child-rearing. The existence of an increase in the hours devoted to unpaid housework is not easily disputed, however and according to the evidence of Gershuny was a tendency of many Western countries in the mid twentieth century. A substantial reduction in the time women spent on housework only occurred from the 1960s onwards and was associated with more women becoming involved in paid work. (For the latter, see Gershuny 2002.)

The Mass Observation survey has another implication. Planning in the 1930s and 1940s was later widely criticised for its apparent paternalism and, as part of this, for its apparent tendency to neglecting consumer preferences (Hebbert 1983). It was also criticised for foisting on women a male-oriented domestic ideal that was only concerned with improving the life of women in their role as wives and mothers (Ward 2004, 284).

Paternalism might be expected as the logical outcome of both the principles of social scientific planning on the Mannheim model and of the 'know best' professionalism of the architects, surveyors and local government officers who would supervise and design the detailed implementation. On the other hand, the existence of a large scale survey such as Mass Observation indicates that consumers were considered, including women, at least in relatively abstract, general terms.

A forward-looking programme?   A desire to satisfy consumer demands was also apparent in the standards adopted in council housing. The impact of the second world war on proposed housing standards was similar to that of the first. Nothing was too good for the returning soldiers and for the mass of the population that had sacrificed so much for the war effort. The Dudley report (MH 1944) assessed the design of the council houses built in England and Wales before 1939 and in this context recommended a continuation of three bedroom family houses rather than flats, though with more variety in dwelling type; the provision of more living space; more modern equipment and fittings in the bathroom and kitchen; and better outbuildings and storage space. A parallel committee, the Westwood Committee, made similar recommendations for Scotland, though with more attention paid to the design of tenement flats (Sim 1993, 50–51)

Dwellings built in the immediate post-war years broadly followed the recommendations of the Dudley and Westwood Committees. Local authorities were carried along by the prospect of building a better future. In addition, the commitment to high standards received political support at a national level. Bevan, the Minister of Health and Housing, was soon under pressure to cut standards as a means of allowing the building of a larger number of dwellings for the same cost. Bevan refused on the grounds that the priority for the moment was to build for the long rather than the short term. In a quotation that has subsequently stood for all those who wish to maintain standards in housing, Bevan argued: 'while we shall be judged for a year or two by the number of houses we build, we shall be judged in ten years by the type of houses we build' (quoted by Foot 1973, 82).

Yet it was also cruel to leave people living in substandard accommodation or sharing with others owing to housing shortages. Bevan and the Labour government faced an impossible dilemma.

Bevan's comments were also prophetic. A failure to complete enough houses, caused in part by a commitment to high standards, contributed to the defeat of Labour in the 1951 General Election. Yet, 60 years or more later, the high quality of the so-called 'Bevan estates' remains apparent. The Bevan houses remained for many years amongst the most popular in the council housing stock. They also figured strongly amongst dwellings sold under the tenants' right-to-buy in the 1980s and 1990s.

They have many advantages, notably a combination of generous floor space standards, good internal equipment standards and spacious surroundings in a way that compares well to any social housing built before or since. The external layouts also contain many distinctive landscaping features – a wider variety of house types, including low rise flats of two or three storeys, the provision of open spaces or 'greens', the retention of existing trees and hedges and the provision of a low brick wall to separate a private garden from the footpath and road.

Not all Bevan houses remained popular or suitable for sale under the right-to-buy, however. The scale of the housing problem led the government to expand production through the use of experimental, non-traditional methods of construction using combinations of timber, steel, concrete and asbestos and intended to avoid the labour and materials shortages of the time. Eventually about 180,000 non-traditional dwellings were completed, mostly in the 1950s, before being terminated for cost reasons (Foot 1973, 81). These non-traditional houses generally used the same type of spacious estate layout as other Bevan houses. However, their construction method and appearance varied greatly. They included some types, especially in the case of the steel and concrete houses that looked unusual or that aged relatively quickly. Many have been demolished or subsequently improved and modernised beyond recognition.

In addition, the same sense of an impending housing crisis led some local authorities, notably those in the big cities, to compromise on the planning standards laid down in the advisory plans. Mixed development remained unusual despite exhortations contained within the Ministry's manuals. In inner London in particular, where land availability remained limited, the County Council built relatively inexpensive four-storey walk-up flats similar to those first built in the 1920s and 1930s and not much else (Bullock 1994; Pevsner 1952, 73).

In Scotland, the pressure to build quickly also led to local authorities to propose the construction of more flats than originally anticipated, but in a peripheral, out of town settings, notably around Glasgow. The estates were located away from existing shops and other amenities, often on sites allocated as green belt land in the regional plan. Grieve (1954, 22), who had participated in the preparation of the Clyde Valley Plan and who subsequently worked for the Scottish Office in defending its provisions later commented of

> The odd picture of a central core of very high density, a diminishing scale of densities through the rest of the City to the immediately pre-war and post-war housing near the outskirts and then a sudden jump to high density building over very large areas on or near the boundaries.

The Glasgow peripheral estates were initially welcomed by the local population. They subsequently required extensive programmes of demolition and improvement.

The Glasgow peripheral estates demonstrate a more general point. The pattern of housing preferences can in part be understood as a trade-off between space and amenity on one hand and accessibility on the other. High density living in or near the city centre, whether in tenements, high density terraces or high rise, balances the environmental disadvantages of high density with access to the facilities and employment opportunities in the city centre. Low density living in the suburbs balances a spacious and green environment with the disadvantages of isolation. In contrast, high density living on the urban periphery provides the worst of both worlds and is especially hard on lower income individuals who are dependent on public transport. High density suburban living is, in other words, always likely to prove problematic as a means of housing those on lower incomes.

Similar problems have arisen in Birmingham where the local authority built high rise in peripheral areas in the 1960s (Jones 2005). They have also occurred in France. In all cases, the outcome has been unpopular estates that have required remodelling and partial demolition.

Community and neighbourhood   An ambiguity in post-war housing policy was whether it concerned individuals and families or communities. The Mass Observation survey consulted residents as individual consumers, not as members of a community. Likewise, the mass housing programmes housed individuals and families in need. On the other hand, the emphasis in the advisory plans was on the community. The County of London Plan, for example, proposed to 'emphasise the identity of the existing communities' (Forshaw and Abercrombie 1943, 28) and it included a map showing the distribution of the main communities in London.

The varied assumptions of planning and housing policy reflected a deeper concern about whether it was worth trying to create communities in twentieth-century Britain. The sociological wisdom of the time going back to Toennies (1971/1925) was that industrialisation and urbanisation had led to the weakening of traditional, tightly knit communities of the type called by the German term *gemeinschaft*. Instead, modern society comprised individuals and families who interacted with others for specific purposes in associations such as companies, bureaucracies or specialised voluntary groups. Community is tradition and is eroded by the individualising, modernising processes of a mass society. Class, as represented by the economic interest of individuals and families, had become the most important source of social differentiation. Community was archaic, pre-modern.

An anonymous author in *Political and Economic Planning* asked:

Do we really want to revive local communities? ... With modern communications there is no need for people to focus their activities on a particular locality. They can pick their friends and can spread their occupational, political and cultural concerns over widely scattered areas. (Anon. 1949, 261)

Communities existed in established towns and cities, it was admitted. However, citing a study of Middlesbrough undertaken by Glass (1948), the anonymous author continued, 'community is not a sign of high but of low social development. Those who do not have educational or material opportunities to widen their horizons are the most likely to cluster around the parish pump'.

In Middlesbrough, and by implication elsewhere, strong communities were associated with poverty. Local meeting places could still be provided, but ultimately, it was up to residents to make uses of the community facilities as they wanted. Who used the meeting places and how these groups related to each other raised questions for which there were 'no predetermined answers' (Anon. 1949, 279).

In this context, as advocated in design guides such as the Dudley report (MH 1944, 58–9) and as used in the first generation of new towns, the neighbourhood became defined as a functional device. The neighbourhood provided a spatial framework for the daily activities of the individual without, however, the assumption that individuals would come together in a community. As such, the neighbourhood remained an influential planning concept throughout the 1950s and early 1960s. The functional neighbourhood was, for example, endorsed in the main textbook of the 1950s and early 1960s *Principles and Practice of Town and Country Planning* by Keeble (1969, 218–38).

There was a complication. If class was the main source of social division, perhaps the creation of social balanced neighbourhoods offered a way of bringing different classes together. For some leading social reformers and advocates of town planning and this included Nye Bevan, the separation of council from private housing meant that the estates built in the 1930s and 1940s could never constitute full communities. Individuals and families from different classes would have to live close to one another. Bevan wanted to build socially balanced communities, 'the living tapestry of a mixed community' (Foot 1975, 75–6). The aims of the Labour government were not completely consistent, however. Bevan also justified council housing as a means of solving the housing needs and problems of 'lower income groups', the implication being that higher income groups would continue to house themselves (Malpass 2003b, 601).

The assumption of Labour policies was that class distinctions were likely to diminish anyway owing to the impact of a series of wide ranging reforms, including progressive taxation and the establishment of the welfare state. Whether this was likely was another question, however. Class distinctions were not just about income. They were also about status and respectability. Mass Observation (1943, 207) reported, 'People liked sociable, but not inquisitive neighbours of the same 'class' as themselves'. It went on to note the existence of two types of complaints when people were not of the same 'class'. 'Some people considered that their neighbours belonged to a lower social grade than themselves and so were dragging the neighbourhood down; while others disliked what they alleged to be the 'snobbishness' of their neighbours.' Given such attitudes, social segregation was likely to reappear at least at the level of individual streets, once policies in favour of social mix were relaxed or abandoned.

For all their limitations, the social balance and social mix policies remain amongst the best remembered of all the measures of the 1945 Labour government. The proposals for social balance and social mix might have led to a different and more popular type of council housing if they had been implemented on a large scale and modified to permit relatively homogeneous streets within the balanced neighbourhoods. The functional neighbourhood remains, moreover, an element of good practice in urban design. For example, the Commission for Architecture and the Built Environment (CABE 2007a, 5) has called for 'Neighbourhoods where it is convenient and safe to walk or cycle to the shops, the primary school'.

The historical specificity of neighbourhood planning in the 1940s must also be recognised, however. Neighbourhoods were planned in the expectation of a housing programme led by local authorities and new towns. Difficulties of coordination emerged from the 1950s onwards with the return of large-scale private house building. The programming of amenities and facilities such as a local school, doctor's surgery or library was more uncertain in the context of private house building and generally lagged behind the completion of the housing estates. In addition, from the 1960s onwards, the greater variety of goods available in town centres and later still in out-of-town centres started to undermine the commercial viability of neighbourhood shops. Smaller household size and a consequent reduction in local population levels also undermined the viability of neighbourhood centres. The environmental case for neighbourhood planning is, as strong as ever. However the means of implementation are weak.

Implementing a Housing Programme

The Conservative governments in power from 1951 to 1964 brought new priorities. In the short-term, in the early 1950s, the priority was to realise an expanded council housing programme. In their election campaign, the Conservatives had promised to out-build Labour. In the longer term, they wished to encourage private house building and to free the land market from the financial restrictions of the Town and Country Planning Act, 1947. The system of house building licences was first liberalised and then in 1954 scrapped. In the same year, the betterment levy was scrapped. Finally, in 1959, the rules of compensation for compulsory purchase were revised so that, other than in a few cases such as slum clearance and new towns, public agencies were required to pay market rather than either existing use values or, in the specific case of slum clearance, site values.

The Conservatives did not go so far, however, as to abolish planning control. The Conservatives accepted town planning as an extension of previous environmental controls and, while they did not publicly debate the point, they accepted in addition that there should be no return to the position prior to 1939 when an approved planning scheme made local authorities liable for compensation for refusal of planning permission. Planning became mostly a means of regulating a process of privately led urban development. Labour returned to government in 1964 and remained so until 1970. By this time, however, the reliance on private developers could not be easily changed.

Densities, Design and Social Patterns

In relation to housing, the main issue was about higher densities, in a way that overlapped though not completely displacing the earlier issue of 'flats versus houses'. Density and the characteristics of the estate outside the home eventually became the most important source of physical distinction both within the council stock and between the council and private housing schemes. At the same time, the internal standards of new council houses were less variable than before 1939. Houses and flats were generally larger and better equipped than those built in the 1930s, even though floor areas fell during the economy drives of the 1950s.

Density was important in part because it impinged on many different interest groups. The initial phase of urban development in the 1940s was criticised as causing an annual loss of agricultural land at the same rate or higher than during the 1930s, before the advent of comprehensive planning (Stamp 1950). In addition, low-density suburban development, including private housing, was criticised for gradually merging town and country into one vast monotonous sprawl or 'subtopia' (Nairn 1956; 1961), without any character as a town or city (Richards and Cullen 1953). Conversely, low densities were defended by housing and planning pressure groups, notably by the followers of the Town and Country Planning Association, as a means of giving people to the type of home that they preferred.

However, the activity of pressure groups was almost certainly not the decisive factor in driving densities higher. Cost factors were another factor. In the early and mid 1950s an economy drive increased densities in council estates in England and Wales. From the 1960s onwards higher land costs increased densities in private housing.

More significant was the impact of land shortages on council housing and a passive acceptance on behalf of central government that higher densities were inevitable. Density is a measure of the intensity of land use. It was inevitable, therefore, that land shortages would affect densities and therefore the form of new housing. Densities increased, moreover, irrespective of whether the proposed schemes were considered as 'slums on the drawing board' as was the subsequently demolished Noble Street flats in Newcastle-upon-Tyne (The National Community Development Project 1976, 20, 54) or as model dwellings as at Park Hill in Sheffield or Roehampton in south London.

Density takes three main forms, as follows:

- the net residential area covering the house and its surroundings, including access roads;
- the gross residential area covering the house, its surroundings, local open space and neighbourhood facilities; and finally
- town-wide densities covering all included in gross density plus industry, the town centre and large areas of open space.

For the most part, the density debates of the post-war years focussed on the net residential areas. It proved too difficult to find ways of saving the amount of land available for non-residential uses.

Higher densities and high rise   The shift towards higher densities is shown most clearly in the guidance provided by the Ministry of Housing and Local Government for local authorities in England and Wales. The Scottish debate is slightly different. By 1950s, many Scottish local authorities had already started to use higher densities in peripheral estates, with three – and four-storey walk-up tenement blocks generally faced in grey roughcast cement render.

In 1952, the Ministry issued a detailed technical review of residential densities. In the context of an economy drive that had already led to the construction of smaller houses, the report accepted that higher densities were justified on cost grounds for peripheral development and could be achieved within conventional spacing and privacy standards, notably the 70 foot (21 metre) rule. However, the report made no firm recommendations and showed, in addition, that, as densities increased, layouts tended to become progressively more regimented (MHLG 1952).

The next official manual (MHLG 1953) was more prescriptive about how 'to raise densities and reduce development costs' in peripheral estates. Amongst the new designs were narrow fronted terrace houses, groups of two-storey flats to fill corner sites and culs-de-sac with footpath access only. The density thereby achieved between 61 and 65 habitable rooms per acre, (or between 25 and 26 per hectare) amounted to a significant shift away from the type of 'open development' that been previously advocated for rural areas and some parts of new towns. However, it was only marginally higher than typical pre-1939 practice or the level advocated in Abercrombie's plans for most suburban zones.

The density of redevelopment areas demanded more radical solutions. The Ministry's review of residential density noted that redevelopment densities were already high – about 120 habitable rooms per acre (about 297 per hectare), with the greater part of the accommodation in flats (MHLG 1952, 50). It made no recommendations about the desirability of increased density in this context.

Nevertheless, when slum clearance started on a large scale in the 1950s, local authorities faced increased land shortages which both they and central government believed could only be fully countered by building higher density schemes with a higher proportion of flats, albeit mostly low rise flats of three, four or five storeys. In *Cities in Flood* Peter Self (1960, 48) noted: 'many cities are in fact already building to higher densities than their original proposals' and that, partly in consequence of these higher densities and partly as a result of unimaginative design practices, most cities had 'preferred to go in for uniform, sanitary barracks.'

Central government could have intervened, but faced contradictory political pressures and largely acquiesced as densities increased. Town planning was largely a passive element in all this. Town planning became increasingly narrow in scope, increasingly concerned with controlling development and increasingly separated from the housing programmes of the time (Glass 1973).

To cover the extra costs of building medium and high-rise schemes, the government introduced additional subsidies in 1956. In the same year, the government started to encourage building contractors to produce non-traditional, industrialised design and build packages in the hope that this might, in the longer term, reduce the costs of high-rise (Dunleavy 1981). Finally, a further housing manual *Flats and Houses* (MHLG 1958) explained to local authorities how flats of various heights and densities might be designed and laid out. Though the manual did not fully endorse high-rise, the implication was that high flats were an acceptable form of housing provision

The alternatives to higher densities were either the promotion of 'overspill' development, from one local authority area to another or the development of new towns. Both overspill and new town schemes went ahead in the 1950s and 1960s but not on a sufficient scale. The proportion of new council housing built as flats increased steadily throughout the 1950s and early 1960s, accounting for about half of output in England and Wales in 1962 (Merrett 1979, 127). The proportion of dwellings in high flats (blocks of five or more storeys) similarly increased, reaching a peak in 1966 of about a quarter of all approved tenders in England and Wales (Gittus 1976, 132).

Where high-rise met a need, it still remained generally popular with tenants. For example, a survey of 692 households living in tower blocks in Glasgow, undertaken in 1968 by Jephcott (1971), showed that, except for households with a child under 5 years old, the overwhelming view was of satisfaction with their home. The main reasons, according to Jephcott, were that tenants had always lived in flats in Glasgow and that flats continued to offer better housing than the available alternatives. Compared to the 'wretchedness of so many of the tenements', the new high flat 'is near enough the dream house of the Ideal Home exhibition' (ibid., 171). Of course, it was another question whether such a favourable view was likely to persist.

The role of builders and architects   Questions of land availability apart, there are alternative explanations for the development of high-rise. Some accounts stress the influence of the construction industry (Merrett 1979, 126–31; McCutcheon 1975). Others point to the role of the architectural profession and in particular the modern movement in architecture.[5] Neither account provides a fully satisfactory explanation, as both ignore the issue of land scarcities and the various interests (opposition of rural interests to overspill, the desire of big city authorities to retain their population) that sought to raise redevelopment densities. At the same time, the role of the building industry and of architecture is important is showing how high-rise became presented as a type of modern best practice, even though it departed radically from the type of housing that most residents had previously lived and probably expected for the future (Dunleavy 1981; Murie and Rowlands 2007).

The influence of the building industry was mostly apparent in the use of building packages. These almost certainly ensured that high rise was more widely developed than might otherwise have been the case. The building packages had advantages of speed; they simplified the development process and also encouraged smaller district authorities, with fewer technical resources to build high. In doing all this, moreover, the building packages spread high-rise to smaller towns where land constraints were not so intense.

The relationship between construction companies and local authorities was sufficiently close to give rise to suspicions about bribery. Norman Dennis, a sociologist active in analysing policies in North East England has commented on 'bottles of whisky at Christmas' being bought by contractors for the technical officers in local government and 'drinks bought at conferences by the officers for the councillors, for which the sozzled [drunk] councillors were sufficiently grateful'.[6] Particular and more serious allegations were also made against T. Dan Smith, the leader of Newcastle City Council, who was later imprisoned for bribery in the award of building contracts. There is no evidence to suggest, however and this is another point made by Dennis that either councillors or officers adopted a policy that they would have otherwise avoided.

Moreover, the building companies had no obvious interest in the development of high-rise as opposed to any other form of housing. Many non-traditional building packages were flexible in their application and could just as easily have been applied to storey terraces and semis, as was the case for Wimpey 'no-fines' housing and Medway timber. If the building packages were not suited to low rise, other packages could no doubt have been prepared. The building companies were adaptable, responded to the calls of government and competed for their own packages, whether high or low rise.

In any case, if given the ability to influence policy, most building companies would have probably preferred a return to the apparently simpler, deregulated system of the 1930s. In 1955, the editor of the journal *The Builder* (4 November 1955) spoke for the industry when he argued that proposals for a change to the housing subsidies were fatally flawed because they encouraged high-rise building, whereas resources should be freed up for building what most people actually wanted to live in – the privately built suburban semi.[7]

The tendency, starting in the early 1960s, for high-rise to be incorporated into building packages displaced the architectural profession from detailed design control (Glendinning and Muthesius 1994, 193). To this extent the architectural profession can disassociate itself from the high-rise building programme in its later stages. Nevertheless, architects were happy to advertise their involvement in high-rise and other types of high-density projects where they were still in control. Throughout the 1960s, the annual preview section of the *Architectural Review*, published in January of each year, contains literally dozens of such projects. The January 1967 edition is particularly notable for the inclusion of projects, at Killingworth (Northumberland), Leek Street (Leeds) and Hulme (Manchester) that were subsequently demolished owing to design and construction failures.

In 1967, the subsidy for high-rise was withdrawn in England and Wales, partly no doubt for cost reasons but also owing to a feeling that the quality of completed schemes did not compare to traditional low-rise housing. The partial collapse in 1968 of Ronan Point tower block in the London Borough of Newham, in which five people were killed, was a further and well-publicised blow to the credibility of high-rise. By this time, however, architectural attitudes were changing. The proportion of dwelling built as high-rise fell rapidly in the late 1960s and new high-rise schemes ceased almost completely after about 1975.

Even so land shortages continued to encourage local authorities to build complex high density/medium (between say four or five and ten storeys) and low-rise schemes until the end of mass slum clearance in the period from 1972 to 1974. In September 1973, the *Architectural Review* published another critique documenting a further wave of mostly medium rise (between about four and ten storeys) potentially unpopular schemes, including the subsequently notorious Aylesbury estate in Southwark.

Housing Contrasts and Segregation

A theme of user research in housing is that people generally judge their home by what is available elsewhere in the nearby locality or by what is available to other people with similar incomes and expectations. This was implicit in the survey of Mass Observation (1943). It was explicit in the survey of high-rise in Glasgow, undertaken by Jephcott (1971). The planning and housing policies of the 1940s had assumed that council housing would remain an object of desire for working-class families. However, from the 1950s onwards, owner-occupied housing expanded to the point that it gradually became the normal, 'natural' type of tenure for respectable individuals and their families (Gurney 1999). In addition, council housing started to acquire significant variations in quality between one estate and another.

Private/council housing contrasts Council estates had always looked distinctive. From the 1950s and 1960s they started look increasingly distinctive. The predominance of flats of various heights from low rise to high-rise was one factor. Flats were still a rarity in private housing outside central London. A lack of interest in the external environment was another, contributory factor. Mass housing programmes of the type pursued by local authorities are well suited to the specification of floor space standards and these were fully discussed, as for example in the Parker Morris report (MHLG 1961). However, the design of an attractive external appearance received less attention, both in official guidance and in practice.

Finally, as part of this neglect of the external environment, local authorities were more likely to use innovative, footpath-based estate layouts and unusual house types with flat or monopitch roofs. In contrast, the basic form (terraces, semis and detached dwellings) of privately developed housing remained much the same as in the 1930s, albeit with a smaller number of bungalows (which are less efficient in their use of land). Likewise, private developers seldom departed from the conventional suburban street or cul-de-sac.

Tenants increasingly disliked the appearance of council estates and this was amply revealed in surveys undertaken by the Ministry and other agencies. One series of surveys was undertaken in 1969 and sought to find out how different types of household reacted to innovative building forms, including high rise. The surveys took six estates in Sheffield and London, all of which had been completed since 1960 and examined in detail the views of the tenants, concentrating as was usual at the time on the views of women. Contrary to expectations, the survey showed that the chief factor in tenants' satisfaction was the appearance of the estate. Appearance included bulk and relation of blocks, colour, design, workmanship and greenery. The official report (DoE 1972, 4) commented:

> Apart from their dislike of very large and massive buildings, which gave an institutional appearance, housewives strongly disliked buildings which they thought looked dull, grey or drab. ... Housewives liked variety in both buildings and the spaces they enclosed and preferred spacious surroundings. Trees, grass and flowers were greatly appreciated ....

The preferences of tenants were modest, even obvious. The fact that they had to be stated at all shows the extent of the gap between the views of the professional designers and those of the public.

Other surveys enabled a comparison of estates designed by architects in accordance with conventional public sector guidelines and other estates that local authorities had bought from private developers in the context of a brief slump in private sales. Two particular surveys may be cited in this context – a large scale, national survey undertaken in the mid 1970s by government researchers (DoE 1981) and a local survey of housing in Sheffield undertaken by Furbey and Goodchild (1986). The former survey examined, in detail, the views of about 3,000 tenants in 55 recently completed council estates in England. The latter examined 426 people on four council estates. Both allowed an assessment of design preferences independently of the tenure status of the respondents. The estates varied in their design principles, but not in their ownership.

The results were similar. Although most residents were satisfied with their home, tenants tended to praise the estates designed by private developers more than the estates designed by local authority housing architects. The bought-in houses were preferred, moreover, even though they were slightly smaller. They looked like respectable suburban owner-occupied homes and possessed layouts of a type that was familiar to residents. In contrast, the architect-designed estates were more likely to possess unusual layouts based on a footpath network with token front gardens and more likely to possess unusual house types.

Contrasts within council housing   Within the publicly-owned housing stock, initial contrasts of design were commonly magnified by the allocations policies and practices of local authorities, that is to say the rules by which they allocated different types of houses in different areas to different applicants and in addition by what might be considered spontaneous processes of social differentiation. In the 1950s, once the slum clearance drives started, local authorities started to formalise their allocation procedures through a rating system, based in part on home visits to the applicants in their previous accommodation. 'Good' applicants, with a favourable rating, received the offer of a good quality home in an attractive area. Less respectable applicants fared less well (CUS 1964, 285; Kirby 1971, 253).

The rating system invariably involved personal or class-based judgements on the part of the home visitor and was later criticised as such (Damer and Madigan 1974). At the same time, the rating of applicants conformed to apparently common sense understandings amongst the respectable working class, about the quality of property that different people did or did not deserve. It also minimised neighbourhood disputes and the likelihood of tenant complaints to the local authority housing department.

The significance of formal rating systems can be overdone. Informal pressures were also made about who should or should not obtain a house on completion of a building project or when a vacancy arose. Mothers would seek to ensure that their daughters could live nearby once they married and established a new household (Young and Lemos 1997, 50–51). In addition, neighbours, friends and relatives would petition the local councillor or the local rent collector or housing manager as to who deserved a property and who did not.

In the 1970s, local authorities mostly changed their allocation policies in favour of assessments of the 'need' of applicants. The main reason was the pressure of the demand from the homeless and, in addition, the tendency for both rating systems and informal, community based systems to work against the interests of outsiders. The search for racial equality and the implications of the Race Relations Act, 1976 were especially important.

Needs-based allocations have remained a key element of housing allocation to the present. They do not promote social balance, however, owing to variations in the pattern of demand and supply between different estates and a tendency for households with the most urgent need for rehousing, and these were generally the poorest and most vulnerable, to accept an allocation in the least popular estates. In London, for example, the trend throughout the 1960s and early 1970s was for the pre-1939 flatted estates to gain an increasingly proportion of low income families with children, often of Irish and black Caribbean origin in comparison with the two-storey cottage estates comprising houses with gardens (Dugmore 1976; 1977). Later, by 1980s, the least popular estates also included examples of tower blocks and other higher density estates (Goodchild 1985).

As the council housing stock grew in size and age, its quality and character became increasingly diverse. The variations were most obvious in large cities, above all in London, with a combination of high rise and low rise accommodation, built over a long period. Even so, even in smaller and medium sized towns, the difference between the best and the worst estates was becoming increasingly obvious. Kirby (1971, 251) commented, for example, of the inter-war council stock in North East England that while some areas had 'matured into as pleasant a residential environment as is found in the private sector, in other localities it has the appearance of twilight zone'.

In general, social segregation was less marked in the post-war new towns and has remained so to the present. (See, for example, Burton 2000, Table A8.) The new towns have generally possessed a relatively uniform housing stock, mostly built within a relatively short period of 20 or 30 years. Probably more important, the corporations responsible for their development attempted to promote a degree of social balance during the 1950s and 1960s when local authorities had mostly ceased to do so.

In addition, in the early 1970s, a few local authorities, for example, Middlesbrough and Norwich continued to pursue social balance policies (Allen et al. 2005). Social balance in the 1960s and 1970s required mixed tenure development of public rented and owner-occupied housing rather than, as in the 1940s, social mix within the public rented sector. However, the resulting social and tenure mix has mostly proved stable. Residents have simply thought that they lived in an ordinary place inhabited by ordinary people.

Council housing in retrospect   The promotion of social balance in Peterborough, Middlesbrough, Norwich and perhaps a few other places was the exception. The typical pattern was for the council estate to become marked off as somewhere different and less desirable than owner-occupied residential areas. The council stock as a whole experienced a process of 'residualisation', to use the term most commonly used in housing studies in Britain. It became progressively occupied by poorer and more vulnerable households and increasingly characterised by poorer physical conditions (Malpass and Murie 1982, 174).

The impact of housing policies in the 1980s and 1990 reinforced this sense of separateness and exclusion. Subsidised house building declined after 1980 in line with a general shift in housing policy in Western Europe, from funding construction and rehabilitation to funding individuals and families in difficulty (Ghékiere 1991, 45–6). Policy shifted because governments believed that previous housing shortages had been largely resolved and that the majority of the population was reasonably well housed.

The scale of reduction was substantial and was almost certainly hastened by the election in 1979 of a Conservative government that, unlike its immediate predecessors, was intent on challenging the post1945 welfare state. For example, in 1978, public sector developers (as social housing agencies were then classified for statistical purposes) accounted for about 47 per cent of the total of a total of 279,760 dwellings. In contrast, in 1986, public sector developers accounted for about 11 per cent of 205,366 dwellings.[8]

However, the general direction of policy was similar to that in other European countries. Social housing in the Netherlands represented about 34 per cent of the total of new housing in 1980, but had fallen to 17 per cent by 2000. In France, the proportion has fluctuated but has mostly been in the range of between 15 and 20 per cent of all new housing since the 1980s (Louvot-Runavot 2001). The proportion of new build completed by social housing agencies in Britain has, moreover, remained relatively low during the period of office of the Labour government elected in 1997. In the financial year 2000/2001, for example, social housing developers completed 14 per cent of a total of 164,881 dwellings in Britain with private developers completing the rest. (Percentages calculated by the author from Table 2.1b, CLG-NS , 2006.)

Indeed, in one specific way, the policy changes of the 1980s and 1990s have involved a degree of convergence with housing policy in continental Europe. After 1919, the house building programme in Britain was unusual in its dependence on local authorities. From the 1980s onwards, in contrast, housing associations took the lead. In particular, after the Housing Act, 1988, housing associations were able to borrow money from private sources and this made them more attractive to governments as the main policy instrument to implement housing policies.

Low levels of new build have meant in turn that the social housing stock and in particular the council stock has become progressively older on average, with few examples of well-designed, up-to-date schemes that might offer a different, more modern image. During the 1990s, in particular, English local authorities fell behind other types of owner in investment in repairs and modernisation work (Davidson 2000).

The 'right to buy', introduced in the Housing Act, 1980, was arguably the most distinctive aspect of housing policy in Britain, one without direct parallels elsewhere in Europe. It gave, as its name suggests, a right to all council and new town tenants to buy their home at a substantial discount that grew with the length of the tenancy. Local authorities had long been able to sell homes if they wished. The creation of a right to buy meant that local authorities had to sell, even if as was generally the case with Labour controlled authorities they did not want to. Housing association tenants received no equivalent right. Housing associations were a minority form of housing at the time. They had a distinctive legal status and, in some case, their finances would not have been able to cope with forced, below market price sales.

Sales increased rapidly once the right became publicised. In England, the number exercising the right increased from 2,328 in the financial year 1980/81 to 167,123 in the financial year 1982/83.[9] Indeed the policy was so popular that the right to buy was retained by a Labour government after 1997. By 2002, the council stock had declined by over 30 per cent as a result of the right to buy alone and by over 50 per cent if all sales are included for example those to housing associations and private developers.[10]

The right to buy appealed to tenants for a variety of reasons. It enabled occupants to escape the restrictions of council housing management and to undertake home improvements. In the 1980s, in particular, the existence of a decorative front door was the typical mark that a house had been acquired by its owners. The possibility of using the discounts for personal gain was also an obvious motivation. In most places, but above all in the case of houses with gardens in attractive, high demand areas, the right to buy enabled occupiers to realise substantial capital gains. Sales were disproportionately concentrated in areas of higher environmental quality, for example in well maintained estates of houses with gardens (Barke and Rowlands 1989). This again reinforced the disadvantaged character of the remaining council stock.

Residualisation involves a reduction in the status of social housing. It does not mean that, apart from specific design issues (for example, high rise) the housing programmes of either the interwar or the post1945 period should be judged a failure. The very popularity of the right-to-buy was itself testament to the long term contribution of council housing to the national housing stock. Moreover, the scale of problems in social housing is easily exaggerated. It is possible to show, for example, that social housing tenants are more likely to say they are dissatisfied with the area in which they live, compared to private tenants and owner-occupiers. Yet the great majority of tenants state they are satisfied (for example, 78 per cent in England in the financial year 2002/3, according to Robinson et al. 2004, Table A7.2). The landscape of social housing includes hundreds and probably thousands of examples of taken-for-granted estates, of varies ages, that have retained their attraction as a home for lower income people. Even the much denigrated high rise block contains hundreds of examples that have avoided serious problems.

Moreover, many of the problems that have affected council (and former council) estates are treatable and more easily treated if they remain in the collective ownership of a social housing landlord. The physical condition of the stock has benefited from a modernisation drive, the so-called decent homes standard drive from 2000 onwards. Likewise, local authorities and other social housing agencies have become more aware of the need for estate and neighbourhood management and improvement programmes than in the past and have successfully pursued policies to this effect. Studies of the most unpopular, deprived estates in the 1980s and 1990s, for example by Power and Tunstall (1995), painted a depressing picture of social landlords failing to cope with increased social polarisation and the management difficulties that this posed. More recent accounts provide a more encouraging picture (Tunstall and Coulter 2006).

Some caution is required. Social housing agencies are generally unable to secure and retain substantial improvements alone. The lesson of exercises in the improvement of deprived estates, from the 1980s onwards, is that the quality of life depends on a wide range of public services (Evans 1998; Page 2006) and depends, in addition, on the level of local unemployment (Tunstall and Coulter 2006). Most likely, now that social housing estates have come to house the most deprived individuals and families, they will remain vulnerable to reductions in public expenditure or increased unemployment.

In addition, the improvement of the social housing stock has not fully eliminated their environmental problems. The English House Condition Survey suggests that the general environment of social housing remains relatively poor compared to that of private housing and relatively poor, in addition, compared to the environment inhabited by poorer owner-occupiers and tenants (namely those in receipt of financial benefits) (DCLG 2007b, 62). Areas that predominantly comprise local authority built flats continue, moreover, to have the highest incidence of environmental problems (ibid., 41).

Outcomes in Terms of Urban Form

Social contrasts in housing mostly operate at the level of specific neighbourhoods and estates. Assessments of the impact of planning on urban form requires a different and more international analysis. Accounts of planning and housing typically focus on the policy framework and practices of a single country. To grasp what is distinctive about one country and what might have happened if other policies had been pursued requires international points of comparison. Two examples may be provided – those of the United States and France.

Comparisons with the United States

In the 1950s and 1960s, the most important point of comparison was with the United States. The higher living standards in the US meant that it seemed to offer an indication of what might happen in Britain in the near future. The US also offered an example of a country with a much weaker framework of public intervention and so allowed a comparison of trends in a contrasting political context.

The impact of public policy is the main theme of a comparison of density policies in London and New York, undertaken by Drover (1973; 1975). Even if planning in London, as elsewhere in Britain, had shifted towards a more pragmatic and less consciously social approach in the 1950s and 1960s, it was still relatively egalitarian if compared to practice in New York. In London, density policy had sought to distribute the population as evenly as possible throughout the metropolitan area. It had sought to reinforce decentralisation from the centre whilst conserving land at the periphery. Despite the development of high flats, for example, planning policies in London in the 1950s and 1960s routinely sought to restrict densities in the inner area (Glendinning and Muthesius 1994, 268).

In New York, in contrast, town planning had originated as a means of protecting and promoting land values and was, as a result, largely subservient to and had reinforced market trends. The desire to protect property values at the centre informed the basis of most early policy decisions, with little consideration being given to land conservation on the periphery. As a result, the range of permitted densities was much greater. In New York, permitted densities varied from over 800 persons per acre at the centre (324 per hectare) to three or four persons per acre (1.21 or 1.62 per hectare) on the periphery. In London, in contrast, the equivalent range was between 200 and 30 (80.9 and 12.1 persons per hectare).

Actual density patterns, as revealed by the 1966 sample census for London and the 1960s census for New York, suggested little difference in the pattern of gross residential densities, that is to say the density at a neighbourhood level. In both cities, gross densities were also similarly correlated with the socio-economic and family composition of the area concerned. The implication, therefore, was that housing and planning policies in London, had done little to promote social balance at the level of neighbourhoods. Moreover, in London, the lower density of the cottage estates was itself a source of social distinction and status. As Taylor (1973, 173) noted independently of the post-war plans for London, 'by protecting the lower densities of the outer suburbs, they cemented class distinctions between inner and outer areas'.

On the other hand the density pyramid in New York was more marked. In New York, market forces had boosted net residential densities where demand was greatest, at the centre and reduced densities where land was more freely available on the periphery. In London, in contrast, the public sector had built to lower densities than the older privately rented stock (despite the trend towards higher densities in the 1950s) and in doing so had redistributed housing space to those in need.

London and New York are exceptional cases in their respective countries. Clawson and Hall (1973) undertook a more extensive comparison of urban growth in Britain and the U.S. in the post-war years, examining typical densities throughout the major urban complexes in the two countries, that is 'urban England' stretching from Leeds and Manchester in the north through the Midlands to London in the south and the north-eastern seaboard of the United States. At the end of World War II, seven or eight houses to the acre was the most common density in new housing in the US (ibid., 130). Thereafter, the density of new housing in the US had declined at the same time that it had increased in Britain. Internal standards of equipment were also higher with the provision of air conditioning systems and higher quality plumbing and electrical circuits (Hall et al. 1973, 188). The main difference between the two countries was increased land price inflation in Britain, twice that of the United States in the 1960s (Clawson and Hall 1973, 238).

The comparisons of Drover and Clawson and Hall have different implications. The comparison of Drover shows the distinctive egalitarian aspirations and achievements of policy in Britain. Clawson and Hall, in contrast, emphasised the disadvantages of planning for the achievement of consumer aspirations.

Subsequent evaluations of US suburbia have focused more on the collective disadvantages of uncontrolled development. Lucy and Phillips (2000, 21) have complained, for example, of the 'tyranny of easy development decisions'. Private developers do not necessarily provide what consumers prefer; they tend to scatter development in a way that increases commuting time; and they encourage continued outward expansion in a way that leaves behind depressed communities. In response, local authorities and states have started to promote so-called 'smart growth' initiatives, though these remain controversial.

Dislike of post-1945 suburban growth in the US has also directly influenced policy in Britain. The report of the Urban Task Force (UTC 1999, 38) includes, for example, an aerial photograph of part of Houston, Texas to illustrate a 'non-sustainable pattern of suburban development'. In the late 1960s and early 1970s, however, the collective disadvantages of US suburbia received less attention than the higher material standards. In *The Containment of Urban England*, Hall et al. (1973, 427) argued that the main losers from planning in Britain were 'the aspirant rural or suburban dwellers. Families who have sought rural life have had to settle for a suburban one – though they still aspire to the suburban acres beyond. Suburbanites have been housed in homes that are smaller and meaner than their equivalents in the 1930s.'

The reference to 'meaner' homes is misplaced. Privately developed homes were at least as well equipped as those in the 1930s. Nevertheless, given the inflation in land prices in the 1950s and 1960s, privately developed homes were smaller and less well-equipped than they might have been. Planning had encouraged inflation in land prices and this led developers to economise in the standards of new housing.

Deregulation on the US model was not the only way of promoting better value for money in the housing market. Given a continued desire to manage and control urban growth, it might have been better, as Hall et al. (1973, 434–6) also recognised, for public agencies to assemble more sites for development at their existing use value. New town development agencies would have provided the appropriate policy instrument. Such a strategy would have countered inflation in land prices, without abandoning an overall growth strategy. Hayek had argued that planning was justified as a means of promoting competition. Within the framework of economic liberalism, it would therefore have been justified for planning agencies to bring forward sites that would break the monopoly or near monopoly power of local land owners.

Efforts were made in the direction of publicly-led development through the establishment in 1967 of a national Land Commission under an Act of the same name. However, the Land Commission achieved little partly owing to the opposition of local authorities, keen to protect greenfield sites and partly owing to its short period of existence prior to abolition by a Conservative regime elected in 1970. Irrespective of the implications of competition arguments, active public intervention in the land market was consistently and, in practice successfully opposed by successive post-war Conservative governments, except for exceptional cases such as new towns. A political dislike of public land ownership took precedence over the economic and planning arguments in its favour.

Comparisons with France

The distinctiveness of the British model of twentieth-century urban growth can be revealed in a different way if compared to patterns of development in France. Here a much higher proportion of development in the 1950s and 1960s was in the form of flats. For example, in 1964, only about 25 per cent of new dwellings were built as flats in Britain, whereas in France, the equivalent figure was 73 per cent (UNECE 1969, Table 7). Although suburban densities were higher in Britain than in the US, they were lower than in France.

Why did the French experience differ so much from that in Britain? Bauer and Roux (1976) point to two distinctive features of processes of urban development in France.

First, owners expected land to be valued in relation to the highest potential density. Because flats in France cost no more than houses to build and because they could achieve higher densities, developers who intended to build flats could usually outbid those who intended to build houses. A vicious circle was established in which most development land was priced as though flats would remain the norm. In the 1960s and early 1970s, land values in Britain did not present such severe problems as in France (ibid., 7).

Secondly, an ideological preference on the part of the French cultural elite for traditional, compact cities tended to undermine political support for measures to reduce densities. The high density, flatted estates of the 1950s and 1960s were the product of a centralised planning programme, itself linked to a system of national economic planning, that organised both private and public developers in mass housing programme. Development proceeded, virtually without criticism or debate, according to specified standards of equipment, in distinct estates that were separated both from other types of land use and from older built-up areas.

The result is a pattern of densities and a pattern of social segregation in France that is unlike the typical urban pattern in most cities in Britain (albeit more similar to the pattern in Scotland). In most French cities, the social house building programmes ensured the construction of high density and often high rise social housing flats in enclaves in the suburbs. In doing so, the French state encouraged the emergence of highly segregated, high density and high rise peripheral estates.

By the early 1970s, French consumers discovered that they could purchase sites in the countryside, build a home and commute to work by car. Planning control, though in operation in France, was not tightly organised into a pattern of urban containment as in Britain. Isolated and scattered development in the countryside was able to go ahead and was often encouraged by local politicians to promote local taxation income. As a result, scattered low density estates and single houses started to appear as a broad diffuse ring outside and around that of the large scale estates. Such exurban scattered development, as it developed from the 1970s onwards, has similarities with dispersed US suburbs and has the same mixture of consumer advantages and environmental and public costs. Exurban development in France also shows that the preference for two-storey houses is not a peculiarly 'English' preference, as Glendinning and Muthesius (1994, 325) suggest. In urban France the preference for living in flats only lasted whilst no alternatives were available.

In Britain, the tendency towards higher densities and towards flats occurred in a contradictory policy framework. Flats and more generally higher density housing appeared in the 1950s and 1960s in the context of increased land shortages for council building projects and higher land prices. However, the development of these high densities also appeared in a cultural and professional context in which town planning still favoured the principle of low densities, especially in relation to private housing.

This concern with reduced densities goes back at least to the Town Planning Act, 1909 and to the powers contained therein to control densities (space around buildings and distance between buildings) without paying compensation for loss of development value (Ashworth 1954, 183–4). These particular provisions of the early planning legislation hardly warrant attention in most planning histories, which generally focus on the Town and Country Planning Act, 1947 as the start of comprehensive planning. They are also ignored by those who look at the general rules for compensation in the pre1939 period rather than the exceptions covering density (see Whitehand and Carr 1999, 494; Cherry 1988, 91).

The tradition of low rise building is older still. It goes back to nineteenth-century styles of urban development and, in particular to the style that Rasmussen (1947; 1969) called 'building speculation' as opposed to the 'land speculation' of continental Europe. As a result, with the significant exceptions of Scotland with its different building tradition and some post 1950 council estates with their high rise blocks, the urban residential landscape in Britain remained a relatively low density landscape of two-storey semis, detached houses and terraces.

Notes

1   Policy Studies Institute (c. 1998) *About the Institute*, http://www.psi.org.uk/.
2   Information gained from a visit to Marseilles in October 2002 and from a website consulted in July 2003 at http://www.culture.fr/culture/inventai/itiinv/archixx/imgs/p54–09.htm.
3   'Pph' is persons per hectare and 'dph' is dwellings per hectare. This figure and all others dealing with the conversion of persons per unit area to dwellings per unit assume the development of three bedroom family accommodation.
4   Given a tendency for Scottish local authorities to build a significant proportion of one and two bedroom dwellings, the figures for dph are probably an underestimate and strictly speaking not comparable to those in England.

5   *High Rise Dreams*, BBC 4, Wednesday 23 June 2004, consulted February 2007 at http://www.bbc.co.uk/bbcfour/documentaries/timeshift/high-rise-dreams.shtml.

6   The quotation comes from a discussion on the web page of Civitas, available July 2005 at http://www.civitas.org.uk/blog/archives/2005/01/the_road_to_a_g.html. The name of the author is not given in the discussion,. However reference is made to 'my books about the Sunderland planners', including *People and Planning* by Dennis (1970), London, Faber and Faber.

7   Jones, P. (2001) The evolution of professional attitudes towards high rise: paper presented at the *International Seminar on Urban Form* in Cincinatti, September, consulted on the web, June 2004 at http://www.gees.bham.ac.uk/research/umrg/membersfiles/phil/ISUF4.pdf.

8   Calculated by the author from successive editions of the *Housing and Construction Statistics*, prepared jointly by the Department of the Environment, Scottish Development Department and Welsh Office.

9   Office of the Deputy Prime Minister website consulted September 2003 at http://www.odpm.gov.uk/stellent/groups/odpm_housing/documents/page/odpm_house_609105.xls.

10 The Office of the Deputy Prime Minister website consulted September 2003 at http://www.odpm.gov.uk/stellent/groups/odpm_housing/documents/page/odpm_house_609105.xls. The figure refers to the number of sales in the period (1 April 1979–31 December 2002) as a percentage of stock at 1 April 2002 plus sales in the same period (1 April 1979–31 March 2002).

Chapter 4

Searching for an Alternative

The post-1945 era of planned housing and planned urban development gradually faded away as the assumptions and practices of comprehensive planning appeared progressively less relevant and feasible. The policies pursued by the Conservative government in power from 1951 to 1964 constituted the first stage of a gradual unravelling, as it meant that private developers became primarily responsible for plan implementation. The abandonment of mass council house building constituted the later stages.

At the same time, during the 1960s and 1970s, disillusion with post-1945 practice initiated a series of theoretical exercises in town planning and its allied disciplines, notably architecture and urban sociology. These exercises led to few concrete results at the time. However, they pointed the way forward to subsequent forms of practice and subsequent ways of interpreting practice. They may be simply divided into proposals about ideal cities and future urban forms on one hand and, on the other, reflections on the character of planning practice.

Redefining the Ideal City

Much of the objection to post-1945 planning was about the assumptions of utopianism, rather than about the details of any specific project. The utopias of modern town planning offered a highly controlled environment that, for the critics, was too orderly. As the novelist J.G. Ballard once noted, we 'need a certain element of ... street level chaos in our lives'.[1] Whatever the details of urban design, it was suggested, the future city had to be open to change and to what later postmodern theorists would call 'difference'.

The Demise of Mass Clearance

This sense of excessive, 'unnatural' order was a particular theme in critiques of slum clearance and redevelopment. Jane Jacobs (1964), writing about the post-1945 redevelopment of New York, was arguably the first to argued against comprehensive planning as inherently insensitive to the diversity of urban life. Later, in Britain, Davies (1972) argued that the planner had become no more than an 'evangelistic bureaucrat'. Planners used an ideology, that is to say a set of fixed ideas, of 'futurism' and progress to justify wholesale urban redevelopment of a type, which was, not only highly disruptive to those affected but which also ignored economic reality.

Increased local resistance to clearance in the early and mid 1970s tended, moreover, to vindicate the views of the critics. Mass slum clearance had moved from areas of privately-rented property, generally in a very poor condition to areas with a higher proportion of owner-occupiers and that, in some cases, retained their attractiveness to local middle-class groups (Henney 1973: Mason 1977). In such circumstances, local authorities encountered increased difficulty in showing that clearance was the best course of action and increased resistance from local residents (DoE 1975). Other than for younger individuals and couples who could raise a larger mortgage, the usual effect of compulsory purchase was to force owner-occupiers into council housing – a move that was seen as involving a loss of status and the removal of any prospect for long term capital appreciation. Older, owner-occupied households living in what they considered an adequate property were particularly unwilling to move (English et al. 1976, 155–68).

The uncertainty and blight of clearance proposals was a further problem. The formal procedure for slum clearance started (and indeed continues to start) with a resolution by the local authority to issue a compulsory purchase order to the owners of dwellings in the proposed clearance area. The resolution then has to be confirmed after a local public enquiry. The period from the issuing of the compulsory purchase order to its confirmation would probably be about two years, with another two years before most people were rehoused. In total, therefore, four years would elapse between issuing the compulsory purchase order and rehousing and this is itself long enough. In addition, however, there was a long period before the issuing of the compulsory order during which the local authority, local estate agents and many property owners knew that clearance was likely. Local authorities started their clearance programmes in the 1950s, knowing that at least a decade would pass before the programme was completed. The result was a long period during which all investment in the built environment, both inside and outside the house, would cease and conditions would deteriorate (Gee 1974). Residents turned to improvement as a way of avoiding many years of neglect. At the same time, once conditions had reached a certain point, clearance was inevitable. So while most community groups began to campaign against clearance, those in the worst areas called for immediate rehousing (Ravetz 1976, 13).

Perhaps in a passive, deferential society, local residents would have put up with their problems and kept quiet. The disruption caused by clearance was not a new phenomenon. However, Britain in the 1960s and 1970s was increasingly less deferential to authority. It was a place, for example, of increasing protest against road building and against insensitive city centre redevelopment.

The campaigns of the local groups, in turn, raised the question of community disruption. To obtain political legitimacy, the groups had to insist that a local community existed and, if they were campaigning against clearance, they also had to insist that most people wished to stay. They argued therefore that slum clearance broke up established communities in a way that damaged the morale and life of residents. Middle-class critics agreed. Slum clearance became a narrative of loss, of a way of life that was disappearing. (See, for example, Konttinen 1983.)

In the long term, clearance was unlikely to influence either the persistence or the break-up of closely-knit communities. In older inner areas, communities were likely to break up in the context of population turnover, irrespective of whether dwellings were improved or demolished. A follow-up survey of improvement areas, undertaken by Niner and Forrest (1982) showed that, by 1980, only 37 per cent of residents remained. Conversely, in the newly redeveloped areas and in the peripheral housing estates, communities were likely to re-emerge amongst those rehoused, if social and economic conditions were conducive (Coates and Silburn 1980).

Nevertheless, the cost and disruption caused to the lives of individuals and families were sufficiently serious to require alternative approaches. Comprehensive clearance tackled large areas at one time through a single policy measure. The main theoretical alternative, gradual or cellular renewal was the opposite (McKie 1971; 1974). Gradual renewal tackled small blocks or 'cells' of housing, in some cases as small as an individual dwelling; it proceeded through a mixture of rehabilitation and minor rebuilding; and it attempted to protect the function of the older housing stock in providing low cost accommodation for lower income groups. To this extent, gradual renewal implied flexibility in the adoption of improvement standards, rather than the comprehensive improvement of a neighbourhood to high standards. Finally, though this is an aspect that was stressed more in the writings of McKie than in official practice, gradual renewal was intended to promote private investment. It was intended to encourage local builders to use vacant sites and involved environmental improvements that attempted to lift the status of the neighbourhood within the town.

In reaction to mass slum clearance, the renewal policies pursued by the local authorities in the 1970s were more differentiated and more sensitive to community wishes. Local authorities experimented with different approaches. Sometimes community groups and voluntary agencies experimented with alternatives, in opposition to the local authority. Various examples can be given.

- In Birmingham, the local authority pioneered an 'enveloping' programme that involved the full repair of the external elements of blocks of terraces (Thomas 1986, 125–34).
- At Byker in Newcastle-upon-Tyne, the local authority converted a conventional programme of mass slum clearance into a community-based programme, with local rehousing (Malpass and Murie 1982, 124–30).
- At Black Road in Macclesfield, Cheshire, a group of residents led by an architect successfully campaigned for a community-designed improvement project (Hall 2002, 291; Walters 2007, 73–4).
- In Glasgow, community-based housing associations were able to persuade owners of the advantages of tenement rehabilitation and undertake local rehousing in circumstances where the interventions of the local authority had previously generated much local resistance (Goodchild 1997, 161–3).

The various approaches showed what could be done, if a government were committed to improving neighbourhoods, whilst also consulting residents. With the exception of the owner-occupied housing at Black Road, they also ensured that the improved housing retained its function of housing low-income individuals and families. However, few local authorities were able to implement the full gradual renewal policy agenda, with its emphasis on fine-grained, sensitive approaches. In the words of one contemporary review, many involved in housing renewal 'questioned whether such an individualised approach was a feasible response to the scale of housing problems' (Thomas 1986, 120–21).

In the meantime, neither the experimental, community based initiatives nor the more routine application of improvement grant aid proved sufficient to improve the average quality of the housing stock at a national level or to tackle problems of disrepair (ibid., 134–5). The experimental initiatives were able to make a local impact. The local housing associations in Glasgow, in particular, succeeded in improving the image of the inner city (Maclennan 1983). In general, however, the scale of their application was heavily constrained by their cost.

Unfinished, Spontaneous Cities

For some architects, the apparent failure of one type of utopia – the comprehensively planned city of the early and mid twentieth century – did not amount to the failure of all utopias. Instead, the answer was to search for something new, to rework utopia into a vision that would be unfinished, spontaneous and open to change and that, in addition, would apply the energy of the 'pop' culture of the 1960s to the city. 'Pop' in this context meant not just the growth of popular music, such as the Beatles but young fashion, photography, magazines and furnishings. Pop also meant experimentation and the promotion of varied innovations. Radical architecture and planning followed suit, some stressing the potential of technology to liberate design from the conventions of the past and others stressing the case for the liberation of the individual from over-regulation.

Plug-in cities and open building   The most notable and widely quoted technological visions were those of an architectural collective called Archigram, founded in 1961. The proposals consisted, in their initial form, of drawings for prefabricated 'capsule' apartments that could be hoisted into position by cranes, so forming large urban complexes in the form of a 'Plug-In City' (Sadler 2000). The cranes were a permanent part of the complex, as opposed to a fixture during the construction phase and would therefore allow piecemeal replacement of elements with the blocks.

Thereafter, proposals became increasingly diverse. Two examples will suffice: a 'Blow out village', intended as emergency housing and that could be erected from telescopic tubes and placed under a dome and an 'Instant City' that, like a travelling fairground, went from community to community, giving each a taste of metropolitan culture (Archigram 2000: Jencks, 1969). Town planning and architecture had previously assumed what might be considered a long term, permanent view of the future. Archigram emphasised the ephemeral, 'throw away' character of consumer society and promoted adaptability as in the plug-in capsule apartments.

Archigram adopted a playful, ironic tone to its proposals. It is unlikely, for example, that anyone would take seriously the idea of fully mobile, instant cities. It did, nevertheless, mark a shift away from the serious, socially responsible tone of virtually all previous ideal cities in the twentieth century.

Proposals for plug-in cities were paralleled in the design of housing, by proposals for 'open building' systems that would allow residents to personalise otherwise standardised homes to their tastes and needs. Open building is based on the design of parts that can be assembled in different ways and is invariably associated with a Dutch architect, Habraken, whose initial proposal was published in 1962 and made available in English in 1972.

For Habraken (1972, 63), the conventional building systems of the 1960s were deeply flawed. They assumed that the final form of the home is known in advance and they denied the possibility of combining different building elements in different ways. Diversity, rather than standardisation was the way forward for house building, but it was diversity generated from combining standardised elements – 'for example, external wall elements, internal partition elements, floor elements, storage elements, doors, kitchen elements, bathroom elements etc.'.

The usual logic of open building was to disentangle the details of design and home equipment, whilst retaining an overall support structure and organisation. Residents participated in design through choosing room arrangements at the design stage and, in the most flexible systems, being able to change their room arrangement and to update electrical, gas and plumbing systems after completion. The developers and owners of rented housing could also use the greater flexibility of open building to change the mix of house types in a block and to delay making decisions about an appropriate mix until late in the development process.

The reference to a block requires clarification. In principle, the separation of the dwelling from its external supports favours development in the form of easily extended detached dwellings, or at least houses with gardens. In practice, however, open building reflected the development context in the Netherlands where the theory originated. Most development, especially of low and moderate income housing in the Netherlands has taken the form of flats and terraces.

Open building was too unusual, too complex and too expensive in the short term to be easily applied. A former Greater London Council scheme at Adelaide Road, Camden is the only fully documented example of open building principles being applied to a flatted estate in Britain (*Architects Journal* 21 May 1975; 12 October 1977). Open building did, nevertheless, identify issues of flexibility and adaptability in housing and these have not disappeared, especially in relation to apartment blocks.

Non-plan Another proposal, simply called 'non-plan', had simpler aims and was much closer to the anti-utopian positions of Jacobs. It sought to promote spontaneity, populism and technological innovation in a way that would promote dispersed urban forms of various types in various regions. Non-plan is generally associated with a series of articles that were published in the weekly journal *New Society* (20 March 1969). Non-plan involved the abolition of planning controls and the acceptance instead of the projects of private developers, neon advertising signs and the landscape of highways such as dominated the landscape of US cities, notably Los Angeles and La Vegas (Barker 2000).

The *New Society* articles, though the best remembered, were not alone in advocating non-plan. In 1967, as an aspect of on-going debates about the failures of council housing, the editors of the *Architectural Review* suggested, 'it is good for architects occasionally to look at housing from the consumer's point of view'. In this context, Cowburn praised the typical privately developed home, not as architecture but as a consumer product similar to a car. The best consumer products were 'objects of choice', with implied meanings and expected values that were more important than functional criteria. Of a typical housing estate road of the type heavily criticised in innumerable planning and urban design guides, both before and afterwards, Cowburn commented that this 'strikes in the popular mind a balance between economic land-use and individuality. The occupants feel free ... to associate only with those they prefer and to live without restraints'.

Self-build, as advocated by Ward (1976) and Turner (1976), offered a further and, from a political viewpoint, more radical interpretation of non-plan. Self-build was a means whereby ordinary people could take possession of land. It gave people a sense of control and therefore contributed to personal and social well-being. At least this was the argument.

Self-build in turn informed in the prospectus for a third garden city, prepared by the Town and Country Planning Association (1979, 4). The first garden city was Letchworth started in 1903. The second was Welwyn started in 1919. The third, based on as yet unidentified site, made reference to the previous examples in its emphasis on combining town and country. Otherwise, this was a small-scale communitarian and anarchist utopia, par excellence – one that emphasised experimentation and the abandonment of large-scale solutions, including large-scale planning. In the words of the prospectus (ibid.),

> In physical terms, large parts of the town will give a predominant impression of greenery and openness, because there would be a larger proportion than in most conventional towns of farming and horticulture. ... Buildings would be on a human scale with probably none above three storeys being necessary. ... Some parts of the town will have what would be recognised as architectural unity. ... The characteristics of informality, variety, experimentation and maximum participation, however, would mean that the garden city would not have a neat of orderly appearance.

There was no overall plan and no spatial vision – merely a series of illustrations of craftsmen at work, of low energy housing, of children playing and of families.

Apart from the self-build element, the third garden city concept failed to be implemented. It proved exceptionally difficult for the Town and Country Planning Association or indeed any similar voluntary agency to obtain a sufficiently large site at low 'existing-use' value. The proposal also encountered disagreements about what the garden city should and should not include (Hardy 1991, 172–202).

Impacts and influences The various proposals for unfinished, spontaneous cities had obvious flaws. The drawings of Archigram looked more like an illustration for a science fiction novel or comic than a realistic contribution to town planning. Many were deliberately based on the style of comic books. The infrastructure in the plug-in cities was as static, monumental and subject to technological breakdown as conventional high rise blocks. Similar considerations applied to open building systems, much of which amounted to little more than an adaptation of the conventional social housing block.

Non-plan was open to other criticisms. The *New Society* group and Cowburn assumed that private developers would always provide the best quality housing, so long as the constraints of the planning system were removed. They were trapped in the images and myths of the advertising industry and commerce.

The anarchist variant of non-plan, as advocated by Turner and Ward, avoided many of the traps of other forms of pop radicalism. The advocacy of self-build involved a rejection of architectural megastructures and equally of commercialism. Self-build is a people-oriented strategy of design and urban development and potentially a liberating approach that by-passes conventional housing providers. It is not an anarchic building process, however. Self-builders generally have to raise finance from banks and building societies. They have to satisfy the financial institutions that the house will be well built and saleable in the case of default and, like all builders, they have to satisfy the building regulations and planning controls. The dependence of most self-builders on borrowed money, together with the skills and other demands of the building process, means that this is not in any case a practical measure for increasing the supply of affordable housing, at least not on a large scale. Typical self-build schemes are undertaken either by relatively wealthy middle-class individuals and families or by those with connections in the building industry (Goodchild 1981). The completed dwellings mostly comprise good quality detached dwellings, mostly with four bedrooms (Barlow et al. 2001).

Despite their weaknesses and limitations, the proposals for plug-in homes, open building and non-plan announced a new era in housing and planning. Proposals for plug-in cities and open building anticipated proposals for the application to housing of 'mass customisation' techniques of the type that combines mass production with the ability of the consumer to personalise the product as appropriate.[2] Likewise, the commercial landscapes endorsed by non-plan soon became a key source of ideas for postmodern architecture (Huyssen 1984, 16–24). Equally and this is also a paradox that affects postmodernism itself, plug-in cities, open building and non-plan were also modern in the sense that they sought innovation and sought to criticise forms of modern architecture and planning that had become stale.

Yet neither plug-in design nor non-plan remained the final word on the design of future city. Another ideal city, that of 'Civilia' (de Wolfe 1971), applied environmentalism to urban development. 'Civilia' used the visual language of pop, but for a more controlling purpose. Civilia comprised a photo-montage with people supposedly enjoying themselves in a city largely dominated by a combination of high blocks and a waterside setting. The underlying theme and aim was, however, about environmental protection and the promotion of an environmentally responsible life style, one that minimised the use of the motor car. Civilia restated that the high density megastructures of the 1960s in the form of a hill town, built around a waste tip in the industrial Midlands.

The contrast between the pop culture and Civilia posed a distinction between market-oriented populist and environmentalist forms of urban development in a way that has persisted, even amongst those who know little or nothing about the originals. More than this, however, the varied architectural experiments and ideal cities suggested that the architectural imagination and more generally the human imagination is capable of a diversity of visions that would outstrip any possibility of a unified urban plan.

New Planning Theories and New Problems

The utopian debates of the 1960s and 1970s undermined the logic of the blueprints that had previously guided town planning. At the same time, the blueprint style was itself less credible than before. The 1960s were a decade of rapid economic growth of a type that implied the constant updating and modification of plans in the light of changing patterns of demand. The 1970s were a decade of a brief boom and then economic recession and growing unemployment, with increasingly localised patterns of prosperity and decline. However, this too challenged the previous assumption that patterns of urban development were relatively stable or at least predictable.

From Blueprints to Processes

In the 1960s, the most commonly articulated criticism was that planning lacked an adequate empirical understanding of the world it sought to manage (Taylor 1998, 55). Planning was too utopian, too concerned with simple models of urban design. It was a lack of social understanding that had led to the failures of slum clearance. Likewise it was a lack of economic understanding that caused a failure to anticipate the effects of increased affluence. Policies and plans could be revised to accommodate changed circumstances, but what was needed was a conceptual model that might prevent such errors in the future, or so it was thought.

The initial response was a shift away from construction, dwellings and urban form to a more abstract concern with planning processes and an understanding of urban development in terms of flows, activities and systems. By the early 1970s, systems approaches to planning, especially as elaborated by McLoughlin (1969), had become the most influential interpretation. In this, planning theory in Britain followed the example of land use/ transport studies in the US and a conceptualisation of transport investment, above all road investment, as the main determinant of urban spatial patterns. Systems approaches said little explicitly about housing and virtually nothing about housing form and neighbourhoods, though they did recognise the significance of repeatedly testing the housing and other assumptions of plans against trends and outcomes. A system is a set of interconnected elements. Systems approaches are, therefore, attempts to identify the main determinants of urban growth, to work out the spatial alternatives in the context of growth trends and to test alternatives against agreed objectives.

The systems view had a series of limitations. First, it proved difficult to identify urban systems, other than for the urban infrastructure (land-use/transport systems, water and telecommunications) and difficult to make long term predictions about how these systems would change. Secondly, systems approaches raised philosophical objections. The systems approach assumes that a consensus would emerge automatically and paid little recognition to conflict and politics. Third, system approaches assumed that local authorities and, in particular, the planning departments of local authorities had sufficient power to control and manage the urban system. In practice, they did not. In particular, during the 1970s, local authorities found that they had to scale back their investment programmes, partly as a result of local opposition, partly as a result of a lack of funds and partly as a result of faltering economic growth.

In this context, systems approach became less appropriate and systems theory gradually faded as a general theory of urban planning. No examples of systems theory are, for example, given in later planning theory textbooks by Campbell and Fainstein (1996; 2002).

However, systems theory has not completely disappeared. Systems theory persists in sociology, albeit in the difference form of communication and linguistic systems (Teubner 1993). These latter continue to have relevance for an understanding of planning as administration and as law. In addition, the notion of the city as a system has persisted in environmental studies. For example, the Royal Commission on Environmental Pollution (2007, 5) has called cities 'complex systems', 'shaped by the trial-and-error accumulation of factors and forces that survive because they fit into and reinforce other aspects of the system'.

Equally, however, as the Royal Commission has recognised, the city understood as a complex system is different from specific infrastructure systems concerned with water or sewerage or the type of ecosystems that are associated with plant and animal communities. Urban systems have socio-technical characteristics, involving a multitude of different, interacting factors (ibid., 86). If systems theory in planning was about land use/ transport systems, socio-technical systems are about the interaction between land use/ transport (and other infrastructure) systems and society.

Within mainstream planning theory, the limitations of systems analysis in its original form led in a different and ultimately unfruitful direction. They led towards a simplified version of the planner as a rational decision-maker. The 'system' was ignored and attention focussed solely on the decision-making procedures that would guide the system. Planning, as presented by Faludi (1973) seeks to ensure that strategic decisions are more rational, more scientific, more sensible and, in general terms more likely to achieve the intended outcomes.

The rational planning models of the 1970s had similarities to the model of planning proposed by Mannheim, about 30 years earlier. They were only new in town planning because the profession in the late 1940s and 1950s had ignored concepts of economic and political planning in favour of an exclusively design-oriented and therefore rigid, blueprint approach. Like Mannheim, the rational decision model was concerned with the application of social science to the work of government. Rational planning did not add to Mannheim's analysis, however. It also lacked the sense of social crisis that had previously provided a justification for planning.

From One Question to Another

In the 1970s, the main challenge to both systems theory and the rational decision model had an explicit political edge. The challenge came from a series of theories that sought to define the role of the state in maintaining a capitalist economy and encouraging its growth. The most precisely articulated theories drew on French structural Marxism especially the work of Castells and Godard (1974) and Castells (1977). As originally conceived, structural Marxism made a series of linked assumptions as follows:

- The process of capitalist development results in under investment in the amenities of working-class life, including housing and related community provision.
- The failures of individual enterprises to invest in social provision leads to a growth of public intervention, though still not necessarily enough to provide satisfactory living standards.
- Protests about the quality of life have the potential to supplement organised action in the factory and can therefore be considered as an aspect of class conflict.

'City changes', by which Castells (1977, 378) meant significant improvements to city life, 'did not emerge under the pressure of city-planning technicians but under that of the conflict process in social groups'.

In Britain, similar structural positions were commonplace in the 1970s. The role of the state emerged as a crucial issue for a national community development project that the Home Office and its Scottish equivalent established to find new ways, apart from simple demolition and dispersal, of tackling urban deprivation. For example, the project team for Coventry declared that, while local protests were always welcome, the results were limited. Protests about the quality of life had to be related to the trade union movement. 'Effective action must bridge the gaps between community politics and industrial politics' (Benington et al. 1975, 68). Likewise, the role of the state became crucial in attempts to conceptualise the history of public sector housing. Merrett (1979, 276), for example, distinguished between two functions of the capitalist state, 'maintaining the economic and political stability of the social formation and, at a more mundane level … promoting the accumulation of capital' (that is to say promoting the profitability of business).

Structural explanations were sufficiently convincing to explain the origins of public sector housing in Britain in the nineteenth and early twentieth centuries. Rodger (1989) explained the continuation of poor living conditions in the period 1780–1914 as a result of a tendency on the part of capital to search for productivity gains and profits, rather than environmental improvements. In addition, Swenarton (1981) analysed the Homes for Heroes programme of 1919 as a means whereby the state sought to pacify working-class unrest through offering the promise of homes that only the middle classes could have previously afforded. Structural explanations were also evoked to explain the absence of large-scale public housing provision in the US. Here the housing problem became defined as one of immigration in the early twentieth century and later as one of race and ethnicity (blacks and Spanish speakers) rather than class (Marcuse, 1980).

In addition, structural explanations had a general influence in restating the importance of economic constraints and the role of interest groups in moulding the outcome of policies. These explanations countered the anodyne, technical emphasis of systems planning and rational decision-making theory. In doing this, they led the way to later interpretations of planning and urban policy as a means whereby the state copes with the growth of flexible, post-Fordist production and globalisation.

On the other hand, structural Marxism was uncertain as to whether economic or political factors had primacy. An emphasis on economic primacy would limit state intervention to the logic of Hayek and other neoliberal economists. State intervention would be limited to those forms of planning that resolved conflicts between property owners, tackled public health problems or in some cases co-ordinated the provision of workers' housing to new industrial projects. An emphasis on political factors helped explain the development of high quality state housing as a means of legitimating the capitalist state, much as Swenarton (1981) had argued. Along similar lines, Merrett (1979, 282) argued since 1945 legitimating function of state housing had become increasingly important, mainly as a result of the increased role of owner-occupation. However, if planning and other forms of state intervention could respond to political pressures, how far could or would this response go before capitalism was transformed into a stable and more socially just society?

Whatever the assumptions, whether economically or politically oriented, the assumption was of the state as a unified, competent planning entity. The experience of economic planning in the 1940s and of public sector building in the 1950s and 1960s gave a different impression. In particular, mass slum clearance and high rise construction served to discredit state intervention, whilst also consuming substantial sums of public money. The building programme had, in particular, acquired a momentum of its own and had reflected a combination of general policy considerations (namely the need to combine speed of production, low costs and high density) and the considerations of specific interest groups (rural conservation groups, urban and rural local authorities, the architectural profession) in a way that lost sight of both consumer wishes and the broader political logic.

With the benefit of hindsight, a further limitation is apparent. The various Marxist theories were mostly about the response to the industrial city. Yet the era of rapid industrial expansion, characteristic of both the nineteenth century and, in a different way, much of the post-1945 era had ceased. The economic context was increasingly one of the collapse of the traditional heavy industries (shipbuilding, steel, coal etc) and localised urban decline. Likewise, the social context was increasingly one of the emergence of unpopular housing estates. The main problem was, in this context, no longer that of providing an adequate or good environment and community facilities for the mass of working-class people. Instead, the problem had become one of integrating marginal urban areas, marginal neighbourhoods and marginal social groups.

The growth, in the 1970s, of such terms as 'the inner cities' or 'urban deprivation' marked the new concerns. The Coventry community project was itself established with the aim of tackling these new problems, though, in stressing links between community groups and the Trade Unions, its report adopted a political strategy that bore no obvious results. The inner city was, in part, a real place characterised by a loss of employment, by a lack of private investment and by a high level of poverty amongst its residents. Such was the analysis of the inner city White Paper, prepared by a Labour government (HMG 1977) and the various programmes of urban regeneration pursued by the government of Margaret Thatcher after 1979. In addition, the inner city was a place of the imagination – a dystopia. Harrison (1986, 21), for example, wrote of the inner city as 'a universe apart, an alien world devoid of almost every feature of an ideal environment … a symbol and summation of the dark side of a whole society'.

Likewise, the political context had changed. The Homes for Heroes programme that Swenarton had shown to be emblematic of class conflict was indeed emblematic but in a slightly different way. The discourse of 'Homes for Heroes' shows exactly that the state was rewarding the working-class for their participation in a mass war. The techniques of war had now changed in a way that no longer depended on conscription, a large standing army and mass working-class participation. Structural Marxism defined one type of *Urban Question*, to cite the title of the major work of Castells (1977). The experience of the 1970s was increasingly of another type (Donzelot 2003).

Notes

1   Taken from a transcript of an interview broadcast on BBC Radio 3, 10 November 1998 and available May 2004 at http://www.jgballard.com/gravenewworld.htm.
2   See, for example, the website of a German research insititute 'TUM Research Center Mass Customization and Customer Integration' consulted January 2005 at http://www. mass-customization.de/index_english.htm.

PART C
New Forms of Modernity, 1980 Onwards

Chapter 5

(Re)tracing the Context

By the 1980s, the old formulas no longer seemed to work. Planning had created cities and housing estates that were now part of the problem rather than a solution. Planning continued, but in a way that largely repudiated its previous style of intervention. Planning had become more fragmented, more varied in its aims and more likely to support market processes (Brindley et al. 1989). Even more importantly in terms of the history of ideas, the shift in direction in planning in Britain paralleled shifts and crises in planning in other countries and overlapped broader doubts about the legacy of twentieth-century culture and politics (Sandercock 1998).

In Britain, the journal *Marxism Today* expressed the mood most succinctly when in October 1988, it announced that politics had now entered a new era, a 'new times' to use their term. The concept itself 'new times' said little about the specifics of planning practice or about cities. The concept has, moreover, subsequently fallen into disuse. However, the sense of difference with the past, including most of the twentieth century, has not disappeared.

Since the 1980s, as applied to urban planning and related aspects of public policy, three main interpretations of the new times have emerged:

- postmodernism, a rejection of the unifying features of modernism in favour of fragmentation and diversity;
- hypermodernism, a theory of consumption and of adaptation to change;
- post-Fordism and related theories of structural change.

Each interpretation throws light on aspects of policy and practice, though none offers a full account.

Postmodernism

In terms of their date and chronology, ideas of the 'postmodern' offered the first interpretation and offers for this reason an appropriate starting point. Hypermodernism and post-Fordism emerged partly in response to the deficiencies of postmodern theory and, in particular, from a desire to base interpretations of contemporary social change on social and economic life. Postmodernism is also both the simplest and the most multidimensional of the various theories and interpretations. Postmodernism is not a single theory. It is not even a series of linked theories. It is instead, to use the words of Jameson (1984a, vii) 'a kind of crossroads in which a number of different themes ... intersect and problematize each other'.

Aspects and Directions

In relation to planning, the simplicity of postmodernism lies in the way that it can be related to its history and to changing spatial patterns. The term town planning, and the various related terms that emerged in Europe and the US in the late nineteenth and early twentieth centuries, were, to cite Choay (1969), 'intended to mark, with the full impact of a neologism [a newly coined word], the advent of an entirely novel relationship between Western man and the organisation of cities' (italics added). Town planning was a product of the big industrial city. Equally, as Choay (1995) later suggested, the cities of the late twentieth century had changed sufficiently to demand new forms of professional practice and new words to describe this practice. The 'urban', as reflected in urban design, urban policy and urban studies and meaning a relatively diffuse and dispersed urban area, had started to replace references to the more concrete and specific concepts of 'town and country'. To go slightly beyond Choay's intention, the invention of the urban marks the passage to a postmodern style of planning.

In addition, the postmodern involved a process of reflection on the past. Planning and more generally other forms of public intervention in the early and mid twentieth century were about rescuing the industrial city from the failures of laissez-faire. From say the 1970s onwards, the various forms of *urban* policy have been about improving cities that are in part the product of planning and other forms of public intervention.

At the same time, postmodernism is not just about planning. It means a narrative of change, a repeated reinterpretation of Western modernism from a variety of different aspects. In relation to planning and related aspects of urban policy, five main themes may be identified:

- the fragmentation of the urban landscape, this being closely related to the origins of postmodernism in opposition to modern architecture;
- discourse analysis, this being associated with so-called 'poststructural', linguistic social theory;
- a process of reflecting on different aspects of reality, this being associated with the implications of discourse analysis;
- the politics of identity, difference and 'performativity'; and finally
- a dialectic in which postmodern ideas have been watered down and absorbed into mainstream policy and practice.

Fragmentation   The logic of postmodernism as fragmentation is apparent in almost all attempts to define the term in contrast to modernism. The modern/postmodern dichotomies produced by Hassan (1985), a literary critic, are typical and widely cited.[1] Postmodernism represents a movement that moved away from, but did not completely reject the unifying features of modern literature and modern Western culture. Postmodernism is a process of unmaking of culture and was associated by a multiplicity of other terms, all of which carried the prefix 'dis' or 'de', for example, 'decreation, difference, discontinuity, disjunction, disappearance, decomposition, de-definition, demystification, detotalisation, delegitimation'. Such terms express an epistemological obsession with fragments or fractures, and, by implication, a corresponding political commitment to minorities in politics, sex and language, to pluralism and to multiculturalism. Postmodernism so described is not just an exercise in description and analysis. It is also a realisation that the production of difference is desirable as a means of promoting cultural and social progress.

The experience of Post-Modern (as it was usually spelt) architecture repeats these same themes. Post-Modern architecture amounted to a rejection of the dogmas of the modern movement, namely that the form of the building should follow its function and, in addition, that simplicity of form was always desirable. For Jencks (1977), Post-Modern architecture involved an exercise in double visual coding. Design had to appeal to a popular audience and it had to work within a market context. Equally, and especially for the most prestigious schemes, Post-Modern architecture had to appeal to professionals and to a critical audience that might appreciate its subtleties. The reference to double coding was misleading, however. The key element in Post-Modern architecture was and remained the reference to coding itself – that is to say to the role of architecture as a form of social communication. Post-Modern architecture liberated the architect from the dictates of form and function, enabled greater experimentation and, amongst other things, allowed designs to express the feel of a place or respond to the preference of its users.

Post-Modern architecture served, in the most general terms, to put architects back into contact with popular views of design and taste. It was a reaction against elitism and as part of this a reaction against the failures of high-rise and modern housing design. Jencks (1977), for example, suggested that Post-Modern architecture originated on a precise day, that of 15 July 1972 when the authorities blew up (or blew down, depending on the preferred terminology) a complex of high-rise homes at Pruitt-Igoe in St Louis in the US. The blocks were considered an irredeemable social failure and one that could not be rectified at a reasonable cost.

The failures of Pruitt-Igoe and of similar blocks elsewhere became part of the standard story in explaining the apparent death of modernism, in Britain as well as the US. They also became implicated in explanations of the problems of social housing in the 1970s and 1980s. Modern architecture in housing became defined as 'contributing to a process of social exclusion' (Brindley 1999, 42).

Yet neither the failure of the blocks at Pruitt-Igoe nor the more general use of modern styles of architecture could be held as responsible for social exclusion, except perhaps as one factor amongst many. In part, the failures of Pruitt-Igoe were caused by the failures of the housing authority to manage and maintain the blocks, rather than by any specific aspect of design.[2] Much the same was, moreover, said about the experience of high density, flatted estates in Britain (Anderson et al. 1985; Power, 1984). Given selective improvements, effective management and the allocation of the properties to people who actually wanted to live there, high-rise had a long-term future.

The desire of Post-Modern architecture to promote better communication was a statement of intent. The extent to which this intent was realised in practice is an empirical question capable of being answered through social surveys and other similar techniques. In the most notable study, Groat and Canter (1979) examined how 30 accountants perceived the meaning of buildings identified as significant in the leading architectural journals. Accountants were selected as an appropriate public since they have similar middle-class attitudes and backgrounds to architects. Yet the accountants did not generally find Post-Modern designs more attractive than the Modern schemes and they sometimes attributed a different meaning to that intended by the architects. In some cases, the perceived meanings were plainly contradictory of the original intent. For example, a Post-Modern old people's home was repeatedly mistaken for a home for transients or a motel.

Groat and Canter's conclusions remain a valid, albeit partial assessment of postmodernism as architecture. Its strength was to encourage an exploration of the meanings and associations in the built environment. However, continued experimentation was not enough. More attention had to be paid to bringing architects, users and others together in an interactive process that would modify the initial design preconceptions. Postmodern architecture was a halfway house on the way to an increased recognition of the importance of user participation in design.

At the same time, Post-Modern as architecture did not stop at the creation of individual buildings. It also led to the creation of cities of difference characterised by buildings of different shapes, styles and visual symbolism. Post-Modern in architecture was, moreover, not just committed to popular culture or the rejection of the angular, cubist styles of the modernism of the 1920s. It was also committed to an acceptance of the logic of commercial development and of the market. For Robert Venturi, for example, architects should not content themselves with an analysis of the environment as it is used. They should also learn from, 'the housing content of television commercials, home journals, automobile advertisements, *New Yorker* cartoons, developers' blurbs and mail order catalogs' (*sic*) (1976).

The association between Post-Modern architecture and commercial development, in turn, changed the terms of the debate. For the supporters of postmodernism in the 1970s and early 1980s, whether as a general cultural tendency or as architecture, the production of difference was a liberating experience. The promotion of difference was a liberation from the dictates of standardisation, simplification and universal solutions. It was also a liberation from the dictates of mass housing, mass slum clearance and the imposition through town planning of some sense of order. Postmodernism supported the local and specific and was consistent for this reason with the various experiments in the 1970s in gradual renewal and community architecture.

In contrast, for the critics in the 1980s, postmodernism summarised a retreat from social responsibility. It was the cultural equivalent of the neoliberal policies of Margaret Thatcher, intended to dismantle the welfare state and to promote the market in urban development. Harvey (1989, 67), in particular, argued that postmodernism involved urban design rather than planning and amounted to a retreat from attempts to mould space for social purposes. Instead, 'postmodernists see space as something independent and autonomous, to be shaped according to aesthetic aims'. Postmodernism summarised the logic of a city where commercial developed had run riot, without social controls. Other critics adopted a similar position. Postmodern urban development involved a process of 'splintering' that planning could not counter, other than through the creation of enclaves (Graham and Marvin 2001, 110); that was divisive and potentially alienating (Jameson 1984b, 89); and that encouraged 'social secession', the opting out of neighbourhoods from their broader social responsibilities (Graham and Marvin 2001, 267; Navez-Bouchanine 2002, 41–4).

Finally, taken to its logical conclusion, fragmentation led to the complete loss of meaning of the type described by Baudrillard (1990). It led to a world dominated by objects and their brand names, by images and by virtual reality. This is a world of infinite or 'bottomless' fragmentation where worth is always judged by appearances or by slogans rather than by substance and where, as a result, the line between the real and the imaginary disappears (Raulet 1984). This also the type of ambiguous, hard to interpret world explored in the film *Blade Runner* first issued in 1982. A hunt for and eventual destruction of a gang of 'replicants', manufactured human beings, provides the main action sequences in *Blade Runner*. The underlying theme, however, is that replicants and human beings, manufactured reality and 'real' reality, are becoming more difficult to tell apart. The setting is also postmodern. The constant presence of intrusive aerial advertising suggests commercialism run riot and out of control.

To an extent, bottomless fragmentation is the mirror image of earlier, modernist fears of standardisation. Bottomless fragmentation is exact opposite, again taken to an extreme. Moreover, like the earlier fears of standardisation, bottomless fragmentation offers a dystopian vision that says something about the experience of living in the contemporary city, but is overly negative. People do not, for example, necessarily find the contemporary city as alienating and difficult to understand. They can to create their own sense of meaning and spatial unity through their own experience and personal development (Werner 1991).

Postmodernism provides a means of reflecting on the distinctive features of the contemporary urban landscape compared to that of the past and, in addition, as a means of reflecting on the distinctive styles of contemporary town planning. However, it is not an inclusive social theory. To say whether the contemporary landscape is desirable or undesirable and to say, in addition, whether contemporary planning styles are progressive or regressive requires further analysis and reflection. It demands an examination of the specific context in which policies are being implemented, together with an assessment of their specific aims. It requires, in addition, the use of other theories, notably those concerned with social exclusion and social disorder.

Discourse analysis   During the late 1970s, postmodernism crossed the Atlantic. In particular, in France, postmodernism was taken up by Lyotard (1984) as a means of making politics and public policy more sensitive to social and cultural difference. For Lyotard and this has become the conventional definition, postmodernism means that no one viewpoint is logically superior to others and that no-one's voice should be excluded from a dialogue (Kitchin and Tate 2000, 16). Postmodern knowledge, it is suggested, is not about looking for universal truths or universal aesthetic standards. Instead, truth and beauty arise from the recognition of difference, from a reflection on the workings of power and from the ability to draw patterns out of chaos and disorder (Cloke et al. 1991, 171; Deleuze and Guattari 1995, 238–40).

Thereafter, and somewhat misleadingly in terms of the history of ideas, Anglo-American social theory has generally associated postmodernism with French poststructuralism. This latter is a school of philosophy that favours social explanations in terms of the motives and beliefs of actors; that focuses on their discourse (their language and vocabulary); and that also assumes that language itself is flexible and subject to change. For example, in the *British Journal of Sociology*, Murphy (1988) equated postmodernism with the ideas of a variety of 'European writers', in fact mostly French, who see language as the source of reality, who reject the typical dualism of modern sociology in which action is treated as a distinct from and largely reactive to structure and who insist that all valid knowledge presupposes explicit value judgements.

The significant aspect of poststructural theory is its emphasis on language and discourse. Discourse means a series of concepts and themes that are associated with one another and lead policy makers and practitioners in distinct directions, whilst excluding others. Discourse analysis is well suited to professional bodies of knowledge that are a combination of science, evidence and socially defined notions of good practice. It is, for this reason, well suited to the typical situation in urban policy and planning where technical and political considerations interact with one another (Feindt and Oels 2005; Goodchild and Cole 2001). Likewise, it is well suited to the analysis of environmental policy where the character of the problem is commonly in dispute (Hajer 1995). Much the same can be said of housing and housing policy. Discourse analysis is used to explore how housing problems are socially constructed, to challenge assumptions and to open-up policy debates to critical analysis (Hastings 2000)

The method of discourse analysis is to highlight contrasts in meaning between people in different positions, for example those representing different institutions and different interest groups. The method therefore assumes the contested nature of most policies and planning proposals, including a consideration of marginal voices that might offer alternative options. The method also allows a reflection of contrasts over time and at different spatial scales, for example between central and local government. In allowing for contrasts, discourse analysis also allows for the likelihood of internal inconsistencies and variations. The planning discourse of the present government provides an example. On one hand, the discourse includes proposals for carefully designed 'eco-towns' and a timetable for the introduction of carbon neutral housing. On the other hand, emanating from different parts of the governments, notably the Treasury, the discourse is about speeding up the planning process and finding ways to reduce the burden of planning on house builders.

Discourse analysis does not mean simply taking language at its face value. It is a critical device that looks for silences and absences, notably in its treatments of different social groups and minorities. For example, most histories of housing and planning said little or nothing about the role of women, until the growth of self-consciously feminist approaches from the 1970s onwards (Sandercock 2003, 41–2). Yet it is still possible to find policy areas where little is said about women. For example, local employment policies in England fail to recognise the specific needs of women, despite a general tendency for women to have lower rates of participation in paid work (Grant and Buckner 2007, 2)

Discourse analysis also tests language against variations in practice and looks to how institutional actors in different contexts use policy concepts for their own purpose. The terms 'neighbourhood' and 'neighbourhood management' offer an example. These have become central to the discourse of housing and urban regeneration of over the past ten years. Yet neighbourhood and neighbourhood management are used to cover a wide range of different practices and are sometimes also used only because the terms have become fashionable or have to be used a condition for funding.

As applied to planning and housing, discourse analysis is mostly about the way in which governments attempt to implement and justify policies and about, in addition, the way in opposition groups seek to make counter proposals or block implementation. It is also about how some specific definitions of a problem become institutionalised in policy frameworks, whilst others are ignored. Environmental discourses provide an example (Lovell 2004). The discourse of low energy housing was, for many years, dominated by the radical ideas and values of environmental enthusiasts. These were individual architects and self-build groups who sought to pioneer alternative lifestyles. Once climate change became a significant political issue, the government adopted a technical agenda of zero carbon housing whilst ignoring the values and lifestyle implications of the pioneers.

Discourse is a more open, less demanding concept than 'ideology' – a term that indicates a rigid or entrenched view. In the 1950s and 1960s, the various justifications for planning, as well as the main planning principles, were commonly called ideological by critics and researchers, for example by Foley (1973). The implication was that the technical body of knowledge associated with planning had become entrenched, rigid and increasingly out of touch with reality. Discourse suggests, in contrast, that policy and planning has subsequently become less fixed and more pragmatic.

At the same time, poststructural discourse analysis implies limits to flexibility. In looking at how problems are defined and solutions determined, discourse analysis has an institutional element. It is about the relationship between ideas, positions of power and the process of governing. As is implicit in the term itself, poststructuralism does not wholly abandon the concept of structure, but instead breaks down the distinction between action and structure. It is about searching for structured ways of arguing, structured regularities and breaks in what is being said or represented. Poststructuralism offers, for this reason, a more flexible and realistic social understanding than the planning theories of the 1970s. These latter were theories that opposed action and structure. Either they gave planning and the planning process almost free reign in seeking to manipulate cities, as in rational decision-making. Or they reduced the planning process to a mere cog in a machine, as in structural Marxism. Poststructuralism offers a middle position.

In addition, poststructuralism is about relating what is said back to a context that is unpredictable and open to multiple interpretations. Applied to urban planning and policy, discourse analysis suggests a constant state of flux. It suggests a process that is attempting to make sense of and to control change, but is also aware that change itself has its own logic and uncertainties (Craib 1992).

Reflections on reality and the 'real'   The analysis of policy discourses begs an almost obvious question. How is discourse related to reality? One answer is to make a distinction between the 'real' and 'reality' and to define what is 'real' as merely the remainder of what is left over after other aspects of reality are understood. Some clarification is required. The distinction between real and reality refers to the work of Lacan, a French theorist of the 1950s and 1960s, who sought to apply linguistic analysis to the development of the human personality and who defined reality as a triadic, that is to say three-sided, structure with each aspect tied to a different stage of childhood development. The real is the first and most basic stage of childhood development and knowledge. The imaginary is the stage when children start to become conscious of themselves as individuals and start to consider alternative images. The symbolic is when they relate to other people (Julien 1994).

In this context, the real remains an uncertain primordial state. In the words of one interpretation, 'the Real is that dimension both of one's own body and of the rest of the world that is neither captured nor controlled by the Symbolic or the Imaginary register'.[3] The real is roughly the equivalent of the unconscious in psychoanalysis, a partly unknowable force that trips up plans and assumptions about how the world works. '"Real" is the point of resistance, the traumatic "indivisible remainder" that resists symbolization' (Žižek 2003, 2).

The real, so understood, denies a sense of certainty. It implies a style of planning based on 'indeterminacy and contingency' (Hillier 2003, 41). The real is disorder and irrationality. The real makes consensus provisional, temporary and conditional. It does this through requiring repeated renegotiation in the context of change.

The real does not, however, as Gunder and Hillier (2004) have suggested completely deny the possibility of making social agreements or coming to a policy consensus. To the extent that social agreements and consensus exist, these belong predominantly to the symbolic realm as this covers politics and policy. Consensus can, in any case, take different forms. Consensus about the procedures used to determine a decision, for example by a majority vote, does not preclude continued disagreement about substantive issues. Consensus can also involve varying levels of agreement, for example from enthusiastic support to passive acceptance.

The estimation of future levels of housing need provides an example of the unknowable aspects of planning practice. Some estimate of housing need is necessary if public authorities are to allocate adequate land for new house building or public funds to help disadvantaged individuals and families. The estimation of need in relation in relation to land allocation is the more simple calculation and it involves the following considerations: the size of the existing stock; average and projected levels of vacancies in the housing stock, projected demolition and the number of future households, based on estimation of population trends and the rate of household formation. The difference between future household numbers and the projected size of the housing stock represents the need for new housing and then requires the use of an assumed density level so that need projections can be turned into calculations of land requirements (Bramley and Pawson 2000).

Counting the number of existing dwellings and making an allowance for vacancies is straightforward. Estimating future household numbers is more problematic. Reductions in household size may not continue indefinitely, beyond a certain point, for example. Migration is particularly unpredictable. At an international level, immigration is dependent a combination of economic factors and policy decisions – for example those covering immigration controls. At a local level, in the context of highly restrictive planning policies, migration is also partly dependent the level of permitted house building.

Drawing attention to the limits of statistical and other analytical techniques has led some critics (Sokal and Bricmont 1999) to suggest that poststructuralism denies the possibility of science and rational thought. Knowledge becomes purely relative to the subject orientation of different actors. The critics' case is strengthened by examples where Lacan and other poststructural thinkers have made naïve comments about science, notably mathematics, as well as by the impenetrable character of some of their writing.

Yet an acknowledgement of limitations and uncertainties does not undermine in principle the case for planners or researchers to push back the boundaries of knowledge, if new techniques can be identified. Another interpretation of poststructural ideas is that the very sense of the real is the driving force for science and research.[4] The unknowns of knowledge and the unknowns of science are a 'productive void', driving along a process of innovation. To return to the example of housing need, a postmodern analysis would not avoid quantitative analysis. It would instead explicitly recognise the limits of quantitative analysis and supplement this with recognition of uncertainties and the views of the relevant interested parties.

At the same time, if knowledge is about pushing back the boundaries of knowledge, the real cannot be regarded merely as a remainder. Were the real to be so considered, it would disappear as an object. It would simply appear as some vague residue once all other forms of knowledge had been analysed.

Amongst those who follow Lacan, another interpretation of the real is available. Considered from a socio-economic viewpoint, the real can be interpreted as capital. This latter is an impersonal force, in the words of Žižek (1999, 276), 'real in the precise sense of determining the structure of ... material social processes: the fate of whole strata of populations and sometimes of whole countries'.

If the real is considered as capital, it is knowable. At least it is researchable. The 'real', defined as need or capital is not an incoherent, undifferentiated mass.

It can be analysed and observed in a way that reveals its internal distinctions, structures, as well as its broader logic. It can also be subject to public interventions of all types, including planning.

Taking all this together, and also taking into account other attempts to apply similar distinctions to the study of urban space, for example by Lefèbvre (1974), Harvey (1989) and Phillips (2002), it is possible to apply Lacan's triad to planning as follows:

- the real, understood partly as the material environment, partly as capital and therefore as the production of cities and urban spaces;
- the imaginative, understood as the imaginary landscapes that enables the representation of space and the making of various, not necessarily consistent proposals for the future;
- the symbolic, understood as the personal and social identities embodied in space and the relation between proposals, communities and significant political actors.

The three spheres of understanding overlap each and are all knotted together (Julien 1994). If one sphere of understanding disappears, the other two become undone. The task of analysis is, in other words, to follow the distinctive logic of each, whilst also recognising their interdependence.

The logic of a triad is as important as the details, as it offers an alternative to the type of binary thinking implicit in such distinctions as Left/Right, working class/middle class, inner city/suburbs. A binary distinction helps identify contrasts, oppositions and antagonisms. A binary distinction also helps clarify what is desirable and undesirable, a term that itself illustrates the pervasive character of binary distinctions in common language. A triad, in contrast, is about triangular thinking. It is about significant effects and interrelationships, including echoes and implications. A triad is moreover not about one element determining the rest, at least not as a universal rule. The relationship comprises a series of mutual dependencies and constraints of a type that precludes the discussion of one aspect without touching on the others (Lefèbvre 1991, 49).

'The triad is only a starting point and only a general classification of practice. It cannot say much importance as of itself. It cannot say much partly because it involves a universal language independent of specific social practices' (Harvey 1989, 222). Historical accounts and accounts of practice have to use the language that is at hand. Classifications of practice are also passive in the sense that they say little about the causes of change. They only become alive and useful when applied to the analysis of events and processes over time or to the analysis of policy issues and proposals.

Identity and performativity   Postmodernism, like the contemporary city, sprawls in different directions. Poststructuralism is mostly about modernity and the analysis of modern literary texts, without specific and explicit references to postmodernism. Lyotard's *The Postmodern Condition* is, in contrast, about contemporary culture and politics and offers an historical interpretation that is otherwise missing.

To provide a brief summary: *The Postmodern Condition* is characterised by a loss of political direction, in which the old ideologies, the 'grand narratives' of Left and Right, have lost credibility and in which 'old poles of attraction', notably the nation state have lost their attraction (Lyotard 1984, 14, 37–41). Instead, postmodernism implies a new type of politics, in part more directly related to the 'life goals' of the self (Lyotard 1984, 15) and therefore to personal identity.

In this context, postmodernism implies the politics of reforming pressure groups and social movements and the 'little narratives', that is to say the discourses of policy and progress that these groups incorporate. The politics of personal identity are generally not little from the viewpoint of the individual. Identity politics includes global themes and global social movements such as those concerned with the environment, religion and the promotion of race and gender equality. Identity politics are, nevertheless, distinct in the way they do away with neat distinctions between Right and Left, conservatism and socialism. Identity politics are more diverse. Moreover, like other concepts of postmodernism as difference, they are deeply ambiguous, leading simultaneously towards liberation and fragmentation.

The women's movement provides an example of how postmodern politics are more differentiated than their modern equivalent. In the early twentieth century, the women's movement had a clear idea of what it wanted, namely good quality family houses, with labour saving features and set in a healthy, low-density garden city estate. (See, for example, Sanderson Furniss and Phillips, 1919.) In contrast, the typical view within the women's movement in the past 20 years has been to argue for diversity and against universal solutions. The headings of a report *Women in the City* prepared by the Organisation for Economic Cooperation and Development (OECD 1995) provide an illustration. The headings include 'Recognising social diversity in the development of cities', 'Planning with a gender perspective', 'Creating liveable environments' and 'Urban services responsive to diverse needs'.

Difference has its limits, however. Recognition of difference in urban planning and policy requires a classification of the current and future users of a place, but the classification itself cannot be too lengthy or complex. Planners, designers and policy makers seldom have the time the resources to investigate all the potential variations (by class, age, ethnicity, gender, disability, income level, relationship with the place and property and so forth) or to assess the complex politics that is likely to arise if all the potential groups seek active participation, whilst stressing their separate needs and identity (Lynch and Hack 1984, 64). Moreover, the repeated subdivision of categories denies those aspects of design and planning – for example the promotion of safety, the removal of environmental nuisances – that are likely to be in the interest of all groups.

The impossibility of a full, outright postmodernism implies some intermediate position. Allmendinger (2001, 257) states, for example,

Can we have a postmodern planning? No. ... Can we have a planning that is more open, sensitive to the needs of the many, radically challenges existing notions and actively seeks to encourage wider participation from those previously excluded .... ? Yes.

The approach may be called either a reformed modernism or a reformed postmodernism, depending on one's viewpoint. Literary theory has put forward another, related term that helps clarify the approach, that of 'constructive postmodernism', meaning the ability to combine an appreciation of difference and an appreciation of the viewpoint of others with a cumulative understanding of the world (Schiralli 1999).

Applied to planning practice, difference means, in addition, a relatively light touch to the regulation of development, not insisting on strong design policies and accepting the place of non-conforming uses and minority groups. Allmendinger (2001, 233–4) for example suggests that postmodern planning practice involves a degree of transparency about its rationale and an assessment of who is likely to gain or lose from any decision. The presumption is that controls on the freedom of individuals should only be applied if they are justified.

If planning is defined in broad terms as a means of providing the social infrastructure of a community, other themes become apparent. Planning becomes a means of meeting the increasingly diverse needs and preferences of different types of community and, in addition, of expressing their identity. Even in what might be considered 'ordinary neighbourhoods', where large-scale public reconstruction is unlikely, it is possible to both enhance local cultural identity and bring people together through cultural activities, for example murals, festivals, exhibitions and other local artworks. Indeed, such projects have become commonplace in neighbourhood regeneration, especially in areas with a multi-ethnic population. Formerly blank gable walls have become covered in colourful murals. Cultural projects encourage the residents of deprived areas to be positive about their traditions. In multi-ethnic areas, it also enables people from different groups to interact with one another.

Issues of identity politics apart, the end of the grand narratives has another consequence. It means that policies are for the most part no longer based on abstract principles of truth. Instead, they are tested against the standard of cost effectiveness or 'performativity' in relation to the system requirements of society. Performativity has a series of aspects. It amounts to a legitimising strategy in which organisations and individuals justify their existence through demonstrating their efficiency (best use of available resources) and value for money in terms of the achievement of predetermined criteria. It means the external auditing of practice and, in relation to urban policy, it means the evaluation of outcomes, measured by such factors as the number of jobs created, the number of dwellings completed or improved or the leverage of private finance, as appropriate. Performativity also means a pragmatic commitment to what works in any given situation. It leads, for example, to the preparation of good practice guides about how to implement policy.

Performativity provides the logic of the evidence-based and target-driven policy of the type that has been influential in Britain during the past decade, during the period of office of 'New Labour'. However, performativity has a broader logic than the specific requirements of a single political party. It is in the interests of all governments to know what is working and what is not and to know, in addition, that money is being spent efficiently. It is also interests of political transparency that the results of policy evaluation are available to the public, even if as is most likely the evaluation is limited in scope.

In addition, performativity can be understood in broad terms as a replacement or supplement for legitimacy by the observance of static, bureaucratic rules. Performativity enables rules to be applied flexibly so that these are better related to political and social aims in an uncertain context. To give an example: until, say 20 years ago, elected local authorities took key decisions within a defined legislation and policy framework. The current pattern is, instead, for local authorities to work in partnership with the voluntary sector, other public and semi-public bodies such as the police or housing associations and the private sector. Lines of responsibility have become less clearly defined and democratic accountability has to be exercised to a greater extent through the clarity of the policy process itself, that it is through a repeated exercise in specifying policy aims, preparing progress reports and undertaking evaluation.

The politics of identity and performativity are, in part, opposing tendencies. Performativity is about treating people as 'human resources' that contribute to an organisation's goal and not as people who wish to express themselves or who interact with one another. Performativity is, for example, about defining work responsibilities in social housing so that managers, caretakers and wardens focus on property related issues rather than on relations with occupants. In urban policy, performativity and identity conflict with one another in other ways. They conflict with one another in the promotion of community involvement. A potential conflict exists between the demands and slow pace of community involvement and a typical requirement for policy delivery within a given time frame. Performativity and identity also conflict with one another in questions of urban design. Performativity means measuring the effectiveness of development control decisions by the speed of decision-making process, rather than by the quality of the completed scheme in relation to its setting or by the effectiveness of consultation.

However, performativity and identity are not always in conflict with one another. Performance criteria can also be modified to take into account the needs of community involvement or design quality. Ho (1999) in particular has argued for a broad 'realist' approach to policy evaluation. 'Realist' policy evaluation makes no explicit references to the 'real', as defined in poststructural theory. It shares a family resemblance, however, in insisting that policy evaluation should tackle the unexpected, as well as the expected, consequences of action. Realist policy evaluation consists of three elements: the context including the character of the locality, the local economy and the level of deprivation of the target population; the programme or policy itself; and the outcomes for the quality of life and well-being of the community.

Otherwise, the lesson of postmodern planning is unsettling. If planning can encourage pluralism, wider participation and can involve more accountability in terms of its consequences, as most postmodern theorists suggest, it can also do the opposite. It can also promote community exclusion, deny public participation and make arbitrary, inconsistent decisions. Policy evaluation, criticism and cultural activities can express the hope for something better, but much is likely to depend on the political context. Planning is not necessarily a benevolent, democratic activity (Yiftachel 2001).

Reassessing Postmodernism

Postmodernism involves a closed, circular version of history that establishes a dialectic between itself and the modernism of the twentieth century. The original thesis, the modern, is negated by its opposite the postmodern. Equally, the postmodern is unstable. It contains the seeds of its own negation and this finally leads to a synthesis that retains aspects of the original, albeit in a different context.

The recent history of planning and housing itself demonstrates the unwinding of the modern/postmodern dialectic. If the thirty years from 1970 to 2000 could somehow be omitted, the history of town planning and housing would appear predominantly as one of continuity rather than a break. In the first few years of the twenty-first century, housing policy is again concerned with the numbers of houses completed each year, as was the case in the 1950s and 1960s. Again, housing development operates within a planning framework that, like that in the 1960s, favours a combination of urban containment and the identification of growth areas. Again, tower blocks are back in fashion, as for example in the building programmes of private developers in and around city centres. Again, governments have promoted non-traditional building methods, or as they are now called modern construction methods, as a means of improving the capacity and efficiency of the building industry. The policy discourse is also often similar to the past. The title of the Parker Morris report, *Homes for Today and Tomorrow* (MHLG 1961) provides, in particular, a suitable summary of current debates about the future of housing design in the light of current concepts of sustainability and sustainable development.

In planning theory, postmodernism continues to be debated, as it does in social philosophy. Postmodernism raises numerous important issues about the relation between knowledge and power, about the contradictory meanings of difference and fragmentation and about attitudes to minority groups. It has left a continuing methodological legacy to social research by virtue of its emphasis on discourse. Finally, it has encouraged a distinct method of argumentation, through the preparation of stories and narratives.

In other respects, however, the dialectic of modernism and postmodernism has come to a pragmatic, uneasy conclusion and synthesis. A postmodern era, by virtue of the prefix 'post' can only last a few years before it begs the question as to what comes next. In architecture, postmodern styles are *passé*. In urban policy, the process of target setting and evaluation has probably gone as far as possible without itself causing inefficiencies. Likewise, the promotion of cultural diversity has gone as far as is likely given the emergence of new policy discourses based on community cohesion and social inclusion.

Flexible Consumption and Production

Postmodernism tends to define the present in relation to the past in a way that hinders generalisation about the present and the future. Its preference for fractured, splintered knowledge has the same effect. Making generalisations and as part of this identifying key issues for plan making, requires a different approach. It requires, in its simplest form, a double analysis, looking first at changing life styles and consumption patterns and secondly at the relation between consumption and the forces of production. This double analysis of flexible consumption and production leads in turn to analysis of changing, more flexible styles of policy making and implementation and then to changing styles of professional practice.

Hypermodernism and the Environment

In relation to consumption and lifestyle, one way of conceptualising the present is as 'hypermodern', meaning a stage beyond the modernism of the past. The prefix 'hyper' means beyond or taken to a higher level. It retains, therefore, the postmodern notion of coming after modernism, whilst also suggesting that the contemporary era is an extension of the modernity of the past and one that is characterised by continued change and innovation. Indeed, the prefix 'hyper' suggests that change is now quicker and more pervasive than ever. 'Hyper' is admittedly not the only possible prefix to express such ideas. Alternatives include new-modern, second modern, neo-modern, super-modern, high modern and late modern. It is, nevertheless, as good as any alternative.

A summary of the main theories Like postmodernism, hypermodern social theory is not so much a specific theory, but a series of themes that are interpreted in different ways to explain and explore aspects of social change. The themes themselves comprise an interest in trends towards individualised, flexible consumption; the social implications of choice; the disconcerting effects of accelerated social change; the emergence of new type of risk-oriented society (Beck 1992); and in some accounts, notably Giddens (1991), the need for a 'third way' political strategy between bureaucratic socialism and the market.

In urban planning, hypermodernism has two main strands. One direction, represented by Virilio (2000, 545; 2005, 113–42), is to envisages the disappearance of modern cities into an impersonal, non-place realm of endless communication networks. Another represented by Ascher (1995) is to envisage a greater diversity of distinct places within a new type of ultra-dispersed urban area, the *métapolis*. Both interpretations would accept, however, that an increased speed of communication is a pervasive feature of modern life, that this poses new questions for the organisation of urban (or perhaps semi-urban) space and, finally, that these questions are more about the internal divisions within a city, rather than the external boundaries which are in any case increasingly difficult to define.

The work of Virilio is, in any case, outside the mainstream of hypermodern theory. Virilio focuses on speed and risks, but almost exclusively in the context of the techniques of warfare, terrorism and security counter measures. The hypermodern city is for Virilio (2005) a 'city of panic' – a city that is designed to install anxiety in its residents and visitors. It is a city divided against itself, characterised by gated communities, policed shopping arcades and widespread networks of security cameras. It is also a city that looks increasingly the same worldwide and that, for all its apparent security, remains vulnerable to disruptions and disasters.

The city of panic is a dystopia, the hypermodern equivalent of the film *Blade Runner*. It illustrates the negative direction of current trends without demonstrating that this negative position has been realised and without also demonstrating that residents and visitors have the same view. The counter argument is that cities have long been objects of attack in modern warfare, that they have survived and have been able regenerate themselves from setbacks and disasters (Thrift 2005).

Crime and insecurity figure as a significant theme in other accounts of the risk society, but mostly at a more everyday level in relation to anxiety about the pace of change. Giddens (1991, 92) for example talks of 'ontological security', meaning a sense of being comfortable, of being at peace with the world and of living in a predictable, reliable environment. People strive for predictability in the context of the uncertainty and rapid pace of change of what he calls 'high modernity', but what is called here 'hypermodernity'. Yet the rapid rate of change, as well as its impersonal character, denies such security.

The 'city of panic' apart, the hypermodern argument may be summarised as follows: An increased variety of labour-saving and timesaving technology, combined with an increasingly wide and more customisable range of consumer services of all types gives people more choice and enables a more varied, more individualised and more comfortable lifestyle. People have much greater choice – of food in superstores, of clothes, of restaurants and of entertainment. People go to private health and recreation clubs; they watch subscriber only television; they use a mixture of free and subscription services to access a huge range of information on the internet.

People also have more choice in how they use their time. Increased car ownership opens up a wider range of travel destinations and increased choice in where one lives. Increased access to the web opens up an increased range of information. Ownership of mobile phones permits more flexibility in mixing work and leisure, in making appointments, in passing on and receiving messages. Other factors, such as changes in family structures towards one person households, the disappearance of stable working-class communities, the requirements of increased labour flexibility and the demands of the women's movement for more independence, push in the same direction of individualisation (Beck 1992, 97–8).

The outcome is similar to that predicted by postmodern social theory, though the causes are more related to increased affluence social and to technology than to cultural change. Individuals are less constrained by class, gender, age and less constrained, in addition, by established notions of lifestyles. Individuals seek to construct their own identity and own lifestyle, with the inevitable result that lifestyles become more varied and diverse.

At the same time, the very existence of choice is also unsettling for many individuals. Increased choice is limited. It is a product of technological and organisational changes to which people have to adapt in their workplace, with all the stresses and strains that this implies. In particular, people have to work to buy all the various labour saving and communication devices. In addition, people are bombarded with a mass of information on the web and on 24-hour television. People have to manage the risks associated with change and they have to cope with the demands of modern life.

Hypermodernity is, therefore, also a period of 'reflexive modernity' in which individuals consciously seek to master their future or at least seek to learn from experience. People have to make many more decisions than in the past and they have to weigh many more considerations into account. For example, in relation to food they have to consider not just whether they enjoy a particular food, but whether they are eating too much or too little or whether there are any health risks. Dieting has become a way of life for many people, especially women, as they seek to control their shape, size and health. Likewise, in relation to housing, people have to consider where they should live in the context of extensive potential commuting areas; what investments to make in the home to maintain its value; and how best to decorate the home to reflect their tastes. Finally, when they leave their home to make visits in the neighbourhood or wider city, they have to consider where they should go or not go for reasons of personal security.

Styles of hypermodern planning   The hypermodern society is based on individual choice and the social networks that link individuals. However, it does not escape the case for town planning outlined by Hayek and other economic liberals, from the 1940s onwards. The urban infrastructure (roads, parks, drainage system, schools and other services) and the environment are consumed collectively as well as individually and need to be coordinated with one another.

The question is, therefore, to define the exact characteristics of hypermodern planning. Ascher (1998; 2001, 96–7) provides a possible answer. Hypermodern planning, for Ascher, is an exercise in which public agencies actively promote modernisation of the infrastructure and built environment, albeit in a flexible, pragmatic manner. Hypermodern planning is about the creation of places that suit current lifestyles, tastes and social relations. It is

- characterised by a concern with specific measures and projects that can evolve over time rather than fixed plans;
- able to reflect on and to mobilise knowledge and forms of understanding before, during and after action;

- precautionary in its treatment of environmental risks, taking into account the requirements of sustainable development;
- competitive and collaborative, recognising that design and implementation results from the intervention of numerous actors;
- flexible, open to negotiation and in phase with the pace of development;
- multivariate, made of hybrid elements, multiple solutions and of differences;
- stylistically open, free from the ideologies and fashions of urban design;
- multi-sensory, encompassing noise and smells as well as appearance and concerned with enriching the experience of urban spaces and therefore of making these more attractive to consumers.

The first characteristic of hypermodern planning is arguably the most important. It is organised around measures and projects that bring together institutional actors and investors, that mobilise support for change and that provide a starting point for negotiation. The plans are, therefore, oriented towards delivery and depend on the ability of a public sector actor to mobilise the relevant funds, either from within the public sector or from private sources.

The list of characteristics is as significant for its omission, for example its lack of reference to need, as for its inclusions. For Ascher (2001, 80) a linear style of planning based upon the prior identification of needs or aims and the subsequent elaboration of a plan is obsolete. Planning has become based on a series of projects that are 'heuristic', that is to say based on the testing of hypotheses, 'iterative', based on successive and progressively more accurate approximations, 'incremental', based on a series of small steps within a strategy and 'recurrent', based on a reflection of the implications of preceding steps.

Though this is seldom discussed explicitly, hypermodern planning theory has points of similarity with earlier concepts of rational planning. Like Mannheim, for example, hypermodern planning assumes the existence of a group of technical analysts able to bring information together, measure trends and predict the consequences of action. Like the latter, it is more of an aspiration than a description of practice. Like Mannheim's model of substantial rationalisation, hypermodern planning is demanding in its scope and demanding of the analytical and synthesising abilities of researchers. Like the systems theories of the late 1960s, moreover, hypermodern planning is based on a cycle of decision-making rather than a single plan.

The points of contrast with earlier forms of rational planning theory are, nevertheless, significant. Hypermodern planning places more emphasis on coping with uncertainty. It places an emphasis, wholly lacking in Mannheim or the systems theorists of the 1960s, on working with multiple partners and multiple sources of information. It offers as a result a more decentralised and flexible philosophy of public intervention. Equally, it assumes that planning and planners are unable to control events. Hypermodern planning is adaptation to change rather than social reconstruction.

Like all historical processes, hypermodernisation has its winners and losers. The winners are those who possess relevant technical and social skills and can successfully negotiate their way around the various social networks that determine access to well-paid employment. The losers are those who cannot cope with economic change, for example those who become unemployed and those who suffer individual mishaps such as illness and divorce. Hypermodern planning therefore implies policies to help individuals and communities to adapt to change, to counter inequalities in the housing market as well as measures to counter the social segregation that is likely to accompany the increased scale of urban areas.

The 'Sustainable Communities' policy plan for England (ODPM 2003b) and elaborated thereafter provides an example of how governments might respond to inequalities in the context of a hypermodern society. The Sustainable Communities policy plan recognises, in this context, the significance of local public services in protecting individuals and families. It remains a 'third way' policy, however, in seeking to adapt communities to a changing context. There is little recognition, as is an implication of other, structural interpretations, that the state should intervene to correct economic imbalances and inequalities.

Three main elements may be identified as follows: First, the idea of a sustainable community offers a general vision of the characteristics of a 'good' community or a good urban place. The sustainable community is one that is 'Active, inclusive and safe', 'Well run', 'Environmentally sensitive', 'Well designed and built', 'Well connected', 'Thriving', 'Well served' and 'Fair for everyone'.[5] In addition, the idea means a long-term programme of action, comprising a combination of regeneration and new build in different parts of the country characterised by different housing market conditions. The plan aims, in the words of a recent summary 'to tackle housing supply issues in the South East, low demand in other parts of the country, and the quality of our public spaces'.[6] Finally, the idea means ensuring that all those concerned with their creation have the necessary skills and can exchange knowledge and experience. This is the policy agenda of the Academy of Sustainable Communities founded in 2005.

Proposals for 'sustainable communities' are neither a blueprint plan of the type that prevailed in town planning before about 1970, nor a publicly-led building programme. The plan is about the strategic management of the housing market and, in relation to low demand areas, is also about promoting the adaptation of communities to change. 'Sustainable communities' are communities that have an economic future and where people want to live.

A qualification is necessary. The term itself 'sustainable communities' is not consistently used even in relation to the programmes originally established under its name. There are signs that the term is going out of fashion in government pronouncements (SDC 2007, 6). The term is also generally not used by the European Union or in continental Europe, other terms being preferred such as 'sustainable urban development' or 'integrated territorial development' (ASC 2007a, 8). In addition, a separate European Union initiative called URBACT has fulfilled a similar role to that of the ASC in providing a network for the exchange of good practice, albeit without using a prior definition of a good community and mostly in relation to community development and urban social policy rather than physical planning (Mboumoua 2007; PRI-CUDEM 2007).

Differences in terminology should not obscure the comment elements, however. Hypermodern planning implies a style of intervention based on the principles of adapting places to change and to conmsumer demands. Such a process is implicit in many aspects of planning and urban regeneration.

Risks and values   In principle, concepts of the sustainable community cover considerations of sustainable development. Whether this is so in practice, is another question. The Sustainable Development Commission, the UK government's 'watchdog' on the subject, has criticised the sustainable communities programme on a series of points – for example that it has done little to improve the energy efficiency in the existing stock, that it has placed increasing pressure on scarce water and land resources and that it has failed to involve integrated public/private transport systems (SDC 2007). The Environment Agency for England and Wales has added a further criticism, namely that local authorities have not completely prevented the development of new housing in areas at risk of flooding, despite its advice.[7]

The criticisms illustrate an ambiguity in hypermodern planning theory and more generally in contemporary environmental politics. Ascher (2001, 26–8) argues that while modern technology and economic development creates new risks, new forms of knowledge enable risks to be better quantified, predicted and controlled. Likewise, modern forms of communications enable people to see graphic details of environmental catastrophes from around the world. Societies, it is assumed, are able to think and act reflexively in a similar way to the individuals and families that comprise society. Individuals enter into a process of rational debate with one another and in the context of a democratically organised society are able to act collectively if this is in the interests of the majority.

However, to say that environmental risks can be predicted is not the same as saying that effective preventative or remedial action will be taken. The logic of the hypermodern society is individualisation. It is about personal consumption and taking care of the self. Translating the care of the self into care of the environment is possible, but people have to be persuaded that it is in their interests. To provide an example, domestic use accounted for about 29 per cent of total energy use in 2005 in Britain.[8] Yet, according to most surveys, most home consumers, other than a small proportion of 'green' or ethical consumers, see no personal responsibility for the pollution and other problems associated with energy production and do not consider energy savings as a major priority when deciding where to live (Goodchild 2005; Hinchcliffe 1997).

Trends in energy consumption are slightly more encouraging than the statements of consumers might suggest. Levels of domestic energy consumption have stabilised since about 2000, after a long period of increases, including sharp increases in the early 1990s.[9] Levels have stabilised moreover in a context of increasing household numbers and population. Stabilisation is probably caused by a combination of higher standards in new build, piecemeal improvements to buildings, for example loft and wall cavity insulation and the introduction of more energy efficient heating, cooking and other appliances. Reducing energy consumption implies more of the same, for example more stringent building standards covering new build and refurbishment, publicly-led programmes to improve the existing stock, selective demolition, more efficient heating systems and energy labelling on appliances and of the dwelling as a whole (as for example in the Home Improvement Pack) (SDC 2006). Higher domestic energy prices would also promote savings, but only in a way that would impinge most sharply on low income individuals and households. However, whatever the mix of measures, progress is likely to be slow.

The ability to measure risks involves the application of scientific knowledge. Yet scientists may fail to reach an agreement when discussing environmental issues and they use a language and method of argumentation that is itself fragmented between disciplines and is often difficult for non-specialists to understand. In any case, the logic of policy making is different from that of science. Environmental experts are able to specify the environmental risks involved, but the economic risks and social consequences will be outside their competence. The risk society is not a society without risks. It is a society in which risks are tolerated. Yet the level of toleration is itself a political, rather than wholly technical question.

Flood risk provides an example: Flood risk has gradually increased as a result of a tendency for towns and cities to grow in locations that are close to rivers and coastlines. It has also probably increased as a result of global warming and associated rises in sea levels and rainfall. The Royal Commission on Environmental Pollution (2007, 61) notes for example that increased rainfall has a disproportionate impact on flooding and that, say, an annual 40 per cent increase in rainfall could lead to a 100 per cent increase in flood volumes and a 200 per cent increase in flood damage.

Maps of flood risk are available for all of Britain. One might argue therefore that the planning system should be used to stop building on the flood plains of rivers and, in addition, on ground liable to sea floods. However, urban development in Britain has covered at risk areas since at least the nineteenth century and in the case of London for many hundreds of years. Stopping all development in at risk areas would blight economic development. Moreover, flood protection regimes of varied quality and effectiveness cover many urban areas. Judgements have to be made about acceptable risk in different situations.

The interaction of technical and political judgements is why environmental politics is best analysed through the discourse of policy justification and evaluation. The discourse of environmental politics is moreover about values, as well as risks. It is about setting priorities and these include care for the environment compared to other concerns.

Post-Fordism and Inequalities

Changes in patterns of consumption and communication presuppose and are associated with changes in the form of production. Hypermodernity is a society characterised by flexible consumption and increased consumer choice. Equally, however, flexible consumption and the possibility of choice require a society characterised by flexible and increasingly global scale production methods.

Naming the present   The terminology is an issue. Changes in the mode of production might imply the use of the term 'postindustrial', meaning a shift towards a knowledge-based, information processing economy and, in addition, a shift towards the provision of human services. The term has advantages. Postindustrial expresses the experience of de-industrialisation in many towns and cities in the 'rustbelt' of northern Europe, including parts of Britain and the north-east of the US. It also expresses the emergence of global cities, such as London, New York and Hong Kong, where employment depends predominantly on finance, professional services and culture (Hamnett 2003; Savitch 1988).

On the other hand, the usual language is to talk of electronic and service *industries*, likewise the tourist industry. The term 'industry' remains commonly used. Manufacturing industry, though less important in terms of employment, has not, in any case, disappeared as a significant element in the economy, for example in medium sized and smaller cities.

Otherwise, from the late 1980s onwards, the most common approach has been to define the economy of the contemporary city as 'post-Fordist' (Albertsen 1988; Harvey 1989; Allmendinger 2001, 64–9; Amin 1994). Post-Fordism means production in the context of globalised consumer goods markets, faster product life cycles and continuing product/market differentiation. It also means the increased emphasis on service industries as a source of wealth and employment, as is a theme of the concept of postindustrial.

For a history of housing, the term 'post-Fordist' raises a specific issue concerned with the construction industry. Fordism suggests a degree of factory-based production that simply did not exist in the house building industry for most of the twentieth century. Conversely, post-Fordism suggests flexibility in the development process on a scale that remains largely beyond the typical private housing developer.

Post-Fordism also suggests a degree of international trade and international competition that does not occur in the house building industry. Cars and consumer products can be shipped around the world. Houses and blocks of flats are constructed or, in the case of prefabricated dwellings, assembled *in situ*. There are some signs that imports and international trade might grow in the future, as it has already in building elements and components. In general, however, the import of fully assembled homes is the exception rather than the rule.

In this context, Fordism and post-Fordism are best understood as economic ideals, rather than as accurate statements of practice. Le Corbusier promoted mass production in a factory in the face of a fragmented process of craft work and unskilled labouring. Likewise the advocates of post-Fordist production methods, for example Barlow (1999) have advocated the use of flexible mass customisation in house building as a means of giving individual consumers more choice in the face of corporate power. Mass customisation is advocated as an ideal, even if, in general, the organisation of house building is insufficiently flexible to cope with individual variations in customer demands.

Two and multiple speed cities   From the viewpoint of urban planning and urban policy, the application of post-Fordism to house building is mostly a side issue.

More significant is that the decline of manufacturing and increased international competition has changed the character of the economy and the character of the contemporary city. Over the past 20 years, Western countries have generally experienced some combination of higher levels of unemployment, as has been typical in Western Europe or of greater income inequalities as has been typical in the US or by some combination of higher unemployment and greater income inequalities. Globalisation has given greater rewards to those with skills or who can offer products and services in demand. Equally it exposes unskilled and semi-skilled workers to competition from low age economies elsewhere in the world.

For Britain, Hutton (1996, 105–10) summarised the situation a '40:30:30 society' where 40 per cent of the population is in secure employment, 30 per cent in insecure employment, and 30 per cent marginalised, idle or working for poverty wages. Since the time of Hutton's comments, unemployment has declined in most of Britain and is also lower than in most other European countries, but it has not reached the same low levels as in the 1960s. In any case, much of the growth in employment has been in relatively low paid service jobs.

The result, in terms of spatial patterns, is the emergence of what is sometimes called a dual, polarised or 'two speed' city. The term itself is associated with Castells (1989, 224–8) and the impact of new information technologies. Similar ideas of two-speed cities, two-track cities or simply two cities are, however, as Castells (ibid.) also notes a common theme in social policy and social debates in most countries, including non-English-speaking countries such as France.

The term itself 'two speed' or 'multi-speed' can, in part be understood as a metaphor for increased inequalities, including increased unemployment, at least in the period from about 1980 to the mid 1990s (SEU 1998, Figures 6 and 7). The reference to speed also has another meaning. Speed, meaning speed of movement and speed of information flow, is a defining characteristic of modernity in hypermodern social theory. To talk of two or multi speed cities is to recognise therefore a more differentiated, more unequal modernity, one characterised by varying degrees of participation in economic and social life.

A series of qualifications is necessary. The reference to 'two speed *city*' is slightly misleading. Dorling et al. (2007) show that social polarisation is most obviously apparent at a national and regional level, with the poor concentrated in larger towns and cities and the rich concentrated in rural areas and small towns mostly, but not exclusively, located in the South of England. To take West and North Yorkshire as an example, social polarisation has involved an increased concentration of wealthy individuals and households living close to, but mostly outside the Leeds urban area in the Harrogate and York districts.

At the same time, aggregate patterns of social polarisation conceal a variety of different tendencies. Ignoring the very rich and the very poor, various factors exist that encourage younger, middle income individuals and households to live in urban neighbourhoods. Some policies have this effect – for example, planning policies that prioritise brownfield development and area-based programmes of neighbourhood regeneration. Probably more important, however, are market-based processes, for example, high property prices that require middle income individuals and households to search for a home in low priced areas; the growth of employment in service and professional industries in and around city centres; a demand for urban living, especially amongst childless couples; and, in the largest cities notably London, the stresses of long-distance commuting.

Counter polarisation is mostly linked to the workings of an inflationary housing market in the context of prosperous cities and regions. It is not surprising that in England, for example, the most intense segregation at the neighbourhood level, whether of unemployed people (NWSP 2004, 19) or ethnic minority households (Turok et al. 2006, 11), is found in the North. This is the region worst affected by deindustrialisation and economic decline in the 1980s and 1990s. However, the difference between the North of England and elsewhere is only one of degree. Even in the most prosperous cities, specific neighbourhoods typically become characterised by a concentration of problems and a concentration of unemployed, low income and excluded individuals and families.

The term 'social polarisation' is not quite the same as social segregation. The former term is unsatisfactory partly because the growth of minority ethnic groups has introduced an additional dimension to patterns of social segregation in urban areas. Ethnic identities are by definition distinct from the type of socio-economic divisions that are at the root of either the two-speed city or the polarised city. Ethnic segregation is related to identity, rather than income or employment.

Finally, the term 'social polarisation' is unsatisfactory because the difference between statistical units of analysis (for example, wards and enumeration districts) is typically a continuum between rich and poor, not a sharp divide. The contrasts between the poorest and other areas mask a multiplicity of variations, of multispeed rather than two speed cities. Poorer neighbourhoods are likely to contain some relatively affluent households and some relatively affluent streets and vice versa (Mooney and Danson 1997). As a result, it is not always easy or appropriate to counter problems by narrowly defined, targeted area-based programmes.

Social polarisation and segregation are, nevertheless, sufficiently permanent, extensive and intense to worry influential public opinion and governments, especially in the context of racial or ethnic tensions. The words of an official enquiry into the riots of 2001 are typical. The riots were caused by a tendency for different communities to operate on the principle of 'parallel lives' (Independent Review Team 2004, 9). The comments were directed towards the different lives of white working-class and Pakistani communities. The notion of parallel lives as a diagnosis of urban disorder could apply almost to any group living in a two-speed or multi-speed city.

There are other, related concerns. For example, Copestake et al. (2005) have explored the views of policymakers and service managers from a variety of sources about future trends in social segregation. Most of those interviewed suggested a continuing trend towards increased socio-economic and ethnic segregation, with a wide range of negative consequences, including – 'lack of trust and compassion for other groups', 'unfulfilled potential, leading to worse outcomes for many individuals', 'violence, isolation, lack of tolerance, narrow-mindedness, discrimination', 'unequal access to resources (housing, education, work, welfare)'. The concerns are also not dependent on increased spatial segregation. It is possible that different groups live in local enclaves and gated communities, pursuing different lives by virtue of different lifestyles, different travelling patterns, the use of different facilities, for example private rather than publicly provided schools and so forth.

Twin-track, two-pronged policies Concerns about social polarisation and segregation have been sufficient to generate a series of policy initiatives that overlap and parallel the sustainable communities policy agenda. The most common policy formulation goes under the names of social cohesion and the 'cohesive community' where, *inter alia,*

- 'those from different backgrounds have similar life opportunities':
- 'strong and positive relationships are being developed between people of different backgrounds' (ICC 2007, 11).

The social cohesion policy agenda came to fore in Britain immediately after the riots of 2001. Its main features predate this date, however. The integration of immigrants and the improvement of deprived neighbourhoods was a theme in the earliest area-based programmes in Britain, implemented in the 1970s and 1980s.

Social cohesion is also not just a British concept. It fits in well with concepts such as social inclusion and social solidarity that originated in discussions in the European Union and ultimately derive from continental European concepts of the welfare state. The European Union has, in particular, pursued a series of policies to promote 'territorial' solidarity. These measures include policies for regional economic development and convergence (such as Objective 1 and 2), a small-scale demonstration programme called URBAN Community Initiative, in operation between 1994 and 2006 (Carpenter 2006) and the URBACT initiative for international information exchange.[10]

The measures for territorial solidarity overlap modernisation measures that are best conceptualised as a response to changing patterns of consumption. However, they also seek to correct structural inequalities. URBAN and URBACT have, in addition, promoted multi-agency, neighbourhood-based initiatives in countries, notably those in southern and eastern Europe, with little experience of this type of working (Frank 2006).

The distinctiveness of European policies can be overdone. Neighbourhood-based policies have been pursued in the US, as for example in the Federally funded Hope 6 programme that has sought to regenerate and break down the isolation of public housing estates (Popkin et al. 2004). Moreover, the British government and British policy makers, probably more so than those in other European countries, have drawn from the US policy experience and policy discourse. For example, the concepts of community empowerment (literally giving decision-making powers to local communities) and social capital (recreating social networks within and between neighbourhoods) both have US origins.

Conversely the European model of urban policy does not involve a single minded emphasis on social cohesion. It also involves a recognition of economic growth and competitiveness on one hand and social inclusion and cohesion on the other as twin principles of urban policy. For the European Union, for example, 'Economic growth makes it easier to achieve social cohesion' (CDCS 2004, 5–6).

To put the point in a slightly different way, urban policies in Britain and more generally in Europe have become twin-track, two-pronged or 'bifurcated'. Policies for urban regeneration provide an example. One set of measures is aimed at deprived, often segregated communities and another set is aimed at prosperous consumers or, in some cases, at wealthy decision-makers who might invest in a place. One set of measures seeks to improve the situation of disadvantaged individuals and families and is mostly based on investment in community development and the provision of public services. The other seeks to improve the infrastructure and property market and to attract people from elsewhere. One set is based on working with communities and generally involves an attempt to promote democratic accountability. The other is based on development and marketing projects such as museums, waterfronts, exhibition halls and parks and business centres and is part of an effort to re-enforce the competitive position of urban economies (Swyngedouw et al. 2002).

Housing policy in Britain, France and Germany has similar, bifurcated characteristics (Kleinman 1996, 175–6). One strand, policies for excluded minorities, comprises measures for income support, for the development of social rented housing and for neighbourhood renewal. Another strand, general housing policies, means tackling housing shortages, minimising inflation in house prices and in the most recent formulations, for example the zero carbon policy of *Homes for the Future* (DCLG 2007c), reducing the environmental impact of house building.

To talk about a twin-track or bifurcated policy is, in some ways, too simple. Urban regeneration policies generally assume that tackling urban deprivation and promoting economic development are linked through the necessity of generating employment and, though this is less often articulated, linked as a means of providing the hope of economic advancement for people from an ethnic minority background. Much of the apparatus and rhetoric of recent initiatives in partnership working and community planning is intended exactly to bring economic and social policy together at a city-wide or neighbourhood level. The Labour government elected in 1997 argued that the policies of the previous Conservative regime placed too much emphasis on competitiveness, too little on social inclusion and were in any case poorly coordinated. The policies pursued by the devolved government in Scotland over the same period have made similar assumptions (McCarthy 2007), as have the urban initiatives of the European Union.

Equally, however and this is where a degree of policy bifurcation is apparent, it is generally admitted that particular measures are required to tackle deprived neighbourhoods, to tackle crime and social disorder and in some areas to bring together individuals from different ethnic and religious groups (Turok et al. 2006). It is practically impossible to integrate measures for deprived individuals and communities fully within general policies, without the risk of diluting their impact.

It is, of course another question as to whether current policies will actually promote social cohesion. Current policies are unlikely to lead to a fundamental change in patterns of social interaction and it is difficult to see how any policy could make a substantial short-term difference to social interaction (Robinson 2005). Changing the spatial distribution of different social groups is a slow process and one that is only partially influenced by public policies. Housing markets have their own dynamic. In any case, irrespective of where they live, people make their own friends. To this extent, the achievement of local social cohesion is probably too ambitious an aim. On the other hand, policies have a better chance, of improving the quality of life of deprived communities, in relation to health, employment and housing for example and in addition, of changing the local political context in a way that might reduce tensions (Turok et al. 2006).

In addition, social cohesion and the promotion of urban compeitiveness are not as complementary to one another as they are presented in the official policy discourse. The comment of the European Union, namely that 'economic growth makes it easier to achieve social cohesion' is a gross oversimplification. Unless checked by policy measures, economic growth tends to create increased income and other differentials. In this context, conflicts about policy aims and priorities will surely continue.

Transversal Working

Flexible consumption and flexible production, taken together, amount to an increase in the complexity of policy. At the same time, processes of flexible consumption and flexible production are linked to changes in the organisation of public services at the local level, including the organisation of planning. Organisational complexity has also increased, with the involvement of an increased number of different agencies and an increased emphasis on transversal, 'post-bureaucratic' styles of public intervention that cut across established bureaucratic boundaries. Transversal practice is a style of intervention that depends on uncertain, 'blurred' professional expertise; responds to relatively broad and sometimes unclear policy aims, uses a multiplicity of policy instruments and, in some cases, assumes a degree of professional autonomy at a relatively junior level (Jeannot 2005).

From government to governance The context may be explained in more detail. The multiplication of measures and agencies is ian extension of long-standing trends. To give the example of housing policy: At the time of World War I, the discourse of housing policy was about the distinction between middle-class and working-class housing and in relation to the latter it was about a three way choice between private developers building for private landlords, independent housing societies and local authorities. In the 1960s, the institutional framework was still relatively simple, with the policy discourse being dominated by the concerns of local and central government, new towns and building societies (Goodlad 1994).

In the first decade of the twenty-first century, new towns have disappeared but have been replaced by urban development corporations, intended to tackle problems of urban dereliction. In addition, a huge number of housing associations have partially replaced local authorities as the providers of social housing. The number of social housing agencies active in any single district has increased many times, working alongside local authorities as strategic actors. In addition, a series of other bodies have appeared – the regulatory bodies for housing associations (which also vary between England, Wales and Scotland), regional agencies, arms-length companies (ALMOs), housing trusts, local investment companies, banks and institutional lenders and so on.

Policy has also been marked by an increasing variety of different spatial scales of intervention. At a local level, various forms of community and voluntary groups have also emerged either to represent a locality or to provide services of various types, for example for the elderly or for young people. At an international level, the European Union has started to pursue independent initiatives for transport, employment creation and regional development, supplementing those of the national state.

From a policy viewpoint, the multiplication of actors has a mixture of positive and negative consequences. On the positive side, the growth of voluntary agencies in the provision of local services, for example in training and local economic development, has brought a competitive edge that, in principle, is likely to promote innovation and keep down costs. A diversity of measures and types of provision also means that policy can better meet different local conditions and can include hybrid initiatives that mix policies from different sources. Likewise, a diversity of scales of intervention means that governments can pursue overlapping policies in accordance with their spatial impact and frame of reference. For example, housing markets seldom conform to the administrative boundaries of local authorities. They require intervention and a regional or subregional level.

The multiplication of actors does not, however, mean that local authorities have more freedom to make decisions. In some European countries, notably in France, the national state has decentralised decision-making responsibilities to local authorities in an effort to make policy more flexible to local conditions. In Britain, in contrast, local government has become more fragmented owing in part to the removal of responsibilities from local authorities, as in the transformation of council housing into social housing or through an increased emphasis on competition, as in the provision of public transport. Where central government has given more responsibilities to local agencies, as for example, in the case of English regional agencies, the principle has been mostly one of *deconcentration* rather than *decentralisation*. Policy has given additional discretion to local officials, without giving decision-making powers to elected authorities or community groups (Goodchild and Hickman 2006). In housing policy, in particular, regional agencies have started to acquire a role of applying and enforcing national building targets on local authorities.

The negative consequences of fragmentation are partly one of omission. The multiplication of housing agencies is largely irrelevant to problems of homelessness and of poor quality housing, including overcrowding. Fundamental inequalities persist unless governments are committed to their elimination or at least their reduction and provide the funds to make a difference.

In addition, the multiplication of agencies tends to complicate the process of policy making. Homelessness again provides an example. In the past local authorities were both responsible for dealing with homeless people and possessed the housing stock to house the homeless. With the disposal of their stock, local authorities have to work with housing associations or other voluntary agencies.

In addition, different agencies start pulling apart in a process of what Mannheim (1971, 52–6) once called functional rationalisation, that is to say pursing a specific organisational agenda that fails to consider the impact on others. The demands of performativity, of target setting in different services, have the same effect. These demands mean that different services tend to pursue priorities related wholly to their principal mission rather than in relation to a local community. Unless checked by deliberate policy requirements, performativity means, for example, that the police look to reducing overall crime statistics rather than working with a housing agency and local residents in tackling a specific neighbourhood problem. It means that highway authorities look for the most cost effective solution to traffic problems rather than one that promotes urban regeneration. It means that recreation departments look at open space provision as a maintenance and management cost rather than as local amenity – and so on.

The multiplication of agencies and measures, combined with an increased emphasis on performativity has the effect of pushing local agencies in different directions. Local government, conceived as a single authority having a dominant role in the social and economic development, becomes replaced by local governance meaning a process of interaction between a variety of different agencies and services of which the local authority has become only one. Transversal practice is a response to such a dispersed process of governance. It is an almost inevitable response if governments either wish to promote coordination at a local level or wish to promote co-ordinated development.

Wicked problems Numerous examples of transversal, area based and neighbourhood-based initiatives can be cited. In England these include the New Deal for Communities and other exercises in neighbourhood regeneration, the establishment of Local Strategic Partnerships and Community Plans under the Local Government Act, 2000 and intended to tackle urban regeneration and neighbourhoods at a city-wide or local authority wide level and the Housing Market Pathfinders first established in 2002 to tackle declining housing markets. These are all cross-cutting in the sense that they imply coordination with one another and impinge on a mixture of housing strategies and physical planning. The New Deal for Communities and the Local Strategic Partnerships are also cross-cutting in the sense that they require the coordination of physical planning and housing policies with those for employment and training, education and crime prevention and usually involve coordination between the private, the public and the voluntary sector. All these are a product of a Labour government elected in 1997 with a mandate to promote 'joined-up government' at a local and national level.

However, to cite specific, formal examples of area-based regeneration measures is, to an extent misleading. Much of the work is informal. It is about consulting various parties as necessary. It is also about *ad hoc* responses to specific problems, for example antisocial behaviour or poor quality public spaces, that require the local coordination of different agencies – the police, social housing agencies, local authority environmental services for example. In addition, transversal working applies to policies intended for specific priority groups. For example, policies for disabled person's housing require implementation in the fields of statutory town planning (dealing with the regulation of new build), environmental health (dealing with the regulation of conditions in the older privately-owned stock), social housing (dealing with subsidised accommodation) and social care and health (dealing specific adaptations).

A further layer of interpretation and theory is necessary. As the various examples suggest, transversal practice is not just a response to governance. It is also a response to problems that defy conventional, single agency solutions. Coordination or, to be more accurate a lack of coordination, has, for example, long been an issue in neighbourhood regeneration programmes, more or less from the first small-scale examples in the 1970s (Stewart 1999, 46–8). It is a structural issue that arises from the way in which neighbourhood regenerations programmes tackle what once called 'multiple deprivation'.

Put slightly differently in terms of the language of organisation theory, neighbourhood problems and the problems of the urban environment are 'wicked problems'. 'Wicked', as opposed to simple or 'tame' problems, are open to multiple, competing interpretations and cannot be pinned down either to a single cause or to an agreed hierarchy of causes of varied importance (Rittel and Webber 1973). In response to wicked problems, it is suggested, organisations should take the following complementary courses of action – they should promote their capacity for learning and joined up action with local residents and with other relevant organisations (Stewart 2000, 58–62); they should encourage cross-boundary working and a concern with comprehensive or 'holistic' thinking (Williams 2002); they should accept a diversity of possible solutions (Harmon and Mayer 1986); they should promote multiple policies 'constituting a portfolio of actions for a variety of players' (RCEP 2007, 9); and finally, they should adopt a pragmatic approach to evaluation using a combination of qualitative and quantitative data that monitors trends over time (Glasser 1998).

Collaborative planning   In planning theory, transversal practice generally goes under the name of 'collaborative planning' and is associated with the work of Healey. Collaborative planning means an institutional capacity to 'discuss the qualities of places and to address the evident reality of conflicts of interest in non-combative ways' (Healey 1998a, 1541). It involves, therefore, a dialogue between 'stakeholders', meaning those who have an interest in a place and represent different parties in processes of urban development and regeneration (Healey 1998b, 7–8).

In some ways, the references to stakeholders is not new. Plan implementation has long necessitated planners working with developers and land owners. Calls for cooperative styles of planning, in the form of cooperation between planners and land owners, can be traced back to the 1970s (Denman 1975) and even to the pre-1914 era (Nettlefold 1908). The originality of collaborative planning, as promoted by Healey, rested on a recognition of the diversity of different stakeholders and in addition on a recognition that local residents, not just property owners, are stakeholders in the future of an area.

Collaborative planning, so defined, has been open to criticism of ignoring political campaigns and more generally of ignoring the role of power. The criticism may have been exaggerated, as has also been argued (Healey 2003). The critique is more a warning about the need to avoid an idealised interpretation of collaborative planning as an open, democratic style of decision-making. Collaborative planning is not of itself democratic. It depends, instead, on some sense of trust on the ability of partner agencies to deliver what they say they will do. Collaborative planning, like concepts of transversal planning practice and governance is a general, international concept that allows significant variations in practice both between different countries and within a country. Whether collaborative planning is democratic or not depends on whom is consulted and whether their views are acted on. In any case, collaborative planning does not exclude politics. It is likely for example that projects will be planned and policies pursued within a political context, with politically determined priorities.

Debates about power, more particularly debates about the power of planning, continue. A recent review suggests, for example, that spatial planning and therefore the voice of the planner tends to become lost in the day to day decisions of local government and regional agencies (RTPI 2007). Another, more neglected issue concerns the potential conflict between professional ethics and power. For example, professional town planning involves an explicit code of conduct that stresses the role of the planner as an expert who 'shall fearlessly and impartially exercise their independent professional judgement'.[11] Collaborative planning or teamwork necessarily compromises the role of the planner as independent professional, especially if the team involves other types of professionals or the partnership involves private sector interests.

The counter argument is that the model of the independent professional has never worked well for professionals working in public sector agencies. In this context, collaborative planning remains useful in recognising that planners work in networks of organisations and that the work of planning is not simply technical. It is also about mediating between different requirements and agencies.

At least four types of mediation may be distinguished in collaborative planning. First and most obviously, collaboration is about bringing together different interested parties and different funding regimes, for example in an urban regeneration or new build project. In addition, it is about linking short-term measures and development projects to a longer vision and strategy. This is planning as spatial coordination, as defined by the profession[12] and endorsed by government (DCLG 2007e). Further, collaborative planning is about adapting high level and sometimes contradictory general policy statements to the specific, concrete reality of a locality. Finally, as part of this exercise in applying high level policies, collaborative planning is about translating abstract and sometimes highly bureaucratic concepts to a different audience, including in some cases community groups.

New occupational skills?   Considered in a historical context, collaborative planning also amounts to a redefinition of the scope of professional expertise. Mannheim postulated the possibility of all-round, all-knowing social scientist planner in the 1940s, but it never happened. The vision of a wide-ranging societal planning such was too broad and too political. Indeed the vision was so broad that its very definition ran into a recurrent problem of being simultaneously everything and nothing (Wildavsky 1973). The alternative market-led view of planning as development control, espoused by Hayek, was more easily placed in a technical box. Development control rests on a clear statutory definition, involves detailed legal knowledge and a relatively precise concern with the physical environment (Allison 1986). Planning as development control is reactive, however to development proposals, says little about the impact of development programmes on deprived and less well-off groups and does not fit easily into current policy preoccupations with urban regeneration, sustainable communities and 'stakeholder' working. Collaborative planning offers, therefore, a middle position between the impossible breadth of Mannheim's societal planning and the reactive, market-oriented definition of planning as development control. It offers a view of planning as place making and spatial coordination, as is also the current professional definition of practice.

Yet, even on this reduced and limited definition, the range of skills and occupational tasks is too wide to be encompassed within a single profession, whether some new super-profession or a redefinition of an existing profession. Place-making is, for example, likely to involve the design of buildings (architecture), the assessment of property values and market analysis (surveying), environmental impact analsyis and project management. And this is only a starting point. A government review established to determine the skills for the promotion of sustainable communities, the so-called Egan Review (ODPM 2004a, 10) has identified over 100 relevant occupations

Different tasks and skills have to be brought together. The ability to make a sythesis of different requirements and to see the 'big picture' has been a repeated theme in town planning since the time that Geddes specified a methodology for plan making before 1914. However, specialist tasks also have to be undertaken and they are often covered by specialist professions. The difficulty of predicting the exact requirements of future government policies also limits the ability of going outside conventional professions and their relatively stable educational requirements.

There are some distinctive British peculiarities in relation to occupational skills. The existence of strong professional organisations in Britain has coloured the debate. In particular, governments have sometimes viewed the existing professions as a break on public sector efficiency and modernisation and have, in this context, sought to promote the role of the general manager (Hutton and Massey 2006). In relation to urban regeneration and physical planning in England, the Egan report (ODPM 2004a) can be understood as a device whereby government has sought to redefine occupational skills in terms of the language of business and management rather than that usually associated with the environmental professions.

In addition, the debate about professional skills has been conducted in a context of overall staffing shortages that is not paralleled in most European countries. In response to these shortages, the government has provided financial incentives to universities to reduce the length of professional full-time postgraduate planning courses to one, rather than two years. In other European countries, the length of postgraduate full-time professional planning courses remains two years. The distinction between old and new occupational roles and between old, closely defined and blurred spheres of expertise is, nevertheless, a European-wide distinction (ASC 2007a; Jeannot 2005).

The growth of collaborative planning and the growth, more generally of transversal practice has led to a proliferation of analyses of relevant skills. The Egan report (ODPM 2004a) is probably the most important. Others have been prepared from the viewpoint of neighbourhood regeneration (NRU 2002), of urban design (CABE 2003) and of professional town planning (Kitchen 2007). Typically these analyses emphasise the need for general analytical skills, general communication skills and general skills in financial management, as well as technical skills. They suggest, as does evidence available to the Academy of Sustainable Communities (2007b), that practice comprises and will most likely continue to comprise a mix of old and new specialisms, established technical knowledge and newer business management skills.

However, an emphasis on skills development alone has its limits. It ignores the organisational context and the role of individual professional workers. Much depends, for example, on whether professionals are allowed to use their use their various skills, including their social skills and their ability to promote a debate and to mediate between different interests. It is the new way of working that poses the challenge for professionals and organisations, not just the possession of skills, many of which are not in any case necessarily absent in long-established forms of professional education (Kagan 2007). For example, communication and presentation skills have long been an implicit aspect of the education of professional town planners.

Conversely, skills require some purpose if they are to be fully employed. There has to be some fixed point in planning and urban regeneration, some sense of direction, if only as a means of avoiding an excessive sense of stress on individual workers. There are limits to the extent that professional workers can or would want to make up initiatives as they go along. Policy frameworks are also necessary, even if they limit the freedom of action of individual professionals.

Some forms of transversal practice, notably those concerned with communities, involve a responsibility to consult local people. In this context, training programmes for residents, and especially amongst community leaders, is a priority, albeit one that is not always recognised in discussions of professional expertise. The promotion of local, community-based accountability is, in principle, a counterpart of coordinated intervention at a neighbourhood level. However, local accountability is also constrained by the vertical structure of conventional public service bureaucracies, as well as by policy presumptions in favour of efficiency in service delivery. As a result, the very process of establishing a coordinating framework for local initiatives may have the effect of pushing out local residents, especially in the context of short time scales and nationally prescribed programme aims (Duncan and Thomas 2000, 5–6; North 2000). Community involvement takes time and probably requires an explicit policy commitment in its favour.

The 'New Times' Reconsidered

Concepts of post-bureaucracy and transversal practice are specific to the mechanics of planning and public administration. However, they also help to define in general terms the extent of change in the 'new times'. Post-bureaucratic styles of intervention are exercises in promoting innovation. Equally, they reflect that existing bureaucracies, including those responsible for housing and planning, persist. Transversal practice, including collaborative planning has not replaced old-style bureaucratic regulation. This latter continues alongside the various partnerships and often involves separate systems of formal consultation.

Likewise, and more generally, tendencies towards social change have to be weighed against tendencies towards stability. The tendency for the modern/ postmodern dialectic to come to an equilibrium is one consideration. More important is the way that social and economic processes operate to maintain continuity as well as change. Patterns of behaviour, including consumer preferences remain in part a product of routine and operate within continuing patterns of inequality. In addition, administrative structures and systems persist owing to the costs, disruption and uncertainties of rapid change (Webster 2005, 481). As a result, the shape of policy and the shape of implementing agencies is likely to change only gradually, mostly through a process in which new aims and new responsibilities are added to those of the past (Malpass and Murie 1982, 22).

Social theory is generally about classifying different views and models of a problem or trend, taking various models to their limits, testing them to destruction and putting them back together in new ways, including ways that reflect changes in practice. An exercise in planning theory would, in other words, only be concerned with the strengths and limitations of different theories of change or theories of stability and resistance to change. A contemporary history cannot take such a pure, theory drive approach. It must merely note their existence and use different theories as and when appropriate.

Notes

1 The web encyclopedia Wikipedia states that the dichotomies of Ihab Hassan have 'helped many students understand the differences, both concrete and abstract, between modernism and postmodernism'. Consulted November 2007 at http://en.wikipedia. org/wiki/Ihab_Hassan.

2 Birmingham, E. (1998) *Reframing the Ruins: Pruitt-Igoe, Structural Racism, and African American Rhetoric as a Space for Cultural Critique* consulted September 2005

at http://www.tu-cottbus.de/BTU/Fak2/TheoArch/wolke/X-positionen/Birmingham/ birmingham.html.

3   Bracher, M. (undated) Lacanian Resources for Organizational Consulting consulted June 2006 at http://www.sba.oakland.edu/ispso/html/bracher.html.

4   Benedikter, R. (undated) *Jacques Lacan and the Discourse of Science*, consulted June 2007 at the website of 'Philosophia' at http://www.philosophia-online.de/mafo/ heft2001–02/benedikter_lacan.htm.

5   Taken from the website of the Office of the Deputy Prime Minister and from a statement *What is a sustainable community?* consulted February 2006 at http://www.odpm.gov. uk/index.asp?id=1139866.

6   The quote is taken from the website of the Department for Communities and Local Government consulted October 2007 at http://www.communities.gov.uk/communities/ sustainablecommunities/sustainablecommunities/.

7   BBC News, 10 February 2006: reported on the BBC website, consulted February 2006 at http://news.bbc.co.uk/1/hi/uk/4699928.stm.

8   Calculated from Table 1.4: Final energy consumption by final user (1) 1970 to 2005, available at the website of the Department of Trade and Industry, consulted June 2005 at http://www.dti.gov.uk/energy/statistics/publications/ecuk/overall/page17954.html.

9   Domestic Energy Consumption Tables, Table 3.2: *Domestic energy consumption in terms of primary equivalents, by fuel 1970 to 2006* available at the website of the Department for Business, Enterprise and Regulatory Reform, consulted October 2007 at http:// www.dti.gov.uk/energy/statistics/publications/ecuk/domestic/page18071.html.

10 URBACT has its own website, consulted November 2007 at http://urbact.eu/no_cache/ home.html.

11 The quotation comes from *The Royal Town Planning Institute Code of Professional Conduct*, consulted January 2008 at the website of the RTPI at http://www.rtpi.org. uk/cgi-bin/item.cgi?ap=1&id=214.

12 'What Planning Does', extract from the website of the Royal Town Planning Institute consulted June 2007 at http://www.rtpi.org.uk/what_planning_does/.

Chapter 6

Quantity and Quality in Housing Development

The process of housing development comprises the material base of the urban landscape, both in the economic sense of the term and the sense of what is real and concrete. The process of housing development also expresses with particular clarity the twin themes of change and continuity that are inherent in any account that seeks to combine history with an account of current practice.

In relation to change, private house building has become increasingly concentrated into larger companies. Larger companies are more likely to possess a variety of specialist skills to deal with a development process that is becoming increasingly complex. They are also better equipped to raise finance for long-term land purchase and for infrastructure investment and more able to pursue marketing campaigns at a regional or national level. Conversely, smaller companies are more at risk of financial problem if the market in a single town or region lags behind others or if a single site has higher than expected development costs. The social housing sector has likewise moved towards concentration, at least in relation to housing development. Successive governments in England, less so in Scotland and Wales, have preferred to work with larger housing associations or consortia of housing associations operating over the area of different local authorities.

At the same time, the distinction between social and private housing developers has started to blur. The larger developing housing associations in England have started to undertake unsubsidised market rent and build for sale schemes. The main constraint is a regulatory framework that, rightly in the view of most people, seeks to minimise any risks for public assets, including the existing social housing stock and for tenants (Calcutt 2007, 28). Conversely, private house builders in England and again mostly the larger developers, have, since the Housing Act, 2004, started to receive public funds for the provision of affordable housing.

On the other hand, in relation to continuity over time, both private and social housing developers work within a combination of market processes, planning frameworks and government policies, as they have done since at least 1945. The government is less influential than at the time of mass building programmes of the 1950s and 1960s. However, development controls operated through the town planning system remain as powerful as ever. In addition, the development industry is aware of the range of potential powers that the state might employ and for this reason is always alert to the direction of policy. Finally, the key policy issues reflect continuity rather than change. As has been a recurrent theme since the establishment of housing and planning policies in the early twentieth century, the issues concern the quantity of new dwellings and their quality.

Numbers and the Development Process

In relation to the quantity of homes, current concerns stem largely from inflation in house prices. In the 1970s and early 1980s, the possibility of home ownership was, in general, open to any individual with either the prospect of long-term stable employment or access to capital. Thereafter, house price inflation, in two waves in the late 1980s and from the late 1990s onwards has limited access or increased the cost of access to home ownership for most first time buyers without capital.

For example, in evidence to the Barker Review, Bramley has estimated housing affordability at different times since the house price boom in the late 1980s. In the period 1986–1991, about 43 per cent of new households were able to buy a home in South East England. In 2002 only about 27 per cent of new households could afford a home. If, in the meantime, bank interest rates had not diminished and if, in addition, the income multipliers had not been relaxed, the loss of greater affordability would have been higher.[1] It is unlikely, moreover, that affordability has increased thereafter. Recent reports have suggested, for example, fewer and fewer first-time buyers entering the housing market.[2]

House price inflation has other adverse side effects. It redistributes wealth into the hands of existing property owners and, as part of this, to middle aged and older people rather than young adults. It has opened up a gap between those families that can help their grown-up children to buy and other families with fewer resources. Finally, and this was a theme in the Barker Review (2004, 7), it has pushed up general rates of inflation and adversely affected the potential for economic growth.

House Building Targets and their Implications

The diagnosis of the Barker Review represents the official orthodoxy about the causes of inflation in house prices. The diagnosis is relatively simple in outline. It consists of three, linked and overlapping causative assertions, that:

• house price inflation has been mostly caused by a lack of house building in response to demand;
• the underlying constraint on house building is 'the supply of land' (Barker 2003, 10); and finally
• planning restrictions are at the root of a lack of development land.

The third causative assertion is a logical consequence of the previous two points. The planning system is the gatekeeper for the release of development sites. However, the first and second assertions are more contentious. The second ignores the way in which the building industry might itself operate to limit the expansion of output. The first ignores the numerous other factors, apart from supply, that might influence house prices. It also ignores inconsistencies in the international experience. In the Irish Republic, for example, a combination of loose planning, high levels of building and high rates of inflation in house prices coincided with one another in the period from about 2000 to 2006 (Paris 2007).

Assessing the shortage   In any case, and more fundamentally, the scale of house inflation has generally been so great that it is unrealistic to expect increased output to have a significant short-term impact. New homes only account for a small proportion of the homes sold in any year. In England and Wales in 2002, for example, the number of dwellings completed by private developers only represented about 9 per cent of the residential property transactions recorded by the Inland Revenue.[3] Housing shortages are the cumulative impact of inadequate building over many years. Supply can be increased, but only slowly and through large increases in the annual rates of house building.

The calculations made in the Barker Review illustrate the problem. Barker (2003, 58–9) estimated that, to bring down inflation in house prices in line with general house price inflation, assuming average European rates of construction and average European price elasticities, an annual rate of 145,000 private sector dwellings additional to recent output was needed in Britain.[4] This amounted almost to a doubling of recent rates. Yet even Barker's estimates have been challenged by those who note that they make no allowance for the recent surge of immigration from eastern Europe or for increased numbers of overseas students at British universities (*The Times* 7 June 2007, 6).

A doubling of output is so ambitious that one might doubt whether it is feasible. Subsequent trends in house building show some increase in output, but not on the scale that Barker suggested was necessary. Annual completions have increased from a periodic low of 115,701 dwellings in the financial year 2001/02 to 145,554 in the financial year 2006/07.[5] Moreover, most current forecasts, at the end of 2007, suggest a likely decline in completions, given housing market uncertainties.

Economic models deal with national or regional aggregates and have difficulty in coping with local variations. Variations in the rates of house building rates are not relevant to the high house prices in inner London where demand outstrips supply owing to a concentration of economic activities, cultural facilities and, in addition, the limitations of the commuter rail network. Anyone who thinks that the low rate of house building in South East England is the main cause of high house prices in London should ponder the example of New York, especially of Manhattan, where high prices coexist with a much more development-oriented planning system.

In any case, the balance between supply and demand is not the only consideration. House prices almost certainly have a speculative element to them, based on a belief in the continuation of previous inflationary tendencies. House prices rose in the mid 1970s and the late 1980s at a rate that was unsustainable and that was later corrected. House price inflation in the first decade of the twenty-first century may also be unsustainable.

In addition, housing has, in part, the characteristics of positional good, that is to say a good whose price is determined by its social position and attractiveness or by its environmental advantages (Hirsch 1977). These positional characteristics are likely to maintain scarcity in attractive and high status areas even in the context of an apparent surplus. The experience of prices in the North of England provides an example. Here, in conditions of an approximate balance between supply and demand, some areas continue to possess what would be commonly regarded as unaffordable house prices, in contrast to the low prices available in unpopular low demand areas nearby. Balancing supply and demand and, as part of this, building more homes does not necessarily lead to a reduction in house prices in all areas.

Uncertainties in the demand/supply relationship have implications for land use planning. They mean that it is not feasible to identify with any precision the amount of land that should be released to reduce house price inflation. Persistent increases in house prices suggest that more homes should be built and that land should be made available for housing, as is current government policy. At the same time, a flexible and pragmatic response is also necessary, for example monitoring trends in house building rates compared to what has been completed recently and looking at the comparative rates of house price increase in one area and one region compared to another. In England, guidance on the assessment of housing markets for planning urges exactly such a pragmatic, market-aware and more regionalised approach (ODPM 2004b).

These same considerations and uncertainties also suggest that measures to promote affordability should not rely wholly on the promotion of private house building. High house prices mean a continuing and probably expanded role for social housing. Yet the development of new social housing remains low by historical standards. To provide an example: in 1970 housing associations completed 15,110 dwellings and local authorities completed 164,978 – a total of 170,088 dwellings for the social housing sector as a whole. In contrast, in 2004, housing associations completed 20,607 dwellings, including shared ownership dwellings and local authorities completed 133 dwellings – a grand total of 20,740 or only about 12 per cent of the total in 1970.[6]

A wide variety of other national policies are also relevant, for example taxation policies, that might reduce the incentive to speculate from house price inflation, policies to reduce housing pressures in inner London through planned decentralisation and policies of neighbourhood regeneration that ensure that home buyers are prepared to live in previously unattractive areas. In other words, managing local housing markets should seek to spread demand over a wide area.

There are examples of all such policies. For example, capital gains tax reduces the incentive of landlords and second home buyers to buy for speculative gain. Neighbourhood regeneration policies already seek to make unpopular areas more popular. Questions persist, however, whether existing policies are sufficiently well coordinated or, in the case of taxation, go far enough in seeking to reduce house price inflation.

Blaming the developers? The significance of land constraints might seem obvious. House builders repeatedly raise land as the main constraint on their operations. Yet the house building industry has itself been frequently criticised for its complacency and uncompetitive practices. The Barker Review (2003, 78) noted, for example, that complaints existed about inefficiencies in production, about failures to meet consumer aspirations and about the ownership of large stocks of unused land. Likewise, the Environmental Audit Committee of the House of Commons (2005a, 57) has complained about 'The lamentable lack of ambition within the industry', both in regard to promoting an expanded output and to maintaining higher environmental standards.

The criticism of land hoarding deserves particular attention as it counters the view of the planning system as the main cause of problems. The Campaign to Protect Rural England (CPRE) has been especially influential in this context, notably in a research briefing entitled *Housing Myths: Housing Solutions*.[7] The myth, according to the CPRE, was that house building was being restrained by a lack of planning permissions. The reality was that 'over recent years the amount of land with at least outline planning permission for new private, for sale homes has been rising, according to the house builders themselves'. Between 1999 and 2002, the number of plots with outline planning permission held by the UK's 15 leading house builders had increased from about 247,000 to about 279,000– an increase of about 13 per cent. Subsequent work by the Royal Town Planning Institute suggests that the numbers have remained substantial. The RTPI has suggested that, according to the 2006 annual or mid year reports, the leading nine developers had 224,383 plots with planning permission.[8]

Land is part of the portfolio of assets owned by a building company and is listed in the annual financial reports that provide the data for the CPRE and RTPI reports. From the notes in these two reports, the data includes sites with outline planning permission only, that is to say to sites that still require full permission and the resolution, as part of this, of various detailed matters. Of the nine company reports examined by the RTPI, for example, only one had sufficient land with either full or outline planning permission to sustain building for more than four years at recent completion rates.[9] At face value, therefore, land banks of private house builders generally do not look excessive. In any case, house builders only own a minority of sites with planning permission for new housing. Evidence cited by Calcutt (2007, 37) suggests that 61 per cent is owned by non-property interests, including the public sector.

On the other hand, one might wonder about the accuracy of the annual company reports. Demonstrating the ownership of sites with planning permission contributes to the value of a company. As a result, it is in the interests of a building company to exaggerate its assets. Conversely, in a stagnant market, it is in the interest of developers to hold land as an option without taking this forward quickly to the stage of applying for planning permission. The RTPI has called, in this context, for the introduction of rules that might lay down a higher level of clarity in relation to land banks in the company reports of house builders.[10]

The debates about concentration and land banking are often highly technical. They miss the point. The house building industry is cautious. Firms make annual targets based on previous experience and expectations. They are not necessarily eager to achieve ambitious targets. Even in the context of high house prices, they continue to build at a rate with which they are comfortable and, so long as they make adequate profits, are not worried about expanding their output. At the same time, developers are sensitive to price signals that might indicate a downturn in profitability and a reduction in their ability to make development gains (Barker 2003, 42; Pryce 1999).

Why is the industry so cautious? Increased concentration is not to blame. Information presented by the Barker Review (2003, 62) suggests that in 2002 three firms, Wimpey with 13,480 completions, Persimmon with 12,352 completions and Barratt with 12,250 completions were significantly larger than any other. These 'big three' firms accounted for about 23 per cent of output. Recent evidence produced by the Calcutt review into house building delivery suggests that concentration has continued. Even so it has a long way to go before it is likely to trigger concerns about monopolies.

Concentration has also not prevented the entry of other companies. Evidence on the scale of entry of new companies is presented in the Barker Review and this shows that a number of new developers entered the field in the 1990s and prospered. The subsequent entry of developing associations in the build for sale market has further increased competition. Entry of firms specialising in new technology is more difficult, however, as these need to acquire either large sites or a portfolio of sites before they can begin. In evidence to the Barker Review, 'First Base', a company that has specialised in commercial construction suggests, for example, that the minimum economic site size is one for 150 units and preferably 200 units.[11]

The concept of 'satisficing' provides an alternative explanation for the caution of private developers. Conventional economic theory assumes that firms seek to maximise their profitability and are always on the look out for ways to expand their market share and reduce costs. Even in apparently competitive markets, however, firms do not generally seek to maximise their performance in the sense of searching out all possibilities. They face too many constraints of time, money and resources. Instead, they 'satisfice', to use a term devised by Simon (1957). They set a level of aspirations and a level of profitability that is satisfactory or good enough in relation to previous expectations and the expectations of significant others, search until an alternative is found that satisfies the aspiration level criterion and then select that alternative as a management strategy. So long, therefore, that the previous performance is good enough, firms do not possess an incentive to innovate.

Satisficing is a tendency within all organisations, not just private firms and not just house builders. It assumes that, in the absence of external stimuli, all organisation will seek to do merely 'enough'. Satisficing therefore potentially applies to the development strategies of housing associations and to the work of local authorities.

However, satisficing applies particularly to house builders as in conditions of rising house prices, these can make satisfactory profits from land development without considering expansion or innovation (Ball 1999; Barlow 1999; Barlow

and Duncan 1994; Carmona 2001, 97–124; Young 1997). In
House of Commons Environmental Audit Committee, one wit
house building industry, 'These are comfortable people doing a
(2005a, 56).

A shortage of development sites has a similar effect in discouraging efficiency
in the construction of social housing. Land shortages limit and sometimes prevent
social housing agencies from organising a competitive bidding process, judging
contractors in terms of value for money. They have to accept what is offered by
developers within the framework of planning agreements. Private developers
own a large proportion, probably most of the potential development sites and
this gives them an enhanced bargaining power in building contracts. Internal
regulation within the social housing sector means that building costs remain
within acceptable limits and that the designs conform to appropriate minimum
standards. However, the incentive for making long-term efficiency gains is either
limited or lost.

Prefabrication   Accepting the case for increased house building, how is the
capacity of the building industry best expanded? One apparently obvious way
might be to promote prefabricated construction methods, with parts transported
to a site from a central factory that can use the most advanced manufacturing
techniques. Prefabrication offers a means of reducing the cost and amount of
labour necessary in house building. It is widely used in countries with different
house building traditions – for example Japan with its tradition of steel frame
construction and Scandinavia with its tradition of timber frame. It is also
commonly used in Britain in commercial projects, including projects, such as the
construction of hotels and hostels, that are close to housing.

Prefabricated systems are currently called 'modern' methods of construction.
They used to be called 'non-traditional', but 'modern' is more attractive for their
supporters. They cover a variety of methods as follows: 'open panel' systems,
covering two-dimensional elements such as walls, floors and part of the roof;
three-dimensional 'volumetric' or modular systems that enclose space; hybrids
between open panel and volumetric systems and finally other techniques adapted
for large, complex schemes. The open panel, volumetric and hybrid systems all
involve a degree of prefabrication, with assembly on site. The volumetric systems
involve the lowest proportion of on-site work.

The short-term financial horizons of private house building have slowed
down the adoption of modern building methods. A story in the industry's
journal, *Housebuilder* (June 2002) provides an example. In 2000, the firm Wilson
Connelly bought a specialist in prefabrication 'Prestoplan' to ensure that off-site
prefabrication, based on timber-frame methods, could be incorporated into its
mainstream business. 'One set of poor results later saw heads roll and the new
man at the top take an axe to the number of timber-framed houses the company
would build.'

A tendency to outsource contract work to contractors is a further constraint.
Extensive subcontracting means that the developer lacks full control over the
construction process and cannot easily train workers in new skills. The developer

.s to use whatever skills and techniques are available at a competitive price in a given locality. Subcontracting is, moreover structural to the workings of the construction industry as it is generally seen as more cost effective and also offers a means whereby developers can reduce fixed labour costs and, in doing this, reduce their exposure to fluctuations in building activity (Ball 1983, 164–77).

In this context and given in addition the dependence of private house builders on land development for their profits, innovation in construction method is most likely to come from two main sources. Piecemeal innovation of the type that is sometimes called continuous improvement will arise from internal reviews of efficiency. Otherwise, more radical changes, including the adoption of prefabrication are likely to arise from external sources. Various examples can be given. Developers might be required to innovate owing to forthcoming changes in the building regulations favouring stringent low energy and zero carbon standards. They might change their construction practices in response to changes in the housing market, as has already occurred in the development of private high rise. Finally, as Roy et al. (2003) have suggested, specialist firms might emerge that can compete with existing subcontractors on value for money. Most likely, these firms will also manufacture building systems and components for non-residential uses.

Social housing landlords are more open to innovation, if encouraged by government. By the financial year 2004/05 and partly in response to government targets, about 48 per cent of publicly funded new social housing in England was completed using modern methods (Housing Corporation Annual Report 2004/05, 11). Equivalent figures for private house building are not publicly available. An official estimate for the year 2003 suggests about 15 per cent of UK private sector output.[12]

The experience of prefabrication in social housing has been subject to extensive evaluation in England, notably by the Housing Forum (2002a; 2002b) and the National Audit Office (NAO 2005). The lessons are as follows:

On the positive side:

- the length of time involved in construction is significantly reduced and this could be important where a developer wishes to initiate its income stream as quickly as possible or where completion is otherwise urgent;
- the build quality of the completed dwelling is also commonly higher than in traditional build. In general, off-site production reduces the range and number of faults (The Housing Forum 2002b);
- finally, residents of the demonstration projects are no more or less likely to be satisfied than the average for all new build schemes (The Housing Forum 2002a, 35).

On the other hand, prefabrication has involved a series of cost and related penalties.

- Overall construction costs remain higher for prefabricated schemes, generally by about 10 per cent (*The Guardian* 20 November 2002; The Housing Forum

2002b, 7). The average conceals extensive variations, however. For example, open panel methods have about the same cost as traditional methods (NAO 2005, 14). Modern construction methods of all types are better suited to building high (ibid.).

- The designs of prefabricated schemes have to be worked out in more detail in advance (Ross 2002, 21). Prefabricated systems have proved less flexible in coping with disruptions in the supply of materials and fittings; less flexible in coping with unexpected problems during the construction process; and less flexible in dealing with particular or unusual design requirements, for example planning requirements that are imposed at a relatively late stage (after the approval of outline permission) (NAO 2005, 10).
- Finally, if faults occur, the use of specialised components increases maintenance costs and delays the carrying out of any remedial work owing to sourcing difficulties and other uncertainties (Ross, 2002).

The supporters of prefabrication often argue that this will prove cost effective in the long term and that it is best undertaken in conjunction with long-term 'partnering' contracts between a client and a builder. An evaluation, undertaken by the Building Research Establishment of prefabricated projects undertaken by the Peabody and Joseph Rowntree Foundation projects suggests, for example, that 'the additional costs can largely be attributed to their prototype nature and higher than normal specification'.[13] Is this so? Future cost savings are, by definition, uncertain, depending for example on the type of site, the type of scheme and the scale of production runs available in any specific case. In this context, the caution of private developers is understandable and rational.

Partnering has become the good practice orthodoxy in the procurement of social housing, since the publication of *Rethinking Construction* (CTF 1998). However, the business case for partnering is not without limitations. Long production runs intended to provide economies of scale and innovation suspend scheme-by-scheme competitive tendering in favour of long-term contracts and negotiation for specific sites. Contractors may, in this context, take advantage of negotiation to avoid market trends towards lower prices. The Housing Corporation's Volume Procurement initiative of the mid 1990s provides an example of this. (Goodchild et al. 1996b).

Long-term building cost estimates are notoriously unreliable, as contractors look on the optimistic side and even ignore known problems to win contracts. Underestimation of future costs may even be endemic to long-term building contracts (Flyvbjerg et al. 2002). For housing schemes long-term contracts are unnecessary, except where the aim is to promote innovation or prefabrication. Given this and given that such aims will also inevitably favour one type of contractor, the larger building companies rather than others, a degree of caution is necessary.

The problems of long-term partnering can, in part, be resolved by regulation. The Housing Corporation has been the main regulatory body for social housing in England. It would almost certainly argue that best value checks prevent building contractors or other interested parties from misusing partnering contracts. Even so, there are limits to partnering. Conventional scheme-by-scheme competitive tendering has a legitimate role in procurement and has probably been undervalued over the past few years.

The promotion of prefabrication has taken place against a background of fears about labour shortages in the construction industry. In evidence to the Barker Review (2003, 14) over 80 per cent of firms reported skill shortages. In contrast, a later survey has shown good rates of recruitment into the building industry and concluded that skill shortages are not a pressing issue (*Housebuilder* October 2005). The extent of labour shortages has fluctuated, influenced in part by immigration from eastern Europe. In any case, improvements in labour productivity do not depend only on the adoption of prefabricated methods. Piecemeal improvements to traditional methods are also likely, including the adoption of hybrid forms of construction that incorporate elements of both tradition and modern methods. Most likely, labour shortages will not hold back future expansion if this takes place.

Alternatives to the Developer

Conventional private and social developers are not the only source of new housing. There is a disparate variety of alternatives, each of which implies a different product and different type of design. Alternatives include the promotion of so-called mobile homes and various types of self-build, including individual development and community self-build, based on self-help groups.

The alternatives came to the fore in the reaction against mass housing in the late 1960s. Mobile homes are an extension of proposals to treat housing as a disposable consumer product. Self-build was a reaction against large-scale planning and large-scale forms of housing provision. In the 1960s, these alternatives were fresh and innovative. The novelty has subsequently worn off, but the alternatives have not disappeared.

Mobile homes/park homes   In relation to technology, the most radical alternative is the humble 'mobile' or 'park' home, that is to say fully prefabricated housing units that are transported as one unit or sometimes as two or three linked units placed on a privately owned and managed site. The names 'mobile' and 'park' are both misleading but have stuck for want of a better alternative. These homes are described as 'mobile' by virtue of their use of a chassis, like a vehicle and their distant origins in the 1930s and 1940s in the caravan industry. They are not mobile in any realistic sense, however. A mobile home requires a large truck if it is to be moved and in most cases requires partial dismantling. Mobile homes are also 'park' homes by virtue of their usual situation in an area that is collectively managed and sometimes landscaped. 'Park home' is more attractive than 'mobile home' from a marketing perspective. It is also not accurate, however. The situation of a typical 'park home' is generally no more park like, than say the situation of a typical tower block.

In terms of the economics of development, a reduced building life expectancy is the most distinctive feature of mobile/park homes. The manufacturers of mobile homes typically claim that a new unit would have an effective life of at least 30 or 40 years (Berkeley Hanover Consulting et al. 2002, 25). The life expectancy has lengthened over recent years due to the use of more durable materials and better construction methods. Even so, it is closer to that of the individual building components in a conventional home, for example window and door frames, rather than the structure as a whole. Conventionally built homes have a longer life expectancy, arguably an indefinite life if subject to regular maintenance and so long as sufficient demand exists.

The potential of mobile/park homes is most commonly argued and demonstrated with reference to the housing market in the US (Abley 2001, 16; Cowburn 1967). Here a similar type of 'manufactured housing' has become a common source of affordable housing for all age groups, especially in rural areas and in the south and west of the country. The construction costs of manufactured homes have proved about 50 per cent less than equivalent types of permanent, site built accommodation in the US and have proved popular for this reason amongst lower income groups.[14]

It is unlikely, however, without a drastic review and restructuring of housing policy, that British or European manufacturers would be able to obtain the same economies of scale as those in the US. Any such review of housing policy would moreover inevitably raise objections from virtually all pressure groups that are connected in some way to house building – not just the conventional house building industry, but the social housing and environmentalist pressure groups. The basic criticism and one that is difficult to refute would be that so-called park homes offer inferior standards of accommodation, are hard to heat, have an inferior structural performance and longevity and are easily stigmatised.

In the absence of government support, park homes possess a limited role in the housing market. Park homes are commonly marketed for retired and semi-retired people and commonly have minimum age restrictions of 50 or 45 years. For middle aged and elderly people, park homes are attractive owing to the way that they combine living in a bungalow with purchase costs around half those of an equivalent sized standard house.[15] As a result, moving from a conventional 'bricks and mortar' home to a park home typically enables middle aged and elderly people to generate substantial cash sums.

However, the experience of living in a park home estate is not always as attractive as the marketing might suggest. The occupants tend, on average, to be more dissatisfied than social tenants, private tenants or owner-occupiers (Berkeley Hanover Consulting et al. 2002, 72 and 74). Admittedly, most residents are satisfied, just as most residents living in privately-rented and social housing are satisfied. However, a minority is dissatisfied and the minority is larger than is generally revealed in general national surveys.

The reasons for dissatisfaction in park homes have not been explored in any depth. Dissatisfaction may be the result of their design limitations. Despite their appeal to older people, they are also not specifically designed for the requirements of disability or infirmity. Dissatisfaction may also be caused by a tendency for the physical condition of park homes to deteriorate more quickly than conventional

Homes, Cities and Neighbourhoods

homes. Short-life homes inevitably cause problems for occupants at the end of its expected life.

Another possibility concerns the legal status of owners. Residents associations have repeatedly complained about lack of value-for-money in maintenance and management charges, about unjustified commission costs, charged by the site owner at the time of resale and about bullying from site-owners if they fail to pay these charges (*The Observer* 27 April 2003). Initial purchase of a park home is less expensive than a comparable new home of the same size, but there are many hidden costs for the resident. It is difficult, moreover, to see how the occupants could acquire an equivalent level of rights to conventional owner occupiers, without also undermining the distinctiveness of park homes as a form of housing. The relatively low legal status of building owners is a logical consequence of their short-life expectancy and the management requirements of living in a park estate.

Further expansion of park homes is restrained, in part, by the difficulties of obtaining planning permission, according to the site operators (Berkeley Hanover Consulting et al. 2002, 67). This is not the only constraint. The mobile home and park home manufacturers specialise in detached bungalows, placed in a simple layout on a spacious site. A survey, undertaken in 1999 suggested that the average density of a park home site is roughly four or five dwellings per acre (10–13 dwellings per hectare) (ibid., 35). This is low by the standards of contemporary practice and, in most parts of the country, would be difficult to justify on either planning or economic grounds. The mobile home offers an alternative to the developer's home, but one that is likely to remain of marginal importance.

Individual development   For a minority of households with sufficient time, resources and determination, individualised housing is achievable through organising the development work themselves. Consumers do not have to do the work themselves. Individual development or possibly self-procurement as this type of development is best called is not necessarily self-build in a literal sense. Individual developers can hire a contractor to do some or all the work and can also hire an architect to undertake the design. Including these latter types of self-development, the VAT returns of HM Customs and Excise showed an increase from around 2,000 in 1978 to an estimated 15,000 in 1999, with a marked increase in the mid 1990s associated with the greater availability of specialist self-build mortgages (Barlow et al. 2001). In 1999, individual development represented more than the output of any single volume house builder in Britain.

No direct, comparable information is currently available about the scale of individual development since 1999. The usual assumption is that numbers have continued to rise (Nicol and Golland 2004, 328). A land-finding website has even given an unlikely estimate of 50,000 homes per year.[16] It is equally possible, however, that completions have started to grow less quickly or have reached a plateau.

Two opposing forces are apparent. On one hand, individual development has become increasingly fashionable, recognised in a peak-time television programme, Channel 4's *Grand Designs*, and supported by networks of specialist private consultants, land dealers, mortgage finders and by journals such as *Build It* and *Homebuilding and Renovating*. These journals, together with a wealth of sites on the web, provide a source of information that did not exist 20 years ago. On the other hand, individual development has faced increasingly severe land and planning constraints.

Elsewhere in Europe, individual development has been more significant as a means of providing new homes. In France and Germany, individuals have been able to find sites more easily and in some cases local authorities have also been prepared to find sites and sell land for once-off schemes. In France, in particular, developers have, for many years, undertaken exercises in plot development – *lotissement* – whereby they provide a serviced site. In Britain, in contrast, house building and site development have been joined to one another in a way that generally leaves individual developers with only a scattering of small infill sites. Barlow and Stockerl (1999) have compared house building patterns in Britain, France and Germany in 1996. Individual development (or 'self-procurement' to use the term of Barlow and Stockerl) accounted at the time for 11 per cent of completions in Britain, 45 per cent in France and 55 per cent in Germany.

Individual development has a reputation for delivering well built, value-for-money homes. Individual development offers a way of increasing the capacity of the house building industry, either by using the labour power of the self-builders or through the use of prefabricated building techniques. It is also potentially consistent with the housing policies pursued through the planning system. For example, local authorities could use planning agreements or the rural exceptions policy to allocate land for individual developers. However, local authorities could do this only if the promoters of self-build and individual development sector dropped their interest in dream homes and paid more attention to building for people in need. If the planning system is made more conducive to individual development, the implications will also have to be publicised and clearly explained. A mere change of policy without publicity would almost certainly not bring forward a large number of applicants.

Community build   Individual development is mostly about owner-occupation. Another, smaller sector comprises the social housing equivalent – low cost, publicly funded group self-build. One model, for example, is for low income or unemployed individuals to come together to complete a shared-ownership dwelling where a housing association owns half or three quarters of the value and the builders own the remaining proportion, this representing the value of their labour during the construction process. It is also possible to offer training to unemployed people during the construction process so that they can obtain qualifications for further work in the building industry.

Community self-build, as this form of self-help scheme is often called, poses a number of obstacles for possible participants – notably the difficulty of organising and maintaining the coherence of the group in the face of the inevitable setbacks and delays. Housing associations, whose cooperation and support are generally needed, are also wary of becoming involved owing to the likelihood of delays and the high administrative cost. All this, combined with the demanding regulatory requirements of publicly funded self-build means that the number of completion is insignificant in relation to meeting overall housing shortages. The Community Self Build agency for England, together with its Scottish equivalent, is the main agency representing and collecting information on groups self-build. The web site of the agency for England stated, in 2005, that the number of groups that have completed is 'over 90' since the start of their work in 1989. Since the size of each group is between about six and 12 dwellings, this gives an average of between about 34 and 67 each year.[17] Even allowing for other schemes completed without the help of the Community Self Build agency, the numbers are insignificant if compared to other providers.

Community self-build is highly significant for those who participate and successfully complete a scheme. It is particularly desirable on policy grounds because it helps people in need. Like individual self-build and customisable development, group self-build is desirable, moreover, as a means of promoting more diversity in house type and design in new residential areas. It is desirable as a minority form of development, but is unlikely to contribute greatly to tackling current housing shortages.

Land and the Planning System

The promotion of greater capacity and efficiency in house building is a necessary, but not sufficient means of promoting affordable homes. Let us pose a hypothetical question. If, in the future as techniques improve, prefabrication is able to reduce building costs by 50 per cent, who would benefit? Most likely, in the context of house price inflation, housing shortages and land shortages, the main beneficiaries would be the developer and the landowner. The cost savings would not be passed on to the consumer.

More land needs to be made available for housing. Development sites exist, at least in principle, in most of Britain. A joint submission to the Barker Review by Gallagher Estates (a private development company) and Roger Tym and Company (a firm of planning consultants) puts the point succinctly.[18]

> The real shortage relates to land with planning consent and capable of immediate implementation. This is evidenced by the fact that strategic studies such as the Cambridge Sub-region Growth Study and the Milton Keynes and South Midlands Study are able to identify strategic directions and locations for growth which are generally unconstrained by environmental or planning policy designations and which are capable of being served by public transport services.

The scale of urban development in South East England, the region facing the greatest development pressures, still remains relatively low if expressed as a proportion of the total available land area. In 2001, the figure for London and South East England taken together was about 17.9 per cent (Barker 2004, 45). The problem is one of making sites available through the planning system.

Commercial and Residential, Greenfield and Brownfield

The significance of planning constraints may also be revealed by comparing the operation of the housing market to that of the property market for offices. Evidence submitted to the Barker Review by London Residential Research suggests that office development in London has been highly responsive to changing demand, that the rate of development has altered accordingly and that, as a result, the price of renting an office declined over the term from the 1970s onwards.[19] The reason was the existence of 'strong policies to promote office development in central London, particularly in the City of London and Tower Hamlets'. The development of housing was a lesser priority and faced stronger environmental and other objections.

The significance of planning constraints applies as much, moreover, to brownfield sites, meaning previously developed sites and sites within urban areas, as to greenfield. For most types of site and in most urban areas, developers have overcome the technical and marketing uncertainties of brownfield of the type that were the focus of previous studies, for example noted by Syms (1997). Technical constraints, such as land contamination, are, in particular, less important than even a few years ago. Technical difficulties alone can be countered through remedial work and design solutions that are charged against the asking price of the site prior to acquisition by the developer. Technical difficulties raise the cost of development. However, in the market conditions that have prevailed over the past few years and with the exception of the most depressed areas, technical difficulties have rarely rendered a site incapable of development. Instead, developers say that planning itself has become the main constraint (Price, 2006) – for example zoning preferences in favour of commercial and industrial use or the detailed complaints of neighbours against intensification or the apparently onerous financial requirements demanded through planning agreements.

From 1997 onwards, partly in response to planning restrictions on the development of greenfield land, the proportion of dwellings completed on brownfield sites in England has increased substantially. In 2005, 70 per cent of new dwellings in England were built on brownfield land excluding conversions, compared to 53 per cent in 1997 (DCLG 2007d, 8). The development of brownfield sites has its limits, however, especially if the government wishes to encourage a rapid increase in the rate of house completions. Setting targets for brownfield development, as is currently practiced at both a national and local levels, constrains overall house building if an adequate supply of brownfield sites is unavailable.

Reforming the Process of Regulation

Failure to allocate sufficient sites for housing has led some critics to suggest the complete deregulation of housing development and the dismantling of the planning system. Another slightly more realistic possibility might be to update and modernise the planning system of the type in operation in the 1930s, giving owners the right to compensation for refusal of planning permission other than for health and safety reasons. For such critics, 'the return of development rights', that is to say making planning authorities liable for compensation as was the position before 1939, is the only feasible way of freeing large quantities of land for housing and would have the further advantages of ending 'nationalised and bureaucratic land use planning as we know it'.[20]

However, the context is different. Proposals for deregulation ignore the greater intensity of demands on the countryside, compared to the 1930s as well as the claims of environmental protection and the need to coordinate housing, transport and infrastructure investment. Such proposals ignore the arguments of Hayek and other laissez-faire theorists who accepted that the environment was an exception where the normal rules of the price mechanism and of private legal control are ineffective. They also ignore the experience of the Thatcher government of the early 1980s, a government that sought deregulation but stepped away once the environmental implications became apparent.

The question is therefore how best to define the principles whereby the planning system might be reformed and made more flexible so that it can take into account current housing shortages. How might this be done?

Promoting a culture change?   The response of government, at least since the election of New Labour in 1997, has been to promote a culture change in planning. In the words of the relevant policy statement,

> Too often the culture of planning is reactive and defensive. We want a culture which promotes planning as a positive tool: a culture which grasps the opportunities to improve the experience of planning, for those affected by its decisions .... (ODPM 2003c, para. 6)

The reactive and defensive character of local planning practice has also been noted by researchers (Carmona and Gallent 2004; Gallent and Tewdr-Jones 2007, 270–72) and by practitioners.[21] The implication is that planning should become more forward and outward looking and should itself set a local development agenda.

Advocating a culture change and realising a culture change are different to one another, however. Theories of reflexive law are relevant in this context. They have two components. First, they argue that the law and public administration take the form of 'autopoietic', or self-reproducing systems that are characterised by an increasingly remote and inward looking technical and professional language (Luhmann 1986; Teubner 1987; 1993). These are systems that grow automatically in complexity in response to external events and challenges. The growth of case law in town planning would provide an example. Second, they argue that the law becomes more detailed and wide-ranging through a 'juridification' whereby governments seek to manage social problems and control the work of local authorities.

The guidance in relation to planning for housing in England provides an example of juridification at work. The most recently published guidance is more market-oriented than its predecessor and it places new requirements on planning authorities. The guidance states, *inter alia*, that local planning should plan for a five years' supply of 'deliverable' housing land, further 'developable' land for years six to 10 and take note of trends in affordability across the housing market (DCLG 2006d). National government has, in other words, identified a specific problem, promoted a new policy in response and has specified rules and guidelines intended to ensure that local authorities follow suit. So, one might argue: why bother with culture change? The crucial question is whether the rules of regulation are appropriate to the task.

Theories of reflexive law are not wholly negative in their assessments of the potential for culture change. They draw attention to the importance of measures that might counter legal rigidities and in this context have called for a combination of 'negotiated regulation' rather than regulation by the book, the extension of consumer rights and increased external scrutiny (Teubner 1987, 33–40). Again, a parallel can be drawn with planning practice. Consultation and negotiation are routine in planning practice and their importance is widely recognised. Moreover, the role of community involvement has been recognised in England and Wales in the Planning and Compulsory Purchase Act, 2004 in a requirement for local authorities to prepare statements of their policy on the subject.

However, consultation and participation in planning operate in a political context where local authorities have to make decisions within fixed time limits and where the main pressure groups have opposing interests. Developers generally dislike consultation with residents because it tends to slow down the approval of projects and favours anti-development objections. Local amenity groups, whilst welcoming their own involvement in planning consultations, dislike negotiation with developers because the negotiation is in private and generally facilitates development.

The political context does not wholly determine the culture of planning. Professional planners also have a responsibility to clarify the basic choices. For example, in relation to planning for housing, Carmona et al. (2001, 35–46) have argued that good practice is simultaneously 'integrative', establishing joint working within and between organisations and 'realistic', recognising contexts and constraints and generating feasible objectives.

Such concepts of integrative and realistic practice have been implicit in planning theory since the 'great debate' of the 1940s. Planning provides a distinctive form of politics that brings together actors and requires them to consider the long-term in a single explicit framework. However, planning alone is unlikely to make much progress in the face of entrenched interest groups. In determining land allocations for housing, local disputes are unlikely to be resolved without a national policy lead.

Zoning, master plans and design   Modernising the planning system requires a consideration of the extent of discretion at the time of each single application for planning permission. The system was described as 'plan-led' in the immediate aftermath of the Planning and Compensation Act, 1991 Act. However, 'plan-led' is not the same as 'plan-determined'. The development plan or development framework is the first, but not the only material consideration in the determination of a planning application. Since, in any case, the development plans have proved slow to prepare and quick to date, other material considerations count for much.

Elsewhere, in most other economically advanced countries, in France and other continental European countries and in the US, the plan is the main or only consideration, together with legal guidance concerning the categories used in different zones contained within the plan. The owner retains a right to develop land so long as the proposal is in accordance with the provisions of the development plan (Davies 1992). Development control in such circumstances becomes an administrative and legal rather than a policy or political decision. In Britain, in contrast, the owner's right to develop land was largely removed in the financial provisions of the 1947 Town and Country Planning Act and only persists for mostly small-scale projects that lie within the definition of the 'general development order' and the 'use classes order'.

This non-discretionary approach has been called a 'binding plan' by the Barker Review (2004, 45). Otherwise, it has been generally called a zoning system in the sense that zoning means a classification of different areas as to the type of development that may suitably take place. It does not, however, mean 'mono-culture', single use zoning or, indeed, any particular pattern of urban development or design. Zoning is an exercise in classification and each class could take almost any form whatsoever. The zoning class could incorporate a combination of mixed land uses or of mixed house types of different prices and sizes as appropriate.

For Barker, the advantages of a zoning plan were to 'front-load' community consultation so that this occurred at the time of plan preparation only and not again at the time of applying for planning permission. A zoning plan has other advantages. It provides greater clarity for all concerned and minimises the extent of delay in the processing of decisions, though a large project and especially a large project would require a separate procedure. In addition, zoning provides a way of integrating environmental risks and health consideration directly into the planning system. Zoning plans consist of detailed maps that would, if their potential were realised, indicate areas subject to flooding, areas subject to risks from industrial processes, areas subject to excessively high levels of noise and so on.

On the other hand, a zoning plan is highly demanding of local authorities in their ability to prepare adequate planning documents and keep these up to date. The record of previous exercises in plan preparation is not encouraging. Local authorities have always encountered problems in the speedy preparation of development plans since the Town and Country Planning Act, 1947 (Kitchen 2002). The counter argument is that local authorities in other countries can manage to prepare zoning plans, so why not in Britain. The planning system in other countries provides examples of procedures for plan revision and exceptions in a way that would largely overcome any tardiness in plan preparation or rigidities in the overall framework.

The search persists of finding ways of speeding up the processing of planning applications and these have inevitably considered the simplification of planning controls. Local authorities have started to produce design-based master plans either to guide large-scale development projects or in a few cases to provide a sense of vision for a variety of different urban neighbourhoods. They have also tended to produce more development briefs to explain how general policies might be applied to a specific site. An otherwise unconnected announcement on the part of government in favour of 'urban codes' or 'community codes', that is to say explicit and detailed design guidelines, suggests a move towards a more formal, less discretionary framework of control.[22]

Master plans, development briefs and design codes provide the most practical way of giving developers more guidance and of ensuring more consistency in the treatment of planning applications. So long as these various devices contain sufficient relevant detail, they also provide a means of improving design quality in new housing (CABE 2007b, 52). However, it remains, unclear whether in practice master plans and development briefs deliver their potential advantages. Master plans and other planning documents can easily become general, illustrative exercises whose contents can be interpreted in various ways. Varying or conflicting statements between development briefs, master plans and other planning documents covering the same area are another potential source of confusion. The application of master plans, development briefs and design codes still depends, moreover on the allocation of development sites at a more strategic level.

Reforming the Financial Aspects of Planning

The rigidities of planning practice involve a double process. On one hand, legal requirements act on the relationship between local planning authorities and developers, necessitating that planning authorities make decisions in accordance with specified procedures and after a range of consultations. At the same time, legal regulation also acts on and restricts the ability of public agencies to intervene directly in the property market through such measures as compulsory purchase and the threat of compensation.

Some discretion remains. A local authority can make a legally binding agreement with a developer to provide services and funds in exchange for the granting of planning permission. This is the 'planning agreement' or 'section 106 agreement' as it is called after the relevant section of the town and country planning legislation for England and Wales. However, as will be explained, pressures exist for greater standardisation and greater accountability in the use of planning agreements.

Compulsory purchase   The planning system, as it operates in Britain, tends to encourage land speculation. The planning system simultaneously restricts development whilst identifying specific parcels of land as appropriate for development. The use of public agencies to bring forward development sites would help prevent land speculation. In principle, powers exist for the purpose. In practice, local authorities use these powers infrequently. The main reasons were identified by the Urban Task Force (UTC 1999, 228) as a 'lack of resources in advance of redevelopment', 'the inherent bureaucracy of the process, uncertainty over powers, a loss of skills and the inadequacy of compensation provisions', these latter being based on inflated valuations for sites in proposed redevelopment areas.

Lack of resources and the problems of compensation go together. In the context of the movement for central planning, the Town and Country Planning

Act, 1947 enabled local authorities to acquire sites at below market values. Those provisions were lost during the years of Conservative rule in the 1950s.

Admittedly, the provisions of the New Towns Act, 1946 have remained in force. These specify that a Development Corporation acquires land at existing use values rather than their development potential value. The provisions have largely fallen into disuse and are probably inoperable. The effect of the Human Rights Act, 1998 and of previous European human rights declarations is that public action, including compulsory purchase should not normally leave a property owner any worse off in comparison to a situation where there is no compulsory purchase. Therefore, if the value of a site is raised by its development potential, this potential has to be considered in the valuation process, irrespective of the actual land use at the time. Values are no longer deemed to be created by the 'community', understood in this context as the planning system, as was the argument of the Uthwatt Report (Ministry of Works 1942).

In addition, exactly because values are created by development potential or development trends, rather than the 'community' it would be inappropriate to allow policy aims and criteria to influence the level of compensation. The Urban Task Force (UTC 1999, 231) noted: 'We have been advised that it is not legally possible to have separate compensation regimes for different areas, e.g. in designated Urban Priority Areas. Neither is it possible to distinguish between property speculators/absentee landlords and bona fide property owners'.

Compensation for compulsory purchase provides an example where legal regulation has not merely changed the details of policy and made policy more bureaucratic. It has restricted the range of policy options.

Even so, compulsory purchase at market prices is still a potentially useful device to bring land into development. Compulsory purchase avoids the situation where owners delay selling expecting that inflation in land prices will bring them even greater rewards in the future. In addition and most importantly, it provides a means of promoting the development of sites in fragmented ownership or sites where landowners refuse to sell.

Planning agreements   Purchase at existing use values apart, there are other ways of limiting the costs of public agencies in urban development and therefore of making savings that could be used to promote affordable housing. Much of the potential value of development sites depends on the provision of public services and infrastructure, provided at public expense. If developers are asked to pay for all or a proportion of the cost of this infrastructure and if they know, in advance before purchasing the site, what they have to pay, they will offer lower prices to the land owner and the burden of payment will fall on the landowner rather than either the developer or consumer (Goodchild and Henneberry 1994).

Planning agreements are the usual way that developers contribute to the costs of public agencies. They do not stop at physical infrastructure, however. Planning agreements have provided a means of generating local community amenities and benefits, including local employment in the case of industrial and commercial projects. In this latter role, they help contribute to neighbourhood regeneration. In addition, in relation to planning for housing, planning agreements have acquired a particular role in promoting social balance and social mix, as is recognised by the relevant professions (CIoH/RTPI 2003) and successive governments in England (DETR 1998) and in addition by the Scottish Executive.[23] In the financial year 2004/05, for example, about half of completed social housing in England was on sites that involved Section 106 agreements (Whitehead 2007, 36).

Planning agreements are a distinctively British device, with few, if any equivalents in most other countries (Whitehead 2007). The planning systems in other countries, for example France and the US, allow local authorities to charge a developer, but the form of the charge is subject to closer legal constraints and is generally concerned only with infrastructure. In the US, the contributions of developers depend on whether a planning agency can demonstrate a rational nexus between the proposal and its effects on public expenditure. In France, the contributions are defined by statute and are silent on the provision of social housing (Goodchild and Henneberry 1994).

The absence of a written constitution in Britain and the consequent absence of constitutional guarantees in favour of private property have given governments greater discretion in determining the detailed logic of planning control. Even in Britain, however, the legality of planning agreements to provide affordable housing was unclear until the 1980s. The legality was only resolved through a ministerial announcement in favour of a small-scale 'exception policy' in rural areas in 1989 and subsequent policy statements in the early 1990s (Crook and Whitehead 2002; Goodchild 1992).

The advantages of planning agreements in securing affordable housing have to be set against numerous limitations and criticisms. Whether used to provide affordable housing or some other community benefit, the scale of benefit is invariably limited by what developers and landowners are able and willing to pay. The leverage of private funds for public uses works best in an inflationary property market, such as has existed in most of southern England from the late 1990s onwards. Even in such circumstances, however, owners may keep land off the market believing that policies will change in the future (Whitehead 2007, 38). For example, in 2003 in evidence to the Barker Review, 'London First', an agency concerned with the promotion of economic development, commented that 'onerous and inconsistent Section 106 obligations' had acted 'as a disincentive for bringing housing sites forward'.[24]

The operation of planning agreements has, moreover, numerous other weaknesses, for example:

- The negotiation and preparation of planning agreements cause uncertainties and delays and takes place in secret, without public involvement (Goodchild et al. 1996a, 165).
- During negotiation, too much emphasis is given to the ability of the developers to pay, rather than to the environmental impact of the proposal.
- The outcome depends too heavily on the bargaining skills of the parties.
- Where the local planning authority is also the land owner, it has a financial interest in the outcome and may reduce the level of requirements to ensure that the site can be easily sold.

The Nolan Committee, established to review the ethical standards of local government, offers perhaps the most damning criticism. The Committee found that more public concern was expressed about the planning system than of any other aspect of local government: Planning obligations were 'the most intractable aspect of the planning system with which we have had to deal (and) have a tremendous impact on public confidence' (HMG 1997, paras 302, 303).

In response, some local authorities have started to specify a tariff of standardised infrastructure charge on a per dwelling basis and have, in addition, specified uniform levels of provision for affordable housing. Tariff-based charges are likely to become more common in the future, given a government announcement in their favour in October 2007 (*Planning* 12 October 2007). Section 106 agreements have evolved in the direction of a formal system of charges, but are still subject to extensive local discretion. Fundamental reform has been blocked by an alliance between developers and local authorities. Developers wish to retain flexibility so that they can develop sites where planning permission would otherwise be refused. They also fear that any new system will lead to higher charges, including charges on schemes that would otherwise have escaped a charge. Conversely, local authorities wish to retain flexibility to deal with exceptions and to maximise their negotiating power with developers.

Whatever the outcome, the case still remains for a clearer statutory framework. The Nolan Committee considered that, irrespective of the quality of circulars and other administrative guidelines, there was 'no reason to suppose' that problems with the system of planning agreements would not happen again in the future. In the words of the report, 'The result is that planning permissions will continue to be 'bought and sold''. 'It appears that the pressures on the ground, particularly the restrictions on the capital expenditures of local authorities are too strong to be overcome by guidance alone' (HMG 1997, paras 310–11).

Land taxes and land pooling   Other revenue raising measures have also been proposed. In particular, the Barker Review (2004, 7–8) suggested the revived introduction of a development land tax, levied at the time of the granting of permission and based on a proportion of land value. For a time, such a proposal was under active consideration in England and Wales under the title of a 'Planning Gain Supplement' (HM Treasury 2005). However, the same government announcement that endorsed tariffs within the existing system of planning agreements also dropped the Planning Gain Supplement.

A development land tax, like an infrastructure charge, generates funds for the public purse. From an economic viewpoint, a development land tax is, in principle and once established, less disruptive than a development charge, as the payment is more likely to be proportional to what the landowner can afford. The main issue is to work out an appropriate charge that would not hinder development and to avoid uncertainties before its introduction.

From a planning viewpoint, in contrast, a development land tax has disadvantages. The revenue of the tax is likely to vary independently of infrastructure costs. Moreover, the proposed development land tax is unlikely to lead to the abolition of the existing system of planning agreements, merely to a limitation in their use. The development land tax would deal with 'off-site' infrastructure costs as opposed to planning agreements whose application would be confined to site-specific requirements. The distinction between off-site and site-specific considerations is not always easy to make. More significantly, planning agreements would probably continue to promote community benefits, including the provision of affordable housing. Therefore, the introduction of a development land tax or planning gain supplement would not have simplified the current system.

The development of complex projects requires some mechanism that links proposals for an area to a combination of compulsory land purchase, voluntary land purchase, public investment and a schedule of charges indicating the contribution of developers. Syms (2002) describes such a combined exercise as one of land pooling because it involves all the landowners pooling their interests to their mutual benefit and for the benefit of the community. Goodchild et al. (1996a) call this a 'coordinated development area', largely on the basis of the *Zone d'Aménagement Concerté* in France. The *ZAC* offers a combined means of first, raising funds for infrastructure from private and public sector developers, of secondly realigning property boundaries, with compensation for compulsory purchase and thirdly of urban design and the coordination of different land uses and buildings. Other European countries such as the Netherlands and Germany have similar procedures (Golland and Oxley 2004)

Such extensive coordination is possible in Britain, so long as the local authorities are prepared to use their powers of compulsory purchase and so long as, in addition, the prospect of financial gain is sufficient to interest developers. The *ZAC* involves a contract between interested parties much as is the procedure for planning agreements in Britain. However, in Britain the various parties have to make up their procedures as they go along and they do this in a way that currently has few safeguards in relation to public accountability. The liberal and neoliberal case for legal regulation in urban development, as stated from the time of Hayek (1944) onwards, is as a means of avoiding uncertainty and delays, whilst also avoiding long-term problems that might arise from disputes. In this context, planning agreements provide an example where a more posituve and structure approach is desirable.

Housing Quality and the Home

The quality in new housing invariably goes together with discussions of quantity. However, quality is more elusive and difficult to measure. In principle, the definition of quality is simple enough. Quality as conceived in business management is about whether goods and services meet the expectations and needs of consumers. The British Standards Institute (BSI), for example, defines quality as 'all those features of a product (or service) which are required by the customer'.[25] The International Organisation for Standardisation likewise gives a list of principles for good quality management in business, with 'customer focus' as the first principle.[26]

Quality in business is a dynamic concept, linked to marketing, management and the consumer. In contrast, the quality of new housing is a static concept, linked to the attributes of an object. It is also characterised by potential divisions between users, the ultimate consumers, producers and the professional groups such as architects, surveyors and building specialists that are involved in the development process.

Definitions of Housing Quality

Various classifications of housing quality are available; for example:

- Goodchild (1997, 32–59) suggests a broad distinction between the 'house as a system', covering such factors as (1) flexibility in use (2) economy in use and (3) access and the 'house as home' covering such factors as (4) privacy and the control of interaction (5) security and (6) appearance and ambience;
- the architectural consultants DEGW have attempted to provide a formal framework of 'Housing Quality Indicators' based on ten factors as follows (1) location (2) site: visual impact, layout (3) open space (4) routes and movement (5) unit size (6) unit layout and landscaping (7) unit noise control, light quality, services (8) accessibility within the unit (9) energy, green, and sustainable issues and (10) performance in use (ODPM 2000);
- finally, architectural and producer groups have established a housing quality benchmark called *Building for Life* comprising four main elements, 'character', 'roads, parking and pedestrianisation', 'design and construction' and 'environment and community'.[27] *Building for Life* was endorsed by the former Office of the Deputy Prime Minister in 2003 and has been used widely thereafter, in England, in undertaking surveys of completed schemes, in awarding prizes and in assessing planning applications.

The existence of different classifications summarises the problem. There is no single overarching definition and therefore no possibility of measuring quality on a consistent, objective basis. Moreover, measurements of some quality criteria, notably those concerned with the external environment remain subject to different professional perceptions and are also likely to vary according to the context. For example, *Building for Life*, the benchmarking system, avoids any reference to floor space standards or car parking standards or any specific model of the external layout.

In any case, the very process of classifying quality criteria is an over-simplification. From the perspective of a consumer, the choice of one home rather than another and the subsequent evaluation of that home involves a bundle of different attributes that are often difficult to disentangle from one another. It is the totality of all the different features that count. Moreover, the consumers' definitions do not necessarily correspond to those undertaken from a relatively narrow building or architectural viewpoint. For example, definitions of housing quality generally cover issues relating to safety, durability and environmental impact. These seldom arise as a significant issue in surveys of consumers' satisfaction in Britain.

Consumer expectations are, in any case, relative rather than absolute and change over time. They are relative partly because consumers generally judge housing in terms of their previous experience and what is available in any locality. They are also relative owing to the significance of affordability and economic conditions. Cost and price are aspects of quality for the consumer. Residential surveyors, responsible for organising the buying and selling process, would argue that cost and price are, together, by far the most important factor influencing consumers, well ahead of location and even more so ahead of design (Goodchild 2005). Yet cost and price do not appear on most quality classifications.

Professional designers sometimes argue that good design is not a function of cost or price and that good design can be found at all price ranges, in social housing as well as in private housing. They would argue in particular that considerations of good layout, the scale of a building and its external appearance are independent of cost variations in development. Examples of good design may well exist at all price ranges. However, the surveys of (CABE 2007b, 16) also show that, other than for social housing schemes 'poorer schemes tended to be found in less affluent areas, either resulting from the lower land values, projected sale values or the attitudes of planners'. Some aspects of good design, for example, the use of non-standard house types, the quality of surface materials and the quality of landscaping are directly related to costs. In addition, quality in the external layout is indirectly related to cost, as it is related to the amount of time and attention spent in the design process. Time is money for a commercial enterprise.

A further complication is that the buyers of new property are probably not typical of housing consumers in general. The surveys of the New Homes Marketing Board suggest that these are people who are prepared to pay a premium for a never previously occupied home, with a 'clean canvas' and no need for decoration, do-it-yourself work or repairs.[28] Most people would prefer not to buy new.[29]

For the 'Sustainable Communities' policy plan, the apparent dislike of new housing suggests that a large majority of the population 'do not consider that current housing developments were well designed' (ODPM 2003b, 13). However, much depends on what is meant by 'quality'. The apparent popularity of most second-hand properties, for example twentieth-century semis, is not necessarily linked to their architectural character or urban design qualities. Another possible explanation is that older properties generally offer better value for money in terms of floor space and the provision of a garden.

Housing Market Types

In the past, the assessment of housing quality could look to national enquiries into housing standards and housing design. *Homes for Today and Tomorrow* otherwise known as the Parker Morris Report (MHLG 1961) and *Homes for the Future* (RIBA/IoH 1983) prepared jointly by senior members of the architectural and housing management professions provide examples. Both documents were aimed mainly at what is now called the social housing sector. *Homes for Today and Tomorrow* was also crudely functionalist in the way that it omitted issues relating to the subjective experience of the home and the external environment.

At the same time, the reports remain relevant in identifying relevant issues and factors. The Parker Morris report, in particular, suggests two sets of considerations:

- first, the emergence of 'new patterns of living', as the report put it, including new domestic technologies that influenced demands made on floor space and equipment within the home; and, in addition,
- the different requirement of different demographic groups, notably 'homes for the families with children', 'homes for persons living alone' and homes for elderly people.

Of these two sets of consideration, the latter, the distinction between different demographic groups provides the basis for distinctions in the type of new housing. An immediate point of clarification is nevertheless necessary. Consumers buy and rent houses as individuals rather than as members of a demographic group. Younger consumers may look to the future and, if they buy, they may search out the type of housing they would occupy as part of a family with children. Older households often stay in the family home or look for somewhere similar to the type of home where they have always lived. The distinction between one type of housing market and another is often blurred. Indeed, the distinctions sometimes seem to have become more blurred over time. Growing diversity means, for example, that housing developers sometimes say that it has become increasingly difficult to say what types of people will buy into a particular scheme (*Housebuilder* October 2001).

General and Family Housing

As a result, the first and largest market category is best described as 'general and family housing' rather than as a single specialised market. This is a market category exemplified by the usual market strategies of the larger volume house builders. The web site of George Wimpey, the biggest volume builder of all, may be taken as typical. It attempts to demonstrate the existence of a variety of properties in different parts of the country and the wide appeal of these properties to different types of consumer. It offers, in addition, a practical guide for homebuyers, with a search engine to find a suitable house and site, information about finance, styling choices and moving as well as more 'inspirational' articles intended to show just how consumers could personalise the home to their own tastes.[30]

In the past, much of the advertising material of the volume house builders has linked the purchase of a home to pictures of a stereotyped nuclear family comprising a husband, wife, children and a dog or cat. Children still figure prominently in websites. However, marketing analysts are aware that most of today's purchasers do not fit the nuclear family category. As a result, advertising images currently include many individuals and couples in their 20s. They also contain more black and brown faces. The imagined purchasers are invariably well dressed and stylish, however. Landlords are an additional target audience and one that has only emerged in the past ten years. The promotional material of Barratt Homes, for example, has included a supporting testimony from a buy-to-let purchaser.[31]

The style of the home is itself a marketing device. Private house builders have always sought to make their homes attractive to as wide a clientele as possible and this means that they present their homes in the most favourable way possible. They continue to do so. In doing this, moreover, they have also sought to juggle competing requirements and competing interpretations of beauty. One market survey suggests, for example, that developers have sought to juggle the twin concerns of 'elegance', often expressed in the development of higher density town houses and 'individuality', generally expressed in a search for detailed house-by-house variations in style.[32] Others have suggested that developers respond to a popular ideal that combines the comfort and convenience of modern technologies with a traditional feel and appearance (Forty and Moss 1980; Morley 2005).

House builders generally promote individual homes, rather than communities. The typical advertising image is that of the home itself or, in the case of flatted property, a block. The home is presented in the abstract without a location context, often with the addition of greenery to mask adjoining buildings.

This emphasis on the home rather than the estate or community is linked to a reliance of standardised house types, that is to say a standardised floor plan with some variation in the use of external finishes. Standardisation provides a focus for market research and simplifies subsequent advertising campaigns. Standardisation has, moreover, other advantages. Because the standard types are marketed at a predetermined price level, their use simplifies the task of assessing the economic viability of a project in advance and of determining the most efficient arrangement in density and value to suit the site and the market. George Wimpey, for example, undertakes an annual review of house types to promote efficiency in design and construction (Annual Report and Accounts 2002).

Standardisation also reduces construction costs through economies of scale in the ordering of materials and in ensuring greater familiarity and predictability amongst contractors. The larger is the output of a house building company, the greater is the potential economies of scale. As a result, standardisation is more common amongst the larger volume house builder and is almost universal for companies building more than 2,000 dwellings (Nicol and Hooper 1999). The only alternative is for house builders to prepare bespoke designs for each site, using either in-house or external architects and this method is generally reserved for smaller, more exclusive schemes.

In any case, there is generally little scope for variation in the design of a typical small home of four bedrooms or less. A small- or medium-sized terrace, or a small semi- or detached dwelling is likely to comprise a box with a pitched roof, for the simple reason that this is the least expensive means of sheltering household activities.

Conventionally designed privately developed estates, based on the repetition of family houses, have long been widely criticised by architects and planners for their standardised, monotonous appearance, a lack of sense of place. (See, for example, Carmona 2001, 91–2.) Estates built since 2000 are arguably less standardised and monotonous than those built in the 1980s and 1990s. Developers have moved away from greenfield sites to brownfield sites that require bespoke design solutions. In addition, the variety of different house types in a single estate has also tended to increase. The surveys of the New Homes Marketing Board suggest, for example, that consumers praise the variety of house types in a single estate.[33]

However, the attitude of professional designers and above all of the architectural establishment remains vehemently critical. CABE, for example, has surveyed and ranked privately developed estates using the *Building for Life* benchmark. The report of survey (CABE 2007b, 4) states that across England 'fewer than one in five schemes could be classed as 'good' or 'very good'. In addition, 'the quality of a substantial minority of developments – 29 per cent – is so low that they simply should not have been given planning consent'.

Such negative comments are overstated. They are based on a particular professional interpretation of quality and do not look, for example, at the extent of consumer demand. They are only the latest in a long history of attacks on private house building, especially suburban house building, dating back at least to the 1930s.

At the same time, the comments raise a question whether *Building for Life* or possibly some other benchmark should be used, as CABE recommends, in planning control. Some local authorities already do so. Most likely, the effect is exactly as intended. Benchmarking prevents the poorest quality schemes. The very process of discussing a proposal against benchmarking criteria requires the use of more time and effort in finding design solutions. However, the use of quality benchmarks does not do away with the use of subjective judgments in quality assessment and does not speed up the decision-making process.

Retirement and sheltered housing   In relation to housing for older people, a review of good practice, prepared jointly by the Planning Officers Society, representing local planning practitioners and the Retirement Housing Groups, representing the house building industry, suggest three main categories as follows (POS-RHG 2003):

- housing designed for the early retired and comprising property of a type that would, most likely, appeal to people of any age;
- sheltered housing, of the type initially developed by local authorities and housing associations in the 1970s, and now extended to private developers and that offers residents a package of estate management services, emergency services, communal facilities and a warden; and finally
- sheltered housing for 'older' elderly people, with a higher degree of care.

A further type of retirement housing, the retirement village, is distinguished by its large scale. It may encompass any combination of the previous three, together with a wide variety of leisure facilities.[34]

The second and third categories, that of sheltered housing with varied degrees of support, is the focus of attention of the specialist house builders. Sheltered housing is generally sold on long leasehold, with service charges payable to cover additional management and other costs. The typical scheme consists of as many as 50 flats, located near to a town centre, with enhanced security and safety, communal facilities such as gardens, a central lounge, a laundry service, a resident or day manager and 24-hour emergency call facilities. Given a typical edge of town centre location, the density is usually about 50 dwellings per hectare, significantly higher than has been usual of typical suburban estates.[35]

Most elderly people prefer to stay for as long as possible in their existing home. (See Tinker 1984, 59, 118.) They generally do not trade down to a smaller home once the family have left and many would, in any case, dislike the institutional feel associated with sheltered accommodation. Growing numbers of affluent elderly owner-occupiers suggest, nevertheless, that private retirement homes will remain a growth area for the future. The growth of private retirement homes is, moreover, likely to occur independently of any trend in social housing where isolated or old-fashioned sheltered housing blocks have sometimes proved difficult to let.

McCarthy and Stone has been the best known and largest private developer of retirement homes, claiming to build 75 per cent of all private sheltered housing units in the past few years.[36] The company's advertising material stresses customer care, quality and the high level of satisfaction amongst purchasers, as shown by independent research.[37] Similar high levels of satisfaction have also been reported in social housing, despite the existence of some problem schemes (Housing Corporation 2003, 16).

A sheltered housing scheme, whether private or public, is generally defined by the availability of additional personal care – for example the availability of warden support. For residents and potential purchasers, however, the attraction of a sheltered scheme depends as much on its environment and its management – for example, on the standard of security measures, on the ease of access to urban facilities and on the absence of responsibility for maintenance and gardening (Heywood et al. 2002, 82). Sheltered housing appeals to those who no longer find their old home suitable, for example owing to its design or location or possession of a large garden and who, in addition, welcome the prospect of living amongst other elderly people in similar circumstances.[38]

It is sometimes suggested that the market for retirement homes is easily overlooked in planning policy, in favour of a concentration on the needs and demands of economically active households (DH-ODPM 2003; POS-RHG 2003, 20). For example, the developers of retirement homes cannot easily provide a proportion of affordable housing in their schemes.[39] Instead, the development of private retirement homes meets the needs of younger households indirectly, through releasing relatively under-occupied family homes for sale. With the exception of large-scale retirement villages, moreover, retirement homes do not pose particular difficulties in relation to land use or siting. The most suitable sites are relatively flat, close to local shops, community facilities and public transport (ibid., 2). In this context, the development of retirement homes provides a means of using vacant and underused sites close to smaller town and suburban centres and in older, lower density suburbs.

City centre housing   A further and final major type of specialised housing market is that for single adults and childless couples and is most clearly expressed in the development of city centre and inner city flats, with communal leisure facilities in the most up-market projects. Such flats do not necessarily comprise an ultimate consumer aspiration, though examples exist of luxury, penthouse flats. They are typically characterised by high levels of household turnover. And this high turnover is linked to the demographic characteristics of the occupiers. Other than in London, there has been no apparent tendency towards the traditional pattern in continental Europe where families live in flats and see this as perfectly acceptable accommodation. City centre and inner city flats are developed for buy to let landlords as well as for home owners and sometimes, in addition, for the larger housing associations that undertake market renting, that is to say commercially-financed projects let at market rents. Developers may sell *en bloc* to a housing association or the association may itself undertake the development.

Market research undertaken for the Joseph Rowntree Foundation provides the best general picture of the pattern of demand at the start of what soon became the city centre housing boom (Oakes and McKee 1997). The study was undertaken in Leeds at a time when the market for city centre flats was still untested. It was based on a series of focus group discussions with middle-income working single men and women and young childless couples. The study found a changed and more favourable attitude to private renting and it noted 'a clear division between those with a propensity to enjoy the 'buzz' and social anonymity of social life and those to whom the suburbs and rural areas remained the preferred option. The main advantages of city centre living were seen as 'less time wasted in travelling, the ability to get around easily without driving, freedom to lead a more cosmopolitan social life and social and leisure opportunities' (ibid., 4).

A later series of focus group meetings, undertaken by Allen and Blandy 2004), suggests that demand comprises two groups: '(a) young people seeking a short 'experience' of city centre life and (b) 'authentic' city centre dwellers that stay long-term'. All this relates mostly to city centre schemes developed in large regional centres in the Midlands and North of England. Similar schemes built on the south coast of England also attract the purchasers of second homes, interested in the leisure pursuits and ambience of a seaside location. Elsewhere, in smaller towns and cities, city centre living has fewer attractions.

The development of city centre housing was at first almost universally welcomed. Substantial city centre residential populations and new residential and mixed-use neighbourhoods emerged almost from nothing. The diversity of the housing stock increased and vacant sites were put to good use. In the Midlands and the North of England, in particular, the development of city centre flats facilitated local authority efforts in marketing and rebranding. The development of attractive, 'luxury' city centre flats became a symbol of a revitalised city, with a new cultural image.

Subsequent evaluations have proved less enthusiastic. Other than in London, the market became increasingly driven by the hope of high rental returns and capital growth. Once developers found that the market existed, they were able to use these high rental expectations to build on a scale that failed to reflect any detailed or realistic market research. The market grew too far, too quickly, with relatively high rents in comparison to those available in older property in the inner city. The design and location of some schemes has also been open to criticism. Once developers thought, wrongly, that a market was guaranteed, they pushed up density to ever higher levels and used less attractive inner city sites.

As a result, and again other than in London, anecdotal reports suggest increasing over-provision of city centre flats, with increased vacancies and examples of falling property values. In Leeds city centre, in particular, the *Estates Gazette* (8 December 2007) the main weekly journal for property investment, has reported that 1,000 of the 6,000 units built in the previous five years were empty in December 2007 and posed a series of difficult management issues. The same edition of the *Estates Gazette* also talked of a breakdown in social cohesion in city centre flats, as respectable tenants left the most unpopular blocks. The market for city centre flats in Leeds and other regional centres may recover in a few years time, depending on trends in demand. However, at the moment, the outlook is uncertain.

The uncertainties associated with city centre flats has another implication. The review of house building delivery undertaken by Calcutt (2007, 25) has reported that house builders have started to examine the possibility of retaining (or selling to a third party) an investment interest in completed schemes. 'In effect,' in the words of the review, 'the developer trades a proportion of the up-front development profit for the opportunity of long-term revenues plus future capital growth'.

The business model used in retirement flats already follows this investment model. However, it would be new for most housing developers who typically use a trader model of development in which they bring a scheme to completion for sale. City centre flats would have been a prime target market for the investment model, owing to the prevalence of rented property. Current uncertainties with this type of market will have reduced average investment values and increased scepticism amongst lenders about whether the model might work.

Comfort, Functionality and Beyond

Whatever the target housing market, the design of the home has to cope with the practicalities of living. The home has to provide an adequate range of facilities for cooking, for personal hygiene and for typical household activities, as, of course, has been a recurrent theme in the history of housing design, the Parker Morris report included. It should, moreover, in doing this, be adaptable to new technologies and to a range of different lifestyles, including the needs of people as they age.

Floor space Whether a home is able to accommodate all its current requirements is the first question and one that immediately raises questions of the adequacy of floor space. General information on trends in floor space is available from the English House Condition Survey. In 2001, according to the survey, the average size of a post-1980 home was 83m², compared to 88m² for those built before 1980 (ODPM 2003a, 16). Admittedly, the available floor space per person in the home has increased, from 38m² in 1991, to 43m² in 1996 to 44m² in 2001 (ibid., 29). However, this increase in the floor space available per person is caused by a decline in average household size, mostly expressed by an increasing number of single person households.

Otherwise, the last detailed survey of housing floor space standards in the private and social housing was undertaken in the early 1990s by Karn and Sheridan (1994). Karn and Sheridan's analysis compared housing association schemes and privately developed schemes in the less expensive and moderately expensive price range. The average size of housing association family homes was slightly smaller on average than that of privately developed homes. A five bedspace housing association house (comprising two double bedrooms, plus one single bedroom) was 82.8 m², while the equivalent for the private sector 85.2m². The average size of family homes, whether developed by housing associations or private developers, was hardly different or even smaller than family houses built throughout twentieth century, from the time of the Tudor Walters report (1919) onwards. In this context, complaints about inadequate size have been a persistent theme in recent consumer surveys. A review of survey evidence, undertaken for CABE (2005c, 21) notes that: 'The criticism about lack of space was expressed by all groups of home buyers with singles just as vociferous as families.'

The small size of new homes has been of sufficient concern for the Town and Country Planning Association (2000, 14) to urge the 'reintroduction', for all new houses, of minimum space standards along the lines of the Parker-Morris standards of the 1960s. Such a proposal forgets that Parker Morris standards did not cover privately developed dwellings. More significantly, it misunderstands the logic of floor space standards. Either, as in the case of the Parker Morris standards, these relate the overall floor space and storage space to the type of accommodation and so permit small dwellings if intended for single people or couples. Or, as is common in continental Europe, the floor space standards comprise controls on the size of habitable rooms rather than controls on overall dwelling sizes. Or, as was the case in Scotland before the abolition of the relevant legislation in 1987, the regulations relate room size and storage space to the number of habitable rooms in a dwelling (Wren et al. 2001).

Whatever the details, floor space controls do not impose overall minimum floor space requirements, except in the case of one bedroom or one person houses that are likely to be relatively small in any case. Conversely, as happened in Scotland after 1987, the deregulation of floor space standards does not necessarily lead to a reduction in the dwelling size. Deregulation in Scotland led, instead, to a redistribution of floor space in different rooms within an overall shell that remained much the same as before. Storage space and the floor area of the third or 'spare' bedroom were reduced in favour of other rooms (Wren et al. 2001).

An alternative to regulation is the provision of better consumer information. Karn and Sheridan (1994), Rudlin and Falk (1995) and Wren et al. (2001) have all suggested floor area labelling as an alternative way forward, the assumption being that more consumer information will encourage a demand for more spacious housing. Karn and Sheridan (1994, 96) add that floor plans should be drawn to scale, with full sized furniture marked on them. Floor area labelling would do nothing to resolve the financial constraints on developers, but it might lead to greater consumer awareness and higher expectations of what is acceptable.

For social housing, the simple solution would be to raise floor space standards, especially in family dwellings. For example, *Homes for the Future* (RIBA/IoH 1983, 15) argued, in a way that recalled the recommendations of Tudor Walters in 1919, for 'two separate living rooms where practical'. It is also likely that the incorporation of higher floor space standards in social housing would encourage private developers to follow suit, at least at the lower end of the market.

Disabled persons' standards   Floor area regulation overlaps the regulation of design for the needs of wheelchair users and other disabled people. Larger homes with more generously sized rooms and hallways are easier to use by people in wheelchairs. They are also more easily adapted to accommodate any additional equipment that disabled people might need. Conversely regulations intended to facilitate wheelchair access or use have consequences for the minimum circulation and room dimensions permitted in a home.

Since 1999 Part M of the Building Regulations for England and Wales has required that 'reasonable provision shall be made for disabled people to gain access to and to use the building' (DETR 1999). This has involved the provision of ramp access to the front door, with some exceptions on difficult sites and has required, in addition, the provision of a downstairs toilet. The revised regulations do not make the home liveable by disabled people, however. For example, the minimum provision for the downstairs toilet is not in accordance with the standards necessary for unaided use by a wheelchair user. The regulations do not include, moreover, a requirement for a lift in blocks of multi-storey flats. They have also not been fully implemented. A study of the implementation of Part M, undertaken by Imrie (2003, 64–5) suggests that a tendency towards higher densities has caused difficulties in the design of level and/or ramped access and that a combination of building regulation staff shortages and a desire to avoid enforcement action, could lead to an acceptance of 'minor transgressions'.

There is another concept of design for disabled person's housing. Since 1997, Habinteg Housing Association and the Joseph Rowntree Foundation have jointly promoted the concept of a *Lifetime Home*, that is to say a home that the occupants can adapt to different stages of their life cycle, including the needs of disability. Amongst its features, the *Lifetime Home* standard specifies the minimum dimensions of the kitchen, bathroom and toilet, together with the space for a potential through-the-floor lift from the entrance level to the first floor.[40]

However, few private developers have willingly adopted the *Lifetime Homes* standard. Most target their product on young adults and families, dislike the additional costs and design rigidities associated with disabled persons' standards and see few advantages in their marketing strategies. Developers assume that consumers will move as their life cycle needs change and that therefore the provision of additional features in mainstream housing is unnecessary (Hooper and Nicol, 2000, 308; Imrie 2003).

Local authorities do not always accept such arguments. An increasing number requires developers to include a specific proportion of *Lifetime Home* standard dwellings. The argument is partly that elderly people move less frequently and as they age they become less and less likely to move (Heywood et al. 2002, 78). A further consideration is that the ageing of the population is on such a scale that rehousing in specialist accommodation is impractical.

However, the *Lifetime Homes* standard is itself limited in scope,. Small terraces and flats are, for example, less adaptable than detached or semi-detached houses. Flats without lifts may be completely unusable for disabled persons. Yet the promotion of easily adaptable detached and semi-detached houses or the inclusion of lifts in multi-storey blocks is outside the standard.

Adaptability also has a general meaning of flexibility in use and has encouraged experiments in designing homes with moveable partition walls. (See, for example, Rudlin and Falk, 1995, 48) As a means of adapting homes to the needs of disabled people, moveable partition walls make sense. A specialist developer of retirement homes, 'Pegasus', has reported, for example, the use of removable wall panels that enable the creation of an additional bedroom for a carer.[41] Otherwise, moveable walls have numerous limitations. For smaller houses and flats, including virtually all the homes built in the past ten years by social housing agencies, a lack of floor space is the main constraint on flexibility of use than a lack of moveable partition walls. Even for larger homes, say over 100m², the advantages of movable walls are marginal. Moveable walls cause complications in heating systems, the position of electrical sockets and in electrical wiring. They also imply a high level of flexibility, perhaps an impossibly high level of flexibility in furniture arrangements.

Home automation   In future-oriented accounts of housing design, electrical systems figure prominently. It is possible to link all the electrical systems (central heating, lights, fire and other security alarms) and specific devices such as television sets, cookers and fridges together in an overall control system, with remote control also being possible. This is the realm of the 'smart home', the 'intelligent home' and more generally of 'home automation' whose advocates claim significant advantages in the ease and safety of running services and equipment and, in addition, significant advantages in enabling disabled people to live at home independently.[41] Examples, already under development, include equipment to monitor old people to identify when they get into difficulty and to ensure, in addition, that potentially dangerous devices are turned off when not needed.[42]

Home automation is generally at the experimental stage and has, as yet, a shaky consumer rationale. One review in the journal *Building* (29 August 2002) commented that 'home technology is proceeding at a snail's pace', partly because of its complexity and partly because, for able-bodied people, many of the cited advantages look unnecessary. The most commonly claimed advantages are about the ability of an individual to switch on the central heating before returning home, forgetting of course that a time-controlled switch does this already or about checking the status of a burglar alarm while on holiday. To go further, to ease the running of the home and to make it safer requires the installation and linking together of a variety of other devices of varied expense, reliability and complexity, for example smoke detectors, integrated security systems, mechanised doors, mechanised windows and curtains and, for disabled people, adjustable height tables and stair lifts. In any case, the very people for whom the technology is considered the most suitable, the elderly and the disabled, are the most suspicious of new technology and the most concerned about failure and technical complexities that they do not fully understand (Pragnell et al. 2000). As a result, the incorporation of home automationa equipment is unlikely to raise property values and prices. It may even cause problems with sales (Golland and Blake 2004, 351).

The question of fully automated homes apart, the flexibility or otherwise of domestic wiring systems has been criticised. In the design of offices, developers have sought to maximise the flexibility in the use of electric power circuits. Duffy (2002) and others have suggested the same in the design of the home. There are, however, obvious objections in the use of office equipment in the home. Lightweight partition walls risk increased sound transmission and other elements of office equipment such as access flooring, suspended ceilings and clip-on skirting boards would require redesign for domestic use. In addition and probably more importantly, communications technology has moved on with the routine application of wireless and plug-in mains electricity distribution systems. So long as an adequate number of safe mains plugs are included, wiring systems are likely to become less of a constraint in the future. Automated homes are therefore unlikely to pose major questions in housing design, at least not in comparison to such considerations as the external layout or floor space standards.

Towards Zero Carbon Homes?

Business definitions of quality refer mostly to consumer demands and needs, including health and safety. What about environmental quality and the modernisation of environmental regulations?

To an extent, government policy is clear and long term. It is to introduce progressively tighter regulations so that, by 2016, that all new homes in England are 'carbon neutral' or 'zero carbon' in relation to energy use. In some ways, the target is relatively modest. A zero carbon home is not what it seems. It is not 'zero carbon' at all times of the year. The definition means that, in the winter heating season, home energy imports from various sources can be set against summer energy exports, presumably to the national electricity grid.[43] The zero carbon home is not an autonomous home that is completely independent of urban services and infrastructure. The definition of a zero carbon home also excludes the embodied energy and carbon emissions involved in construction, for example in the manufacture of cement.

To an extent, moreover, zero carbon housing design can incorporate a variety of low energy design techniques and technologies in use since at least the 1970s and mostly pioneered by environmental activists and housing associations. Low energy design typically involves a combination of passive solar (maximising the heat gain from the sun); high levels of insulation and draught-proofing; and various types of renewable energy (for example wind turbines, solar panels and bio-mass fuel heating systems). In addition, the proposal for zero carbon homes can draw on the experience of measures to improve thermal efficiency in new homes through progressively tighter building regulations. According to a recent official report energy efficiency standards for new homes in England are 40 per cent better than those before 2002 and 70 per cent better than in 1990 (DCLG 2006a, 10).

The proposal for zero carbon homes is, nevertheless, very different and more ambitious than previous exercises in environmental regulation. The proposal is for the routine use of zero carbon housing, not just for experimental schemes and not just for households who have a sympathetic attitude towards low energy lifestyles.

Amongst the most obvious obstacles are the following:

- The Home Builders Federation has expressed concern that overhasty attempts to promote zero carbon building will result in the introduction of unreliable technologies, cause complications in relation to building insurance and will also lead to substantial increases in construction and maintenance costs.[44] It is arguably in the interests of the HBF to exaggerate the problems. Nevertheless, sufficient examples exist to suggest that the fears are not grossly exaggerated. To give a specific example, the 'BedZED' (Beddington Zero Energy Development) scheme at Sutton, South London is a well-known example of zero carbon housing. It is a mixed use, mixed tenure scheme of 99 three-storey terraces and incorporates a collective heating system that uses sustainable biomass sources of fuel.[45] BedZED's district heating boiler has, however, been out of commission for long periods.[46]
- Recent reports suggest that, in an urban setting, small-scale domestic renewable energy technologies are largely ineffective and 'grossly overhyped' (Monbiot 2006). Wind turbines and solar panels do not at present generate sufficient energy savings in relation to the cost of installation and maintenance. Biomass heat generation is more viable for groups of dwellings in the short term, say over the next five years. However, biomass heat generation has other limitations concerned with obtaining, transporting and burning the biomass material – for example woodchips. One might wonder about the practicality and impact (on woodlands, on air quality and in relation to the transport implications) of the operation of large numbers of wood burning boilers in an urban area. Biomass burning does not meet the full preconditions of sustainabillity, even if it meets the technical requirements of zero carbon. The continuing management, including the collection of relevant charges, of communal energy systems also needs to be considered. Other than in social housing, there are few examples of community management agencies that might undertake the work (Calcutt 2007, 91).
- The variability of renewable energy sources suggests a case for discretionary regulation with local variations. Discretionary and variable environmental regulation is the field of planning rather than building regulation. Some

local authorities have already pursued such flexible control, albeit mostly in relation to commercial development. They have required that on-site renewable production accounts either for 10 per cent of future energy demands or for 10 per cent of future carbon emissions. The policy was initiated by the London Borough of Merton in 2003 and is, for this reason, sometimes known as the Merton rule. It was subsequently endorsed by government in national planning guidance for England (ODPM 2004c, 10). However, most developers dislike the use of planning controls in relation to low energy and zero carbon housing, owing to the variable costs and design implications. They would also argue that planning professionals do not know enough about the economics of low energy housing to apply controls on a consistent or sensible basis.

- Low and zero energy building may require inspection on completion to check levels of workmanship and not simply inspection at the time of plan submission, as is current practice. The House of Commons Environmental Audit Committee (2005a, 43–5) and The Royal Commission on Environmental Pollution (2007, 134) have complained that the building regulations are failing to achieve adequate compliance, even under the existing standards.

Even if not fully achieved, the zero carbon target is likely to have benefits in promoting higher environmental standards and in encouraging more experimentation with renewable energy. However, a broader uncertainty persists as to whether experimental technologies can be applied on a large scale. In the past, high development costs led governments and local authorities to face a recurrent conflict between quality and quantity in social house building programmes. The comments of Nye Bevan in 1946 provide the most striking example. The conflict between quality and quantity persists, but has been largely displaced into private house building and considerations of environmental standards.

Notes

1   Bramley, G. (2003) *Barker Inquiry on Housing Supply: affordability and the intermediate market* (p. 6) consulted December 2007 at http://www.hm-treasury.gov.uk/media/B/6/ Glen per cent20Bramley.pdf.

2   *First-time buyers 'at fresh low'*, reported on the BBC News website, 22/12/07 and consulted in December 2007 at http://news.bbc.co.uk/1/hi/business/7156906.stm.

3   Housing completions are taken from Table 2.5c and 2.5d of the Housing Statistics of the ODPM, consulted November 2004 at http://www.odpm.gov.uk/stellent/groups/ odpm_housing/documents/page/odpm_house_026202.pdf. The number of residential property transactions is taken from Table T16.1 of the Inland Revenue Survey of property transactions in England and Wales, consulted November 2004 at http://www. inlandrevenue.gov.uk/stats/survey_of_prop/menu.htm.

4   The term elasticity means the rate at which an increase in supply reduces prices or vice versa. The rate varies between different goods and between different countries.

5   Data taken from the live house building tables, consulted July 2007 at the Department for Communities and Local Government website at http://www.communities.gov.uk/ index.asp?id=1156032.

6   Taken from Table 243 *Housebuilding: permanent dwellings completed, by tenure; Great Britain, historical calendar series* available at the website of the Department for Communities and Local Government, consulted June 2006 at http://www.odpm.gov.uk/index.asp?id=1156032.

7   Available at the CPRE website, consulted September 2005 at http://www.cpre.org.uk/resources/pub/pdfs/planning-and-development/housing-sprawd/hgusing-myths.pdf.

8   MacDonald, K. (2007), *Opening up the Debate: Exploring housing land supply myths*, London, RTPI consulted June 2007 at the website of the Royal Town Planning Institute at http://www.rtpi.org.uk/item/912/23/5/3.

9   Since the Planning and Compulsory Purchase Act, 2004 planning permissions in England and Wales expire after three years, unless work has started. Presumably, those firms with three or more years include sites where work has started, but not finished. The legal definition of starting work is, at present, not onerous. Merely digging a trench would, for example, meet the definition.

10 Ibid.

11 Information gained from a statement available on t`e web in February 2004 at http://www.hm-treasury'.ov.uk/mddia//8B3DD/barkresp_StanhopeEL_0103_99.3kb.pdf.

12 Parliamentary Office of Science and Technology, *Postnote*, December 2003 Number 209, Modern Methods 0f House Building, consulted July 2007 at http://www.parliament*uk/documents.upload/postpn2 9.pdf.

13 Building Research Establisment press release available at http2//www.bre.co.uk/pressservice/articles/process1.html.

14 Bovis Lend Lease Consulting (2002) Manufactured Homes for Moderate Income Groups Market and Product Potential Study, consulted January 2005 at the site of the public development agency for New South Wales, Australia at http://www.landcom.nsw.gov.au/landcom/nsw/RESOURCES/IMAGES/images_mih/Exec_Summ_Rev150702.PDF.

15 The Park Homes trade association site available May 2004 at http://www.parkhome-living.co.uk/buying/index.php.

16 Taken from the website of 'Building Plot', consulted August 2007 at http://www.building-plot.org.uk/self-build-home.asp.

17 The figures are taken from the Community Self-Build website consulted May 2006 at http://www.communityselfbuildagency.org/agency1.html#far. The relevant page on the community self-build website has subsequently disappeared.

18 Available February 2004 at http://www.hm-treasury.gov.uk/media//EE012/barkresp_GallagherRogerTymBB_0903_99.6kb.pdf.pdf.

19 Available February 2004 at http://www.hm-treasury.gov.uk/media//DFAB9/barkresp_LondonResidentialResearch_0903_40.3kb.pdf.pdf.

20 Abley, Ian (2002), *Time to take on the anti-development lobby*, article available on the web May 2004 at http://www.audacity.org/Construction per cent20inertia per cent2004.htm.

21 Planning Officers Society (2001) Planning For Change: The Planning Officers Society's View on The Reform 0f The Planning System, consulted September 2003 at http://www.planningofficers.org.uk/shared/files/POS/postscript/13–12–01.pdf).

22 Office of the Deputy Prime Minister, News Release, 20 November 2003: available November 2003 at http://www.odpm.gov.uk/pns/DisplayPN.cgi?pn_id=2003_0249.

23 Planning Advice Note: PAN 74 *Affordable Housing* consulted July 2007 at the website of the Scottish Executive at http://www.scotland.gov.uk/Publications/2005/03/20796/54075.

24 *Kate Barker Review of Housing Supply, Response by London First*, p. 7, available June 2005 on the website of the Barker Review (other business responses) at http://www. hm-treasury.gov.uk./consultations_and_legislation/barker/consult_barker_othindresp. cfm.

25 As stated on the British Standards Institute website, consulted February 2005 at http:// www.bsi-global.com/Quality_management/Management/bseniso9000.xalter.

26 *ISO 9000 Quality Management Principles* consulted February 2005 on the International Organisation for Standardisation website at http://www.iso.org/iso/en/iso9000–14000/ iso9000/qmp.html.

27 The *Building for Life* website, consulted October 2007 at http://www.buildingforlife. org/buildingforlife.aspx?contentitemid=384&aspectid=15.

28 See a consumer survey undertaken in 2002 and reported at a joint website of the New Homes Marketing Board and the House Builders Federation and consulted January 2005 at http://www.new-homes.co.uk/customer_survey/preference.html.

29 A survey undertaken in 2001 and also reported on the joint website of the New Homes Marketing Board and the House Builders Federation indicated that 24 per cent of new homes purchaser would 'prefer' to buy new (consulted January 2005 at http://www. new-homes.co.uk/customer_survey/preference.html).

30 Taken from the companies website consulted April 2004 at http://www.georgewimpey. co.uk/.

31 Barratt Homes website, consulted June 2004 at http://www.barratthomes.co.uk/wobs_i. html.

32 Taken from the website of the New-Homes Marketing Board, consulted June 2003, at http://www.new-homes.co.uk/customer_survey/higher_density.html.

33 2002 Customer Survey, reported by the New Homes Marketing Board and consulted April 2004 at http://www.new-homes.co.uk/customer_survey/affordable_2002.html.

34 As described on the web page of the New Homes Marketing Board, consulted April 2004 at http://www.new-homes.co.uk/why_buy_new/retirement_living.html.

35 McLaren, J. and Hakim, M. (2003?), *A better life: private sheltered housing and independent living for older people*, unpublished but available on the web October 2004 at http://www.mccarthyandstone.co.uk/pdf/McCarthyStone_Final.pdf.

36 As reported at the following website, consulted November 2004 http://www.hemscott. com/hstoday/Focus per cent202002/mccarthy_0611_2002.htm.

37 From the company's website consulted October 2004 at http://www.mccarthyandstone. co.uk/default.asp The survey report is by McClaren and Hakim (2003?).

38 McLaren, J. and Hakim, M. (2003?) *A better life: private sheltered housing and independent living for older people*, available on the web October 2004 at http://www. mccarthyandstone.co.uk/pdf/McCarthyStone_Final.pdf.

39 'Building Homes' May 2003, consulted April 2006 at the website of *Building* at http:// www.building.co.uk/story.asp?sectioncode=32&storycode=1028751 .

40 The Lifetime Homes design concept and standard is described at the Habinteg webpage, consulted June 2004 at http://www.habinteg.org.uk/lifetimehomes/ and in addition at the Joseph Rowntree Foundation website at http://www.jrf.org.uk/ knowledge/findings/foundations/2.asp.

41 A British application is documented in a Joseph Rowntree Foundation presentation *Smart Homes: what the house can do*, consulted June 2004 at http://www.jrf.org.uk/ housingandcare/smarthomes/what.asp.. A more general account of smart homes is available from the website of Smart Homes, Netherlands, consulted September 2007 at http://www.smart-homes.nl/engels/index.html.

42 'Smart homes offer a helping hand' *BBC News* (19 May 2004) available June 2004 at http://news.bbc.co.uk/2/hi/technology/3715927.stm. The website of Accenture Technology is also relevant, consulted June 2004 at http://www.accenture.com/xd/xd.asp?it=enweb&xd=services\technology\tech_home.xml.

43 Department for Communities and Local Government press release, 13 December 2006, consulted May 2007 at http://www.communities.gov.uk/index.asp?id=1002882&Press NoticeID=2320.

44 Calcutt review of house-building delivery, Submission by Home Builders Federation, 2007 London, HBF, consulted November 2007 at the website of the HBF at http://www.hbf.co.uk/index.php?id=1837.

45 Twinn, C. (2003) *BedZED*, The ARUP Journal (1) (available June 2004 at http://www.arup.com/DOWNLOADBANK/download68.pdf).

46 Fry, D. (2006) *Design for Living*, article available May 2007 at the website of The Institution of Engineering and Technology at http://www.iee.org/oncomms/magazine.cfm?issueID=133&articleID=0D9DD6EB-0176–F0C7–3F496358443C9BBB.

Chapter 7

Urban Design and the Environment

The repetition of houses forms neighbourhoods and then towns and cities. However, towns and cities are qualitatively different from either individual dwellings or the process of housing development. Towns and cities are simultaneously spatial fields that people have to navigate from one point to another and places of the imagination imbued with meaning and values.

The role of towns and cities as places of the imagination may be emphasised. Places of the imagination are essentially places that change and can be designed. Places of imagination lead therefore to the practice of urban design, defined as 'the art of making places for people' (DETR 2000a, 8). Urban design is about imagining alternatives, above all about imaginary landscapes and showing how places might be in the future. Governments promote urban design exactly for this reason as 'central to the delivery of sustainable communities'.[1]

Official enthusiasm for urban design is relatively new. It has arisen for a variety of reasons – to market places to consumers and investors, to provide a clearer planning framework for developers, to find some common ground between the planning and architectural professions and finally to facilitate urban conservation. All this has demanded a greater attention to how buildings fit together with one another and with the existing urban fabric.

The issues involved in urban design are not new, however. The early town planning movement, as for example represented in Britain by the textbooks by Triggs (1909) and Unwin (1909), saw urban design as a core professional activity. These textbooks drew, moreover, on earlier nineteenth-century traditions. Likewise, the most influential planning textbook of the 1950s by Keeble (1969) focused on physical layout and physical form. To an extent, therefore, the concern with urban design is a return to earlier preoccupations, albeit in a context in which the significance of markets and of public involvement is more readily admitted than in say the period before 1960.

Qualitative and Functional Interpretations

Urban design, like the city itself, is about the organisation of urban spaces, about land uses, about the layout of groups of buildings and streets and ultimately about urban form. It is in part about 'the quality of public realm', largely meaning the space between buildings, as Carmona et al. (2003, 1) suggest. The terms 'public realm' and 'public space' are generally used interchangeably in urban design and refer to a combination of streets, footpaths, parks, recreational areas and the area around canals and other open water. Shonfield (1998), for example, defines public space as all the places where public time is spent and public time is all time outside of work or home.

The reference to 'public realm' and 'public space' are consistent with treatment of urban design in the early pre-1914 textbooks. Unwin (1909) and Triggs (1909), for example interested themselves in the design and layout of streets, albeit with a significant difference in emphasis. Unwin was more interested in the design of residential streets as part of a housing programme. Triggs (1909) was more interested in the city beautiful and adornment.

However, the reference to public space is a departure from the typical assumptions of town planning at the time of full-blooded modernism. The language of Abercrombie in the plans for London was, for example, about streets and 'public open space' with this latter conceived as fulfilling a separate hygienic function. Interest in the term 'public space' is most likely explained by the increased emphasis, from the 1980s onwards on urban regeneration. Once policies started to focus on the improvement of urban areas and once, in addition, policies started to look at the quality of urban areas for pedestrians, not just cars, architects and planners started to consider the external environment as a continuous matrix of spaces and places.

The role of public space in defining the quality, in all senses of the word, of urban and suburban areas remains its main importance. Sandercock (1998, 207–15) offers one influential interpretation, suggesting that the language of planning should encompass 'the city of memory', concerned with history and conservation; 'the city of desire' concerned with excitement and consumption and finally 'the city of spirit', as represented by places that people can gather and relax and represented in addition by public art. However, the cities of 'memory', of 'desire' and of 'spirit' all refer to town and city centres and to tourist destinations, not necessarily to the inner city and suburban areas that most people call home. It is particularly important, in this context, not to define 'public realm' in a way that neglects the complaints of those living in poor quality residential areas. Moreover, a large-scale consumer survey, commissioned by the Commission for Architecture and the Built Environment (CABE 2005d, 32–5) has suggested that residents place less emphasis on the public realm than is commonly supposed in urban design. For most residents, the home is essentially a place for a private, individual and family-based lifestyle.

Urban design need not stop at the space between buildings. As was a major theme in modernist architecture, urban design can also consider the public and private implications of large-scale urban development. It is about building *en masse* and, in the context of urban regeneration, rebuilding and improvement *en masse*. The advice from CABE, to put the point simply, is that 'housing should be: functional, attractive, and sustainable'.[2]

Towards Liveable and Sustainable Cities

The planning and urban policy literature uses slightly different, but consistent terminology to that of CABE. The main aim is to ensure that cities are liveable (functional and attractive) and sustainable (Brook Lyndhurst 2004). Liveability is the contemporary equivalent of long-standing town planning concerns with amenity, pleasantness and health. It implies an ability on the part of the urban designer to empathise with users, to put oneself in their position and to assess whether a proposal meets their demands and wishes (Lynch and Hack 1984, 98). Empathy in turn implies exercises in user participation and user research. Sustainability is subject to its own definitional uncertainties, but generally includes an assessment of the long-term environmental impact of proposals.

Liveability and sustainability are obviously not the same and are sometimes in conflict with one another. It is likely, for example, that, for most people, a liveable city is one where they can move around easily, without traffic congestion. However, increased mobility does not necessarily promote sustainable lifestyles from an environmental viewpoint and is in conflict with sustainability if car use is increased.

The relation between liveability and sustainability is made more complex, moreover, in Britain, more particularly in England, by a recent tendency to define 'liveability' in narrow operational terms as factors relating to local environments. This is the 'cleaner, greener, safer' policy agenda for neighbourhood environmental improvements (ODPM 2002)

The international definition of liveability is broader and generally encompasses long-term environmental issues associated with sustainability. A submission to the United Nations World Urban Forum gives for example six definitions of liveable cities (Timmer and Seymoar 2006). None exclude environmental sustainability and most consider sustainability as an aspect of liveability. Older British accounts are similar. Gibson (1994, 43–6) considers liveable neighbourhoods and sustainable planning as complementary to one another, without reflecting on any distinction.

It might be tempting, therefore, to lump liveability and sustainability together. This would probably help gain political support from as wide a variety of sources as possible. However, planning is not just about searching for compromises. It is also about searching for realistic policy choices. For the most part, liveability and sustainability are best treated as twin criteria in assessing models and proposals.

The Ideal City Revisited and Applied

Testing sustainability and liveability requires strategic models and this, in turn, implies ideal cities. Urban design is an exercise in imagining alternative models of the future and applying these to existing towns and cities. Ideal cities are a logical extension, one that enables the full implications of alternatives to be worked out in advance. The imagination provides a sense of coherence and direction to individual action and thought. Imaginary ideal cities provide the collective equivalent. Ideal cities show how people may live in harmony with one another, in harmony with technology or with nature.

The imagination does not necessarily lead to ideal cities. Though this is seldom recognised in the planning literature, imagining the future can also lead to dystopias, nightmare scenarios of cities and neighbourhoods gone wrong. Dystopias provide statements of what to avoid rather than ideals to be achieved.

Dystopias are sometimes merely a long-term negative mirror image of ideal cities. For example, the prospect of environmental disasters is an argument for the pursuit of an ecotopia, based on environmental sustainability. However, at a practical level and ignoring long-term or remote scenarios, most urban dystopias refer to landscapes of fear, excessive commercialism and dereliction. Examples include the postmodern visions of fractured, fragmented cities and the city of panic of Virilio (2005). Urban design and planning has a role in countering dystopia, for example in the creation of a safe environment and socially mixed neighbourhoods. However, countering the landscapes of fear is a different, more consultative exercise and is best considered as an aspect of neighbourhood regeneration.

In some ways, dystopian thinking is well suited to contemporary conditions. Postmodernism suggests, in particular, that people are increasingly suspicious of authority, increasingly sceptical towards grand narratives of progress and increasingly sceptical about the possibility of a single over-arching utopian vision (Gunder 2005). Postmodern critiques of ideal cities also raise numerous questions about the power of different parties. Who is involved in the process of designing and then building the ideal city plan? What is the source of their legitimacy? Who will manage and regulate services after completion (Liscombe 2006, 28–9)? Likewise, the hypermodern vision of endless change, uncertainty and personal anxiety precludes the possibility of implementing an ideal city, other than as an isolated project.

However, utopian thinking has not disappeared. The postmodern search for identity has led to experiments in the development of small-scale communities, alternative lifestyles and alternative technologies, independently of the proposals of government. Likewise, the hypermodern concern with futures has led governments to propose new types of housing and new types of urban development as a means of simultaneously meeting consumer demands and minimising environmental pollution and risks.

There is a difference in how ideal cities are discussed. Most planning theorists consider ideal cities as work in progress, rather than as a fixed blueprint. The 'ideal', ideal city, if this term is permitted, would arise from the accumulation of knowledge and experience, from reflection on previous experience and from a pluralist dialogue with different communities (Liscombe 2006; Perrault 2003).

At the same time, contemporary ideal cities have points of continuity with the past. Postmodern grassroots activism has revived the principle of urban dispersal, as advocated in particular by the garden city movement from the start of the early twentieth century. Proposals for eco-villages have, for example, a broad physical and social similarity to the experimental 'third' garden city proposed by the Town and Country Planning Association in the 1970's. More generally, environmental activism means promoting a green matrix in existing urban areas and, as part of this, protecting green areas in existing cities, for example using vacant sites as nature reserves and using private gardens to promote ecological diversity and domestic food production (Baines 1985; Davidson 1988). Conversely, hypermodern solutions tend to favour higher density, compact city proposals that reduce energy consumption and the impact of human activities on the countryside and that revive the modernist visions of the 1920s and 1930s.

Eco-villages and eco-towns   Proposals for eco-villages and eco-towns illustrate the logic of environmental identity politics. For the eco-village movement, urban dispersal is a vehicle for the creation of different types of settlement and different forms of social organisation. In part, the aim is simply to get away from the problems of the big city. The intention is to build 'communities that attempt to get away from the waste, pollution, competition and violence of contemporary life'.[3] In addition, the aim is to provide a positive alternative to current lifestyles – an antidote to the centralised state and to globalisation. Eco-villages are self-sufficient, small-scale communities that self-consciously seek to reduce their ecological impact.[4]

The web site of the *Eco-Villages Network UK* provides a list of examples. [5] These include:

- the Findhorn community in northern Scotland established in 1962 and committed to sustainable lifestyles since the early 1990s;
- an energy self-sufficient earth sheltered housing scheme at Hockerton in Nottinghamshire, comprising five houses in an estate of 25 acres;
- Sherwood Energy Village also in Nottinghamshire, this comprising the development of a former colliery site for mixed housing and industrial use with an emphasis on renewable energy and self-build; and
- Tinker's Bubble, a small mixed-use farm in Somerset, founded in 1994 and comprising 40 acres of conifer plantation, orchards and gardens.

The Findhorn, Hockerton and Sherwood experiments are intended to pioneer new, sustainable forms of urban development. The Findhorn project has involved the development of a wind farm, a biological system for sewage disposal and the provision of short courses for those interested in sustainable development. The Hockerton scheme is widely cited as an example of zero carbon housing, albeit a model that is only feasible for a low density, rural or semi-rural setting. Tinkers Bubble involves local building materials and seeks to promote small-scale organic agriculture and sustainable woodland management.

As demonstration exercises, eco-villages have had a long-term influence. Lovell (2004) has, in particular, argued that the experiments of environmental activists from the 1970s onwards laid the basis for the subsequent low energy and zero energy housing proposals of government. Likewise, the example of eco-villages in Britain and elsewhere in the world have provided a rationale for current proposals in England to build a series of eco-towns of between 5,000 and 10,000 homes.[6]

The eco-towns, like the most eco-villages in Britain, are 'new settlements, with a 'separate' identity (DCLG 2007a, 12). Likewise, they are intended as a laboratory for low energy and zero carbon housing.

However, eco-villages do not offer a sustainable model of urban development. The small scale of eco-villages means that they cannot support a range of facilities. What exactly is a minimum 'critical mass' in relation to new settlements is a matter of debate, though far more than say a dozen or even 100 dwellings of a typical eco-village. The most detailed British study is by Breheny et al. (1993, 50–51) and this suggests two possible minimum levels – at least 3,000–5,000 dwellings (or 7,500–12,5000 people) if the aim is to support a secondary school and 10,000 dwellings (25,000 people) if the aim is to minimise the need for journeys by car. Household size has declined since the date of Breheny's study and is likely to decline further in the future. Therefore, the thresholds will need to be adjusted upwards. In addition, the high cost of land with planning permission requires relatively high density forms of development, such as terraces and flats, rather than the low density earth sheltered houses and self-built cottages that are the usual rule in eco-villages.

Finally, the usual preference for rural locations means that eco-villages can only be developed on a small scale and enjoyed by a privileged minority. Otherwise, they run counter to planning policies in favour of countryside protection, as has been the fate of many such proposals. Eco-village residents are not privileged in an economic sense. Their websites often emphasise their frugal lifestyle. Moreover, the eco-villages network reports that their proposals have a particular appeal to poorer, third world and developing countries. The residents of eco-villages are, instead, privileged in the sense that, in Britain, many more people would wish to live this way if given the chance. The development of eco-villages could easily lead to a scramble of development in the countryside, without the strict controls and respect for sustainable development that the eco-village movement has promoted. Likewise, eco-village development does not tackle problems of affordable housing. Eco-villages are too small. They also offer no obvious, long term way of preventing new dwellings from being occupied in the future by rich urban incomers.

The preference for rural locations means, in addition, that proposals for eco-villages commonly run counter to planning policies that restrain greenfield development. In some cases, including Tinkers Bubble, development has gone ahead without planning permission and this has only been granted retrospectively, after a long period of uncertainty. Essentially the residents of the eco-villages have had to demonstrate a special case for their continued existence.[7] Most likely other eco-villages and other similar projects would have gone ahead, were it not for the opposition of local planning authorities and the risk that any unauthorised development might have to be demolished.

Development in the countryside can be justified if it meets environmental objectives. The 'lowland crofting' initiative pursued in the West Lothian area of central Scotland since about 1994 provides an example. In this, housing and small scale workshops are developed through the subdivision of marginal farms in areas of poor environmental quality, with the condition that developers improve the landscape, that buildings are screened by new woodland and that the land is well managed thereafter.[8] However, such a proposal is only suited to regions where population levels are stable or declining and where vacant sites and marginal farmland are plentiful.

Green Infrastructure and Green Space

Irrespective of the future of eco-villages and eco-towns, it is still possible to use community efforts to protect and enhance the green environment of existing cities. There are numerous examples where local voluntary groups manage urban farms, children's play areas, local parks, community arts events, food-producing allotments and so on. There are also examples where voluntary groups have used environmental works to help unemployed people learn new skills and to enable young people to make a positive contribution to their community. 'Groundwork' is the best example of this.[9] Clean up and tree planting campaigns, remain popular and have provided a repeated focus for local community-based action. Moreover, the core idea of 'green cities' retains its popular appeal and continues to attract practical support from volunteers and local groups. It also offers a practical way of giving local communities a greater sense of control over their local environment and encouraging a greater sense of environmental care.

However, voluntary action is only a starting point. Strategic, citywide intervention, otherwise known as, 'green infrastructure' planning is also relevant. Infrastructure is necessary to maintain an adequate quality of life, but is generally taken for granted. Green infrastructure planning is similar. It is about recognising the positive qualities of green spaces, about linking disparate green areas together and about finding ways to maximise their impact through a combination of environmental enhancement, environmental conservation and, in some places, the provision of recreational areas (Kambites and Owen 2006).

The avoidance of flood risk has been a particular concern. Undeveloped green areas offer a soak-away for surplus water, whereas paving forces water into drainage systems. Undeveloped green areas also counter flooding, moreover, in a more effective manner than is general possible through 'green' roofs (roofs covered with vegetation).

In addition, some proposals involve the use of relatively large-scale sustainable drainage systems ('SuDS') that involve a combination of porous pavements that hold rather than discharge water, grassy depressions for the collection of floodwater and wetlands.[10] SuDS slow run-off and reduce pollution in watercourses. When not containing floodwater, they also provide a community asset. SuDS are an established technology, widely practiced in continental Europe. They are recognised as a necessary aspect of housing schemes in Scotland and are proposed in the form of a green grid in the Thames Gateway growth area. SuDS require integrated forms of drainage and open space management. It is unclear whether current practice in SuDS, realises its potential advantages (RCEP 2007, 79–83).

As a side effect, green infrastructure proposals imply a reworking of the green belt. As commonly imagined since the publication of the advisory plans for

London in the 1940s, the green belt comprises a concentric ring around a built-up area. The green belt is mostly about protecting the countryside from urban growth. In contrast, the eco-alternative is about creating a hybrid alternative, of green wedges and corridors and sometimes about creating new types of semi-urban, semi-rural uses. As an example of the latter, Wood and Ravetz (2000) have proposed turning the Manchester green belt into an 'eco-belt', characterised by a combination of environmental enhancement and conservation, informal leisure facilities, smallholdings and low impact eco-housing.

Existing green belts are commonly fragmented, occasionally discontinuous and sometimes of a poor environmental quality. Therefore, notions of a green mosaic, green infrastructure and an eco-belt make good sense. Whatever the technical and planning advantages of the green mosaic, however, green belts stand as a symbol of environmental protection in Britain. Mostly likely, in the context of eco-proposals, green belts will be absorbed into a broader strategy for green infrastructure. They are unlikely to be abandoned or substantially reduced in size without opposition.

Support for green spaces has not been a priority in the policies of government. Much of the efforts of volunteers and voluntary organisations have been undertaken against a background of neglect. The Urban Green Spaces Taskforce, set up by government in 2001 to develop a vision for open space and parks in England, concluded in particular that many had suffered from underinvestment in the previous 20 years and, as a result, had a poor image (DTLR 2002).

Neglect of open space and parks can be corrected, though it remains uncertain as to whether previous underinvestment will be corrected. Local authorities continue to face numerous conflicting and high priority demands on their expenditure programmes. Another trend, urban intensification, is less easily reversed. There are no official statistics on the subject. However, Pauleit and Golding (2005) have provided a detailed case study of the trends in Merseyside. Here a progressive loss of green space was apparent over the period 1975–2000 with a concomitant increase in the amount of space devoted to buildings and paved or asphalt areas. The reduction in green space was not large in relation to the overall distribution of different types of land use, but more significant in terms of environment and visual impact. The reduction generally measured between 1 and 3 per cent for different types of green space (turf, rough grass, shrubs and trees in different neighbourhoods.

In the context of high house prices and extensive urban development pressures, some loss of green space is almost certainly inevitable and in some cases may be desirable – for example if the green space is not used by local residents or is poorly maintained. It still remains possible to find neighbourhoods with a surplus of green space – for example council estates that were designed and built between about 1920 and 1950 at relatively low densities, with each estate surrounded by local green belts that are largely unused. The loss of green space has to be considered carefully, however and needs local consultation if it is to go ahead.

Compact cities – their definition From the 1990s onwards, and with the partial exception of current proposals for eco-towns, environmental policies in Britain has favoured in the words of the report of the Urban Task Force 'the compact, many-centred city of mixed uses which favours walking, cycling and public transport' (UTC 1999, 40). Influenced by a combination of considerations, notably the promotion of public transport and a reaction against urban sprawl, the most common position has endorsed notions of the compact city, characterised by a combination of higher densities and a continuous built-up area.

The promotion of urban compaction has, moreover, not been confined to Britain. Countering the problems of urban dispersal and fragmentation are repeated themes in the policies for sustainable development pursued in the European Union and its predecessor the European Community (CEC 1990; CEC 2006). The policies are advisory on individual European states, but have set a tone for national discussions. In the US controlling and avoiding 'urban sprawl' is a policy objective of the new urbanism movement.[11] In the US, however, policies to counter sprawl remain more contentious, with significant disagreement between different political parties and variations amongst different states.

At the same time, some obvious differences exist in the standards implied by compact city polices in different countries. The compact city is a relative rather than absolute concept. The Congress for New Urbanism is the main professional advocacy group for compact cities in the US. The plans and policy statements prepared under its name allow extensive flexibility in density levels and include schemes for conventional suburban single-family houses (Bohl 2000, 781). At the same time, the compact city as generally envisaged in Britain, implies lower densities than proposals to intensify urban development in French cities such as Bordeaux, Marseilles or Lyon. Here proposals exist to increase densities impact on inner city areas that are already dense by the standards in Britain, especially English rather than Scottish standards.

The compact city in the US and France differs in another way from that in Britain in that it has been more project-oriented and more oriented towards the promotion of public transport. In the US, proposals for 'Transit-Oriented Development' concentrate new development and infill around public transport stations and corridors, offering a mix of land uses within walking distance of the station. In France, proposals to raise urban densities have likewise been tied into programmes of public transport investment, notably in tramways and a downgrading of investment in roads (Pouyanne 2004, 50). In Britain, in contrast, the compact city generally means merely a framework for organising development.

The compact city has to be carefully and precisely defined. It is more than just high-density housing. The compact city is a model of urban development. Density is an indicator. Density is, moreover, not the only indicator. Continuity of urban development, the absence of breaks, is another. Together a combination of relatively high density and contiguity of development may be considered as constituting a minimum definition of the compact city (Pouyanne 2004).

At the same time, the compact city does not imply uniform density levels. New urbanism involves, in part, a revival of the density gradient between the city centre and the periphery. The relevant technical term is the 'transect', an imaginary cross-section through a city of concentric density zones (Duany 2002). Likewise, the Urban Task Force (UTC 1999, 53) advocates clusters or 'pyramids' of higher densities around subcentres as well as the main urban centre and in which each subcentre contains a mix of housing, employment and other land uses. This is also the preferred model in official planning guidance in England (DCLG 2006c, para.76). For these reasons density itself requires separate examination in terms of its social impact.

The compact city is also associated with a series of other policy indicators and aims. In principle, the compact city brings people and activities together. It promotes pedestrian access to facilities; promotes the mixing of different land uses; and promotes in addition the social mixing of different types of people. Again all these considerations, pedestrian access, land use and social mixing should be considered separately.

Urban form and ecological efficiency   The compact city, understood as a combination of relatively high density and contiguity of the built environment, has a narrow rationale. It is about promoting in the words of the European Commission the 'sustainable use of natural resources' (CEC 2006, 10). It is about the promotion of ecological efficiency in urban form. In particular, it is about promoting efficiency in the use of land and efficiency in the use of energy, especially in transport.

The rationale in relation to the use of land is relatively simple. Compact cities reduce the impact of urban development, both through their higher density and through reducing the contact between urban development and the countryside. Reducing the contact between urban development and the countryside diminishes the risk of conflict between urban activities on one hand and agriculture, wildlife and natural habitats on the other. It means a diminution of the impact of urban noise, light and human intrusion.

The main qualification, at least at a technical rather than political level, concerns the impact of density. Savings on land take are more marked through preventing low residential densities, say below 25 or 30dph rather than to seek uniformly high densities, say of 40 or 50dph. In addition, non-residential uses are more resistant to higher densities. For example, the amount of land occupied by schools and parks is generally fixed by means of standards in relation to the population. The area devoted to commercial uses, though not documented in official statistics, has almost certainly increased over the past 20 years as a result of the prevalence of single-storey warehouses, factories and shopping centres.

The political limitations of the land take argument are more important. Reducing the contact between urban development and the countryside is about environmental sustainability, not liveability. Many people like walking in the countryside and would welcome, for example, an opportunity for a direct footpath link between a residential area, local parks and the open countryside. Conserving agricultural land for food production has not been a major policy priority for some time. In any case, the advocates of the green mosaic turn the compact city argument on its head. They propose the creation of 'community gardens', spaces within towns and cities capable of local use for intensive food production (Hopkins 2000).

The crucial argument in favour of the compact city is instead about energy efficiency, in the use of buildings and in transport. Though it is difficult to obtain consistent statistics, the energy use in buildings, including the use of dwellings is almost certainly more significant than the energy involved in personal movement in urban areas. Steemers (2003) estimates a ratio is about 2:1, with an even higher ratio in London where personal movement is more dependent on public transport.

However, it is difficult to trace a relationship between building energy use and urban form. Different factors work against each other in a context characterised by disagreements about the best strategy for energy reduction. Many would argue that low energy and zero energy housing and towns should incorporate renewable energy sources, for example solar panels of various types and wind turbines. Others argue that small-scale domestic renewable energy technologies are largely ineffective in an urban setting (Monbiot 2006).

Much of the impact of urban form on energy use depends on the density of development. Low-density housing forms such as detached houses and semis have more external wall space than high density housing forms such as terraces and flats. As external walls are more exposed to the weather, a logical implication is that low-density dwelling forms are, in principle, less energy efficient. Much depends, however, on levels of insulation, the size of the dwelling and the number of occupants and their lifestyles.

Higher density residential areas are also better suited to energy efficient combined heat and power systems. On the other hand, high-density housing encounters layout restrictions that may prevent orientation towards the sun and are also more likely be over-shadowed by adjoining buildings. In the case of flats, the energy used in lifts is another complication. Conversely, low-density dwellings have more space around the home and on the roof for the installation of active solar devices such as small wind turbines, ground-based heat pumps and solar collectors, assuming of course that these are sufficiently viable to merit installation.

Energy consumption in urban transport, though less in absolute terms than consumption in the use of buildings, has a series of implications that are themselves important for policy.

- Energy use in transport is sensitive to the transport mode. Public transport involves less energy use than private cars. One estimate is that cutting the use of cars by about 60 per cent and shifting the journeys to public transport would cut energy consumption in transport by about 26 per cent.[12]
- Traffic is a general, almost universal environmental nuisance in urban areas and one that has steadily increased in importance in the views of residents, according to the reports of the English House Condition Survey (DCLG 2007b, 44). Traffic also serves to isolate communities, severing pedestrian movement. For individuals and families without easy access to a car, traffic

problems are therefore an aspect of social exclusion (Fotel 2006; Jain and Guiver, 2001).

- Car ownership and use has tended to increase as incomes have risen, whilst walking and the use of public transport has tended to decline.[13] Car use tends to encourage a sedentary and potentially unhealthy lifestyle.

How might people be discouraged from using the private car? Car-free cities cannot be implemented in a literal sense. Even in new housing areas, limited vehicular access is necessary to cope with emergencies, refuse disposal and the delivery and removal of bulky household items and necessary in addition to provide mobility for disabled people. Car-free cities, such as promoted by Crawford (2000), have no prospect of implementation other than in carefully defined and limited pedestrian zones.

Moreover, where car-free housing projects have developed, they generally cannot command the same level of rent or price, if sold, than schemes with car parking. Even in city centre housing schemes, where one might have thought that car dependency was less than elsewhere, consumers are generally prepared to pay a premium for secure and convenient car parking. Landlords are able to charge higher rents. Likewise, in inner city areas, owner-occupiers see the provision of car parking as enhancing the value of their property and offering an additional selling point (Stubbs 2002). Another potential problem, mostly affecting social housing schemes, is that car-free schemes might become labelled as poor people's housing, used only where car ownership levels are low owing to the low income of residents.

In the longer term, however, different urban forms almost certainly have an impact. Urban dispersal more or less requires car use. Conversely higher densities are at least more likely to facilitate the economics of public transport provision. A typical rule of thumb, for example, is that a minimum of 25 dwellings per hectare is necessary for a viable bus network and that 60dph is necessary for a tram service (CABE 2005a; Rudlin and Falk 1999). The precise minimum standards deserve more critical scrutiny and examples. However the rationale for some form of public transport threshold is logical.

In addition, general statistical correlations are apparent between population density and car use. The higher is the population density of an urban area, the lower is the reliance on car use. The correlation was first demonstrated in a widely cited study by Newman and Kenworthy (1989) who compared car use in a large number of cities in Europe, Asia and North America. The correlation has been repeatedly demonstrated thereafter, for example in Britain by ECOTEC in a study that compared travelling patterns in eight case study areas (Bozeat et al. 1992); by a study comparing bicycling and walking in Milton Keynes New Town and Almere New Town in the Netherlands (Whitelegg and Williams 2003); and by a study of energy use in the Paris region (Fouchier 1997).

A correlation is not a cause, however. It is just as likely that high population densities are caused by low car use rather than vice versa. Moreover, residential density is not the only relevant physical and probably not the most important variable. In some cities, for example London, variations in the spatial arrangement of employment are at least as significant as population density in influencing car use (Bozeat et al. 1992). A centralised employment distribution facilitates public transport use, whereas a dispersed pattern favours the car. The availability of public transport is a further consideration. In Britain, high-density housing is generally located in and around city centres where public transport facilities are concentrated. (Hildebrand et al. 2006).

Finally, the compaction of uses into residential areas risks, in the absence of public transport investment, a growth in traffic congestion in a way that is in conflict with both the principles of the competitive city and those of sustainable development. Congestion leads to a loss of time in business activities and causes pollution that impinges most heavily on those living in higher density areas (Fouchier 1997). As a side effect, congestion also encourages firms and individuals to relocate to less intensively developed areas on the periphery or the countryside.

All this does not undermine the case for the compact city as a means of curbing the impact of urban activities on the countryside. It also does not undermine the case for developing higher density housing near to public transport nodes where reduced car parking is more feasible. Otherwise the implication is that public transport is best encouraged and private transport best discouraged by coordinating traffic and transport measures with the implementation of compact city policies. The compact city alone is unlikely to have a significant impact.

Options for urban growth   The dispersal/compaction distinction is a continuum rather than a sharp divide. Elements of the two may be combined together. The Royal Commission on Environmental Pollution (2007, paras 4.6, 4.7), for example, favours a combination of high residential densities, mainly based on the use of traditional housing forms (rather than high rise) and the provision of green spaces within urban areas. Promoting green spaces in turn implies a process of opening up densely built urban areas. As in any ideal city or emergent ideal, the purity of the ideal becomes muddied when confronted with the conflicting requirements of practice.

Debates about dispersal and compaction are, in any case, abstract and hypothetical. The landscapes of Britain consist of neither an empty plain, as is implied by dispersal proposals nor a series of large cities surrounded by empty countryside, as is implied by the compact city model. South East England, in particular, 'essentially consists of a series of suburbs superimposed on a historic pattern of market towns and villages' URBED (2004a, 1). In many places, moreover, the distinct identity of these former market towns has been maintained and reinforced by the use of long-standing green belt and related types of planning policy (Longley et al. 1992, 446).

The existing, highly varied pattern of urban development means that no single model of urban growth provides an adequate framework. Previous policy commitments have a similar effect. Most statements of good practice in planning suggest that a variety of solutions is required. The Town and Country Planning Association (2000, 8) has advocated, for example 'a portfolio approach to housing land allocation' including 'urban and city sites, urban edge sites, infilling and modest extensions to rural towns and selected villages as well as ... new settlements or new towns'.

Of these different options, a series of surveys and focus group meetings undertaken in South East England by Cambridge Architectural Research suggests that none is particularly welcome to local residents, but that the least unpopular are 'densification' (meaning the intensification of existing urban areas), 'urban extensions' and 'new towns'. These were marginally more liked than disliked. 'Village growth' and 'new settlements' (that is to say on a smaller scale than new towns) were more heavily disliked (CAR 2004).

The assessments of urban growth options are mostly based on general questions relating to the planning futures of an area. The assessments of those living next door to a housing proposal may, of course, be even less well-disposed. A backlash against intensification was reported in the London suburbs immediate aftermath of the 1980s property boom by Crockett (1990) and Munro and Lane (1990). Similar reports were made by developers in their submissions to the Barker review. The intensification of suburban areas encourages, as one developer CALA Homes stated in 2003 in evidence to the Barker review, a conflict between density and character.[14] According to the evidence of another developer, First Base (2003), the resistance to higher densities is, moreover, not simply confined to higher income groups, but also to the residents of council and former council estates.[15] Tenants groups sometimes argue, for example, that lower density estates are less likely to be characterised by antisocial behaviour.

The views of residents as consumers are different again. Surveys of consumer preferences invariably find support for a detached home or a country cottage rather than a flat or terrace in an intensified suburb. Questionnaire surveys involve a degree of role playing. Asking people in their role as residents generates different answers from questions about their aspirations as consumers.

Managing urban growth   The suspicion and likely opposition of local amenity groups and the need to combine a variety of options over a wide area mean that policies have mostly been determined at a subregional (that is to say county), regional or national level. The adoption of regional spatial strategies in England under the Planning and Compulsory Purchase Act 2004 is an example. The region is not necessarily the best level to coordinate spatial planning policies, however. Regions tend to cover more than one urban area and more than one housing market area. They favour general policies that do not necessarily amount to a coherent spatial framework for urban growth.

The experience in central Scotland offers an example. Here the abolition of second tier local authorities has led to the fragmentation of spatial planning. Continued implementation of spatial plans at an urban or subregional level has depended on the voluntary cooperation of different unitary authorities, with occasional intervention from the Scottish Executive (Bramley and Kirk 2005).

Spatial fragmentation also tends to perpetuate previous trends and spatial policy commitments, with modifications at the margins of the status quo. It is generally easier for local authorities to generate support for marginal rather than radically different changes of direction. The techniques used to estimate land allocation for housing have a similar effect, usually favouring cautious, marginal adjustments. In their simplest form, allocations of housing land have generally started from trend-based demographic projections for a series of different districts (Bramley et al. 2005, 11). These demographic projections are then converted into the allocation of housing development sites, after making an assumption about typical density levels and taking into account a combination of physical constraints and opportunities such as the difficulty of finding new sites in London, the existence of pre-established policy commitments in favour of environmental protection and various urban regeneration opportunities. In addition, supplementary studies in land availability have been undertaken in cooperation with the house building industry.

This was a style of planning that was subsequently and crudely characterised as 'predict and provide'. It was a highly technical approach and one that could be only challenged on technical grounds, for example through challenging the forecasts of household growth. As a technical projection, however, the results were often flawed. Throughout the 1990s the planned levels of development sites often fell short of projected household numbers in the growth regions of South East England while it exceeded the actual growth in household numbers in the northern regions (ibid.). Merely projecting previous trends did little to recognise changing patterns of regional economic and demographic growth.

The predict and provide approach fell out of favour in the late 1990s when predictions in South East England suggested house building on a scale that was politically unacceptable to local districts and counties. The replacement policy, introduced in 2000 and commonly called 'plan, monitor and manage' incorporated an additional requirement in the determination of land for housing, that of 'capacity'. 'Plan, monitor and manage' was not an invention of central government, however, merely the transfer to national policy of previous local authority and regional planning initiatives.. Urban capacity studies measure the development potential of any area in relation to future numbers of homes and population. Development potential covers in this context, the intensification of existing urban and suburban areas and sometimes the potential for development in the immediate surroundings of towns and cities.

A good practice guide for local authorities in South East England indicates the range of approaches used in capacity studies (Baker Associates 2004). Shepway District Council provided an example of a market-oriented approach. The council used an independent firm to assess sites in terms of their market desirability as a residential location and the likely level of interest from house builders. Brighton and Hove Council used a design-led approach to provide a reliable means of estimating site capacity, as well as to illuminate some of the key policy choices (in relation to density, car parking and other design standards). Finally Hastings Borough Council looked, amongst other things, at the record of private developers in bringing forward small sites to determine whether the number was likely to increase or decrease.

These assessments of urban capacity could not escape being highly subjective. At first, architectural and environmental pressure groups argued that the capacity studies did not go far enough. The former 'UK Round Table on Sustainable

Development' noted its annual report for 1998 that many authorities were reluctant to change their old perceptions about housing densities, design or parking.[16] In contrast, for other pressure groups, more concerned about retaining the conventional low density suburb, the urban capacity studies risked going too far in encouraging intensification. The Town and Country Planning Association (2000, 15) stated, for example, that there was 'an urgent need to define and set standards ... to decide the criteria by which capacity is to be judged'.

At the same time, the use of capacity studies generated suspicion amongst private house builders who accused local authorities of using, or possibly misusing, the approach merely to find ways of reducing greenfield land availability. In evidence to the Barker review, the House Builders Federation complained that urban capacity studies did nothing to promote house building. The HBF suggested, instead, their replacement by realistic studies of land availability, much as operated previously in the 1980s and 1990 and continue to operate in Scotland and Wales.[17]

The Barker review (2004, 49) accepted the house builders viewpoint. However, urban capacity studies still remain in place and 'capacity' itself still remains part of the official discourse of land allocation. There was not, in any case, complete unanimity amongst the submissions of private house builders to Barker. CENTEX, a firm of consultants acting on behalf of the industry, commented, 'There is nothing intrinsically wrong with this approach provided that there is a reasonable certainty that a substantial element of the land will come forward for development'.[18]

The involvement of the Treasury in questions of housing and planning, notably as expressed in the publication of the Barker review in 2003 brought new factors into consideration. On one hand, in an attempt to counter under provision in growth areas, local authorities are asked to assess housing market trends, as for example expressed in trends in house prices (DTZ Pieda 2004). The implication might be read as a partial return to the previous predict and provide approach, except that the assessment of demand is an inexact science and itself requires the use of professional judgements.

On the other hand, local authorities in South East England and in other nearby growth regions have started to assess infrastructure capacity as well as environmental capacity in their housing land assessments (County Council of Essex 2005; Roger Tym & Partners 2005). Without further public investment and in the context of continued house building, the analyses show, existing deficiencies are likely to become worse, especially in relation to transport, social housing and community facilities. The Royal Commission on Environmental Pollution (2007, 28–9) has added to such concerns. It has argued that house building programmes should better recognise the existence of environmental constraints 'in the areas of water quality, water resources and flooding as well as air pollution, climate change' (ibid., 133). The Royal Commission (ibid., 90) also notes that in greenfield growth areas, the provision of public transport tends to lag behind house building and is characterised by uncertainties about its timing. Of course, without coordinated public transport investment, the development of new greenfield housing of whatever density will merely lead to greater car dependency and probably longer commuting.

Higher Residential Densities

The liveability and social implications of higher residential densities deserve closer scrutiny. Carmona (2001) has provided the most detailed account of planning control in relation to housing development in England, at least as operated in the early and mid 1990s. At this time, the typical aim of planning practice was to encourage lower density development, usually with the retention of more trees and greenery, than would otherwise have been preferred by developers. The assumption was that developers would always raise densities to squeeze the maximum development potential from a site and that planning was necessary to control any such tendency.

Minimising density in new housing itself has long roots in the history of town planning, going back to the first town planning legislation in 1909. In the context of urban containment policies, however, the promotion of lower densities was also a palliative. The logic of urban containment was to increase density through denying greenfield sites for new housing.

In contrast, since 2000, planning policy especially in England (DETR 2000c, para. 58) has assumed that developers are reluctant to raise densities to a level commensurate with what is desirable. Guidance has specified that net housing densities (the density of the residential site itself) should be raised from what was in the late 1990s a national average for England of about 25 dwellings per hectare (dph) to no less than 30dph and, as stated in the first range of guidance in force from 2000 to 2006, up to 50dph if possible (DETR 2000c, 316–18). Planning policy in Scotland has been less prescriptive and has suggested that a range of density levels to promote a choice of housing types and to suit different types of neighbourhood (Scottish Executive 2003). However, supplementary guidance in Scotland has also favoured increasing densities compared to that of typical suburban development in the 1980s and 1990s.[19]

Density and affordability In relation to the affordability of new housing, the case for higher densities is relatively strong. For example, for existing urban areas, especially those subject to development pressures, the promotion of higher densities increases the supply of properties in desirable neighbourhoods and, in doing this, moderates trends towards inflation in land and property prices. In London, in particular, higher densities are inevitable if an expected growth in population, households and housing need is to be accommodated (GLA 2003). The main qualification is that urban intensification is a complex form of development, one that is more likely to raise public objections and one therefore that is likely to cause more refusals.

Elsewhere, for greenfield sites, density controls in their existing form, that is to say with a general minimum of 30dph, have a role in promoting affordability so long as they are combined with planning policies to ensure the adequate release of greenfield development sites commensurate with demand. Combining density controls with greenfield land release promotes affordability in housing more effectively than the release of more greenfield sites and a deregulated density policy. Economic models of the house building industry in the South of England and the West Midlands suggest that the latter (more sites allocated to housing, plus the deregulation of density controls) would, most likely, lead to increases in plot sizes and, to some extent in house size and thus to an accelerated expansion of urban areas, but with less improvement in affordability, as measured by the price of dwellings (Bramley 1993, 14–16; Cheshire and Sheppard 1989). The models deserve repeating, but there is no obvious reason why their findings should have become out of date and unreliable.

In general, the relationship between residential density and land consumption takes the form of diminishing marginal savings as densities increase. Ever higher residential densities generate fewer land savings. The greatest gains in land savings and this is already recognised in government policy is to avoid low density housing, of say under 20 or 25 or at the most 30dph. The greatest contribution to affordability is in the same range. Further savings in land costs are possible at higher densities, but become less and generally have to face either increased complexity of design or, in the case of high rise, increased costs.

Though the impact of compact city on housing affordability is beneficial in principle, a qualification is necessary. The implementation of policies for higher densities has taken place in the context of urban containment policies that have prevented the development of affordable housing on greenfield sites. The compact city as a discourse and ideology may lead to a no-development policy with negative impacts on affordability. Partly for this reason, there is no necessary connection between existing patterns of population density and the distribution of affordable housing. To the contrary, measurements of variations in the urban population density at the time of the 1991 census show that those English cities with the highest population densities offered low income households the least amount of effective living space (Burton 2000, 1983).

Density and user preferences   The impact of higher densities on the quality of life is less easily measured than the impact on land take and is more controversial. Much depends, for a start, on the extent to which densities are likely to increase. Higher density is a relative concept that implies a variety of different types of environment at different density levels (see Table 7.1).

The existing minimum density urged by central government on schemes in England, that is to say of 30 dwellings per hectare (net), is not far outside historical precedents and is, in any case, in line with recent trends whereby developers have provided a higher proportion of higher density dwelling types such as low rise flats and terraces. The statistics of the national House-Building Council (NHBC) show, for example, that the proportion of detached houses built by private house builders in England declined from 45 per cent in 1999 to 32 per cent in 2002. The proportion of flats almost doubled from 17 per cent to 32 per cent over the same period. [20]

The National House Building Federation, the main pressure group representing the house building industry has argued that the increased proportion of flats is

Table 7.1   The implications of various densities

Units per hectare[1]	Indicative dwelling type(s)[2]	Comments
20 and less	Detached bungalows and two-storey houses with ample gardens: semis with ample gardens.	Houses for the affluent. Typical of 1920s and 1930s individualistic suburbia. Less common after 1945 and less common in Britain than in the US and France. Still a popular ideal.
21–30	Bungalows on small plots: two-storey detached, semis or wide-fronted terraces.	The average for new housing in England in the 1990s. Typical for suburbia throughout the twentieth century, from the time of the Homes for Heroes estates onwards. 30 is recommended as the maximum by the garden city movement before 1914 and by the Tudor Walters report in 1918 for Council housing. Recommended as the *minimum* for England by DETR (2000c) in 'PPG3'. 30 is also about the limit of detached houses (Diamond 1976).
31–40	Two-storey terraces with small plots. Typical for three-storey terraces.	36 is suggested as the practical maximum for two-storey terraces by MHLG (1952) using generous external standards.[3] This is a common range for suburban estates built in England immediately after 'PPG3' (FPDSavills 2003, 10).
41–50	Narrow-fronted two- and three-storey terraces with smaller front gardens, often but not always with grouped car parking. Terraces are usually combined with low rise (up to five storeys) flats.	This range is suggested by McConnell (1969) as the maximum for garages in terraces. Also suggested as the desirable maximum for family houses, as revealed through surveys of council and new town tenants in the 1960s, 1970s and 1980s (Goodchild 1997, 241; Smith and Burbidge 1973, i). 45 is the limit of achievable density for two-storey family dwellings according to Colquhoun and Fauset (1990, 171). This range also includes high density/low rise Council schemes of the 1970s and recently completed privately developed retirement dwellings.
51–75	Low rise flats with communal gardens, with narrow fronted two- and three-storey terraces on small plots. Generally grouped car parking for both flats and houses.	Typical of the range favoured by recent urban design theorists. A minimum 50 is preferred by Rogers and Power (2000, 191) and by the SDC (2007, 15). 60 is commended by Rudlin and Falk (1995, 55) and by Schoon (2001, 246–52). Also typical of 1950s and 1960s council estates with more flats than houses (McConnell 1969). Pre-1914 four-storey Scottish tenements are mostly between 65 and 80dpa (Hildebrand 2006).

Units per hectare[1]	Indicative dwelling type(s)[2]	Comments
76–100	Blocks of four and five storeys. Includes higher blocks, if these are surrounded by open space.	At this and higher densities it is generally impractical to provide ground level parking for every dwelling, even as grouped car parking. The GLA (2003) gives an example of nineteenth-century terraces developed at 80 with a modest front and back garden and direct road access to every dwelling. However, the GLA's measurement excludes surrounding access roads in the definition of the net area.
100 plus	Either high rise (six storeys or more) or low rise with reduced or no access to daylight for some rooms or some combination of high rise and reduced daylight.	Typical of council high rise built in the 1960s and 1970s, together with recently completed city centre high rise. Historic areas of many European cities are in this range, including Georgian and early Victorian London. Fashionable areas in Notting Hill, comprising subdivided four and five-storey terraces, are about 280 (GLA 2003). Most low rise British examples were condemned as unfit and demolished in the twentieth century.

Notes

1 Refers to the net residential area, defined as is conventional throughout the post-war era as the dwelling, open space around a dwelling and half the width of surrounding access roads up to a maximum of 20 feet (about 6.1 metres), excluding everything else. The definition of surrounding open space is subject to varied interpretation and inconsistencies. Moreover, where blocks include a significant non-residential element, for example ground floor shops, the measure is misleading. Recent definitions, notably DETR (2000c), exclude surrounding access roads.
2 Generalisations about the relationship between density and house types can only be approximate. This is partly because of the vagaries of the net residential area. It is also because specific sites pose different constraints. The maximum densities for any specific type will only be encountered on large, flat, rectangular sites.
3 MHLG (1952) uses habitable rooms per acre for a layout of family houses. The figures have been converted into dwellings per hectare assuming each dwelling has five habitable rooms.

a response to planning guidance.[21] The NHBF would almost certainly add that house builders want to complete more detached houses, in accordance with popular preferences. For example, an opinion poll of 1,000 people and reported in *The Guardian Jobs and Money* (27 July 2003) found that a thatched cottage, the seaside villa and the detached suburban homes remain the ideal types of home for most people. Popular aspirations for the detached dwelling are, moreover, not simply an English or Anglo-American cultural ideal. Surveys in France show the same tendency and also link this to a preference for owner-occupation.[22] Home ownership and the detached house give the occupants more autonomy and more scope for personal adaptations.

Market trends are also relevant, however. Flats and terraces tended to appreciate more quickly in value in the 1990s. For example, the Halifax House Price Index suggests that, between 1992 and 2002 the price of flats, including maisonettes increased on average by 149 per cent and that of terraces by 120 per cent. In contrast, the price of detached dwellings only increased by 102 per cent and the average price of all properties increased by 112 per cent.[23] (Recent trends would almost certainly show a different picture.) In any case, developers had little choice but to raise densities in the face of ever more expensive land acquisition costs, a tendency that has itself been partly caused planning policies. Most likely, planning policy and market considerations have interacted together to produce a more rapid and marked shift than would have been caused by either alone.

As a result, the average density of new housing has experienced literally a step change. According to official estimates, the national average density in England for new build since 2004 has been about 40dph, with little year-on-year change (DCLG, 2007d, 6). The highest densities of all are built in London and on previously developed sites in a way that is to be expected given high land values and high site acquisition costs in London. However, densities are also slightly higher than average in the North of England (ibid., 20) even though land values are generally lower here.

New, higher density estates look and feel different from the typical suburban estate of previous decades. They have also started to generate adverse reactions. The most common problems, as reported by consumers, are lack of car parking, lack of a garden or too small a garden, increased noise and decreased privacy. A review of recent survey evidence undertaken for CABE (2005c, 10, 15, 16), an organisation otherwise favourable to higher densities, notes, for example:

> The reduced parking standards of Planning Policy Guidance 3 on housing (PPG 3) have produced a high degree of frustration .... It was the most frequently mentioned of all problems encountered by the buyers of this type of housing. In the survey of those living in schemes designed to PPG3 standards.

> ... some frequent, specific and sometimes harsh criticism of higher-density projects directed against noise transfer between rooms and through walls shared with neighbours.

> ... studies testing the market for higher-density housing have found a great resistance to smaller gardens. The desire for a larger garden was often the motive for moving house.

Car parking is the most visible problem for visitors to recently completed estates. Roads, car parking and hard surfaces dominate these estates, with little space for greenery and planting.

Alternatives to car-dominated estates are available. It is possible, for example, to place grouped car parking on the edge of a scheme, with pedestrianised streets or landscaped green space at the centre. This is the approach generally preferred by the advocates of new urbanism design principles. It is also possible to place car parking underground. However, both grouped car parking and underground car parking have disadvantages and are rarely used. Grouped car parking, though common in higher density council estates of the 1960s and 1970s, is inconvenient for carrying shopping and other heavy loads and is generally disliked as it increases the risk of car-crime (theft of, theft from the car, vandalism to the car).[24] Underground car parks are expensive to construct and manage. If undertaken on a large scale, both grouped car parking and underground car parking are also ugly and have an off-putting, unsafe appearance.

The existence of car parking problems is a reminder that suburban or exurban high density estates, developed without public transport links, will, most likely, remain dependent on the private car. The intensification of existing low density, car dependent suburbs will likewise not reduce car dependency, in the absence of public transport investment.

Less visible than the problems of car parking, but at least as important, are the problems faced by families with children in higher density estates. Families with children remain the most sensitive to design failures, for example a loss of privacy or an inadequate private garden size or an absence of communal pay areas. Children are the most intensive users of outdoor space in residential areas and so deficiencies are likely to fall particularly on this group (Coffin and Williams 1989). In addition, in some recently completed estates, a lack of space within the home compounds problems of privacy and children's play (Mulholland 2003).

The defenders of higher densities commonly point to the existence of successful higher density schemes, notably in London. (See, for example, GLA 2003.) However, demonstration of particular examples of success does not constitute evidence for the general application of a policy. Moreover, the experience of living in London is different from that elsewhere, owing to a combination of circumstances – the limited alternatives that are affordable to most people, the existence of numerous local attractions that compensate for high density living and last but not least the existence of a relatively extensive and frequent system of public transport.

Low rise versus high rise   At densities between about 40 and 75dph two main alternatives are available – low rise/high density comprising houses with gardens and blocks of flats up to five storeys and high-rise/high density. The former is generally preferred by advocates of higher density in Britain. It is more traditional in terms of its impact on the townscape, provides a means of retaining a proportion of conventional family houses in inner city areas and, in doing this, promotes a degree of age balance to such areas. The most influential and certainly the most systematic statement in favour of low rise/high density is that of Cooper Marcus and Sarkissian (1986) who rightly note that success in design depends on paying attention to a large number of detailed considerations. Maintaining and increasing the numbers of family houses is especially important for social housing landlords in London where pressures for higher densities are also especially intense.[25]

Low-rise/high density is not a panacea. The most land efficient way of placing low-rise housing on a site is through a rectangular layout of long rows of terraces. This is the layout adopted in most pre-1914 working-class streets. The results can look bleak and monotonous, especially if they lack a front garden. Alternative forms of low rise/high density of the type built by local authorities in the 1970s have proved unpopular, owing to their use of non-conventional house types and layouts (Goodchild 1984; Furbey and Goodchild 1986). These non-conventional low rise/high density layouts also use separate footpath networks of a type that has been associated with higher risks of burglary and is generally disliked by the police for this reason.[26]

High-rise/high density has the advantage of providing the highest densities of all and is more easily standardised. High-rise has become increasingly used for private housing in and around city centres and has been taken up in big cities other countries, such as the US and Australia, as a means of taking the best advantage of views. Some high-rise apartments command premium prices as luxurious accommodation.

High-rise has admittedly had a poor reputation owing to its association with poor quality or poorly managed local authority built schemes. The reputation of these schemes has started to change, however, especially in London. Some blocks, notably Keeling House in Bethnal Green (East London), have been carefully conserved and improved and sold off to a relatively up-market clientele (Franklin 2006, 154–60). In addition, individual local authority built flats have started coming on to the market, mostly as a result of the exercise of the right to buy during the 1980s and 1990. These former council flats are generally less expensive than their privately constructed equivalents and have much more generous floor areas.[27]

The disadvantages of flats, and especially high flats fit, into three main categories.

First, other than in the most up-market schemes with integral secure car parking, flats do not escape the car parking problems that affect all high-density housing. The implication is that they work best close to public transport facilities.

Secondly, flats are less suited to children owing to the lack of easy access to ground floor play areas, to the tendency for children to cause more noise and therefore annoyance to neighbours, to the risk of falls from windows and balconies and last, but not least, to the stress that all this places on mothers (Littlewood and Tinker 1981). High-rise in some other countries, notably in the Far East, has proved more popular and more acceptable for families with children. Cultural expectation and lifestyles influence perceptions of what is acceptable. In Britain, accounts of housing in London also give a more favourable impression of the suitability of flats for families with children than would be likely elsewhere. Even in London, however, the acceptability of flats depends in part on the existence of low child densities (Cope 2002; Westminster City Council 1980). High child densities increase the noise on estates and also increase wear and tear on the environment and in relation to vandalism have an impact that is probably larger than variations in physical design (Wilson 1980).

Thirdly, flats and especially high flats generally have higher than average management and maintenance costs than houses with gardens. The likelihood is moreover that these costs will rise in the future as the blocks age. The extent of these higher costs is not always recognised. There have been examples in the past where local authorities have sought to cap the cost per dwelling of maintenance and management work in a way that failed to recognise the particular problems of tower blocks and other expensive to maintain property (Davidson 2000). It is also possible that homeowners living in newly completed private blocks are unaware of the likely long-term cost implications.

The higher than average maintenance and management costs are, moreover, a product of the physical form of the accommodation, rather than the legal arrangements. In English law, a specific legal arrangement that of leasehold involves a separation of the ground landlord and the owners of each flat and also gives the ground landlord the ability to require leaseholders to contribute to repairs. Leaseholders have felt vulnerable to rapacious ground landlords who have, in their view, insisted on excessively high rents, service charges, insurance and maintenance bills. [28] Exploitation of leaseholders by ground landlords certainly exists in specific cases. At the same time, the opposite risk also exists, namely that the difficulty of ensuring agreement on repairs amongst all the occupants in a block leads to under investment and disrepair.

General lessons of density   To summarise the varied evidence: neither density nor the different house types, with which density is associated, are a direct indicator of quality. The popular perception of density does not follow, with any precision, physical measurements of density (Bishop 1985). Much also depends on neighbourhood characteristics, including in this context the use or misuse of the built environment, issues relating to location, management and maintenance (Cope 2002; Tunstall 2002, especially 13–15) and questions related to security in the home, noise, neighbours and friendliness (Parkes et al. 2002; 2434–5). Housing quality is a package of different factors that interact with one another and that operate in different ways in different places in different cultural contexts (Rapoport 1982). As a result, it is not easy to make generalisations about the influences on quality as consumers see this.

The very difficulty of making generalisations has its own implication for policy and practice, however. The difficulty suggests a degree of caution towards any desire to determine an optimal density. Density criteria should not be imposed over and above the detailed requirements of a residential area, for car parking, privacy, open space and so on.

At the same time, some generalisations are possible.

*   Higher densities have, in general, been associated with increased difficulties for children. Problems include a lack of accessible outdoor space (as in high rise), the noise and other problems associated with high child densities or the competition between children's play areas and car parking, as in high density low rise.
*   Higher densities are also associated with the development of flats. While flats can provide good living environments, this is not the same as saying they will do so, given their higher management and maintenance costs.
*   Finally, the house with a garden represents a consumer ideal that local authorities would ignore at their peril if they wish to promote competitiveness

and social balance. In many inner city areas, consumers would almost certainly welcome a wider choice than the combination currently available of city centre flats and older terraces or, in Scotland, tenements (Bramley and Morgan 2003).

A further issue concerns the impact of recent trends on the property market. There have been examples in the past – for example Scotland in the pre-1914 era and France in the 1960s – where high land prices and high densities interacted with one another in an endless circle. High land prices pushed up densities, whilst high densities raised owners' expectations about the possibility of high land prices. Planning policy in favour of higher densities, together with the trend towards flats, rather than houses, has almost certainly acted to raise land prices since about 2000.[29] If owners' expectations are to be reduced, it may be insufficient merely to adopt a less prescriptive and more flexible density policy. Instead, it would be sensible for planning authorities to prepare a clear planning framework in which local densities are specified in advance, albeit in a way that enables a variety of types of scheme in different locations and neighbourhoods.

The Details of Urban Design: Mixing People and Activities

In relation to layout and the other details of urban design, conceptions of the ideal city have mostly amounted to a continuing reaction against the blueprints of modern architecture and modern town planning. For community-based activists, the reaction means a return to nature and an acceptance of a degree of untidiness, as for example in proposals for rural eco-villages. For the supporters of the compact city, in contrast, the reaction means a self-conscious exercise to mix together different types of people and activities.

The urban village The original urban village proposal made by Aldous (1992, 23) amongst others provides an example. It is subtitled 'a concept for creating mixed-use urban developments on a sustainable scale'. Within the context of a relatively high-density urban framework, where most accommodation takes the form of flats, the proposal rejects earlier principles of 'monoculture planning' and 'rigid compartmentalism'.

The term itself, 'urban village' has a tortuous, almost accidental origin as an urban design concept. The term refers to the name of a group of architects, housing and property professionals – the Urban Village Group – who in 1989 were asked by Charles, Prince of Wales to find ways of improving the quality of architecture and new building (Aldous 1992, 11). The term arose at a high level in the British establishment, but outside government and the professions.

The group envisaged a proposal along the lines that Leon Krier, himself a member of the group, had previously made for mixed-use 'quarters'. The term, 'quarter' is Krier's transliteration, that is to say a letter-by-letter substitute, for the French *quartier* or subdivision. Planning urban areas in terms of quarters is, for Krier (1984), a means of providing local identity and avoiding standardisation and sprawl. The quarter is a 'city within a city'.

'Quarter' does not make sense in the English language, however. The group established by the Prince of Wales used 'urban village' instead. They chose the term 'for want of a better label', as they stated in the second edition of the book of the same name. The fact that Prince Charles had previously used the term was probably another factor that enhanced its acceptability (Franklin and Tait 2002).

'Village' is hardly better, however. Both 'quarter' and 'urban village' imply traditional forms of urban living and a degree of local self-sufficiency that is outdated given current levels of mobility (Biddulph 2000). For residents distance is measured by time rather than by distance and time, using whatever form of travel is most convenient.

The provision of local facilities does not, in any case, mean that residents will travel more frequently on foot or by bicycle or by public transport, unless other factors discourage car use. Stead and Marshall (2001, 123–4) have summarised recent studies and suggest that the provision of local facilities reduces trip length, but not its mode. Much is also likely to depend on distance from a town or city centre. Residents living close to a town or city centre tend to travel less far compared to those living in suburban locations (Næss 2006).

The Urban Villages Group no longer has a presence on the web. It has probably ceased to exist as a separate pressure group. The term 'urban village' has fallen out of fashion, as have proposals for self-sufficient neighbourhoods. Yet other aspects of the urban village proposals, notably the theme of mixing, remain a recurrent theme amongst those who wish to work out alternatives to contemporary patterns of urban development.

Three types of mixing are apparent:

*   mixed land uses, meaning a combination of vertical mixing as in houses over shops and horizontal mixing in the form of a juxtaposition of housing, industry and other uses within the same area;
*   social mix, including a mix of tenures, and
*   mixed use of roads and streets, otherwise known as shared surface, streets, open to pedestrian as well as vehicular use and enabling pedestrians to walk round and through urban areas.

Each type of mixing raises its own questions.

Mixed land uses   As initially implemented, the main impact of the Urban Villages Group was to provide a rationale for mixed-use urban rehabilitation and new build schemes in and around city centres. The Covent Garden and Soho areas of central London were cited as possible examples in the original proposal. Other, subsequent schemes have included the Jewellery Quarter in Birmingham and Glasgow's Merchant City. These schemes and many others have brought empty property into use, promoted the development of city centre housing and in doing this have ensured that more people can live near to public transport centres.

Mixed use development is typically supported as a means of giving city centre and other streets more interest and character and to ensure that it has some life at all times of the day and the evening. It has also had a role in making made city centre streets feel safer. It offers additional surveillance of the streets and of commercial property and has as a result received support from housing managers, local authority officials and the police (Goodchild 1998). Residents living above a shop or a bank are, for example, likely to be quickly aware of a noisy break-in on the ground floor. This is not to say that the development of flats in city centres has an appreciable effect on the local crime rates. The statistics are too difficult to interpret and whatever effect exists is probably small in comparison with other influences on crime. However making streets feel safer is itself important.

As a result, the promotion of mixed use schemes has become the staple of policies to promote sustainable development. Even in city centre and inner city locations, a degree of caution may be necessary, however.

- Noise and light, especially at night, can contribute to a sense of stress. In 1998, for example, the Royal Town Planning Institute suggested that the development of high density, mixed use schemes requires stricter controls than is typical in suburban schemes, including additional 'restrictions on some uses (even within the same use class) and on hours of operation, and careful consideration of soundproofing, the position and design of windows, walls, fencing and landscaping'.[30] To this extent, a potential conflict exists between the proposals to encourage city centre housing and other proposals to promote a so-called '24-hour' city.

- Partly as a response to potential land use conflicts, the plans for many of the larger city centres, for example those for Manchester, Birmingham, Sheffield and Leeds, seek to differentiate areas as distinct 'quarters'. The quarters of Manchester city centre, for example, comprise 16 different areas, including the retail core, Chinatown, the gay village and the higher education precinct (Manchester City Council 2003). The different quarters in Manchester and elsewhere implicitly accept a degree of land use zoning, based on the existing character of each area and often specify areas that are most suitable for housing and mixed use schemes.

- Finally, some older residential areas continue to possess a mixture of uses, but in a way that causes a nuisance to residents owing to pollution, a lack of maintenance to the industrial buildings and the noise and the need to service the premises with large delivery vehicles. The Report of the English House Condition Survey states that in 2004 'Households living alongside commercial property have the greatest likelihood of living in a poor quality environment' (DCLG 2006b, 15).

Away from city centres and despite the apparent frequent use of the term 'urban village' as a marketing device, mixed land uses have been more difficult to achieve. Biddulph et al. (2003) have examined three self-proclaimed urban villages at Bordesley (Birmingham), Garston-under-the Bridge (Liverpool) and West Silvertown (London Docklands). The authors note patchy, uneven results, without a significant level of mixed use in any project. The consumer advantages of mixed use schemes are also likely to be less away from city centres. Public transport links are usually less convenient and cars are more likely to be needed for the journey to work, so placing a premium on the provision of suitable car parking arrangements

The experience of the urban villages, as developed, is a reminder that economic forces, as well as planning, favour land use separation. Some sites are better suited to one purpose rather than another. In addition, developers generally dislike the additional complexity of mixed land use, unless they see some positive reason for doing so. Developers dislike, moreover, the extra complexity of mixed use even if they endorse mixed use in principle.

At the same time and despite the advocacy of mixed use schemes, governments at both local and national level have been generally reluctant to constrain the location and design of employment generating activities outside town and city centres. For example, local authorities will generally keep in reserve a number of sites that they consider attractive to employers and these will usually include edge of town and greenfield sites away from housing.

Mixed use means the juxtaposition of homes and other uses either in the same building (for example on different floors) or in nearby buildings. Mixed use, in other words, assumes that homes and businesses retain a distinct identity. Live/ work schemes, in contrast, take the theme of mixed use further so that home and business uses co-exist within one another in the same property. To an extent, of course, all homes are capable of business use if they are equipped with a high speed internet link or if they possess a spare room for use as an office. However, live/work describes accommodation whose interior is specifically designed to enable both residential and business use. It differs from ordinary home working in the intensity of business use that is permitted and is also sometimes associated with shared services provided in a local business centre.

Live/work housing was invented as a specific type of scheme by planning authorities in east London as a means of better controlling warehouse conversions (*Estates Gazette* 9 October 2004, 148–9). It is promoted by a dedicated organisation, suitably called the 'Live/Work network', as a means of promoting sustainable development in towns and rural areas.[31] It is also promoted by some housing associations and by specialist property developers and agencies as a particular type of urban housing.

From the viewpoint of consumers, live/work schemes, raise questions about flexibility in use. For example, what happens if a resident obtains another job or if his or her business goes bankrupt? Does this mean that they lose their home, either under the tenancy conditions of a landlord or under the terms of a planning permission? Likewise, what happens if a resident wishes to move into a larger home? Do they lose their business space? If a restrictive definition of live/work is adopted, namely that such property has to be used as joint residential/business space (and not as either residential or business), the likely effect will be to reduce effective demand for this type of property, as well as to cause disruption for those who already live and work in such property. Live/work schemes almost certainly have a continuing role in marketing exercises. As a device for controlling the use of property, they are too elaborate and too restrictive.

Social balance and mix In relation to social balance, the Urban Village and related proposals are more a rejection of modern patterns of urban development, rather than strictly speaking a rejection of the aims of modern town planning. The official aim of town planning in Britain, at least in the 1940s when social idealism was most influential, was to promote social balance and social mix in the face of economic and social tendencies that pushed in the opposite direction. The role of the Urban Village is similar. Urban sprawl, it is suggested, encourages social polarisation through separating one social group from another. Higher density compact cities, in contrast, bring people together.

Social balance and social mix as envisaged in the Urban Village relates to both the age composition and the socio-economic composition of a locality. In relation to age composition, the Urban Village poses a contradiction between its desire to attract a mix of all different household and family types and its preference for higher densities and mixed uses. The usual experience is that high density/mixed use schemes are disliked by families with children, so long as there is a choice of accommodation. Ramwell and Saltburn (1998, 35–49) have documented the redevelopment of Hulme in Manchester. Here the initial intention was to increase the proportion of families. Social balance meant a population structure that conformed to the city average and avoided a concentration of mobile single adult households. Once the redevelopment programme started, however, the partnership committee that supervised the project came to accept that single adults were likely to offer the largest source of demand and that, for practical reasons, the housing stock should be mostly built with this group in mind. The experience of 'housing over shops' schemes is similar (Goodchild 1998). Where, for example, housing associations have developed mixed-use schemes with flats, the usual client group comprises single adults and childless couples.

The characteristics of the housing stock are not the only constraint on demand from families, however. Higher density mixed use schemes are mostly developed in or near city centres in areas usually with little or no childcare provision, few doctors' surgeries and few, if any well-regarded schools.

The disadvantages of families living in flats have led to suggestions that the best prospects for socially balanced communities lie in the inner suburbs and that resources should be directed here (Nathan and Urwin 2005, 55–6). However, inner city neighbourhoods are already commonly home to families, predominantly low income and sometimes ethnic minority families living in the older housing stock. Redevelopment of the inner suburbs would most likely involve the displacement of an existing population, with all the disruption and local opposition that this would involve.

In relation to socio-economic composition, social balance is advocated for reasons of social policy as well as for the aesthetic and environmental reasons associated with the Urban Village and similar concepts. Since 1997 and the election in that year of Labour government, promoting mixed communities has also been a central theme in national housing policy, expressed for example in England in the New Deal for Communities and the National Strategy for Neighbourhood Renewal (HM Treasury-ODPM 2005, 8). Numerous studies suggest, moreover, that living in segregated neighbourhoods has a series of damaging consequences for disadvantaged individuals and families – for example, higher rates of criminal behaviour, poor educational achievement and lower career aspirations (Bennett 2005; Beruba 2005; Maurin 2004; Oreopoulis 2003; SEU 2004). The main qualification is that the social characteristics of the family and individual are probably more significant as an influence on behaviour than the neighbourhood (Fitzpatrick 2005).

In Britain, the typical pattern of recently competed mixed tenure schemes is one of what might be called 'micro-segregation' by different streets, rather than 'pepper-potting', the complete mixing of different types of people next door to one another. Developers typically believe that complete mixing of social housing and owner-occupied housing on the same street would encounter consumer resistance. As a result, they typically set aside distinct sites for social housing within or more likely on the edge of a project. Residential surveyors also say pepper-potting reduces the marketability of a house. Most say, for example, that they have encountered prejudice amongst homeowners against living amongst or near to social housing tenants, though the prejudice is less marked in relation to shared ownership schemes (Goodchild 2005).

Newly developed estates generally possess few community-wide social networks that might allow residents to interact with one another. Almost certainly, for this reason, most residents of newly completed mixed tenure estates do not feel strongly about whether tenure mix and balance is desirable or not (Jupp 1999). Where residents do express a view, however, these are not always favourable. Living next door to a social housing tenant risks a loss of status, stigmatisation (Mulholland 2004).

In all this, there are few differences between the results of recent surveys and those undertaken in the 1940s and 1950s and concerned with the implications of class-based policies of social balance (Kuper 1953). If given a choice, people would prefer to live next door to those whom they would consider good neighbours.

There are examples of relatively stable pepper-potting, stable in the sense that it has persisted and has co-existed with a popular, in-demand housing stock. For example, in London in the 1970s housing associations mostly expanded their stock mostly through the acquisition of individual properties. Micro-segregation by streets is, nevertheless, more likely to prove stable in the long-term.

Street layout and crime   A further aspect of the Urban Village agenda, its preference for shared surfaces, pedestrian-friendly streets and footpaths, requires some background explanation. The Urban Village and similar new urbanism approaches favour so called 'permeable' street layouts in which one street links to another. These facilitate pedestrian movement and minimise the length of pedestrian journeys (Duany and Plater-Zyberk 1996, 210). They are also consistent with eighteenth- and nineteenth-century and earlier townscapes that Urban Village generally favours. In contrast, for many years, culs-de-sac have offered the preferred model of suburban street layout.

Culs-de-sac provide a simple form of traffic management and so long as the number of dwellings served is not too many, say less than 30; they also permit the dual use of road surfaces by vehicular traffic and pedestrians, as well as a land efficient form of development. For example Design Bulletin 32, concluded that shared surface culs-de-sac schemes were 'highly regarded by residents' and that '... no accidents at all had been recorded on shared surface roads' (DoE/DT 1992, 13). [32] Examples of shared surface culs-de-sac can be found in private and social housing from the 1970s onwards, both in new estates and in housing improvement areas. Shared surface courtyards provide a particularly efficient means of coping with car parking requirements in low rise schemes comprising terraces or low rise flats. They can also be designed to promote privacy. The main limitations concern the cost of the landscaping, the complex implications for underground services and sometimes the expectations of residents for a clearer boundary between the pavement and the road area. These are limitations of shared use, however, rather than of culs-de-sac versus permeable street layouts.

In the meantime, urban design moved on. Especially in continental Europe, innovations in what is now called traffic calming, based on a combination of revised traffic regulations, the use of speed humps and extensive landscaping, provided shared use street surfaces on any type of street and not just culs-de-sac, so long as vehicle volumes were not too high and car parking requirements not too demanding. The Dutch *Woonerf* or housing area was the most widely cited example and this was eventually given legal recognition in England and Wales in the form of 'Home Zones' introduced in the Transport Act, 2000.

In this context, and against the advocacy of permeable street layouts, the role of street layout in crime prevention has assumed an additional importance. In addition to the role of culs-de-sac in stopping through traffic, they also promote the principles of 'defensible space', as advocated by Newman (1973) and Coleman (1985). Culs-de-sac reduce pedestrian and vehicular access to a single point and promote visibility and surveillance within the controlled access area. Reducing access reduces the number of escape routes for offenders, reduces opportunities for crime by casual passers-by and, in addition, makes it easier for neighbours to identify strangers.

Defensible space principles have proved sufficiently convincing to be endorsed by the police, both in the advice given by most individual crime prevention officers and more generally under the *Secured by Design* label of good design practice (*Planning* 10 January 2003, 22). Most new social housing requires to be approved under *Secured by Design* if it is to go ahead. Admittedly most private developers do not apply for the label, almost certainly because they doubt its effectiveness as a marketing strategy. Nevertheless, police crime prevention officers may still become involved if they are consulted during the determination of a planning application.

Secured by Design includes other security requirements apart from street layout. It also includes guidance on the details of design and the way this can hinder or facilitate access by intruders. For example, *Secured by Design* includes guidance on the standards necessary to stop break-ins through the front door and windows or through the avoidance of climbing aids. It is, for this reason, insufficient to point to the success of *Secured by Design* as evidence for defensible space. For example, a study by Armitage (2000) has shown that *Secured by Design* estates in West Yorkshire have a lower incidence of recorded crime than other estates. However, the variation may have been due to a variety of different factors, not just the external layout.

The supporters of the cul-de-sac can point, nevertheless, to evidence in its support.

- An evaluation of a so-called 'alley-gating' project in Liverpool, found that burglaries in the enclosed areas fell by more than 55 per cent, in the same year as a 10 per cent increase occurred in all Liverpool Police Districts (Landman 2003; Young 1999). In an alley gating initiative, the back alleys of rows of terraced houses are closed off by the provision of lockable steel gates at all exist and entry points, with the residents being given a key.
- A detailed mapping exercise of incidents of burglary, theft of or from a motor vehicle, criminal damage, arson, public disorder and antisocial behaviour in a series of representative locations in Bedfordshire found that most, but not all culs-de-sac were free of incidents, in contrast to nearby streets. This same study also noted how the construction of railings across a street in Redwood Grove, Bedford led to a reduction in crime and antisocial behaviour (Knowles 2003?).
- The British Crime Survey whose 1997 survey included information on road type shows that culs-de-sac to be less at risk of successful burglaries than side roads or main roads. 4.3 per cent of those living on main roads experienced a successful burglary in the previous year, compared to 3.5 per cent living in a side road and 2.1 per cent living in a cul-de-sac (Budd 1999, Table A.3.6). This same survey also showed that the risks of an attempted burglary are as high in culs-de-sac as along main roads (ibid.). It is possible, therefore, that the design of culs-de-sac increases the likelihood of burglars being disturbed during the act.

The evidence is not wholly on the side of the cul-de-sac. The alley gate initiative is about back alleys rather than culs-de-sac. The mapping exercise in Bedfordshire relies on the visual impression of a pattern. It does not correlate the number of incidents to the number of dwellings in each type of street layout. Finally, the British Crime Survey also shows that the risk of burglary varies by many other factors – for example, by income (with higher income households being less at risk), by tenure (with private tenants being more at risk), by the type of area (with inner city households being more at risk) and by the presence or absence of signs of physical disorder such as graffiti, vandalism and rubbish and litter in the street (with areas of high physical disorder being very much at higher risk). Much is likely to depend on whether and how these different factors interact to produce a specific context.

Another study, by Poyner (2006, 31) sought to test the varied burglary rates in areas consisting predominantly of grid streets and those consisting predominantly of culs-de-sac. The study, based on 1987 data from Northampton, showed confusing patterns, with markedly different results for the burglary of electrical goods and the burglary of cash and jewellery. The most likely explanation is that other factors are at work.

Tests of the opposing permeable approach have been less common and less encouraging as a crime prevention initiative. Hillier and Hanson (1984) and Hillier et al. (1987) have noted that relatively isolated council estates in London have both higher than average crime problems and lower than average numbers of pedestrians on the street. Therefore, the argument goes, integrate neighbourhoods into the broader urban street network and this would itself counter crime and antisocial behaviour on streets (Colquhoun 2004, 72; Osborn 1993, 40–41).

In contrast, other studies have tended to give contradictory results (Nubani and Wineman 2005).or have gone against permeable layouts. Osborn (1993, 41) has provided an example from the improvement of the Studley Estate in Lambeth in the late 1980s. Here Hillier argued in favour of the creation of integrated routes through the estate to promote pedestrian movement. In fact, before Hillier's proposal was implemented, an independent crime survey showed a concentration of crimes against the person and thefts against the person on the edge of the estate, especially near an underground tube station. High integration of the urban street network and high pedestrian encounter rates coincided with a high crime rate.

A compromise between permeability and defensibility can sometimes be worked out. Closing or gating back alleys is, for example, a point on which both the permeable street advocates and the advocates of defensible space are likely to agree. A preference for short rather than long, branching culs-de-sac is also a point on which it is possible to find agreement (Hillier and Sahbaz 2005). Long culs-de-sac are less effective in providing local supervision of access points. Finally, most of those involved in the assessment of designing out crime would accept the importance of clear boundaries between private and public space (Crouch, Shaftoe and Fleming 1999, 12–16). The establishment of clear boundaries facilitates the control of space around the home and clarifies where pedestrians are (and not) permitted.

Another, simpler but more radical way forward might be to adopt different design principles for different parts of a city and different building types. The principles of permeable street layout are better suited to town and city centre locations and, in addition, to locations around public transport hubs where pedestrian flows are likely to be relatively high and where flats are most likely to be developed for density reasons. Most blocks of flats have, moreover, additional security features, notably electronic door entry systems that compensate for any supposed loss of security associated with a permeable street layout. In contrast, culs-de-sac best are better suited to a suburban environment with lower pedestrian flows and where houses with gardens are the norm rather than flats.

To an extent, new urbanism already supports, through the concept of an 'urban transect', a variety of different layouts according to the centrality of the proposal (Duany 2002). It would only be a relatively modest modification to incorporate an explicit reference, within the transect, to permeable street layouts in a high density centre and culs-de-sac in the suburbs.

A further series of qualifications are necessary. Studies of the impact of street have been narrow in its scope. The mapping and correlation exercises have been mostly about the relation of crime to street layout rather than pedestrian movement as an intermediate or independent variable. Assuming that people should be encouraged to walk around a city and will do so anyway, it would be better to measure variations in the ratio between the crimes committed and the number of pedestrians on the street. CABE, in particular, has argued for the provision of pleasant, safe streets as a means of promoting walking and healthier lifestyles.[33]

Finally, the focus of research on street layout has meant a neglect of community organisation and traffic calming measures, as in a Home Zone, as influences on crime and crime prevention. The supporters of Home Zones suggest, for example, that traffic calming prevents crime through promoting pedestrian use of the street and, more generally, through promoting community life.[34] Such claims are not supported by systematic evidence and are, in any case, not contradictory to the use of culs-de-sac. For example, a Home Zone may comprise a series of culs-de-sac opening off a through route. However, the reference to the role of community life is a recurrent theme in crime prevention. The reference suggests the importance of the use of space around the home and not simply its design. It also shows the limitations of a top-down approach to urban design, especially in the context of proposals to improve existing neighbourhoods

The gated community   In terms of street layout, it is simple to turn a cul-de-sac into a gated community. The cul-de-sac discourages access and places visitors under informal surveillance. The gated community physically restricts access and requires visitors to ask for formal permission to enter.

Like the cul-de-sac, moreover, except even more so, the gated community has been subject to attack from those who prefer free pedestrian movement and permeable street layouts. The context is different, however. The debate about culs-de-sac is between the supporters of the status quo and the advocates of an ideal city. The debate about gated communities is about avoiding a claimed dystopia. For their critics, gated communities represent, in the most concrete terms, the contemporary landscape of fear, privatisation and division (Graham and Marvin 2001, 267–76; Marcuse 1995). Likewise, for many local residents living outside, gated streets and gated communities send out an unwelcome message. They declare that a neighbourhood is unsafe, at least that is perceived as unsafe by those who live behind its walls. The walls themselves suggest separation and division, a desire to opt out of a local neighbourhood and a desire to be apart from other local organisations.

For their supporters, in contrast, gated communities are commercial products that have responded to consumer demands and to the practical difficulties involved in financing and maintaining a high quality of local environment. They are a response to concerns about antisocial behaviour and security fears of a type that are not confined to the rich and that should be respected (Manzi and Smith-Bowers 2005). For other supporters, they are a means whereby local residents can manage their own affairs and manage their local environment. For Webster (2001a), in particular, gated communities are little than a twenty-first-century, urban equivalent of the pre-1914 garden city estates that likewise sought to combine privately financed development, home ownership and collective estate management.

The provision of gates, their supporters would also argue, are not unprecedented. The gate is no more than a functional alternative to the concierge or door entry system long used in blocks of flats and the gated street is no more than a hybrid between an apartment complex and a conventional street. The existence of a gate is an obvious marker and an obvious way of deterring access to a residential area. It is not the only way, however. The layout of streets and paths can itself serve to isolate residential areas, as has been a common observation of the flats and high density low rise estates built by local authorities for much of the twentieth century.

In addition, the supporters argue, the development of gated communities allows middle-class and rich households to live in high-density inner city urban areas that they would otherwise avoid. It reduces the flight of the middle classes to the suburbs and so contributes to population stability in areas characterised by decline and social problems. The ability of gated communities to promote population stability amongst middle-class households is more of a hypothetical than an actual advantage in the context of trends in British cities. Gated communities have not existed for sufficiently long in sufficient numbers to enable an assessment of population trends over time. However, Newman (1980) has shown exactly such an effect from the existence of gated streets in the inner city areas of St Louis in the US.

In Britain and other European countries, gated communities are mostly a recent phenomenon and remain less common than in the US or elsewhere in the world. The garden city estates, with their distinctive co-partnership forms of property ownership, always accounted for a tiny minority of housing. Co-partnership, in any case, died out in the 1920s and 1930s, with the growth of conventional home ownership and council renting. Most likely, as Jaillet (1999, 147) has suggested, the long history of local public administration in Europe, combined with the intensity and detail of this administration and the existence of a strong national government, inhibits the possibility of conceiving of autonomous private communities. Homeowner and resident associations have long been stronger in the US than in either Britain or France. Attitudes towards policing are also very different in Europe with less dependence on private guards, let alone private armed guards of the type that Davis (1998, 248–50) states is typical of the more expensive gated schemes in Los Angeles.

The attitudes towards public administration are significant in another way. Depending on the scope of their ambition, gated communities involve a higher level of charges for their residents, for example, for street lighting and maintenance, but a potentially lower level of costs for public authorities. One reason why the number of gated communities has grown in the US is that local authorities may encourage and sometimes require the creation of private residential associations as a means of reducing public infrastructure costs (McKenzie 2003, 208). Of course, once residential communities start to provide local services, for example recreational facilities, they are also likely to take an interest in controlling public access. Charmes (2005) has reported a similar, albeit smaller scale tendency in France where local authorities have refused to maintain local streets. The result has been to force local residents to choose between long-term deterioration or, less likely, an independent self-funded road maintenance programme.

The claimed disadvantages and advantages do not permit *a priori* judgements about whether gated communities are desirable or undesirable. Much is likely to depend on the visual impact of a scheme, on the characteristics of the surrounding area, for example whether predominantly residential, industrial or commercial and in particular on whether it is seen as acceptable or not by local residents. Much is also likely to depend on whether any proposed gated communities cuts established or proposed footpaths or whether it cuts access to green space. Finally, much depends on the scale. The gating of a single apartment block of say 20 units is likely to have less impact than multiple gated streets or the gating of complete suburbs.

In relation to planning permission, an official study of their role in England states, 'the gating of developments should only be considered as a last resort' (Llewelyn Davies 2004, 30). The study does not say, however, what might be 'a last resort'. Local authorities have to make development control decisions within a given time limit. They are also generally eager to promote development on brownfield sites, eager to promote urban regeneration and eager to meet house building targets. In the absence of local objections, they are likely to let gated housing projects go ahead. Nevertheless, the long-term implications of gated communities and in particular large-scale projects, remain of concern.

Notes

1   Taken from the website of the Department for Communities and Local Government, consulted June 2006 at http://www.odpm.gov.uk/index.asp?id=1127930..
2   Taken from websitse of CABE, consulted June 2007 at http://www.cabe-education. org.uk/default.aspx?contentitemid=384.
3   The quotation is taken from the website of Global EcoVillage Network – Europe, consulted February 2007 at http://www.gen-europe.org/.
4   'What are eco-villages?' Available at the Findhorn Eco-village website, consulted October 2007 at http://www.ecovillagefindhorn.com/what/index.php. Gilman, R. (1991), *The Eco-village Challenge Living Together*, Summer 1991: reprinted at the website of the Context Institute, consulted October 2007 at http:// www.context.org/ICLIB/IC29/Gilman1.htm.
5   Consulted February 2007 at http://www.evnuk.org.uk/projects.html.
6   'New eco-towns could help tackle climate change', press release by the Department of Communities and Local Government, consulted October 2007 at the DCLG website at http://www.communities.gov.uk/news/corporate/newecotownscould.
7   This is the message of the advice given a specialist, not for profit planning consultancy called Chapter 7, 'The Planning Office of the Land is Ours', consulted February 2007 at http://www.tlio.org.uk/chapter7/preced.html.
8   Information is available from a number of sources on the web, including the Scottish Government site, consulted October 2007 at http://www.scotland.gov.uk/library/pan/ pn60–11.asp.
9   The website of Groundwork, consulted April 2007, is available at http://www. groundwork.org.uk/.

10 'Sustainable Urban Drainage' consulted August 2007 at http://www.swel.org.uk/suds. htm.

11 The website of the new urbanism movement has a section entitled the 'sprawl costs', consulted August 2007 at http://www.newurbanism.org/newurbanism.html.

12 'Energy and Transport Re-designing our need to move around' Version 1, July 2007. Produced by the Free Range Energy Beyond Oil Project consulted August 2007 at http://www.fraw.org.uk/ebo/index_info.shtml.

13 National Travel Survey: 2002 Section 2: Trends in Personal Travel, consulted August 2007 at the website of the Department for Transport at http://www.dft.gov.uk/pgr/ statistics/datatablespublications/personal/mainresults/nts2002/.

14 CALA Homes Ltd (2003) *Report on the Progress of Planning Applications– a House Builder's perspective* (available February 2004 at http://www.hm-treasury.gov.uk/media/ F644B/barkresp_CalaGroupRB_0903_32.0kb.pdf.pdf.

15 Letter addressed to Kate Barker and available February 2004 at http://www.hm-treasury.gov.ui/media/8B3DD/barkresp_StanhopeEL_0903_)9.3kb.pdf.pdf.

16 Available at the website of the UK Roundtable on Sustainable Development, consulted June 2004 at http://www.sd-commission.org&uk/roundtbl/report2/04. htm#housingandurbancapacity.

17 Consultation response available on the Barker Review section of the website of the Treasury consulted June 2006 at http://www.hm-treasury.gov.uk./consultations_and_ legislation/barker/consult_barker_profresp.cfm.

18 Consultation response available on the Barker Review section of the website of the Treasury consulted June 2006 at http://www.hm-treasury.gov.uk/media/E55/49/ barkresp_CentexDB_0903_54.5kb.pdf.

19 *Sustainable Housing Design Guide*, Chapter 2 *Planning, Community and Sustainability*, consulted June 2007 at http://www.archive2.official-documents.co.uk/document/deps/ cs/shdg/ch02/index.html.

20 Published in a national House Building Federation press release available July 2003 at http://www.hbf.co.uk/press_releases/hbf 11.html.

21 See a press release issued by the House Builders Federation in 2003 or 2004 *Flats: The Homes of England's Compact Future* and consulted October 2004 at http://www.hbf. co.uk/press_releases/hbf_11.html.

22 See, for example, '*le home sweet home idéal*', *Madame Figaro* 20 May 2004, available on the web September 2005 at http://www.madamefigaro.fr/deco/20050412.MAD0002.html. A report prepared on behalf of the association of the developers of individual homes in France *l'Union Nationale des Constructeurs de Maisons Individuelles* and available September 2005 at http://www.uncmi.org/rubbique.php3/id_rubrique=147.

23 HBOS Press Release *Flats Out Perform All Other Types Of Property* [6 December 2002] consulted on the web November 2004 at http://www.hbosplc.bom/media/ pressreleases'articles/halifax/2002–12–06–00.asp.

24 ACPO – Association of Chief Police Officers (2004) *Secured by Design – New Homes* consulted June 2004 on the secured by design website at http://www.securedbydesign. com/guides/index.asp.

25 See the National Housing Federation press release dated 14 October 2004 and available on the web at http://www.housing.org.uk/library/viewfile.asp?fid=3170.

26 ACPO – Association of Chief Police Officers (2004) *Secured by Design – New Homes* consulted June 2004 on the secured by design website at http://www.securedbydesign. com/guides/index.asp.

27 As reported on BBC News Friday, 7 May 1999, consulted in February 2005 on the BBC website at http://news.bbc.co.uk/1/hi/uk/336884.stm.

28 The main campaigning body is CARL, the Campaign for Abolishing Residential Leasehold. Their website, consulted September 2006, is at http://www.carl.org.uk/index.htm.

29 Calcutt review of house-building delivery, Submission by Home Builders Federation, 2007 London, HBF, p.14: consulted November 2007 at the website of the HBF at http://www.hbf.co.uk/index.php?id=1837.

30 Memorandum dated 19 January 1998 by the Royal Town Planning Institute to the United Kingdom Parliament Select Committee on Environment, Transport and Regional Affairs: para. 57 (available June 20004 at http://www.parliament.the-stationery-office.co.uk/pa/cm199798/cmselect/cmenvtra/495–vi/8040103.htm).

31 The website address is http://www.liveworknet.com/.

32 As reported on BBC News Friday, 7 May 1999, consulted in February 2005 on the BBC website at http://news.bbc.co.uk/1/hi/uk/336884.stm.

33 CABE's response to the Royal Commission on Environmental Pollution Urban Study, consulted October 2007 at the web site of Royal Commission on Environmental Pollution 'Written evidence submitted to the study on the Urban Environment' at http://www.rcep.org.uk/urbanenvironment-evidence.htm.

34 As stated at The Home Zone website, available January 2004 at http://www.homezonenews.org.uk/html/what_ahz.htm.

Chapter 8

Neighbourhoods of Choice
and Constraint

Urban design makes repeated reference to villages, neighbourhoods and communities. The neighbourhood is also an aspect of urban policy, for example in policies for social cohesion. Why should this be? What is the significance of the neighbourhood in planning and urban policy? What exactly is the neighbourhood in any case?

The neighbourhood and community can be distinguished from one another on the grounds that the former refers to an area and the latter to a social group. The question still remains, however, as to the relationship between neighbourhood and community.

The Neighbourhood in Theory and Reality

Difficulties of definition are compounded by a tendency for neither the community nor the neighbourhood to figure strongly in current theories of social change. To recap, these theories can be summarised as cultural theories, organised around various interpretations of postmodernity; theories of flexible consumption (otherwise known as hypermodernism) and theories of flexible production (otherwise known as post-Fordism and globalisation). Postmodernism partially admits community through notions of cultural diversity, but is also suspicious of community as too inward looking and divisive. Sandercock (1998), for example, favours cosmopolitanism rather than community. Theories of flexible consumption and flexible production say little on the subject. The former are concerned with individualisation and consumer choice, the latter with globalisation.

The Neighbourhood as an Intermediate Type of Space

One simple way forward is to look at the neighbourhood in relation to the concepts of 'public' and 'private', defining it as an intermediate type of space, distinct from either. In this context, Webster (2001a; 2001b) uses the term 'club realm', mainly as a means of showing how a neighbourhood provides services for its members and how these services cut across the conventional distinction between the private and public sectors. A club provides services to its members for a price and often subject to entry requirements. The neighbourhood has similar characteristics. The entry requirements of a neighbourhood comprise the price of the houses located there or their rent or, in the case of social housing, the eligibility requirements for access. The services are the facilities and amenities located there.

The reference to a club is more like an analogy than the strict application of economic theory. The club theory, as promoted by Webster (2001b), assumes that neighbourhoods are the product of individuals interacting with one another. It amounts to what might be called the 'spontaneous combustion theory' of community life and community organisation. Neighbourhoods and communities, it is said, emerge naturally as a means of coping with the uncertainties of urban life. Such an interpretation ignores the way in which the neighbourhood has political as well as economic aspects and is also commonly more informal and variable in its social organisation than the term 'club' would suggest.

The local, publicly provided school is a good example of the strengths and weaknesses of the club analogy. Different neighbourhoods lie in the catchment area of different schools, the quality of which typically varies substantially from one to another. Parents with children of school age or nearing school age will often pay a premium for access to a good quality school, with the result that house prices are higher in those neighbourhoods where the schools have a good reputation. As one might expect, the price of family houses is influenced more by the reputation of the local schools than the price of single person accommodation. For family houses, however, the difference is substantial. The additional cost of buying an equivalent home varies, according to one estimate of the market in Reading in the South of England, between about 19 per cent and 34 per cent of the average (Cheshire and Shepherd 2004, F416).

The state provides public education free of charge. However, inequalities within the housing market and the state education system turn the neighbourhood into a club the entry to which involves a charge. At the same time, the neighbourhood as club is not a product of the purely spontaneous action of individuals. The quality of schools and the terms under which children have access to those schools is also dependent on policy decisions. Political considerations are also relevant.

The gated community has similar implications. The gated community has frequently been interpreted as a type of club good (Webster 2001a; 2002; Manzi and Smith-Bowers 2005). However, the recent growth of communities should not be regarded as a natural tendency, of people coming together in the way that is implied by spontaneous production. The development of gated communities is tied to the political culture of a country and is therefore, in part, a product of political choice, for example, whether it is permitted under planning rules and whether it is encouraged by the arrangements for infrastructure financing.

The club analogy is too specific. The broad implication of the club analogy may be retained, nevertheless, namely that the neighbourhood provides some form of service for its members. Two alternative, but largely complementary interpretations are available in this context:

- One interpretation is that of the community of limited liability, as suggested by Hunter and Suttles (1972). The community of limited liability allows an understanding of the community as a series of social relationship that are intermediate between a traditional, pre-industrial close-knit community, itself a highly public set of social relations and a purely impersonal, individualised, economic businesslike relationship. The local community offers a potential escape from the world of work. However, it also has businesslike aspects. Communities are bought and sold on the housing market.

• Another interpretation, represented, for example, by Simonson (1996), is of the community as civil society, that is to say a type of organisation that is intermediate between the state and the market.

Concepts of the community as 'limited liability' and as 'civil society' have different roots in social philosophy. The community of limited liability has its roots in attempts to understand the impact of urban life on traditional forms of community life of the type that Toennies called *Gemeinschaft*. The community as civil society has its roots in political ethics and in the concept of *Sittlichkeit*, broadly meaning the customary, everyday and often taken for granted morality that arises through the participation of individuals in public life (Taylor 1979). The neighbourhood in this latter sense is about shared values and shared standards of behaviour. Taken together, concepts of 'community of limited liability' and as 'civil society' provide an understanding of the neighbourhood as arising from the way in which people remain dependent on the locality for aspects of their social life and the way, in addition, in which the specific characteristics of a neighbourhood arise from the interaction between residents, other social groups and the institutions of local and central government.

Types of Community Organisation

Concepts of the community as limited liability and as civil society imply a variety of different neighbourhood types that can, as an initial step, be classified as indicated in Table 8.1.

The typology is based, in part, on a distinction between a neighbourhood as merely a collection of people living together, sharing some sense of physical proximity and a neighbourhood as a group of residents conscious of shared concerns and seeking to act communally. The typology is also based, in the latter case, on one of scale. It is a distinction between those communal groups that act at the level of blocks and streets mostly in relation to the management of buildings, external spaces and behaviour in external spaces and expanded community groups that represent a locality to powerful external agencies. These latter types of group comprise the community of limited liability, properly (or narrowly) defined.

The self-conscious communal groups define what Suttles (1972) also calls the defended neighbourhood. Suttles confines the term to blocks and streets that residents defend against unwelcome visitors, unwelcome types of behaviour and unwelcome signs of physical decay or mismanagement. Equally, however, the expanded community of limited liability has a defensive element. This expanded community defends strategic external threats, for example an unwelcome development proposal or a reduction in public funding.

The typology is not intended to suggest that every town and city has or ought to have examples of each type. The typology is merely an exercise in attempting

Table 8.1   Types of neighbourhood group

		Smaller.....................................larger spatial scale	
	Site specific	**Groups, blocks and streets**	**The wider neighbourhood**
Sources:			
Hunter and Suttles (1972)	The face block	The defended neighbourhood	The expanded community of limited liability
Simonson (1996)	Local communities of public space	Lifestyle enclave	Voluntary association
Other relevant concepts and examples	The grassroots community Neighbourliness	Gated community Housing co-op	Neighbourhood committees Community Trusts
Main basis of grouping?	Physical proximity	Shared activities, shared management, exclusion of others	Shared political interests and identities

to classify different types of neighbourhood and community groups as and when they exist.

The grassroots community   The simplest and least self-conscious type of neighbourhood, the grassroots community, arises in any setting where people are aware of each other. It arises from the simple fact of people living close to one another or, in the case of strangers, undertaking leisure activities or working in close proximity to one another. The term 'face block', as used by Hunter and Suttles, is misleading as neighbours may also be aware of each other through sounds and even smell, for example of cooking, rather than through visual contact. In the case of groups who meet each outside the home, this type of local community is essentially informal and comprises a combination of 'regulars' who frequent a public space or communal meeting place or who live in the vicinity and strangers who happen to be in the vicinity. The neighbourhood so defined includes the 'third places' that Oldenburg (2007) calls the heart of a community and comprises local cafes, bars and pubs.

The grassroots community is the type of neighbourhood that has most obviously weakened in the past half century. For older residents in particular, the decline of the grassroots neighbourhood is part of their personal history. It is a part of their life and is used in this context to explain the decline of neighbourhoods over time. Older residents look to the loss of supportive networks, the loss of familiar, friendly faces and then see a link between this and processes of physical decay in a neighbourhood or the growth of irresponsible behaviour amongst residents. However, the sense of community loss is not confined to residents living in declining or run-down neighbourhoods. Interviews undertaken by Phillipson (1999) in different neighbourhoods in London and Wolverhampton in the West Midlands show that older people in general sense a loss of the grassroots community.

The loss of community amongst older people is based on subjective judgements. It is also experienced in almost purely negative terms. Yet the loss of the local community is also a product of the opportunities for longer distance social communication, opened up by modern technologies such as the car, the telephone and the internet. It is not necessarily an indication of a declining quality of life.

In any case, a good neighbourhood is not necessarily one where people are friendly in the sense of knowing all about each other or where interaction is strong and frequent. The usual picture of good neighbour relations in Britain is one where people keep a respectful distance whilst being friendly and helpful in emergencies or in giving occasional advice and information (Abrams and Bulmer 1986).[1] A 'good' community is, therefore, a place where neighbours have a mutual respect for the privacy of each other, do not cause a nuisance, where they look after their property and look out in addition for the interests of each other. (See, for example, Forrest and Kearns, 1999, 120.)

There is no long-term series of surveys to provide a quantifiable picture of change in the grassroots community in Britain. US data suggests that the decline in local neighbouring is easily exaggerated.[2] It is possible, however, to indicate current levels of neighbouring from a study undertaken as part of the General Household Survey 2000/01. The report (Coulthard et al. 2002, 27) states, for example,

> More than one in four adults (27%) spoke to neighbours daily. ... Just under a half of respondents (46%) said they knew most or many people in the neighbourhood, 48% said they knew a few people and 6% said they knew nobody.

Some social variations are apparent. Older people, unemployed people and those not searching for work are more neighbourly. Likewise, the longer someone has lived in their neighbourhood, the more likely they are to know and speak to their neighbours. Residents in South East England and especially in London are less likely to know their neighbours than elsewhere. People in the most deprived areas are more likely to speak to their neighbours on a daily basis. Equally, the same survey shows that social factors are not always associated with variations in the level of neighbouring. For example, those living in the *least* deprived areas are just as likely to state that they know most people or at least many people in the neighbourhood.

If the quality of neighbour relations is considered, rather than just the quantity, a different picture emerges. Those living in the most deprived areas have less trust of their neighbours. Taking the sample as a whole over half (58 per cent) felt they could trust most or many of the people in their neighbourhood. Some residents evidently have a 'generalised trust' of local people even if they do not know them personally. Only 40 per cent of those living in the most deprived areas trusted most or many of their neighbours compared to 73 per cent in the least deprived areas. Perhaps for this reason, those living in the most deprived areas also have lower levels of 'civic engagement', meaning lower levels of involvement in local voluntary associations.

The defended neighbourhood   The second type of neighbourhood, the 'defended neighbourhood'/'lifestyle enclave' is organised around shared activities and a shared concern with managing the local environment. In part, it may be understood as a positive desire amongst like-minded people to live together 'a gathering of like-minded individuals typically united by shared taste' (Simonson, 327), for example organised around sporting or leisure facilities. Equally, it may have negative aspects arising from a fear or dislike of other types of people or as a means of providing protection against problems and disruptions to daily life, for example against crime, antisocial behaviour and undesirable others.

The defended neighbourhood, in particular, involves mechanisms to exclude others and maintain internal social cohesion. Suttles (1972, 34–7) suggests that cohesion is maintained through the activities of local gangs, through restrictive covenants and most commonly of all through a commitment to local traditions and local establishments. Atkinson and Flint argue that the mechanism of control are likely to vary by class and that affluent residents are more likely to use formal and official means such as the police and the neighbourhood watch groups that provide a formal liaison with the police.[3]

At the same time, there are similarities between how the residents of deprived areas and affluent areas seek to control behaviour. Tenants groups in deprived social housing estates often arise to campaign over housing issues such as repairs, management and proposed remodelling or improvement schemes. However, once established, they invariably prioritise the prevention of crime and antisocial behaviour and will make contact with the police.

The lifestyle enclave/defended neighbourhood takes an almost infinite variety of forms. Much depends on whether the community is temporary, as for example in a seasonal student community or persistent over many years; whether it is informally or formally organised, as in a gated community; to what extent in the case of formally organised communities, a system of local services and of private environmental regulation is in place; whether, in the case of formal relations, the legal basis takes the form of a co-operative or some other legal arrangement in which a specific person or entity enjoys superior rights in relation to others (for example, a ground landlord in a leasehold arrangement); whether it is relatively open or relatively closed to new members; whether its residents belong to a privileged elite or an excluded minority; whether it has been established for an altruistic purpose, as in the case of eco-villages and so on.

Within a lifestyle enclave or defended neighbourhood, social networks are likely to be more intensive than elsewhere, or so one might think. The residents are likely to have more in common and more to say to each other. There is, however, a lack of systematic or detailed survey evidence to show this is so and much is likely to depend on the type and motives of the residents for living there and the obligations imposed by the community itself.

The expanded voluntary association   The final category of neighbourhood, the expanded voluntary association or expanded community of limited liability, has the strongest political presence. Voluntary associations are sometimes described as community partners or stakeholders in the language of local government and again they take various forms – community development agencies, community development trusts, elected parish councils, area forums, area committees; user forums, user management committees; tenants and their representatives.

From the viewpoint of planning and urban policy, expanded communities comprise two broad categories. First, they comprise those groups that have arisen as a means of defending local amenities against unwanted development. Such groups stand as material evidence against the view of deregulation-minded theorists such as Pennington (2003, 255) that spontaneous communities have the potential to replace top-down planning. The usual, almost unanimous call of community groups is for more effective planning in the form of measures to control the activities of developers and to protect the quality of the local environment.

These defensive groups are often characterised as 'NIMBYs'. The term itself is of recent origin, not being encountered before about 1980, despite its current widespread use.[4] It is typically used pejoratively, as a means of undermining the case of objectors, especially of middle-class objectors, to development proposals, including proposals for new housing (Bedford et al. 2002).

Treated as an aspect of consumer demand, in contrast, NIMBYism is central to the politics of positional goods. Residents want the best of all worlds. They want electricity, airports, motorways and the other accoutrements of modernity. Equally, they want to live somewhere without the impersonal landscapes of electricity pylons, high-speed roads and huge sheds that accommodate factories and distribution centres.

The outcome of NIMBY resistance is to encourage a tendency for the least desirable forms of development in those neighbourhoods least able to mount an effective counter campaign. In the case of housing, a further risk is to block development completely, so restricting supply. Housing consumers, for example first-time buyers, tend not to form organised groups. Counter measures include

• the preparation of clearly articulated city-wide or broader policies that can override local objections;
• the use of various educational and conciliation measures that might prevent overly antagonistic and adversarial positions; and finally
• the use of detailed design measures that might mitigate or avoid local environmental impacts and that also show a willingness to compromise.

The second type of expanded neighbourhood group comprises those that have either arisen as a means of pressurising local service providers or have been established by service providers to increase their accountability. Public service providers in many different fields, including social housing, education and the police, have to consider local variations and differences if they wish to reach people throughout a city. These local variations are, moreover, likely to become more marked where lower income and ethnic groups live in segregated communities.

Some voluntary groups have acquired direct delegated responsibility for the provision of public services, for example local job training, the management of parks and open spaces, the organisation of cultural and artistic projects, out-of-school education and other, more commercially-oriented services. Community Development Trusts, local not-for-profit business agencies provide an example. These and other similar service-provider groups are qualitatively different from protest and representational groups. They have to be formally organised, with fully paid, trained staff and internal systems to ensure financial viability and accountability. As a result, community service providers have similarities with both public service bureaucracies such as local authorities and business companies. Moreover, the establishment of a service provider group typically requires training and the support from the local authority and other institutional actors (Purdue et al. 2000).

The development of neighbourhood associations is also often limited by a shortage of effective and strong community leaders. However, the opposite weakness is also sometimes apparent. Community leadership itself can, over time, become too strong, too rigid and too embracing with the same people occupying leadership positions in a range of different groups. Even with exceptional leadership, the strength of local groups is likely to depend, in part, on the availability of public funds to cover the employment of staff. Many of these projects depend on time-limited funds of say, three or five years and, as a result, their future is likely to be uncertain and dependent on public policy.

The Community as a Space for Debate

The interaction amongst voluntary associations and community groups, including both NIMBYs and public service oriented groups as well as the interaction between these groups and other institutional actors constitutes the public realm as understood in theories of deliberative democracy, applied in particular to planning by Healey (1992) and Forester (1993). The public realm is the realm of political debate and public involvement, as distinct from the private world of the family and individualised consumption. Deliberative democracy is democracy as community involvement and, in the case of strategic decision making, as a community of community groups, arranged at a variety of different spatial scales, not just the neighbourhood but the city as a whole and, in some cases, the region. It implies a new and more fluid style of politics, one that is, in particular, less dependent on party-political allegiances and more on a repeated process of consultation.

Rationales   To an extent, deliberative democracy has a pragmatic rationale, given the complexity of urban policy, the need to ensure that public agencies remain informed of local needs and local differences and the need of public agencies to ensure a degree of cooperation and support from local residents. For example, neighbourhood regeneration in France involves methods for local consultation, even through the assumption of French urban policy goes against so-called Anglo-American 'communitarianism' in favour of a more standardised, centralised approach. French urban policy has tended to downplay the representation of ethnic and religious groups in favour of local neighbourhood committees and councils and favours, in addition, public/public partnership arrangements without involving the private and voluntary sectors at a strategic level as is typical in Britain.

In Britain, various arguments have been advanced in favour of community involvement. The Urban White Paper *Our Towns and Cities* (DETR 2000b) sees, for example, community involvement both as a type of collective social right and therefore as an end in itself and also as a means to other desirable social outcomes – overcoming alienation and exclusion, improving the delivery of public services, promoting coordinated policies at the local level and generating a commitment to the area amongst local residents.[5] In part, the rationale is to promote the modernisation of public services, ensuring that these are better adapted to diverse social needs. In part, the rationale is to reinstate social relations that are assumed to have decayed as a result of the decline of community and the process of social exclusion.

The reinstatement of social relations is often expressed through the concept of 'social capital'. This latter has various definitions and various themes, including social support from friends and neighbours, involvement in local social networks and participation in civic institutions and voluntary groups. However, the most distinctive aspect of the concept of social capital is to specify a series of benefits of community involvement, both to the individuals who participate and to society in general (Putnam 2000). In particular, areas with high levels of participation in voluntary groups have, to use the words of the Office for National Statistics (2001), a 'well-established' relationship with a wide range of benefits, better employment prospects, better health, lower risk of offending. Promoting participation in voluntary groups, such a statistical relationship suggests, promotes the individual welfare of residents and keeps them out of trouble.

The case for social capital is not wholly convincing. Informal groups vary in their quality and character. Some informal groups are, for example, criminal or semi-criminal in character. Membership of a group can also serve to exclude others, as for example in the 'defended neighbourhood'. Applied to the neighbourhood, moreover, concepts of social capital tend to confuse different types and spatial levels of organisation.

However, the conceptual uncertainties associated with social capital do not undermine the general case for participation and the promotion of community involvement. Deprived individuals and groups are less likely to possess the personal resources to make effective individual complaints and are less likely to possess the financial resources to move elsewhere. As a result, direct community involvement is generally the only practical way for less affluent groups, including unemployed, elderly and low-income groups to influence the administration of public services at a local level. Conversely, direct public involvement offers a means whereby neighbourhood service providers of all kinds – social housing agencies, parks and recreational departments, the police, for example – can better understand local problems and ensure that they are meeting local needs.

Community involvement has, moreover, a specific justification as a means controlling proposals for the remodelling of deprived neighbourhoods. So long as residents have an effective influence, their involvement will automatically counter any enthusiasm for bizarre ideas on the part of professional designers and will, in doing this, reduce the risk of subsequent stigmatisation. To an extent, the risk of bizarre designs has lessened with the demise of the modern movement and the rise of new urbanism, neotraditional and similar design concepts. Many of these latter ideas involve an adherence to a set of specific design rules, however and were often worked out with a generally affluent client group in mind. The tendency of new urbanism and neotraditional urban design to ignore the implications of designing against crime is an example. Community involvement remains necessary as a means of applying urban design concepts to the specific problems associated with different neighbourhoods.

Despite the arguments, governments seldom pursue community involvement as a single overriding priority. Community groups routinely argue that local authorities are not committed to participation and are only prepared to promote involvement if required to do so. Community groups and local authorities have a major and obvious disparity in terms of power and resources. The attitude of the local authority is therefore crucial and this varies from place to place. The time and frequency of consultation are also important. Some types of intervention, for example master plans and other plans prepared within the statutory planning system can take years to implement. Initial consultations, undertaken during plan preparation, are likely to become outdate unless maintained through repeated dialogue.

In addition, some types of area and some types of regeneration scheme are outside the framework of community-based initiatives. Economic costs are likely to rule out community uses for high value sites of significant commercial potential, for example in and around city centres. These sites are subject to policies to promote urban competitiveness rather than local democracy or to reverse neighbourhood decline. The future of sites of strategic or policy importance, such as conservation areas, are also likely to be determined outside a local community. Residents may be consulted, but with the final decision being made elsewhere.

Budgetary constraints and the requirements of financial accountability are a further consideration. It is, for example, not generally acceptable for a government agency to give local communities a budget without some direction about its use. The provision of public funds is itself likely to lead to decisions, targets and accounting systems being imposed on local programmes.

Finally, at both local and nationals level, community-based initiatives have a political limitation in their low profile and their tendency to take credit away from elected politicians. Perhaps for this reason, governments also promote large-scale apparently prestigious projects that turn attention away from local communities. The so-called 'Northern Way', a strategy for regional development in the North of England published in 2004 (Goodchild and Hickman 2006) provides an example. The government went for growth and big gestures, when previous policies had focussed on local initiatives. The difficulty with big gestures is, of course, that these can easily become remote and irrelevant.

Bringing different parties together   Community involvement takes place in a context where the world of residents and the world of government is separated by a gap, arguably a chasm, of different concerns, different vocabularies and different interests. The gap is structural. It reflects broader social and economic inequalities. It is, for example, not so marked for those neighbourhoods where a high proportion of residents have experience of professional work. Conversely, in deprived areas, community representatives working on a voluntary basis sometimes express resentment of having to work alongside highly paid professionals (McCulloch 2004, 82).

The gap between professional and local worlds means that, at a theoretical level, the limitations of participation can be interpreted as a product of the systems of class and other forms of domination, as for example in the social models promoted by Bourdieu (1984) (Cabin 2004). Either participation is limited by educational and related cultural constraints that deter the involvement of low-income residents. Or, in a slightly different interpretation, participation is a means whereby decision-making elites manipulate situations, maintain their hold on power and justify their decisions and employment (McCulloch 2004; Mercier 2006).

The impact of class and similar structural constraints can be tested through surveys of resident participation. The New Deal for Communities (NDC) initiative, started in 1998, is the most thoroughly researched of all local exercises in community involvement in Britain. Surveys of community involvement in the various NDC areas suggest that, on average, participation rates in local organisations in NDC areas are only about 60 per cent of the national average. Such a pattern is consistent with the pattern in which poorer and more deprived areas have less 'social capital' than others. The surveys also show that in 2004, six years after its establishment, about 19 per cent of the residents who had heard of the initiative had participated in some form of consultation or other local activity connected to the project. Those most likely to participate were women, older people, those with educational qualifications and those who had not moved home in the last five years (Grimsley et al. 2005).

The tendency for older and more educated households to participate more frequently is a common observation. It has, moreover, undesirable consequences. Middle aged and elderly residents sometimes find the behaviour of local youths to be threatening. Any failure to involve young people is likely to exacerbate any such fears.

Nevertheless, a minority of residents is prepared to become involved in participation projects. If participation were merely an aspect of domination, what would motivate anyone to participate? The answer is obvious. People become involved because they can see the possibility of influencing change. Residents participate because they can see the prospect of neighbourhood improvements that they want to influence or because, in the case of redevelopment projects, they wish to represent people at a stressful time or in the case of planning schemes, they are pursuing the possibility of reducing the local impact of development projects.

The targeting of resources on specific neighbourhoods raises other issues. Targeted programmes can cause a sense of resentment amongst those who do not benefit especially where local rivalries involve ethnic tensions. In the North of England in particular, residents in predominantly white working-class neighbourhoods have tended to see local communities in terms of a sharp 'us and them' divide and have complained that funds are mostly directed towards Asian areas. In the run-up to the riots of 2001, the propaganda of extreme right-wing political parties further encouraged tensions.[6] However, the reverse argument is also sometimes heard namely that areas of black or other minority ethnic group are neglected exactly because of their minority status.

The logic of the complaints about over-favourable treatment is to move away from highly targeted programmes to a city-wide view that might spread out renewal projects over a wider area. There are, moreover, other reasons for a broader city-wide view – the expense of targeted area-based programmes in relation to the relatively small number of beneficiaries, the fragmentation caused by a different initiatives and areas, the need to pursue policies across extensive labour market and housing market areas and, finally, a desire to allow representation from interest groups that are poorly represented at the neighbourhood level, for example those representing young people or smaller minority ethnic groups. The Local Strategic Partnerships established in England under the Local Government Act, 2000 are the most important vehicle for such a city-wide view.

However, specific neighbourhood-based interventions do not disappear in the context of a Local Strategic Partnership. The differential treatment of different areas and different communities is inevitable in any strategy that seeks to counter disadvantage and as part of this to tackle racial disadvantage. Some groups and some neighbourhoods are simply poorer than others and their members are more in need. Area-based priorities have to be based on needs if they are not to contradict the principles of the Race Relations legislations and the principle of equal treatment of all. The answer therefore is to prepare the evidence to counter criticism and to open up the debate to different community groups so that they can better appreciate the issues.

The diversity of different types of community organisation, the rivalries between different areas for limited funds, the frequently diverse social composition within any expanded neighbourhood, the problems of local leadership and of financial uncertainties and the finally the problems of coordination between different public bureaucracies, all these factors hinder the pursuit of coherent long term local strategies. The Local Strategic Partnerships have, for example, varied greatly in their effectiveness, with some being criticised as no more than strategic talking shops, with little practical impact. The relationship between community plans and the development control function of town planning has, in particular, appeared tenuous. Likewise, progress in implementing the New Deal for Communities project established in 1999 in 39 neighbourhoods in England was, at first, slow and patchy, owing to disputes within the boards established to manage the programme and to tensions between residents and other agencies, including external consultants brought in for their advice (Polly Toynbee, *The Guardian*, 17 September 2003).

There is no simple way, no direct footpath towards community harmony. Communities divide as well as bringing people together. Moreover, the 'community' as neighbourhood in any specific place is not necessarily a single community in a social sense. It is often a loose collection of different types of local social groupings.

Yet the involvement of community groups, even on a patchy basis, is surely preferable to their exclusion. Even a process of muddling through keeps public bureaucracies in contact with their users in deprived communities. In addition, the same process requires different groups to meet one another so fostering mutual trust. It requires different groups to negotiate priorities and to come to terms with their differences (Allen and Cars 2001). Negotiation requires the devolution of power, however. Involvement in local partnerships and similar bodies requires different parties to see their involvement will make a visible difference.

In addition, the process of community involvement encourages people to reflect on where they live and to take an interest in places and issues that they had previously ignored or, in the case of issues, had previously considered insoluble. The process of community politics is, in this context, as significant as the outcome or agreement. Community involvement is not a panacea, but, where determined efforts are made, the benefits generally outweigh the negatives (Burton et al. 2004, vi).

A deregulated, market-oriented approach is also no answer. Calls for total local control imply communally provided public services as a supplement or replacement to the welfare state, depending (Beito et al. 2002; Pennington 2003; Webster 2001a). This is the pure 'bottom-up' approach in which communities help themselves without financial support and without the regulatory framework that such support implies.

However, the abandonment of the welfare state, and as part of this the abandonment of publicly financed community development, leads to other dilemmas. In such a context, the income of local community groups become dependent either on commercial projects or on the preferences of private benefactors and charitable organisations. Neither commercial projects nor private sources of funds necessarily correspond to local community needs any more than a conventional welfare state approach.

There are exceptions. In Sheffield, a local community business, the Community Development Trust for Manor and Castle has been able to use its ownership of land to generate community funds, albeit in circumstances where land values increased from very low levels (Interview with Director in 2007). However, an exception should not form the basis of general policy recommendations.

A joint public sector/voluntary and community sector approach, though one that is open to private sector participation as is current practice in most of Britain, remains the most satisfactory way forward. However, the precise approach adopted at any time or place is likely to vary. Moreover, working out the details of any approach involves judgements about the extent to which any single funding programme is concentrated in specific neighbourhoods.

Policy and Practice in Contrasting Housing Markets

Variations in income level, status and ethnic composition ensure that different neighbourhoods have different characteristics and different types of problem. The difference is magnified moreover by trends within the housing market. The housing stock is durable and inflexible in face of relatively rapid rates of change in the housing market. The neighbourhood considered as home likewise appears as a point of stability to residents in the face of the impersonal workings of the housing market (Cooper Marcus 2006, 203–6). Yet change is almost inevitable. Some neighbourhoods decline in the face of weak demand, so generating one set of problems and policy responses. Others go upmarket in a process of gentrification that generates a distinct pattern of losers and gainers.

Low Demand Neighbourhoods

The former type of problem, that of low housing demand, is concentrated in the North of England and parts of the English Midlands (ODPM 2003b). Here, the extent of the problem is potentially substantial – perhaps as many 1.5 million homes according to one official estimate in the North of England alone (NWSP 2004, 56). These are also the regions where the government's main policy response, the nine 'Housing Market Renewal Pathfinders' have been active since 2002. Similar problems have also been reported in Scotland with increasing market segmentation in the owner-occupied sector, between an increasingly low demand lower end and the rest (Craigforth and Newhaven Research 2004). Outside England, however, low demand has not been the subject of a separate policy initiative.

Characteristics and causes   The problem can be summarised as a combination of the following:

• an obsolete or obsolescent housing stock (housing that fails to meet contemporary lifestyles);
• a surplus housing stock (an excess of available stock in relation to the scale of demand); and
• unpopular neighbourhoods (with a poor environment, poor reputation and concentrations of deprived individuals and families).[7]

The causes are various. An almost inevitable consequence of choice in the housing market is that higher income individuals and families move to more attractive areas, whilst low income and often poorly qualified individuals move into relatively inexpensive properties in low demand areas. Once started, moreover, the process of market differentiation and localised decline may acquire its own logic and momentum. Neighbourhoods become trapped in a 'spiral' or 'vicious circle' of environmental deterioration, poor reputation and withdrawal of investment in private housing (Andersen 2002; Hall 1997; Lee and Murie 1999; Power and Tunstall 1995). Continued building on greenfield sites exacerbates local problems, notably through offering a more attractive alternative for families, say those aged between about 25 and 45 years of age.[8] However, the problem is not simply caused by processes within the housing market. In the North of England, low demand is associated with local concentrations of unemployment (NWSP 2004, 19), an absence of business activity (Troni and Kornblatt 2006) and localised long-term population decline (Leather et al. 2007, xiv, 27).

The impact of low demand varies between different tenures. It has a particularly severe impact on owner-occupied housing. Low demand in owner-occupied housing means house prices that decline either in absolute terms or in relative terms compared to elsewhere. Low demand traps owner-occupiers and causes a collapse of investment. In 2005, according to the English House Condition Survey, about 49 per cent of households in Pathfinder areas lived in owner-occupied homes. Equally, however, low demand causes problems for social and private landlords, causing a loss of income from vacant properties and sometimes increased management costs. In 2005, about 38 per cent of households in Pathfinder areas lived in homes owned by social housing landlords and 14 per cent lived in privately rented homes (Calculated from DCLG 2007b, Table A).

In the privately rented sector, the impact of low demand has some positive features from the viewpoint of landlords. Low priced property commonly generates higher yields (that is to say a higher rental return in relation to capital purchase cost) than higher priced property. Such property is therefore particularly attractive to landlords prioritising a rental income rather than capital gains. As a result, landlords are often active in low priced areas, buying up properties and converting them for rent (Hickman et al. 2007).

Existing residents, especially long-established owner-occupiers often blame landlords for the contributing to neighbourhood decline. They argue that landlords let their property to tenants who have no long term interest in the future of their area; that landlords do not control their tenants in the case of antisocial behaviour and that the landlords' neglect on investment and repair itself brings down the value and reputation of an area. The concerns of residents often extend, in addition, to doubts about the good character of the landlords and the agents they employ. However, without investment by private landlords, it is likely that prices would be even lower. It is also possible that, contrary to the complaints of residents, private landlord investment follows rather than causes an increase in house prices (Leather et al. 2007, 61). It is difficult to believe that, without some prospect of future capital gains, landlords would wish to invest in neighbourhoods characterised by high levels of vacant properties.

Though estimates indicate that substantial numbers of property are at risk, it is easy to exaggerate the problem of low demand. The problem is patchy, localised, variable over time and less marked than, say, five years ago. The term 'low demand' does not, in any case, do justice to the variety of housing and environmental problems in the North of England. In Bradford in West Yorkshire, for example, problems of poor location and relative unpopularity have affected the larger, mostly peripheral local authority built estates in a way that corresponds to the typical low demand scenario. At the same time, other types of housing problem have emerged in the older terraced property in the inner city. Here house prices are relatively low and declined relative to those in the suburbs in the 1990s. Yet low prices in Bradford's inner city are associated not with small households and an elderly population as might be expected from an area of population decline, but with a relatively high occupancy rates and a relatively young and growing Asian population. Low prices in the inner city of Bradford, like similar Asian areas elsewhere, reflects low purchasing power, rather than a surplus housing stock.[9]

The experience of the inner area of Bradford suggests, in turn, a more general lesson. House prices and housing demand are not ends of policy. Both low prices and high prices can trigger problems – the former because of environmental deterioration and a lack of investment and the latter owing to increased problems of affordability. Instead, the crucial questions concern the quality of housing and neighbourhood and the degree of access for different economic and social groups (Hickman et al. 2007).

The response to low demand   Where problems of low demand have occurred, much of the initial responsibility has fallen on social housing agencies. If the problems are not too severe, social housing landlords have various options. Typical measures include:

- physical works and investment that offer a visible and tangible sense of improvement and that modernise the property, for example in relation to bathroom and kitchen facilities, heating or insulation (PAT7 2000, 39–40);
- management, remodelling, clean-up and policing measures that tackle problems of crime and antisocial behaviour;
- lettings initiatives and stock adaptation and conversion projects that open social housing to new sources of demand such as students, young professional workers or ethnic minorities; as part of this increasing the proportion of minority, usually Asian households that have been under-represented in council and former council estates;
- selective demolition and sale of sites and properties for private housing development, with a view to reduce vacancies and to establish a mixed tenure and mixed income community; and finally
- for estates in multiple ownership, reducing management and maintenance costs through combining the efforts of different social housing landlords (PAT5 1999, paras 164–73).

The extent to which a single social housing landlord or even a single local authority can counter low demand is limited. Housing markets operate over extensive areas and low demand itself is caused by a combination of housing and economic forces. The promotion of private housing development provides an obvious example. From the viewpoint of a private developer, the acquisition of an empty block or empty site in a depressed estate or neighbourhood is subject to risks and constraints, especially if the estate is located in an economically depressed town or city. For many years, and with the exception of locations close to town and city centres, the general experience has been that private investment is only forthcoming after an area had first significantly improved (Goodchild et al. 2002).

Partly owing to the caution of private developers, social housing agencies generally lead redevelopment projects, building for sale as well as for rent. Local authorities generally also favour social housing agencies as partners in the development and redevelopment of sites in their ownership. Social housing agencies have a series of advantages. They have experience of delivering to minimum design standards, including the provision of specialist housing such as mobility housing and lifetime homes. They often have mechanisms in place to deliver subsidiary benefits for local people such as construction training and employment. Finally, they can provide affordable rented housing without the necessity of a partner organisation and with less apparent impact on the sales price of the land on disposal.

The role of the 'Pathfinders' has been to supplement the work of local authorities, to provide a strategic context and direction and to relate housing improvement to the characteristics of a place. This latter has been a particular innovation. For example, the Pathfinder for South Yorkshire has sought to give 'a clear sense of place and function'. Likewise, the Pathfinder for Tyneside has sought to organise interventions in relation to specific neighbourhoods and in doing this has sought to differentiate one neighbourhood from another.[10] Looking at housing improvement in the context of place making has, in turn, led to an increased concern with design quality in new housing and other types of new development, with conservation, green space and the improvement of local commercial areas.

The housing measures of the Pathfinders are, in contrast, similar to those commonly used by local authorities and other social landlords, albeit often with more emphasis given to interventions in the privately owned housing sector. The Pathfinders have mostly sought to diversify the housing stock in relation to demand, to promote home ownership to national average levels and to achieve this have relied on a combination of physical works, such as improvement, selective demolition and new build, and selective sales to developers and private individuals.

Some policy measures remain beyond the scope of the Pathfinders. Two examples will suffice.

- Local authorities continue to exercise controls under the town planning legislation and have, in general, not scaled back planning permissions for new housing in a way that is directly coordinated with measures for neighbourhood regeneration. Economic development policies generally favour the creation of high quality housing stock, including the development of new housing. Most local authorities and other agencies want to show attractive, high quality new housing to prospective investors, irrespective of whether this is located in a Pathfinder area or not. In addition, even in the more depressed areas of the North of England, the housing market is typically characterised by a juxtaposition of low and high priced neighbourhoods. As a result, subject to policies about the use of brownfield sites, political pressures continue to exist to release housing land where house price inflation is apparent.

• It remains difficult to take action against irresponsible private landlords, given the need for prior consultation, the staffing limitations in local authorities and the possibility of legal challenge. Action can also have negative consequences. It can lead to a reduction in supply for people in need. It can also encourage landlords to invest elsewhere, outside a designated low demand area.

In terms of results, the Pathfinders have at least prevented the targeted neighbourhoods from falling behind other equivalent areas. Since the establishment of the Pathfinders, house prices have risen in absolute terms, vacancies have fallen, and the previous surplus of housing stock has disappeared (Leather et al. 2007, viii). It is possible, however, that the improvement in market conditions in the Pathfinder areas has been due to general changes in the housing market in the North of England, rather than any specific initiatives. Housing markets have their own logic and their own cycle of boom and bust. In addition, over the past few years, housing demand in the North of England, as elsewhere, has been transformed by increased immigration from overseas and, in addition, in the case of the social housing stock, by national policies for the dispersal of refugees.

Demolish or improve? The role of demolition merits particular attention. If extensive programmes of piecemeal housing improvement and modernisation have already failed to increase demand, demolition is probably the only option that remains. Likewise, once significant numbers of properties fall empty, there is often no choice but demolition. Empty houses are a source of nuisance – for example a home to drug users and to rats – and a source of danger, for example fires, for residents, especially to children. Even if securely boarded, as is usual in social housing, empty houses are still a symbol of neglect. Demolition also reduces the stock of unpopular dwelling and was, for this reason, was widely regarded by local authorities as an effective way of dealing with surplus stock in the 1990s (PAT7 2000, 9).

Demolition has negative as well as positive consequences for neighbourhood renewal, however. In dramatising the existence of a problem, demolition can merely publicise that an area is on the slide. It also makes local shops less viable, creates ugly and neglected open spaces and, as various national conservation groups, notably English Heritage, have argued, destroys traditional townscapes. Some of the factors that contribute to weak demand and poor conditions, for example vandalism and antisocial behaviour, are, in any case, unconnected to physical condition and the case for demolition.

Demolition in the 1990s remained relatively small-scale and largely reactive to problems on the ground. In contrast, the Housing Market Renewal Pathfinders sought a more ambitious approach that anticipated trends in the market and that, as part of this, adopted demolition as a strategic measure. Other policy plans for the North of England, notably the relevant section of the 'Sustainable Communities' policy plan (ODPM 2003b) and the Northern Way also envisaged demolition a strategic policy intervention and one that would be undertaken on a large scale. The Northern Way plan 'Moving Forward' stated for example, that the then current demolition rates of about 16,700 homes in the North of

England were 'well below' that required (NWSG 2004, 56). It also urged local authorities to make a clean break with the past, to distinguish clearly between those 'sustainable' communities with a long term future and those without. The implication, though not always stated explicitly, was that the housing market in large areas of the North of England was on the verge of collapse.

The assessment of the case for strategic demolition raises many more technical and social difficulties than reactive piecemeal demolition. It is possible to rank types of dwelling and types of neighbourhoods in order of popularity. However, this says nothing about whether unpopular neighbourhoods should be demolished or not. House prices can change and have changed rapidly. Owners are, moreover, aware of the uncertainty of housing markets. As a result, unless the market in an area has been depressed for many years, with extensive evidence of abandonment, residents are unlikely to support a programme of planned demolition.

For local residents, whether owner-occupiers or tenants, demolition is a stressful process. For older people, in particular, demolition and the subsequent rehousing process are disconcerting exercises that lead to a loss of personal autonomy. Individuals find that their friends and acquaintances move away, that they become subject to a municipal or housing association rehousing timetable over which they have little control and that may be delayed at short-notice. They also find themselves living in a deteriorating environment of increasing numbers of empty and probably vandalised properties and streets.

If clearance involves the use of compulsory purchase (CPO), as is likely for privately owned property, demolition is likely to be particularly slow. A House of Commons report (2005b, para. 25) noted, 'The CPO procedure is long and complex and can take up to six years'. In the meantime, the property is blighted by a lack of investment.

The valuation procedures for owner-occupied property are a further source of concern. Owner-occupiers are entitled to a level of compensation that includes home loss payments up to an additional 10 per cent of the market value of a property. However, the level of compensation is likely to prove insufficient to enable owner-occupiers to buy a decent home elsewhere, unless they can find additional funds. Particular types of owner-occupiers, for example older and long term residents and members of black and minority ethnic groups face particular difficulties (SHU 2006).

Owner-occupiers in proposed clearance areas do not, moreover, greatly benefit from recent trends towards higher house prices. There are some hypothetical exceptions – for example those who move into the rented sector and treat their compensation as a capital asset for investment elsewhere and those who move abroad. Displaced owner-occupiers who want to buy another property nearby will, in contrast, generally find that the asking price of this other property has also increased. House prices have risen generally in the Midlands and the North of England. In contrast, landlords interested in capital gains have been able to benefit directly from increased house prices.

The complaints of owner-occupiers have striking parallels with the complaints made of mass clearance in the 1960s and 1970s. Clearance remains a slow process, characterised by considerable personal uncertainties, community disruption and disputes about the levels of compensation. The problem can be rectified, but only by making what is already an expensive process even more expensive.

A combination of political opposition and increased costs has ensured that the scale of demolition is lower than once envisaged. Improvement has been more important than demolition. In the first round of pathfinder programmes, which ran from 2002 until March 2006, about 20,000 homes were refurbished, 3,000 new ones built and 10,000 demolished (DPM 2005, 6). More importantly, changes in the housing market have transformed the context and, in most areas, have undermined the previous rationale for large-scale demolition. The collapse in local housing markets, feared in the late 1990s, has not occurred. Vacancies in the social housing sector have also reduced.

The experience of the pathfinder programme shows the limitations of housing market analysis as a basis for demolition proposals. Housing market analysis is not an exact science. A responsive and targeted rather than a strategic approach to demolition is needed.

However, the experience of the pathfinder programme is not the end of large-scale demolition. At some point in the future, the application of national energy targets will again lead to debates about the merits of demolition versus various types and levels of improvement. Putting aside questions about the energy implications of the process of demolition and redevelopment, technical assessments of the quality of the older stock have implied very extensive demolition on a scale that would rival and go beyond earlier programmes in the 1950s and 1960s. For example, one estimate, based on the 1991 English House Condition Survey, is that over 1 in 5 of all dwellings are incapable of being improved to a reasonable minimum standard of energy efficiency (defined as a Standard Assessment Procedure – SAP – level of heat loss of 30, where one is highly inefficient and 100 is highly efficient and the national average is 35) (DoE 1996, 2, 248). Another more recent report, published in 2005, makes a similar diagnosis and recommends that the worst 14 per cent of dwellings should be removed, with an increase in clearance to four times current levels, rising to 80,000 per year by 2016.[11]

Given the cost, disruption and likely local opposition to large-scale demolition, no government has as yet wanted to confront the full implications of estimates of poor energy efficiency in the existing stock. Government action has been confined to low level measures to improve insulation, especially in the loft. Moreover, these piecemeal measures generally have no impact on energy consumption in what might be termed the older, high energy housing stock. Residents, many of who have relatively low incomes, use the benefits of higher insulation to maintain higher comfort levels. The problem of obsolete high energy housing is, therefore, unlikely to go away.

Gentrification and Related Processes

The opposite of low demand is high demand and gentrification, that is to say 'the rehabilitation of working-class and derelict housing and the consequent transformation of an area into a middle-class neighbourhood' (Smith and Williams 1986, 1). Gentrification involves a change in the local population. It also involves a change in the appearance of local houses, shops and other commercial property as these go up-market. Slater gives an example.[12]

> Gone are the working classes and the establishments that served them. XX Road now has delicatessens, wine bars, picture galleries, 'alfresco' diners and three estate agencies with window displays chanting 'location, location, location'. Terraces of Mid-Victorian cottages show no evidence of the uniformity which existed twenty years ago – not one house has the same façade.

In Britain, the clearest examples of gentrification come from London. Extensive areas of inner London (from Wandsworth in the south and Hammersmith in the west, through to Camden to Islington in the north) have become predominantly middle class in way that was not the case in the 1960s (Hamnett 2003). In addition, significant minorities of middle-class households have emerged in East London.

Gentrification is not wholly an urban phenomenon. Specific parts of towns throughout southern England and elsewhere, together with villages in the countryside, have experienced similar processes. Cottages once built for railway workers, fishermen and agricultural labourers have become 'bijou' residences, as estate agents might call them.

Explanations and causes   The causes of gentrification have been extensively debated in urban studies and related disciplines. Gentrification has represented one of the most obvious ways in which the urban residential landscape has changed over the past twenty years. More than this, however, gentrification has become tangled in broader philosophical issues in urban geography and not necessarily in a way that has promoted clarity. The diversity of processes of change is another complication. The term was first coined by Glass (1964) to help understand how and why upper-class families were starting to move into working-class neighbourhoods. It has subsequently been used as a portmanteau term that covers almost all types of neighbourhood upgrading in a variety of different countries, including the upgrading of commercial properties, the development of city centre flats and gated communities, the emergence of student neighbourhoods and in some cases the promotion of social mix in deprived estates. It is at least open to question as to whether the term itself is adequate to cover such a wide variety of processes and contexts (Atkinson 2003).

Excluding publicly-led programmes of neighbourhood upgrading, three particular models of gentrification may be cited, as indicated in Table 8.2.

The workings of the property market provided the basis for the first systematic explanation of gentrification. In particular, N. Smith (1979, 1982) sought to locate the potential of gentrification in a cycle of local property devaluation and re-investment and the creation as part of this cycle of a temporary or semi-permanent 'valley' of depressed land values and abandonment between a city centre and outer suburbs. Capital depreciation in the inner city would eventually reach the point that a gap appears between the potential value of the site or property and its current value. The gap, in turn, attracts a combination of

Table 8.2   Models of gentrification

Explanation	Main concepts	Key arguments	Themes in the narrative
Property market	Flows of capital; uneven development; property cycles; the inner city as undervalued urban space	Gentrification occurs because capital returns to the inner city in search of profitable schemes	The rent gap, i.e. the gap between existing and the potential property value; class conflict. Displacement of an working-class existing population
Consumption and culture	Postindustrial urban culture; counter culture; roles of race, gender and sexuality; role of art and artists as a force for innovation	Human agency is prioritised over economic structure. Gentrification occurs owing to the increased attractiveness of urban neighbourhoods	Types of property and types of area; quality of shops and restaurants; marketing and culture, increasing proportion of childless households; impact of students
Labour market	(Sometimes presented as a subsidiary of consumption and culture) Postindustrial service economy; growth of 'new middle class', including creative industries	Gentrification is caused by an influx of middle-class people who seek properties near to their workplace	Macro-economic restructuring; urban regeneration policies intended to modernise and diversify local economies. Replacement of a working-class population owing to job losses

Source: Adapted from Ambrose (2005).

professional speculators, buy-to-let landlords and individual home owners who see the possibility of making substantial capital gains.

The issue is whether either the land value valley or processes of industrial decline and recovery provide either a universal model or a sufficient condition. The property cycle model appears to work best for big cities that have experienced a recovery from industrial decline and large-scale counter-urbanisation. The narrative is as follows: Closures and changing patterns in manufacturing meant that industrial cities experienced large scale employment loss in the 1970s, 1980s and 1990s, at a time when the average national trend was one of increased employment. Job losses were significantly higher in the older provincial conurbations such as Glasgow, Merseyside and Manchester than elsewhere and particularly marked in the core areas of these cities. However, job losses were also higher in Greater London than elsewhere in the South East of England (Turok and Edge 1999). In contrast, since about 1995, the fortunes of the larger cities have changed (Parkinson 2004, 15–16). Many of the most rapidly expanding sectors of the economy – health, higher education and research, culture, finance – have been based in or near to city centres and have shown few signs of moving.

As is usual in portraying spatial trends, a series of qualifications is necessary, however.

- Patterns of employment growth are not uniform between different cities. London is a case apart, by virtue of its status as a world city and the concentration of wealth and high paid private sector jobs. Amongst provincial cities, some such as Liverpool and Hull have weaker labour markets than others. Further, the reference to an inner city land value valley makes less sense in the context of medium sized and smaller towns that have enjoyed unbroken prosperity from the 1960s or 1970s onwards – for example Cambridge.
- Employment growth at the centre has generally been accompanied by a growth of commuting in a way that diminishes the impact on inner city housing markets. In Birmingham, Manchester and Leeds, for example, rail commuting has, for example, increased by over 60 per cent in the period from 1994/95 to 2004/05. In London, in contrast, rail commuting slightly declined during the same period, despite employment growth at the centre.[13]

Beyond particular qualifications, the property market model makes over simple assumptions. Private investors exploit rather than create markets. Most investment in gentrification in Britain is undertaken by individuals and small investors and these are simply not large or powerful enough to manipulate property markets. Even larger investors, for example, house building companies have to acknowledge established patterns of demand and are, for this reason, notoriously conservative in where they are prepared to invest.

A later account (N. Smith 1996), whilst continuing to emphasise property market trends, admits the cultural significance of gentrification. Gentrification, it is said, is the triumph and dominance of middle-class values and respectability over those of either the old working class or over excluded groups such as immigrants, the homeless and squatters.

Reference to triumph and domination is a reference to conflict. It is also a recognition that gentrification has winners and losers. However, conflict is not necessarily linked directly to class. Conflict may be based on ethnic distinctions or generational differences or tenure, notably whether or not the resident is an owner occupier or tenant. There is, in any case, little evidence to suggest that many residents think or talk about gentrification processes in terms of class.

To talk of the 'triumph of middle-class values' is, in addition, an admission that history, architectural quality and style count in the housing market. There is much anecdotal evidence to support this. Most obviously, the general experience is that a street of Georgian or Victorian terraces or tenements is more likely to be subject to middle-class demand than a street of standardised semis. In general, older inner city property is attractive to consumers because it possesses a distinctive character, as opposed to the 'samey' detached and semi-detached houses of twentieth-century suburbia (Bridge 2003, 2552)

Artistic activities also count. Artists act as pioneers in gentrification (Ley 1996; 2003; Zukin, 1989). They seek out relatively inexpensive, but attractive places to live and work. Once established, moreover, in a residential area, artists show its suitability for other and probably more affluent types of middle-class households.

In Britain, the most commonly cited example of artist-led gentrification concerns the 'BritArt' phenomenon of the late 1980s and 1990s and its impact on London's East End. Individual artists used empty warehouses in the Docklands for temporary exhibitions and then moved to moved more permanent displays in galleries concentrated in the Shoreditch and Hackney (While 2003). It is unlikely, however, that artists were solely or even mainly responsible for the gentrification of London's East End, given the scale of commercial and government funded development in the vicinity.

Family-based gentrification is another type and this depends more on the location of an area and its social networks. Professionally employed women typically have to juggle the competing claims on their time of child rearing, looking after the home and of paid work. They are arguable the most hard pressed of all gender and occupational groups in terms of time (Gershuny 2002). They therefore have to live in places that with good access to facilities of all kinds and with, in addition, easy access to their work and to other people in a similar situation. Family type gentrification is best documented in inner London. In the words of one reviewer, talking about gentrification in Islington and other nearby areas in the 1970s: 'Living in the inner city, closer to work and closer to your peers, acquired an appeal for ambitious professionals that went beyond a taste for Victorian brick and period fittings' (Beckett, *The Guardian* 9 December 2004).

The choice of explanation depends in part on the level of analysis. At a city-wide level, a turn round in the local jobs market is probably a prerequisite for gentrification. Hamnett (2003), in particular, has linked gentrification in London to the emergence of a postindustrial jobs market. In contrast, at a local neighbourhood level, it is unlikely that any single factor could be identified as a universal trigger or cause of gentrification. At this level, gentrification is more likely and is more likely to be dramatic in places with a combination of attractions – a favourable property market, an attractive local identity and a strong professional and managerial labour market.

Consequences and implications   Gentrification is an ungainly and value-laden word. It is an alternative to the equally value-laden, but positive term 'regeneration'. It offers a means of turning the apparently positive implication of regeneration into a social critique. It is moreover a particularly useful means of summarising local campaigns to preserve the character of working-class and poorer residential areas, especially against proposals to sell off all or part of social housing estates. A report from 'Indymedia UK', an independent radical news network, provides an example. Talking in 2006 of a local campaign in the inner city of Leeds, the report carries the headline: 'Campaigners gear up to save Little London from gentrification.'[14]

The use of the term 'gentrification' in social research has been similarly negative. In urban studies, for example, evaluations of gentrification generally show more negative than desirable consequences (Atkinson 2002). The experience of gentrification in the US has contributed to this. In the US a lack of social housing and a highly selective and limited system of income support leaves tenants in a relatively unprotected position in the housing market.

Yet it would surely be wrong to conclude that gentrification is inherently undesirable in Britain. In areas where the main problems are low demand, it is arguable whether gentrification is a problem at all. Gentrification offers a means of bringing empty sites and properties into use, of countering social stigmatisation and promoting social balance.

Even in prosperous growing cities, gentrification has a series of benefits. It benefits the older housing stock through an injection of private capital in improvement and repairs. It commonly attracts people who are likely to remain longer in a neighbourhood than those who rent from private landlords. Gentrification therefore promotes population stability. For the local economy, moreover, gentrification has further benefits in stimulating service jobs.

In addition, gentrification benefits existing property owners, including owner-occupiers, through increasing the value of property. Residents, irrespective of whether they are tenants or owners, are also likely to welcome gentrification if this suggests that their neighbourhood is acquiring a degree of social respectability or if accompanied by environmental measures that improve the appearance or safety of their neighbourhood.

On the other hand, gentrification does not generally increase urban population levels, unless development takes place on vacant sites or involves the rehabilitation of empty properties. Higher income groups generally demand and obtain more floor space per person than lower income groups. In London, for example, the type of family based gentrification described by Glass (1964) proceeded through middle-class families converting houses in multiple occupation back into a single dwelling house. Gentrification therefore generally works against the compact city policy agenda.

In addition, gentrification does not necessarily promote social mixing between middle-class and other households, except perhaps through the most casual encounters in shops and other public and semi-public places. Butler (2003) has analysed the living patterns of middle-class households in Islington, north London and shown an almost total absence of interaction with working-class or other types of household. The most significant example concerned education. Only about half of the sample of middle-class children attended local primary schools and none attended a local secondary school.

The most obvious losers from gentrification are those dependent on affordable rented housing. Gentrification involves a loss of affordable housing both directly and indirectly. It involves a direct loss of affordable housing through a combination of direct physical displacement involving the eviction of tenants at the end of their tenancy or through harassment of tenants by landlords. In addition and almost certainly more importantly, gentrification involves an indirect loss through the workings of the market and a tendency for increased rents and house prices.

Long-established 'down-market' businesses are another potential group of losers. Their rents may increase to the point that they are no longer viable. They may face the prospect of losing their premises for upmarket redevelopment. Their activities and appearance may also be regarded as unacceptable in a quiet, respectable residential area. Richards, writing in the *Society Guardian* (20/04/05), has documented the effect of gentrification in Newington Green, East London. Here, the most striking complaints were those of two local businesses whose trade had been adversely affected by the parking restrictions caused by local environmental improvements or by an increase in residents' car parking. Another local business, a Turkish-owned café, also complained that it had wrongly been accused, by the local residents' group, of permitting the presence of prostitutes.

Given all this, a pragmatic policy stance offers the best way forward. It is unlikely that in an economically prosperous city, any policy could stop gentrification. It is equally unlikely that a government would wish to stop gentrification for fear of the disruption that this would cause to the housing market. Instead, the aim should be to mitigate the negative effects of gentrification through a series of measures to protect the size of the social housing stock, this being the only substantial amount of housing developed and managed outside market processes. Various methods are available, for example:

- using planning agreements and other policies that ensure social housing is provided within new private developed estates;
- the acquisition by local authorities and housing associations of scattered dwellings in streets and blocks that are otherwise privately owned (Holmes 2003);
- the development of shared ownership and related housing forms of property arrangements that are partly owned and partly rented;
- limiting or abolishing any sales of social housing to private investors or occupiers.

The various policy mechanisms are well-established. No new legislative or other measures are required. The key issue is partly one of political priority. It is also about ensuring that selective measures are appropriate to the circumstances of a locality.

Student Areas and their Problems

Inner city housing demand is not just from people in employment. In the 1990s and early years of the twenty-first century, demand was boosted by the growth in the number of students living away from their parental home. In larger regional centres, distinct student neighbourhoods have emerged, largely based on a shared lifestyle, shared leisure facilities and proximity to higher educational facilities (Chatterton 1999).

The growth of student areas, or 'studentification' as it is sometimes called, has some parallels with gentrification. Studentification has pushed up house prices and rents in specific neighbourhoods and has promoted new types of urban social segregation (Smith and Holt 2007). However, studentification also has distinctive features. It has affected established middle-class neighbourhoods as well as poorer areas. In addition, studentification typically amounts to the intensification of use of the housing stock, with a number of unrelated adults living in family houses.

For non-student residents, the problem has been the student lifestyle, with its noise and night-time activities and the type of commercial facilities – pubs and fast food outlets – that student lifestyles support. In most forms of land use, intensification of use is subject to planning control. If this was so in the use of a home, studentification could also be controlled. However, the provisions of the 'use classes order' mean that planning permission is generally not required so long as the property is not occupied by more than six people, as specified for England and Wales or five people as specified for Scotland and, in addition, so long as conversion to multiple occupation does not involve significant alterations to the exterior of a building. Otherwise, unrelated groups of the adults can live together without the need for planning permission.

Pressure groups representing the residents of inner-city university neighbourhoods, together with some local authorities have campaigned for more control over student housing and tighter planning restrictions over the creation of houses in multiple occupation. Various examples may be given of local pressure groups – the Nottingham Action Group, the Leeds HMO lobby and the Hillhead Community Council in Glasgow, as part of the 'Sustainable Communities Scotland' (SUSCOMS) lobby group.[15] However, tightening planning legislation in relation to multiple occupation is not easy and as yet the campaigns have had little impact on this particular issue. Multiple occupation generally involves no obvious changes to the exterior of a property. Its control would require the employment of additional enforcement staff, probably diverted from elsewhere. In addition, if the creation of multi-occupied housing were stopped, the question would arise as to where students and other young people would live.

Controls are available under various Housing Acts. In England and Wales larger houses in multiple occupation (three or more floors including the attic and basement) and in Scotland all houses in multiple occupancy are subject to local authority licensing procedures. These licences are intended to control the management and physical quality of the property and do not cover issues relating to the community impact, such as the loss of family houses, the loss of community facilities that are suitable for families and the growth of pubs, fast-food restaurants. However, established forms of planning control are available to tackle most of these latter community impacts.

Most likely, therefore, the problems of studentification are best tackled, like other types of neighbourhood problem, through a combination of coordinated management and consultation. The issue of studentification is, in any case, unlikely to grow in the future. The growth of student numbers was almost certainly a one-off event. Student numbers in most universities are no longer forecast to increase. In addition, many universities have started to provide an increased number of purpose-built student flats and this will reduce the impact on the privately rented housing market.

Suburban and Intermediate Neighbourhoods

Declining and abandoned neighbourhoods on one hand and prosperous gentrifying neighbourhoods on the other cover most of the policy issues. They have also captured most attention in political discussions and in research. However, the concentration on specific types of area and specific types of issue has not been universally welcomed. Local authorities and other pressure groups have also pressed the government to consider the needs of suburbia and have encouraged research studies to look into these needs. *Sustainable Suburbs* by the Civic Trust (1999) is usually considered the first such national study, followed notably by studies of the suburban areas in London and South East England, undertaken by URBED, a firm of private planning consultants (2004a; 2004b).

As the scope of these studies suggest, the future of suburbia is particularly important in South East England. However, it is likely that suburbia remains the single most important type of suburban landscape throughout Britain. For example, Echenique and Homewood (2003) have used a spatial definition of suburbia as an electoral ward that is neither the urban core nor located in rural areas. On this basis, suburban areas contained about 84 per cent of the population of England at the time of the 1991 census. What might be called 'proper' suburbia, namely the suburbia developed in the twentieth century and excluding both nineteenth century, mostly inner urban suburbs and dispersed exurban growth accounted for about 44 per cent of the population of England (ITC 2004, 8).

Long-standing stereotypes of suburbia suggest that these are largely middle class, stable and largely without problems in a way that has almost certainly reinforced their policy neglect. The stereotype has an element of truth. To put the point in negative terms, social conditions (such as life expectancy, level of educational attainment and employment levels) remain relatively poor in English cities, especially the larger cities, compared to the national average. Conditions in English cities have improved, but the gap has not disappeared (Turok et al. 2006, 273–4).

At the same time, suburbia is varied and is becoming more varied over time. Suburbia includes examples of council and former council estates, as for example around Glasgow, Sunderland and Hull and a variety of predominantly owner-occupied neighbourhoods – leafy Edwardian and Victorian areas; working-class suburbs developed in the nineteenth century around factories that have disappeared; middle-class commuter suburbs; and affluent car-based suburbs (GLA 2002a). Suburbia also contains neighbourhoods in virtually all market conditions from the most depressed to the most prosperous.

The possible risk of decline and abandonment was, for example, noted by the Civic Trust (1999) in its case studies. 'Some suburbs', the report noted, 'show significant 'stress' with deteriorating community facilities, declining local centres, car domination, and monotone housing that does not reflect population and social change'. Council and former council estates and pre-1919 suburbs provide the main examples. However, in the North of England, the so-called 'pathfinder areas', these being areas at risk of further deterioration and abandonment, also commonly contain privately owned suburban areas developed in the 1920s and 1930s.

In addition, in the South of England suburbia contains neighbourhoods of deprivation in the midst of prosperity and high housing demand. URBED's report for the Regional Assembly for South East England has noted, for example:

> there is also evidence that some of the worst pockets of deprivation are now to be found on isolated suburban Council estates, like Preston in Reigate and Banstead or Leigh Park in Havant, which formed two of our case studies. Isolated without good public transport, and with large numbers of children, plus the problems of concentrated poverty, a number of suburban housing estates are candidates for Neighbourhood Renewal. (URBED 2004a, 6)

The deprived areas include relatively recently constructed social housing, as well as older estates. Page (1993) has, in particular, commented adversely on the relatively isolated, high child density housing association estates built in South East England in the late 1980s and early 1990s.

Areas of suburban deprivation require the familiar package of multi-agency working, housing improvements, community development and involvement, youth and training programmes and crime prevention exercises. Business development is generally less important, other than in suburban low demand areas. Instead, economic development is more likely to rely on training programmes and sometimes the provision of better transport links. The mix of measures is likely to vary from place to place and remains subject to different assessments. Page (2006, 5) has argued, for example, in a series of case studies covering both high demand and low demand areas that 'ill health, poor standards of literacy, and antisocial behaviour' are the 'most important factors contributing to the quality of life on estates, stronger even than the estates' physical state of repair and lack of modern amenities'. However, tackling physical problems remains a means of promoting participation and bringing people together. Remodelling of an estate is, moreover, probably essential to any exercise that seeks to change the image of an estate.

The existence of existing problem areas is not to say that less or no social housing should be built in the suburbs. The housing needs of many suburban areas are often greater than elsewhere, given the existence of high house prices. Moreover, the decentralisation of population away from inner London remains the only practical way of offering more low rise and lower density housing to people in need. It also continues to offer, in many cases, the prospect of a better quality of life.

Enabling people in need to move to the suburbs requires investment in social housing. Therein lies an obvious and major constraint. Investment has collapsed since the heyday of planned decentralisation policies in the 1960s. For example, in 1969 housing associations and other public sector developers together completed about 185,000 dwellings, slightly more than private developers. In contrast, during the five year period 2000–2004, social housing agencies completed an average of about 23,350 dwellings each year or 13 per cent of the number completed by private developers.[16]

In some other countries, local opposition to social house building or to other forms of low income house building has led to the use of legal measures to unlock suitable sites. In France the law *Solidarité et Renouvellement Urbain* 2000 has enabled the government to impose fines on local authority districts (mostly small *communes* of the size of a suburb or village) that fail to house their quota of social housing. In the US political campaigners have taken legal action against exclusionary zoning practices that limit development to low density, in effect high price housing in suburban areas. Perhaps similar measures might become necessary in Britain if social house building grows in scale. For the moment, however, the main constraint on social house building remains a lack of public investment.

Tackling Landscapes of Fear

Much of the policy agenda for deprived and unpopular neighbourhoods is about planning as coordination and policy analysis. At the same time, planning as urban design remains important in policies for community safety. Crime, both as experienced and as feared, is a significant source of stress. According to the 2006/2007 British Crime Survey, for example, 'fear of crime had a high or moderate impact on the quality of life of 37 per cent of respondents' (Nicholas et al. 2007, 101). Crime and the fear of crime also varies between different types of neighbourhood. Economically deprived neighbourhoods (low income areas, social housing estates and high rise inner city estates) tend in general to possess the highest incidence of both (ibid., 119–20).

The Measures

The role of urban design in crime prevention is relatively simple if stated in general terms. It is to help make a safe and secure environment, alongside a wide variety of other potential measures that include enforcement (police action and action against antisocial behaviour) and community development. Three categories of measures are typically used (CEN 2003; Goodchild 1997, 49–57).

- Macro level planning strategies are mostly concerned with the location of activities and street layouts and generally involve a mix of public surveillance and defensible space principles that control access to residential streets and other sensitive areas.
- Micro level urban and building design strategies are mostly concerned with target hardening measures and the promotion of natural, as opposed to electronic, surveillance around buildings.
- Finally, management measures are concerned with manipulating the appearance of an area, making the area feel more safe as well as with policing, electronic surveillance and the enforcement of rules of conduct (for example in areas of public space or between neighbours).

The range of crime prevention measures is potentially large in any specific case and generally larger than can be implemented within budgetary and other constraints. Some measures also raise potential problems. For example, controlling access can easily go too far and isolate an estate. As a result, effective crime prevention and similar strategies have to be proceeded by a diagnosis of the problem and extensive consultation with residents, local businesses and others to see what might be done. Evaluation of the impact after completion is also important.

However, evaluation of the impact of a local crime prevention initiative is seldom straightforward. The effects of design are often inseparable from other factors in a locality, the number of pedestrians, the social composition of an estate or the local youth subcultures. And so on. In addition, efforts at crime prevention in one locality can sometimes lead to displacement elsewhere or to another type of offence.

For residents, evaluation is even more problematic. In most residential streets, for example, burglaries and physical assaults are rare or sporadic in any single year. Yet, from the viewpoint of the individual, the threat remains and the consequences are potentially severe. Residents are likely to rely on hearsay from neighbours and from reports in the media, both of which may be misleading. Once established, therefore, the fear of crime is likely to persist or to fall away only gradually, unless improvements can be represented in some obvious visible form and unless, in addition, the local authority or some other body is able to publicise its successes.

'Normal' Appearances

Though policy makers and designers would not necessarily use the same language, the fear of crime and measures to tackle such fear involves what Goffman (1971) calls 'normal appearances'. Normal appearances are likely to involve an element of social respectability. They are more than this, however. They are also a product of familiarity and routine. According to Goffman, people negotiate their world by monitoring it for signs of danger – that is to say visual and other non-visual cues that they have learnt to detect, interpret and respond to. When the signs of danger are missing, the world is normal and everyday life can proceed as usual. When the signs of danger are present or when the world is difficult to interpret, the individual feels fear or uncertainty as appropriate (Warr 1990). That uncertainty or fear is, moreover, likely to be heightened by a knowledge that potential offenders can read the same signs and exploit any opportunities that might exist.

In relation to the urban environment, the interpretation of appearances has two main aspects.

• Interpretation involves, in part, the presence or absence of signs of disorder. Some signs are social. They relate to the type of person present in a street, for instance drug addicts, youth gangs or prostitutes. Others are essentially physical. They comprise signs of vandalism, graffiti, litter, dilapidated exteriors and empty property. These are warning signs, moreover, of an increased risk of crime. They are not merely about residents' fear of crime. The 1998 British Crime Survey showed that 'where there is more physical disorder (levels of litter and vandalism as judged by interviewers) crime risks for residents are higher' (Mirrlees Black and Allen 1998, 2).

• In addition, interpretation involves a set of images of safe and unsafe places. Unsafe places are typically dark places, lonely places without the possibility of public assistance, small enclosed places without obvious escape routes and sharp corners in footpaths where on-coming pedestrians cannot be observed. Areas that cannot be observed are characterized by what Goffman (1971, 293–300) calls 'lurk lines or blind spots'. They constitute a part of the environment in which an individual cannot see and thus exhibit the realm of the unknown.

The interpretation of appearances has specific lessons for estate-based and neighbourhood-based improvement programmes. Many practitioners would probably say that these various indicators of risk are what residents point to consultation exercises.

At the same time, the fear of crime is not just about a specific and unchanging set of indicators. It is about the classification of the familiar and unfamiliar. Places that look strange or are unfamiliar are also likely to be perceived as dangerous. As a result, people generally regard their own home or neighbourhood as safer than other neighbourhoods or areas in a city, even when this is palpably untrue (Warr 1990, 893). Equally, people are likely to be suspicious of strange looking, innovative layouts, as was a problem with the non-conventional council housing of the 1960s and 1970s.

Moreover, judgements about risk interact with the community context in which they are made and with a person's attachment to a place. Residents who feel attached to a place are more likely to take of their surroundings, to remove incivilities where they can and to cooperate with their neighbours in watching for signs of trouble. In doing all this, they are moreover likely to deter some types of offenders, for example, burglars who are aware that a well maintained, well cared for neighbourhood is also one where neighbours are likely to react to their presence (Brown et al. 2004). The community context is again not just about the perception of crime, but its incidence.

Conversely, the absence of community is likely to cause a sense of distrust, whether this is warranted or not and so increase the fear of crime. The more that people come to believe they live in an 'urban jungle', the more wary residents will be of their surroundings. Intrusive, fortress-like security measures (such as steel grills over windows and doors or along the galleries of balcony access flats, the bricking up of windows in empty properties or putting razor wire on flat roofs) are moreover likely to have the same effect of intensifying any sense of insecurity.

The role of community in controlling crime and the fear of crime is apparent in the advocacy of low speed traffic zones. It is also apparent in other studies: For example: a study of crime prevention in a series of relatively deprived estates found that the most effective were those that involved a broadly-based programme of measures, intended to improve the quality of life, rather than focussing wholly on design or on housing management (Osborn 1993). Likewise, a recent study of four relatively deprived areas in England suggests that conventional security measures, based on a combination of cameras, physical measures and targeted police action, are a necessary, but not sufficient precondition for residents in a high crime area to recover a sense of security. Informal social controls are also necessary and have to be encouraged by a variety of different social actors (Innes and Jones 2006, 39–49). Community remains important in social life.

Notes

1   Also see: Smith, G. (1996) *'Community-arianism': Community and Communitarianism*: Concepts and contexts published on the Web by UK Communities Online and available July 2003 at http://www.astoncharities.org.uk/research/community-arainism/gsum. html.

2   Forrest, R. (2004) *Who Cares About Neighbourhoods?* CNR Paper 26 available at the Economic and Social Research Council Centre for Neighbourhood Research consulted October 2007 at http://www.neighbourhoodcentre.org.uk/research/research.html.

3   Atkinson, R. and Flint, J. (2003) *Locating the Local in Informal Processes of Social Control: The Defended Neighbourhood and Informal Crime Management*, CNR Paper 10 available at the Economic and Social Research Council Centre for Neighbourhood Research consulted October 2007 at http://www.neighbourhoodcentre.org.uk/research/research.html.

4   As reported in *The Word Detective*, 27 April 2002, citing the *Oxford Dictionary of New Words*. Consulted March 2006 at http://www.word-detective.com/042702.html.

5   A textual analysis of the rationale for community involvement, as stated in the Urban White Paper has been published as *Community Involvement: The Roots of Renaissance?* (Urban Research Summary no. 5), consulted May 2006 on the website of the ODPM at http://www.odpm.gov.uk/index.asp?id=1128595.

6 Oldham Independent Review (2001) *Panel Report, One Oldham, One Future* (otherwise known as the Ritchie Report) (no publisher given), consulted December 2007 at http://www.oldhamir.org.uk/.

7 The description is adapted from a presentation by Brendan Nevin, director of RENEW North Staffordshire pathfinder, at a conference *Low Demand Housing: Stopping the Rot* (Manchester 8 July 2004). It is reported in Audit Commission (2005) *Housing Market Renewal*, consulted at the Audit Commission website August 2007 at http://www.audit-commission.gov.uk/reports/accessible.asp?ProdID=184E49B1–6B96–4efc-9D85–A004C6E9E9B0#note4.

8 As stated in various reports on the Pathfinder areas available at the website of the Audit Commision and consulted May 2006 at http://www.audit-commission.gov.uk/reports/GUIDANCE.asp?CategoryID=&ProdID=694CE869–6CAD-41B4–BB1C-1172221C24DE#pathfinder.

9 City of Bradford/Bradford Housing Partnership (2003) *A Decent Home in a Decent Neighbourhood Joint Housing Strategy for Bradford 2003–2010*, available March 2007 at the City of Bradford District Council website at http://www.bradford.gov.uk/housing/housing_strategy_and_research/housing_strategy_and_research.htm.

10 As documented on the website of the Department for Communities and Local Government, consulted July 2007 at http://www.communities.gov.uk/index.asp?id=1140279.

11 Consulted April 2005 on the website of the University of Oxford Environmental Change Institute at http://www.eci.ox.ac.uk/lowercb/40house.html#report.

12 Slater, T. (2002) *What is Gentrification*, available July 2003 at http://members.lycos.co.uk/gentrification/.

13 Estimate taken from the Department of Transport website, consulted October 2007 at http://www.dft.gov.uk/about/strategy/whitepapers/whitepapercm7176/multideliversustainrailway?page=16.

14 Taken from the Indymedia UK website, consulted September 2007 at http://www.indymedia.org.uk/en/2006/03/335666.html.

15 Relevant websites, consulted September 2007, are http://www.nottinghamaction.org.uk/, http://www.hmolobby.org.uk/leeds/and http://www.hillheadcc.org.uk/documents/24_ezgedit.php?action=show.

16 The data has been taken and recalculated from Table 243 *Housebuilding: Permanent Dwellings Completed, by Tenure, Great Britain, Historical Calendar Year Series* available on the website of the Office of the Deputy Prime Minister, consulted January 2006 at http://www.odpm.gov.uk/index.asp?id=1156032.

PART D
Conclusions

Chapter 9

Looking Back and Looking Forward

What general lessons can be drawn from the history and contemporary experience of housing and planning? The question is apparently simple, the answer less so. History is open ended. It comprises a narrative that continues into the future. Giving history an end, a set of conclusions is a logical impossibility. The history of planning itself demonstrates the point. Abercrombie's plans for London displayed far more certainty about the future than has been typical of recent thinking in planning. Even so, within about 15 years, the detail of Abercrombie's proposals, though not its imagery was obsolete.

A complete synthesis is not required, however. History can be examined in terms of the cumulative pattern of trends over time in a way that first looks back and then forward. Housing and, in particular, trends in housing conditions are best tackled through looking back. Most, though not all housing conditions can be measured by statistical indicators that are suited to time series and an assessment of historical trends. Planning is more future-oriented. Yet neither housing nor planning is exclusive in their orientation towards time. The assessment of historical trends implies a consideration of future directions and vice versa.

Trends in Housing Quality

Assessing trends in housing conditions involves some further subdivisions. It means looking at global trends in the condition of the dwelling itself, as measured by conventional indicators of fitness and occupancy. The former refers to the physical standards and quality of the home and the latter to its intensity of use. In addition, an assessment of housing conditions means measuring the changing quality of neighbourhoods, notably as rated by surveyors and residents. For reasons of published data limitations the discussion mostly refers to trends in England, rather than Scotland or Wales. Survey information about trends in Wales is particularly deficient.

Fitness and Amenities

In relation to conditions of the dwelling itself, progress is apparent from at least 1900 and has continued to the present. Housing conditions have improved gradually and steadily and, since the start of the first national house condition survey in 1967 in England, they have improved according to each successive five yearly survey. For example, the proportion of households living in unfit conditions – a basic public health test – in 2001, the latest date for which data on fitness has been published, in England was 3.8 per cent (ODPM 2003a, 10). The equivalent figure for 1991 was 7.5 per cent (DETR undated) and for 1981, using a less stringent definition, 6.3 per cent (DoE 1998, 72). In Scotland, the number of dwellings that fail to meet the equivalent minimum – the tolerable standard – is less than 1 per cent (Communities Scotland 2002, 70).

The definition of a minimum housing standard is a moving target that responds to rising living conditions. In England and Wales, for example, the statutory definition of unfitness was tightened on two main occasions in the twentieth century in the Housing Acts 1955 and the Housing and Local Government Act 1989. Even apart from changes in the legal definition, minimum standards tend to become more stringent over time. The judgements offered by surveyors generally become more demanding as standards improve. For example, the figure for unfitness 1981 is an underestimate, if the homes were judged by later, more stringent interpretations. As a result, the real improvement in housing standards is larger than that suggested in the official statistics.

Improvements in housing conditions have not taken place in every single decade. In England, the proportion of unfit dwellings remained largely unchanged during the period from 1971 to about 1986. Mass slum clearance finished in the early 1970s. In the context of depressed inner city housing markets, the area-based improvement programmes made little headway in countering further deterioration in the privately owned housing stock. The area-based programmes were narrowly drawn and highly selective. In 1981, for example, area-based programmes covered only about a quarter of the dwellings that were located in potentially suitable areas (DoE 1983, 23; Thomas 1986, 93). The area-based programmes also had a slow impact. Even as dwellings were improved, others fell into disrepair and unfitness (though not as rapidly or on such a large scale as in areas without improvement area status). The subsequent decline in the proportion of unfit dwellings marks a recovery in many inner city housing markets, combined more recently by repairs and modernisation programmes in the social housing stock.

As the proportion of unfit dwellings has fallen, the fitness standard has become mostly obsolete, other than as a component of other, broader measures. Most recent accounts have used the concept of a decent home as a test of acceptability. A decent home is one that meets the fitness standard and is also in a reasonable state of repair, has modern facilities and services (mostly related to the age, size and layout/ location of the kitchen, bathroom and WC and to noise insulation) and finally provides a reasonable degree of thermal comfort (related to insulation and heating efficiency). In 2005 the proportion of English households living in non-decent housing was 27.5 per cent (DCLG 2007b, 12). Failure on the thermal comfort criterion is the most common reason for homes failing the decent homes standard. About 73 per cent of non-decent dwellings lack effective insulation or sufficiently efficient heating (DCLG 2007b, 13).

The opportunity to live in a decent home varies significantly between different social groups. The English House Condition Survey lists a series of what might be called 'housing disadvantaged groups'. These include ethnic minority households, households in poverty (those in receipt of some form of benefit) and older households. Equally, however, in the period since 2000, trends show a degree of narrowing in the difference between housing disadvantaged groups and others. For example, the proportion of households in poverty (defined as 'a household with income below 60 per cent of the equivalised median household income, before housing costs') and living in non-decent homes fell from 54.9 per cent in 1996 to 31.2 per cent in 2005 – an annual rate of improvement of 2.6 per cent. In contrast, the proportion of other households living in non-decent homes fell from 40.7 per cent to 25.4 per cent – an annual rate of improvement of 1.7 per cent (DCLG 2007b, 52)

The reasons for housing disadvantage, though not discussed in the English House Condition Survey, may be readily identified. Ethnic minority individuals and families, though diverse, include a high proportion of relatively low income households and recent immigrants. They also commonly live in areas with the oldest housing stock. Individuals and families in poverty have the fewest financial resources to rent a property or, if they are owner-occupiers, to maintain the property thereafter. They are dependent on social housing to obtain good quality accommodation and this is of limited availability. Finally, older people and even more so elderly people, over 75 years, have fewer financial, psychological and health resources to initiate and manage home improvement and repairs works, if they live in owner-occupied property and are, in any case, less able to cope with the disruption of building work (DoE 1979).

The reason for a narrowing of disparities is also not discussed. Most likely, a general improvement in living conditions is one factor, combined with a technical limitation in the survey methodology. The condition surveys focus on poor quality housing. They say little about continuing parallel improvements in the quality of up-market housing. In addition, publicly-funded improvements to the social housing stock are relevant. In 1996, there was a 10 per cent gap between the average level of non-decent homes in the social housing sector (52.6 per cent) compared to the average of privately owned homes (42.6 per cent). By 2005, in the context of a general improvement in the quality of the existing stock, the gap had reduced to 2 per cent (29.2 per cent in social housing, compared to 27.1 per cent in private housing).(DCLG 2007b, 12).

Overcrowding

Another indicator of poor housing conditions, overcrowding has also steadily reduced over many years. The census definition of overcrowding is more than one person per habitable room and severe overcrowding is a household with more than 1.5 persons per habitable room. A habitable room means in this context any room other than a bathroom or toilet, hallway or kitchen. The percentage of households living in severely overcrowded conditions fell steadily throughout the twentieth century. In England and Wales, for example, it fell from 16.9 per cent in 1911, the first occasion for which reliable data is available to about 0.6 per cent in 2001 (Hole and Pountney 1971; ONS 2003, 103).

The fall in overcrowding is enormous and is generally taken for granted. Yet the impact must have been substantial for living conditions and privacy. As was a repeated theme in the survey reports in the early twentieth century, it is difficult, sometime impossible to maintain standards of civilised family life in an overcrowded home.

There are qualifications, however. First, the general overcrowding figures conceal significant variations in the available space per person by tenure, household size and ethnicity. Those living in social housing, larger family households and minority ethnic households have, on average, less floor space than others (ODPM 2003a, 29). The reasons are as follows:

- Social housing tenants have less space owing to allocation rules that generally insist that applicants should not be given a property with a 'free' bedroom.
- Larger family households have less space because they cannot afford larger properties with four or more bedrooms or, in the case of social housing, such properties are unavailable. Much of the gain in the reduction of overcrowding has been caused by a long term reduction in the size of families amongst lower income groups, rather than through the greater availability of large homes. A low income family consisting of say two adults and four or five children is unlikely to be much better off than say 50 years ago.
- Finally, minority ethnic households have less space either because they are concentrated in social housing, as is the case for black households or because they comprise relatively large low income families, as is the case for pakistani and bangladeshi households (ibid., 31–2).

Secondly, detailed analysis of trends in London where in any case overcrowding is now concentrated, suggests that the declining trend has ended. The analysis undertaken by London Housing (2004) suggests that, between the censuses of 1991 and 2001, overcrowding in London rose by about 20 per cent and by almost 50 per cent, if the standard of severe overcrowding is used. In 2001 5 per cent of households of London was overcrowded to some degree and 2 per cent was severely overcrowded. The problem is concentrated amongst poorer, larger families, especially those belonging to immigrant ethnic groups, notably Bangladeshi, black African and Pakistani groups. Overcrowding was associated in the early twentieth century with poor health conditions and this remains the case. In a direct parallel with nineteenth-century analyses, the maps prepared by London Housing show that areas with high overcrowding are also areas with a high incidence of tuberculosis.

Thirdly, average occupancy rates remain higher than if housing were more affordable and more widely available. Occupancy is increased by so-called 'concealed households', that is to say individuals, couples and families who share with friends, parents or relatives, but who would prefer to move out if given the choice. For obvious reasons, concealed households are likely to be concentrated amongst more deprived social groups. However, the number of concealed households remains impossible to calculate, other than on a broad indicative basis. The proportion of one person households in Britain can be compared to that in other European countries, using for example the figures for 2003 as collated by Boverket (2005, Table 1.10). The proportion of one person households is significantly higher in Scandinavia (Denmark, 37 per cent: Finland, 39 per cent: Sweden, 47 per cent) than in the UK (31 per cent). And this would suggest a large unmet need. On the other hand, the UK proportion is broadly similar to that of the near continent – for example, Belgium, the Netherlands and France.

Average occupancy rates and household size are closely related to one another and are both an indicator of the size of the housing stock in relation to population. In *Decent Homes for All*, Gallent and Tewdr-Jones (2007, 109) ask whether, in the context of recent trends in house building and projected household growth, England might be facing its 'deepest' ever housing crisis. The question shows a lack of historical perspective. There is no general housing crisis in terms of the availability of housing. There is, however, a growing crisis for poorer individuals and families and those from excluded groups.

Neighbourhood Quality

Trends in neighbourhood quality are more difficult to assess than trends in physical condition or occupancy. There is no longitudinal record of standards, such as is provided for overcrowding and house condition by the census or the English House Condition Survey. Systematic attempts to measure changes are relatively recent and mostly date from attempts to measure the impact of the social inclusion and social cohesion policy agendas since 1997.

Neighbourhood quality has been measured in three main ways. Successive editions of the English House Condition Survey provide measures of environmental problems as assessed by professional surveyors. The problems are those of 'upkeep', including such factors as vandalism, litter and building maintenance; 'traffic' including air quality and noise; and 'utilisation', including vacant sites and boarded-up buildings. In 2005, 16 per cent of households lived in homes with poor quality environments. There had been no significant change over the previous two years (DCLG 2007b, 39).

Other surveys, notably local studies of community development and urban policy, have sought to measure variations in quality of life indicators, for example crime rates, educational attainment, life expectancy and employment. A national evaluation by Parkinson et al. (2006 vol. 1, 154) suggests, that 'there has been improvement in social cohesion in most cities in recent years', based on most indicators of quality of life. The gap between the most deprived neighbourhoods and others has narrowed (Parkinson 2006, vol. 2, 137). The main qualification concerns life expectancy and health. People are living longer everywhere and there is little evidence that the gap between rural areas and the cities, where most deprived neighbourhoods are concentrated, has narrowed (Turok et al. 2006, 12).

Finally, surveys of the subjective assessments of residents reveal an inconsistent, varying pattern. There is evidence from the Survey of English Housing of a fall in the proportion of households reporting certain types of problems in their area, at least in the period from 1994/95 onwards. In particular, contrary to the reports in the media, problems with crime and vandalism have on average declined (Bates et al. 2001, 96; NCSR 2006, 148–9). On the other hand, complaints about traffic have increased. In 2004/05, traffic replaced crime as the most widespread neighbourhood problem according to the views of those interviewed (NCSR, ibid.).

However, a reduction in reported problems has not led to a widespread feeling that neighbourhoods have improved. When asked whether their area has improved, the Survey of English Housing suggests that most people can see little difference. Moreover, the proportion of residents saying that their area is becoming worse is nearly always more than the proportion saying that it has improved. The 2002/03 Survey of English Housing suggested, for example, that nearly a quarter (24 per cent) thought their area had got worse, whereas less than one in ten (9 per cent) thought it had got better (Robinson et al. 2004, Table A7.2). Anxieties about the future, combined with rose coloured comparisons with the past, tend to colour interpretations of neighbourhood trends.

Likewise, the reduction in reported problems has not led to an increase in the satisfaction of residents living in deprived areas. The Survey of English Housing suggests that, during the financial year 1999/2000, 19 per cent of those living in the most deprived electoral wards stated that they were dissatisfied with the area in which they lived (Bates et al. 2001, Table A7.3). The equivalent proportion in 2004/05 was 21 per cent.[1] Satisfaction is related to expectations. It is likely therefore that improvements in the quality of a neighbourhood are only just keeping pace with increased expectations. It is also possible that expectations of what is a satisfactory neighbourhood are a reflection of changing standards in a way that is unlikely, ever, to lead to substantially increased average levels of satisfaction, at least not in circumstances where variations persist between neighbourhoods.

Successive editions of the Scottish Household Survey use a slightly different question. They ask whether a neighbourhood offers a 'fairly poor' or 'very poor' place to live. Recent trends in the period from 1999 to 2004 suggest that 'perceptions of neighbourhood are becoming somewhat less negative over time for these areas'.[2] The difference is not large, however. The proportion declined from, in 1999, about 26 per cent of those living in a deprived neighbourhood to about 22 per cent in 2004.

Specific area-based programmes have stimulated a parallel set of policy evaluations, again using a mixture of physical, quality of life and subjective measures. The evaluations generally suggest that positive gains at least in the short-term (Kintrea and Morgan 2005, 6). The national evaluation of the New Deal for Communities suggests, for example, that typical neighbourhood incivilities (drugs, litter, teenagers, vandalism, abandoned cars) have been reduced compared to other similar areas (Lawless 2006). Local neighbourhood programmes also enable more public involvement and consultation than is possible in a top-down, centrally organised policy.

Local neighbourhood programmes have a series of limitations, however. They have typically been targeted on a minority of people in need, even on a minority of areas in need. The variable effectiveness and achievement of different priority areas are other limitations. Progress is partly dependent on local leadership and organisational effectiveness and this is often highly variable.

To summarise: in relation to the physical environment, the pattern is too mixed and the statistical record is too fragmentary to permit an overall assessment.

In relation to the subjective assessment of neighbourhood conditions, the pattern is again too mixed and too fragmentary to permit overall assessment. In relation to the social inclusion and social cohesion policy agenda, the signs of a narrowing on quality of life indicators and the experience of area-based programmes are encouraging. The quality of life indicators refute over-pessimistic, over-deterministic interpretations of globalisation and post-Fordist production. Targeted expenditure on public services can make a difference to those living in deprived areas. Even in the context of local improvements, however, deprived neighbourhoods remain relatively deprived.

There are theoretical reasons why neighbourhood inequalities might persist. Neighbourhood inequalities are a different type of inequality compared to those associated with the standards and use of a dwelling. The physical standards of the housing stock relate mostly to the qualities of the home as a material good. They are likely to increase on average as living standards and the wealth of the economy increase over time. Likewise, general levels of overcrowding are related to the overall supply of housing and this again can be increased. In contrast, the neighbourhood relates mostly to the qualities of the home as a positional good, to its relative social status and environment. Tackling such relative inequalities requires a particularly broad range of social policies.

Directions for the Future

The question remains about how to conceptualise strategic policy directions in urban planning. The professional definition of planning is about futures, places and spaces. It is, in particular, about adopting a longer term view that would be generated through market transactions alone. What therefore might be said about the future and in particular about the role of planning in creating that future?

Growth, Decline and their Implications

In *Housing and the Urban Environment*, the present author (Goodchild 1997, 287–97) distinguished between four scenarios, whilst also suggesting that scenarios are most useful if they can be organised into a simple, coherent framework. One scenario, 'sustainable development' was explicitly based on environmental policy values. The other three scenarios were based on different states of the economy. The implications of sustainable development remain important and topical. However, sustainable development, like other aspects of planning policy, is best understood in relation to different states of the economy and different levels of economic growth and not just as an independent category.

For example, jobless growth would offer a particularly unwelcome economic scenario, possibly the most unwelcome scenario other than outright decline. Jobless growth would lead to increased disparities in the living conditions of one neighbourhood and another, much as occurred during the 1980s and early 1990s (SEU 1998). It would also encourage increased competition between different ethnic groups for whatever jobs remain and provoke youth unemployment of a type that does little for social stability or crime prevention.

Jobless growth is, moreover, not just a theoretical possibility. A recent report on trends in Liverpool has noted: 'low skills and other factors have ensured that the population of the inner areas ... has not benefited proportionately from recent economic growth and there is a danger that this will remain the case in the future.'[3] The same report adds that similar tendencies are apparent in parts of Greater Manchester.

If these local trends were to become more general, the economy would go in two directions at once, with labour market demand growing at the top end, for highly skilled and qualified workers and labour market supply mostly being confined at the bottom. How exactly such divergent trends would be reconciled with one another is unclear. Most policy assumptions are that the labour force will become increasingly skilled to meet the new demand and that this will be aided by increased spending on education and by various community-based initiatives. It is also possible that communities might attempt take matters in their own hands and to tackle local unemployment through self help and community businesses. The difficulty would be to avoid educational and community initiatives being swamped by increased economic inequalities and a sense of exclusion from mainstream society.

Low growth with population decline is a different and, in some ways, even more extreme scenario and one that is disruptive and costly for infrastructure provision and public services. Population decline increases the cost of providing public services per head. It means that existing services, for example libraries, schools and public transport, are used less efficiently and these efficiency losses lead, in turn, to restructuring exercises that are themselves expensive in the short term. A tendency for population loss to be unbalanced in the sense of leaving behind older and more vulnerable people, to be accompanied by physical dereliction and partial housing abandonment and to be accompanied, in addition, by a loss of local taxation revenues is likely to compound the problems faced by the providers of local services, above all local authorities. Low growth, with population decline is the scenario that affected depressed regions and inner city areas in the 1970s and 1980s (Cameron 1980, 7–10), as well as the most depressed low demand neighbourhoods in the North of England, Scotland and Wales. It is not a scenario that is to be recommended.

Despite regional variations in prosperity, low growth with population decline is also a scenario that in Britain is unlikely in most places, according to most estimates of short-term change (over the next five years) (Ove Arup Ltd et al. 2005, ES5). Rates of anticipated population growth vary with the largest increases in the South. Rates of anticipated population growth are also dependent on the scale of net international immigration and this is both difficult to predict and partly dependent on political decisions. However, some population increase is also expected in most regions. Even the large regional cities that have experienced decline for decades, have seen population increases in the past few years.

With or without population decline and ignoring unemployment, a local or national economic downturn would have a series of consequences. On a positive note, a downturn would probably reduce house prices in expensive areas and ease access into owner-occupation for those in work, much as for example did the depression of the 1930s. It would ease development pressures in both the countryside and towns in a way that would probably be welcomed by some environmental groups and it might facilitate a revival of what might be called 'green dispersal' proposals with an emphasis on energy-efficient housing in a low density context.

On a less positive note, however, a downturn would cause problems for those who bought their homes at the peak of the housing boom. It would also lead to problems for banks and building societies, denying them security for their loans. This is exactly the problem that has started to emerge in the last few months of 2007.

More generally, an economic downturn would probably slow down programmes for the regeneration and modernisation of older areas and the older housing stock and would, in addition, probably undermine public investment in infrastructure and services of all types, including the provision of new social housing, environmental improvements and public transport. Faced with a downturn, the state would adjust its spending plans accordingly or divert funds into income support for the unemployed.

It is not, therefore, easy to envisage a future that is characterised by a combination of low development pressures and high levels of public investment. This was the diagnosis of possible urban futures for London (GLA 2002b). The diagnosis elsewhere is likely to be similar. The scale of infrastructure investment at any time is subject to competing political priorities, including reducing the tax burden. Even so infrastructure spending presupposes economic growth and economic development.

Promoting growth at the local level and within London is, of course, not the same as promoting growth equally in different regions. Infrastructure capacity of all kinds (water, roads and public services) is greater away from London and South East England. In addition, the potential for brownfield development is greater away from London and South East England (Entec UK 2005). It is, therefore, in the interests of governments to promote the housing market in those regions where development is easier, less expensive and has fewer environmental impacts.

However, the ability of governments to even out regional variations in growth has long been limited and is probably more limited than in the past. Much of the growth in London is generated by financial services and cultural industries (publishing, film. theatre, music etc.). Compared to a manufacturing plant, post-industrial economic activities are inherently less easy to shift around from one region to another. The most obvious way in which governments can influence the location of economic activity is through the relocation of its own offices. Whether this can or will be done on a sufficient scale is uncertain. There is no indication that either the present government or the main opposition parties would consider the type of major coordinated investment programme that might attract economic activity away from London and the South East. Variations in regional growth rates might also be expected to diminish over time as a result of self-correcting market mechanisms (HM Treasury 2001, 3). Recent trends suggest little convergence, however (Ove Arup Ltd et al. 2005, ES1).

House Building Delivery

A context of growth and economic development means a continued tension between the role of planning as a mean of protecting the countryside and planning as a means of providing sufficient land for future house building. Therein lies the most commonly noted negative aspect of planning control as operated in Britain since World War II, as for example stated by Hall et al. (1973) and the most contentious issue in contemporary planning, as for example explored in the Barker review (2003; 2004). If taken too far, protecting the countryside reduces or stops house building and has inflationary effects throughout the housing market, including the provision of social housing.

The scale of the impact of land restrictions on housing costs and prices is difficult to quantify in relation to other factors (for example, the scale of immigration from overseas, the scale of speculative land purchase, the taxation system in operation at any time, interest rates and so on). In the short term, say over two or three years, releasing more land within the planning system probably has little impact on affordability in housing. The impact of new house building on the size of the existing stock is simply too small. In the longer term, the impact is likely to prove more substantial, though the impact is itself likely to vary from place to place.

Nevertheless, whatever the timescale and whatever the local variations, the planning system should release more land, including more greenfield land, for the provision of affordable housing. Most likely, the planning system will release more land for housing, given current political concerns and the current policy framework. Suitable sites need to be defined moreover at a local level. Regional plans are too general to permit specific land allocations. Density limits also indicate a need to allocate more land for housing. In England, it is not easy to see how average densities could be significantly increased above recent levels without further reducing the proportion of family houses in new build projects.

Whether the mere release of land is sufficient to counter problems of affordability is another matter. An expanded social house building programme may also be necessary. In England, annual completions by social housing agencies have fluctuated between about 9 per cent and 13 per cent of all completions in the period since 2000. In Wales, the proportion has fluctuated in the same period between about 6 per cent and 12 per cent and in Scotland between 14 per cent and 21 per cent. The proportions, though consistent with the range in most European Union countries, are far below those in the 1970s and 1960s when social housing agencies generally accounted for about or more half of annual completions.[4]

Social housing agencies continue, moreover, to have key advantages over private developers and other private institutions as a means of providing affordable housing. They provide below market rents in a way that avoids the administrative and financial complications of means tested benefits. Their not-for-profit status means that they are well suited to the task of managing rented property for lower income and vulnerable people (Hills 2007). Most likely, housing associations rather than local authorities would continue to complete all or nearly all of new dwellings, given their advantages in raising private finance.

An expanded social house building programme may imply a change in the market role of housing associations. As is summarised in the notion of residualisation, both local authorities and housing associations have increasingly concentrated on the most deprived individuals and households. An expanded building programme implies that housing associations will house a wider range of individuals and households, including those on moderate incomes. Housing associations could also expand their new build programmes through the provision of more shared ownership homes or even through building for sale. However, the latter would lead housing associations into competition with private builders and in the context of limited demand would limit private sector output.

In relation to the design of social rented housing, it is commonly accepted that social housing agencies should provide what might be termed 'normal' looking schemes if they wish to avoid stigmatisation and facilitate renting by or sale to individuals and families on moderate incomes. To avoid stigmatisation, social housing landlords should, in addition, work with planning authorities in promoting social balanced neighbourhoods, probably involving clusters of different income groups living in different streets or housing groups. In relation to achieving social balance, an analogy might be drawn between future building programmes, for example in growth areas and the role of new town development corporations in the period from about 1947 to 1975. The lesson of the new towns is that the targeted beneficiaries should be explicitly specified in terms of their social characteristics and the consequent implications for house types and tenure (Bennett 2005).

The regulatory costs of development deserve to be reassessed. Development has focused on brownfield sites and as part of this on infill projects in existing urban areas. These are inherently more complex to develop and more likely to generate objections from neighbouring property owners and from local residents. Developers have also been urged and, in some cases required to adopt higher design standards, including higher energy efficiency standards. Finally, developers are required to negotiate planning agreements for the provision of infrastructure and a proportion of social housing.

Of the various types of regulation, the detailed workings of the planning system can be made clearer through the greater use of design briefs, design codes and master plans. It might also be possible to encourage design quality through quality labelling rather than regulation. The label would be attached to the advertising material and other documentation produced by a housing developer. It could incorporate elements of external estate layout and environment, internal design, such as floorspace and sustainability in relation to water and energy use.

However, the detailed regulation of design is not the main issue. Planning agreements are the most contentious and, in some ways, the least satisfactory aspect of current forms of regulation. The use of negotiated planning agreements is out-of-line with practice in most other countries. It is time-consuming, often incompatible with the principles of open government and counterproductive in the context of measures to promote house building. If the aim is to promote house building, it is counterproductive for the planning system to take resources away from private housing, except where this is necessary for the development to go ahead. In addition, if the aim is to promote efficiency in the procurement of social housing, it is sensible to give housing associations the ability to choose the contractor through the competitive tendering for projects.

Planning agreements have the advantage of securing socially mixed schemes. They have been widely endorsed by housing pressure groups for this reason. Social mix in new and redeveloped housing schemes could, however, equally well be achieved through other forms of planning regulation.

The use of planning agreements can be defended on the grounds that, in the context of an inflationary housing market, the cost is mostly paid by the landowner. However, much depends on the scale of the charge and the overall market conditions. What, for example, is likely to happen in a deflationary housing market? What happens to social housing conditions if the infrastructure charges of new housing increase, as is the desire of many local authorities? Finally, what happens as the cost of new housing increases as it surely will do as a result of the search for ever greater energy efficiency and self-sufficiency. Social housing and the provision of urban infrastructure need to be properly resourced from the public purse, if development is to be encouraged.

Finally, more attention needs to be given to promoting a pro-active, positive role for local planning authorities. It is insufficient merely to call for a culture change in town planning. If a more positive role for planning authorities is to become a reality, their statutory role needs to be revised. Local planning authorities need to be given a positive duty to facilitate development in accordance with an approved plan and, to do this, given effective means to promote coordinated development, including site assembly.

Sustainable Growth and the Planning Process

Attempts to reconcile growth with environmental priorities generally envisage some process of 'uncoupling'. The idea is to uncouple growth from the use of resources, especially the use of energy resources and, in addition to uncouple growth from its negative environmental consequences. The aim is therefore not abandon growth, but to pursue some form of sustainable urban growth.

The implications for planning are relatively easy to specify as an imaginary urban landscape. Since the report of the Urban Task Force (UTC 1999), good practice in urban planning has involved what might be called an amended compact city, with following characteristics:

- high residential densities on average, say in the range of 40–50dph, but probably with higher densities in the city or town centre and lower densities for suburban areas;
- mixed land uses, social mix and social balance, including the provision of affordable housing; and

- a spatial focus on development around public transport, notably rail and tram, access points.

Recent discussions have added two further themes.

- the use of zero energy housing as a building block for new development; and
- green corridors and communal gardens between and within urban development.

The landscape of sustainable urban growth has parallels with the vision of the planned city of the period from 1945 and 1970s. Like the earlier vision, proposals have emerged as a political compromise between opposing forces – between those who wish to promote environmental conservation on one hand and those who wish to meet large-scale housing needs and demands on the other. Again, like the earlier vision, much of the detail has been worked out by architects and reflects a professional rather than popular definition of quality and good taste (Murie and Rowlands 2007). Fewer architects work for local authorities than at the time of mass house building programmes. However, the emergence of CABE as an influential advisory body has provided an effective replacement. Finally, like the post-1945 planned city, sustainable urban growth has led to an apparent failure of policy. The advisory plans led, amongst other factors, to the failures of high rise flats in the 1970s and 1980s. Sustainable growth has involved the development of unpopular 'ghost blocks' of city centre flats, to use the language of an editorial in the *Estates Gazette* (8 December 2007).

However, the parallels between sustainable urban growth and the earlier period are not exact. The ghost blocks are as yet a local phenomenon, confined to a few city centres. There is, moreover, no direct equivalent to the lengthy flats versus houses debate that characterised proposals for redevelopment from 1900 to at least the 1950s (Murie and Rowlands 2007). The excesses of the city centre flats boom were, in any case, as much a market-driven as a planning phenomenon. The enthusiasm was driven by a boom in buy-to-let property and a failure on the part of professional valuers to see the limitations of this boom.

For all these reasons, the recent experience of city centre flats is unlikely to damage the broader planning vision. Yet the vision itself is looser and less detailed than the proposals that emerged after 1945. The vision also amounts to less of a positive policy consensus, though care must be taken not to exaggerate the extent to which the advisory plans of the 1940s received universal support. Current proposals for sustainable urban growth amount instead to a *de facto*, passive and sometimes reluctant consensus of the type that arises when the options are limited and that has to be worked out over and over again to take account of local considerations. A huge number of questions remain – about the choice and mixture of strategic growth options, about the role of high rise and low rise/ high density, about the detailed design options and last but not least about how to programme and phase development sites in the context of an uncertain and ever changing housing market.

In addition, issues remain about how quickly governments should move towards a full environmental agenda in housing and whether sustainable towns and cities are achievable without a change in lifestyles. Some environmental critics, including the House of Commons Environmental Audit Committee (2005a, 3) would argue, for example, against an expanded house building programme. They argue that it is better and more sustainable to build slowly so that new housing can achieve the highest design and energy efficiency standards. Others argue, in contrast, that the promotion of quantity in house buidling should have priority over environmental issues. The amended compact city is a compromise and the opposing forces that led to the compromise have not disappeared. Again, parallels may be drawn with the post-1945 era.

Making proposals for the future invariably tends to focus on issues of new build and new residential areas. Sustainable urban growth is no exception. City centre flats are mostly proposed for sites previously used for commercial purposes. Zero carbon homes and zero carbon towns are proposed as new settlements or new suburbs.

Yet new build and the existing stock cannot be viewed in isolation. Even on the most optimistic rates of house building, the existing stock will account for most dwellings for many years into the future. Moreover, the very process of raising the standards of new build, as is an explicit aim of the zero carbon housing proposals, will make the existing stock obsolete and will raise at some point questions about the future of dwellings that cannot be improved at a reasonable cost.

In this context, clearance and redevelopment offer an obvious partial solution. However, the history of programmes of clearance and replacement is overwhelmingly dismal, from the earliest experiments before 1918 to the latest experiments undertaken in the context of the Housing Market Renewal programme in England. The history is dominated by concerns about personal and community disruption on one hand and excessive public sector costs on the other. Clearance is best avoided, especially mass clearance. If clearance is necessary, the lesson of the past is to ensure adequate compensation for the disruption involved, to ensure that the process is managed to a predictable and realistic timetable and to ensure, in addition, sensitive local rehousing.

The most appropriate models for the worst areas are the various experiments in gradual renewal and community-based redevelopment undertaken in the 1970s. Community-based programmes are particularly appropriate to the promotion of sustainable housing, as this will almost certainly require mechanisms for the collective management of renewable energy production and may, in addition, require mechanisms for the collective management of green spaces. At the same time, evaluations of the community-based programmes of the 1970s, for example by Thomas (1986, 135), suggest a continuing and probably growing need for general measures to stimulate individual private investment in the older housing stock.

Social balance is another policy aim where action for the existing stock and for existing urban areas is likely to provide the most effective way forward (Hills 2007). Social housing agencies can and no doubt will promote social balance through the piecemeal redevelopment of their estates. Redevelopment and new build are only likely to have a slow impact, however. To achieve faster results, social housing agencies will have to promote social balance through a combination of allocations policies and the selective sale and purchase of property. They will also have to work with other public agencies to ensure that neighbourhoods attractive to people of all income levels and backgrounds.

The imaginary landscape of the post-1945 planned city coexisted with a style of planning that emphasised blueprints. Planning at the level of towns and cities ignored issues relating to the planning process, probably because planning at the level of the central state was assumed to deliver a stable context. Current proposals for sustainable growth coexist, in contrast, with a planning style that, according to most statements of good practice, has to promote diversity and efficiency in service delivery, has to anticipate and measure environmental risks, has to combine social inclusion and social cohesiveness with the promotion of competitiveness and has, in doing all this, has to work in partnership with other agencies and local communities. Planning, according to these postmodern and hypermodern interpretations, is less ambitious in terms of its hopes for transforming cities into some new entity. However, good practice in planning is exceptionally demanding. Good practice requires high levels of technical knowledge, an ability to experiment and to learn from experience and a democratic framework that can encourage debate (Ascher 2001, 97).

As a result, planning remains characterised by a disjuncture between its potential and practice. It is easy to fault existing practice. In Britain, for example, the statutory planning system remains limited to the regulation of proposals and the allocation of land for different uses, including housing. It is not easy to use the statutory planning system in its present form to generate a practical vision of the future or to stimulate public interest, other than where conservation issues are involved. In addition, various forms of planning and regeneration partnerships and strategic bodies exist at different spatial scales, from the neighbourhood upwards. These have the potential to provide a more positive direction for planning than the statutory system. However, these latter tend to vary in their effectiveness. Some are little more than talking shops. Moreover questions remain about how best to tie the statutory system and broader strategic policy and community planning frameworks together.

The disjunction between the ideal and practice has led Thomas (2007) to suggest 'planning, as institutionally defined at any given time, may not be a particularly useful category for understanding the world and its dynamics'. Planning as an administrative system and profession is too narrow, whilst planning theory is too remote from the world of politics and the forces that promote social change.

Planning as an institutional system does have an impact, whether for good or bad. It has an impact on the availability of housing, as the debates about land availability and planning agreements. Likewise, planning has had an impact, mostly in conjunction with the architectural profession and private interests, in determining specific forms of urban development. Various examples can be given, not just the present wave of high density city centre schemes, but earlier examples of the garden city and low density suburb. Planning theory, at its simplest level, is a means of enabling a critical analysis of practice. Moreover, like any form of critical analysis, some standard is necessary. To this extent, a disjuncture between good practice and actual practice is not necessarily undesirable, so long as the statements of good practice enable a process of social learning and identify directions for change.

However, it is surely correct to argue that the institutional forms of planning are narrowly defined. Definitions of planning as a decision making and policy making process are broader. These are definitions as a style of government, as was the rationale of the advocates of central planning in the 1930s and 1940s or as a style of governance, as is the implication of the dispersed, fragmented systems of administration of the contemporary city.

Governance implies, in turn, the persistence of two main types of planning. First, governance suggests planning as a specialist exercise of various types – for example, regulation, plan-making, financial appraisal, environmental impact analysis, policy evaluation, project implementation. The tasks themselves would not necessarily be led by professional planners. Second, and this is the most demanding type of practice, governance suggests a transversal exercise that attempts to reconcile, balance and coordinate the claims of different agencies and as part of this to negotiate what Campbell (1996) has called the triangle of requirements – economic, social and environment – involved in sustainable development. Campbell goes on to suggest that planners can, in this transversal role, either seek to mediate between different positions or enter a political arena with their own opposing vision of an environmentally sustainable city. Both positions are necessary for the future, Campbell suggests.

Yet the choice between mediation and opposition is itself an oversimplification. A triangle of requirements defies bipolar oppositions and blurs the distinction between opposition and mediation. Triangular thinking requires instead a repeated process of examining the past, present and future in terms of interactions, constraints and dependencies. It requires imagination, but also the capacity to deal with the material aspects of housing and urban development and with the environment as lived and used.

Notes

1   Table S708, available at the website of the Survey of English Housing (live tables) consulted July 2007 at http://www.communities.communities.gov.uk/index.asp?id =1154799.

2   *High Level Summary of Statistics: Key Trends for Scotland 2006: Housing*, p. 9, available at the Scottish Executive website, consulted July 2007 at http://www.scotland.gov.uk/ Publications/2006/06/20135022/0.

3   ECOTEC Research & Consulting Limited (2005) *Understanding the Drivers of Housing Market Change in the New Heartlands Housing Market Renewal Area A Review of the Evidence Base – Discussion Paper*, p. 23: available at the website of the Liverpool Housing Market Renewal Area, consulted June 2007 at http://www.newheartlands. co.uk/PAGES/PRESS_REL/schemeupdate2005.

4   The figures for England, Wales and Scotland have been calculated from CLG-NS (2006) Table 2.1. The comparison with European Countries is derived from Louvot-Runavot (2001).

PART E
Supplementary Information

A Note on the Terminology of Social Housing

The term 'social housing' covers all forms of not-for-profit and limited profit housing independent of the legal character of the provider. The term itself is of relatively recent origin. Social housing has taken different forms at different historical periods.

Pre-1919 accounts refer to council housing on one hand and on the other to a miscellaneous collection of philanthropic and semi-philanthropic agencies, including housing trusts, model dwellings companies and other housing societies, that were collectively known as public utility societies, if they registered under the Industrial and Provident Societies Act (RCHS 1917, 269). Co-partnership, sometimes called co-operative housing is a specific form of public utility society in which tenants owned a share. These latter were closely associated with the garden city movement.

Council housing is, of course, a term that has persisted and that refers to housing developed and managed by local authorities. The term is also used loosely to cover housing developed by new town development corporations after 1945. Public utility societies were independent housing providers, subject to a separate legal regime and separate regime of public financial aid, if this was available. The term 'housing association' only came into use in the 1930s and was given explicit recognition in the Housing Act, 1935 (Malpass, 2000b). Thereafter, public utility societies became known as housing associations. However, the term 'housing society' remained in professional use until given a more specialised role under the Housing Act 1964. A further term 'public sector developer' refers to any combination of publicly funded agencies (local authorities, new towns and other government bodies) that provide urban infrastructure or, in the past, have undertaken direct housing provision.

This term 'housing association' remains in common use and is used here. Strictly speaking, however, the correct legal term in England and Wales is 'registered social landlord', meaning a landlord that is registered with the relevant regulator.

References

Abercrombie, P. (1935), 'Slum Clearance and Planning', *The Town Planning Review*, XVI, 195–208.

—— (1939), 'Introduction', in Abercrombie, P. (ed.) *The Book of the Modern House*, London, Hodder and Stoughton, vii–xx.

—— (1945), *The Greater London Plan, 1944*, London, HMSO.

Abercrombie, P. and Matthew, R.H. (1949), *The Clyde Valley Plan, 1946*, HMSO.

Abley, I. (2001), Introduction, in Abley, I. and Heartfield, J. (eds) *Sustaining Architecture in the Anti-Machine Age*, Chichester, Wiley-Academy.

Abrams, P. (1968), *The Origins of British Sociology: 1834–1914*, The University of Chicago Press.

Abrams P. and Bulmer M. (1986), *Neighbours, the Work of Philip Abrams*, Cambridge, Cambridge University Press.

Academy of Sustainable Communities (Corporate Author) (2007a), *European Skills Symposium*, Leeds, The ASC.

—— (2007b), *Evidence Base Review of Skills and Cross Occupational Learning for Sustainable Communities Professionals*, Leeds, The ASC.

Adams, D. and Watkins, C. (2002), *Greenfields, Brownfields and Housing Development*, Oxford, Blackwell Science.

Adorno, T.W. (1967), *Prisms*, London, Neville Spearman (original published in German in the late 1940s).

Adshead, S.D. (1916), 'The Standard Cottage', *Town Planning Review*, Vl(4).

Albertsen, N. (1988), 'Postmodernism, Post-Fordism and Critical Social Theory', *Environment and Planning D: Society and Space*, vol. 6, 339–65.

Aldous, T. (1992), *Urban Villages*, London, The Urban Villages Group.

Aldridge, H. (1915), *The Case for Town Planning*, London: The National Housing and Town PLanning Council.

Allen, C., Camina, M., Casey, R., Coward, S. and Wood, M. (2005), *Mixed Tenure, Twenty Years On – Nothing Out of the Ordinary*, London, The Chartered Institute of Housing: York, Joseph Rowntree Foundation.

Allen, C. and Blandy, S. (2004), *The Future of City Centre Living: Implications for Urban Policy*, Centre for Regional Economic and Social Research, Sheffield Hallam University.

Allen, J. and Cars, G. (2001), 'Multiculturalism and Governing Neighbourhoods', *Urban Studies*, 38:12, 2195–209.

Allison, L. (1986), 'What is Urban Planning For?', *Town Planning Review* 57:1, 5–16.

Allmendinger, P. (2001), *Planning in Postmodern Times*, London, Routledge.

Ambrose, A. (2005), 'Gentrification, Urban Policy and the Restructuring Lower Order City', a dissertation submitted in partial completion of a MSc in Urban and Regional Planning at Sheffield Hallam University.

Amin, A. (1994), 'Post-Fordism: Models, Fantasies and Phantoms of Transition', in Amin, A. (ed.) *Post-Fordism, a Reader*, Oxford, Blackwell, 1–40.

Andersen, H.S. (2002), 'Can Deprived Housing Areas Be Revitalised? Efforts against Segregation and Neighbourhood Decay in Denmark and Europe', *Urban Studies*, 39:4.

Anderson, R., Bulos, M.A. and Walker, S.R. (1985), *Tower Blocks,* London, Polytechnic of the South Bank and the Institute of Housing.

Anon. (1949), 'Can Communities Be Planned?', *Planning (PEP)* XV:296, 259–79.

Archigram (2000), 'Instant City' in Miles, M., Borden, I. and Hall, T. (eds) *The City Cultures Reader*, London and New York, Routledge, 125–8 (original 1972).

Armitage, R. (2000), *An Evaluation of Secured By Design Housing within West Yorkshire*, London, Home Office Briefing Note, 7/00.

Ascher, F. (1995), *Métapolis*, Paris, Editions Odile Jacob.

—— (1998), *La République contre la ville*, La Tour d'Aigues, Editions de l'Aube.

—— (2001), *Les nouveaux principes de l'urbanisme*, La Tour d'Aigues, Editions de l'Aube.

Ashworth, W. (1954), *The Genesis of Modern Town Planning*, London, Routledge and Kegan Paul.

Atkinson, R. (2002), *Does Gentrification Help or Harm Urban Neighbourhoods? An Assessment of the Evidence Base in the Context of the New Urban Agenda*, ESRC Centre for Neighbourhood Research, CNR Summary 5.

—— (2003), 'Introduction: Misunderstood Saviour or vengeful Wrecker? The Many Meanings and Problems of Gentrification', *Urban Studies* 40:12, 2343–50.

Baines, C. (1985), *How to Make a Wildlife Garden*, London, Elm Tree Books/ Hamish Hamilton.

Baker Associates (2004), *Assessing Urban Housing Potential – A Good Practice Guide*, Guildford, South East England Regional Assembly.

Ball, M. (1983), *Housing Policy and Economic Power: The Political Economy of Owner Occupation*, London, Methuen.

—— (1999), 'Chasing a Snail: Innovation and Housebuilding Firms' Strategies', *Housing Studies* 14: 9–22.

Barke, M. and Rowlands, J. (1989), 'Environmental Quality and Council House Sales', *The Environmentalist* 9:3, 185–96.

Barker, K. (2003), *Review of Housing Supply, Securing our Future Housing Needs Interim Report – Analysis*, London, HM Treasury.

—— (2004), *Delivering Stability: Securing Our Future Housing Needs: Review of Housing Supply – Final Report – Recommendations*, London, HM Treasury.

—— (2006), *Barker Review of Land Use Planning – Interim Report – Analysis*, London, HM Treasury, HMSO.

Barker, P. (2000), 'Thinking the Unthinkable', in Hughes, J. and Sadler, S. (eds) *Non-Plan: Essays on Freedom, Participation and Change in Modern Architecture and Urbanism*, Oxford, Architectural Press, 2–21.

Barlow, J. (1999), 'From Craft Production to Mass Customisation', *Housing Studies* 14:1, 23–42.

Barlow, J. and Duncan, S. (1994), *Success and Failure in Housing Provision: European Systems Compared*, Oxford, Pergamon.

Barlow, J, and Stockerl, K. (1999), 'Brave New World: German Self-build', *Building Homes*, April, 62–3.

Barlow J. et al. (2001), 'The Current State of the Self-build Housing Market', *Findings*, York The Joseph Rowntree Foundation, No. 951.

Bates, B., Joy, S., Roden, J., Swales. K., Grove, J. and Oliver, R. (2001), *Housing in England 1999/00: A Report of the 1999/00 Survey of English Housing carried out by the National Centre for Social Research on behalf of the Department for Transport, Local Government and the Regions*, London, DTLR.

Baudrillard, J. (1990), *Fatal Strategies*, New York, Semiotext(e), London, Pluto Press (French original 1983).

Bauer, G. and Roux, J.M. (1976), *La rurbanisation ou la ville éparpillée*, Paris, Editions du Seuil.

Bayliss, D. (2001), 'Revisiting the Cottage Council Estates: England, 1919–39', *Planning Perspectives* 16:2, 169–200.

Beck, U. (1992), *Risk Society: Towards a New Modernity*, London, Sage Publications.

Bedford, T., Clark, J. and Harrison, C. (2002), 'Limits to New Public Participation Practices in Local Land Use Planning', *Town Planning Review* 73:3, 311–32.

Beito, D., Gordon, P. and Tabarrok, A. (eds) (2002), *The Voluntary City*, Ann Arbor, University of Michigan Press.

Bennett, J. (2005), *From New Towns to Growth Areas, Learning from the Past*, London, Institute for Public Policy Research.

Benington, J. et al. (1975), *CDP Final Report: Part: Coventry and Hillfields: Prosperity and the Persistence of Inequality*, Coventry, The Home Office and City of Coventry Community Development Project.

Beresford, M. (1971), 'The Back-to-Back House in Leeds, 1787–1937' in Chapman, S.D. (ed.) *The History of Working-class Housing: A Symposium*, Newton Abbot, David and Charles.

Berkeley Hanover Consulting et al. (2002), *Economics of the Park Home Industry*, London, ODPM.

Berube, A. (2005), 'Transatlantic Perspectives on Mixed Communities', *Findings*, York, Joseph Rowntree Foundation.

Bhatti, M., Brooke, J. and Gibson, M. (eds) (1994), *Housing and the Environment – A New Agenda* Coventry, Chartered Institute of Housing.

Bhatti, M. (1994), 'Environmental Futures and the Housing Question', in Bhatti et al., op. cit., 14–33.

Biddulph, M. (2000), 'Villages Don't Make a City', *Journal of Urban Design*, 5:1, 65–82.

Biddulph, M. et al. (2003), 'From Concept to Completion: A Critical Analysis of the Urban Village', *Town Planning Review* 74:2, 165–93.

Birchall, J. (1995), 'Co-partnership Housing and the Garden City Movement', *Planning Perspectives* 10:4, 329–58.

Bishop, J. (1985), 'Never Mind the Density, Feel the Space', *Housing Review* 34:2, March–April.

Board of Trade (1908), *Report of an Enquiry into Working Class Rents, Housing and Retail Prices*, London, HMSO.

Bohl, C.C. (2000), 'New Urbanism and the City: Potential Applications and Implications for Distressed Inner-City Neighborhoods', *Housing Policy Debate* 11:4, 761–800.

Booth, C. (1903), *Life and Labour of the People of London, Final Volume, Notes on Social Influences and Conclusion*, London, Macmillan.

Bourdieu, P. (1984), *Distinction: A Social Critique of the Judgement of Taste*, London, Routledge and Kegan Paul (translation of French original 1979).

Boverket (The National Board of Housing, Building and Planning), together with the Ministry for Regional Development of the Czech Republic (collective authors) (2005), *Housing Statistics in the European Union 2004*, Karlskrona, Sweden.

Bowley, M. (1945), *Housing and the State*, London, George Allen and Unwin.

Bozeat, N. et al. (1992), 'The Potential Contribution of Planning to Reducing Travel Demand', *PTRC European Transport, Highways and Planning, XXth Summer Annual Meeting*, Environmental Issues, Proceedings of Seminar B.

Bramley, G. (1993), 'Planning, the Market and Private Housebuilding', *The Planner*, January.

Bramley G. and Kirk, K. (2005), 'Does Planning Make a Difference to Urban Form? Recent Evidence from Central Scotland', *Environment and Planning A* 37:2, 355–78.

Bramley, G. and Morgan, J. (2003), 'Building Competitiveness and Cohesion: The Role of New Housebuilding in Central Scotland's Cities', *Housing Studies* 18:4, 447–71.

Bramley, G. and Pawson, H. (2000), *Local Housing Needs Assessment: A Guide to Good Practice*, London, The Department of the Environment, Transport and the Regions.

Bramley, G., Fitzpatrick, S., Kofi Karley, N. and Monk, S. (2005), *Evaluation of English Housing Policy 1975–2000 Theme 1: Supply, Need and Access*, London, The Office of the Deputy Prime Minister, The Stationery Office.

Branford, V. and Geddes, P. (1917), *The Coming Polity*, London, Williams and Norgate.

Breheny, M., Gent, T. and Lock, D. (1993), *Alternative Development Patterns: New Settlements*, London, Department of the Environment, HMSO.

Bridge, G. (2003), 'Time–Space Trajectories in Provincial Gentrification', *Urban Studies* 40:12, 2545–56.

Brindley, T. (1999), 'The Modern House in England: An Architecture of Exclusion', in Chapman, T. and Hockey, J. (eds) *Ideal Homes?*, London, Routledge, 30–43.

Brindley, T., Rydin, Y. and Stoker, G. (1989), *Remaking Planning*, London, Unwin Hyman.

Brook Lyndhurst (2004), *Liveability and Sustainable Development: Bad Habits and Hard Choices*, Final Report for the ODPM New Horizons Programme.

Brown, B.B., Perkins D.D. and Brown, G. (2004), 'Incivilities, Place Attachment and Crime: Block and Individual Effects', *Journal of Environmental Psychology* 4:3, 359–71.

Brown, T. and Bhatti, M. (2003), 'Whatever Happened to "Housing and the Environment"?' *Housing Studies* 18:4, 505–15.

Budd, T. (1999), 'Burglary of Domestic Dwellings: Findings from the British Crime Survey', *Home Office Statistical Bulletin*, Issue 4/99

Bullock, N. (1994), 'Ideals, Priorities and Harsh Realities, Reconstruction and the LCC, 1945–51', *Planning Perspectives* 9:1, 71–98.

Burgess, E.W. (1925), 'The Growth of the City', in Park, R.E., Burgess E.W. and. McKenzie, R.D. (eds) *The City*, University of Chicago Press, Chicago, 47–62.

Burnett, J. (1986), *A Social History of Housing*, London, Methuen (second edition: first edition 1978).

Burton, E. (2000), 'The Compact City: Just or Just Compact? A Preliminary Analysis', *Urban Studies* 37:11, 1969–2001.

Burton, P., Goodlad, R. and others (2004), *What Works in Community Involvement in Area-based initiatives? A Systematic Review of the Literature*, Home Office Online Report 53/04.

Butler, T. (2003), 'Living in the Bubble: Gentrification and its "Others" in North London', *Urban Studies* 40:12, 2469–86.

CABE – see the Commission for Architecture and the Built Environment.

Cabin, P. (2004), 'Dans les coulisses de la domination: la sociologie de Pierre Bourdieu', in Cabin , P. and Dortier, J.-F. (eds) *La Sociologie: histoire et idées*, Auxerre, Éditions Sciences Humaines, 181–97.

Calcutt, J. (2007), *The Calcutt Review of Housebuilding Delivery*, London, Department for Communities and Local Government.

Calder, A. (1968), *The People's War*, London, Cape.

Calvert Spensley, J. (1918), 'Urban Housing Problems', *Journal of the Royal Statistical Society* LXXXI: II.

Cameron, G. (1980), 'Introduction', in Cameron, G. (ed.) *The Future of British Conurbations*, London, Longman.

Campbell, S. (1996), 'Green Cities, Growing Cities, Just Cities?', *Journal of the American Planning Association* 62: 3.

Campbell, S. and Fainstein, S.S. (eds) (1996, 1st edition: 2002, 2nd edition), *Readings in Planning Theory*, Cambridge, MA and Oxford, Blackwell.

CAR – Cambridge Architectural Research Ltd (collective author) (2004), *Housing Futures: Informed Public Opinion*, York, The Joseph Rowntree Foundation.

Carmona, M. (2001), *Housing Design Quality*, London and New York, Spon Press.

Carmona, M. and Gallent, N. (2004), 'Planning and House Building: A Step Change from the Bottom Up?', *Town Planning Review* 75:1, 95–122.

Carmona, M., Carmona, S. and Gallent, N. (2001), *Working Together*, London, Royal Town Planning Institute and Tonbridge, Thomas Telford.

Carmona, M., Heath, T., Oc, T. and Tiesdell, S. (2003), *Public Places – Urban Spaces: The Dimensions of Urban Design*, London, Architectural Press.

Carpenter, J. (2006), 'Addressing Europe's Urban Challenges: Lessons from the EU URBAN Community Initiative', *Urban Studies* 43:12, 2145–62.

Castells, M. (1977), *The Urban Question*, London, Edward Arnold.

—— (1989), *The Informational City*, Oxford, and Cambridge, MA, Blackwell.

Castells, M and Godard, F. (1974), *Monopolville*, Mouton, Paris-La Haye.

CDCS – European Committee For Social Cohesion (collective author) (2004), *Revised Strategy for Social Cohesion* approved by the Committee of Ministers, Strasbourg, Council of Europe.

CEC – see Commission of the European Communities.

CEN – European Committee for Standardisation (2003), *Prevention of Crime – Urban Planning and Design – Part 2: Urban Planning*, Brussels.

CHAC – Central Housing Advisory Committed (1944), *Private Enterprise Housing: Report of the Private Enterprise Sub-committee* (chaired by Sir Felix Pole) London, HMSO.

Charmes, E. (2005), *La vie périurbaine face à la menace des gated communities*, Paris, L'Harmattan.

Chatterton, P. (1999), 'University Students and City Centres: The Formation of Exclusive Geographies: The Case of Bristol, UK', *Geoforum* 30, 117–33.

Cherry, G. (1988), *Cities and Plans*, London, Edward Arnold.

Cheshire, P. and Sheppard, S. (1989), 'British Planning Policy and Access to Housing: Some Empirical Estimates', *Urban Studies* 26, 469–85.

—— (2004), 'Capitalising the Value of Free Schools: The Impact of Supply Characteristics and Uncertainty', *The Economic Journal* 114 (November), F397–F424.

Choay, F. (1969), *The Modern City: Planning in the 19th Century*, London, Studio Vista (translated from an unknown French original).

—— (1995), *Le règne de l'urbain et la mort de la ville*, in Roman, J. (ed.) op. cit., 366–8 (original 1994).

CIoH/RTPI – Chartered Intitute of Housing and Royal Town Planning Institute (collective authors) (2003), *Planning for Housing: The Potential for Sustainable Communities*, Coventry and London, CIoh-RTPI.

Civic Trust with Ove Arup & Partners (collective author) (1999), *Sustainable Suburbs*, York, The Joseph Rowntree Foundation, Findings.

Clawson, M. and Hall, P. (1973), *Planning and Urban Growth: An Anglo-American Comparison*, Baltimore, Johns Hopkins University Press.

Clay, G. (1994), *Real Places: An Unconventional Guide to America's Generic Landscape*, Chicago and London, University of Chicago Press.

Cleeve Barr, A.W. (1958), *Public Authority Housing*, London, B.T. Batsford.

CLG-NS – Communities and Local Government and National Statistics (Collective Authors) (2006), *Housing Statistics 2006*, London, Department for Communities and Local Government, Crown Copyright.

Cloke, P., Philo, C. and Sadler, D. (1991), *Approaching Human Geography: An Introduction to Contemporary Theoretical Debates*, London, Paul Chapman.

Coates, K. and Silburn, R. (1980), *Beyond the Bulldozer*, Nottingham, University of Nottingham, Department of Adult Education.

Coffin, G. and Williams, M. (1989), *Children's Outdoor Play in the Built Environment*, London, National Children's Play and Recreation Unit.

Cohen, S. (1969), *Modern Capitalist Planning, the French Model*, London, Weidenfeld and Nicolson.

Cole, G.D.H. (1943), *Plan for Britain*, London, Routledge.

Coleman, A. (1985), *Utopia on Trial: Vision and Reality in Planned Housing*, London, Hilary Shipman.

Colquhoun, I. (2004), *Design Out Crime*, Oxford, The Architectural Press.

Colquhoun, I. and Fauset, P. (1990), *Housing Design in Practice*, Harlow, Longman Scientific and Technical.

Commission for Architecture and the Built Environment (collective author) (2003), *Building Sustainable Communities: Developing the Skills We Need*, London, CABE.

—— (2005a), *Better Neighbourhoods: Making Higher Densities Work*, London, CABE.

—— (2005b), *Creating Successful Neighbourhoods: Lessons and Actions for Housing Market Renewal*, London, CABE.

—— (2005c), *What Home Buyers Want: Attitudes and Decision Making Among Consumers*, London, CABE.

—— (2005d), *What it's Like to Live There: The Views of Residents on the Design of New Housing*, London, CABE.

—— (2007a), *Actions for Housing Growth: Creating a Legacy of Great Places*, London, CABE.

—— (2007b), *Housing Audit. Assessing the Design Quality of New Housing in the East Midlands, West Midlands and the South West*, London, CABE.

Commission of the European Communities (1990), communication from the Commission to the Council and the European Parliament, *Green Paper on the Urban Environment*, Brussels, Com (90) 218 Final.

—— (2006), Communication from the Commission to the Council and the European Parliament, *Thematic Strategy on the Urban Environment*, Brussels, 11.1.2006 COM(2005) 718 final, SEC(2006) 16.

Communities Scotland (2002), *Scottish House Condition Survey Report 2002*, Edinburgh, The Scottish Executive.

Competition Commission (1991), *Structural Warranty Services in Relation to New Homes: A Report on the Existence or Possible Existence of a Monopoly Situation in Relation to the Supply within the United Kingdom of Structural Warranty Services in Relation to New Homes*, London, The Competition Commission.

Conzen, M.R.G. (1981), 'The Morphology of Towns in Britain during the Industrial Era', in Whitehand, J.W.R. (ed.) op. cit, 87–125 (original published in German in 1978).

Cooper Marcus, C. (2006), *House as a Mirror of Self*, Berwick, ME, Nicholas-Hays (US original 1995).

Cooper Marcus, C. and Sarkissian, W. (1986), *Housing as if People Mattered*, Berkeley, CA, University of California Press.

Cope, H. (with Avebury International) (2002), *Capital Gains*, A Report for the London Housing Federation, London.

Cornes, J. (1905), *Modern Housing in Town and Country*, London, B.T. Batsford.

Coulthard, M., Walker, A. Morgan, A. (2002), *People's Perceptions of their Neighbourhood and Community Involvement. Results from the Social Capital Module of the General Household Survey 2000*, The Office for National Statistics, London, The Stationery Office.

County Council of Essex (corporate author) (1973), *A Design Guide for Residential Areas*, Chelmsford, The County Council.

—— (2005), *Infrastructure in Essex: Costing Infrastructure Provision on Three Housing Growth Scenarios*, Chelmsford, The County Council.

Copestake, P., Rudat, K., Coffey, R., Ahmad, S. and Oothuizen, R. (2005), *An Exploration of the Challenges Posed by Future Trends in Segregation and Polarisation*, London, ODPM New Horizons.

Cowburn, W. (1967), 'Housing in a Consumer Society', *Architectural Review* 142:849, 398–400.

Craib, I. (1992), *Modern Social Theory*, London, Harvester (second edition).

Craigforth and Newhaven Research (2004), *Understanding the Dynamics of Low Demand in Owner Occupation in East Ayrshire and North Lanarkshire*, PRECIS, No. 46, Edinburgh, Communities Scotland.

Crawford, J.H. (2000), *Carfree Cities*, Utrecht, International Books.

Crockett, D. (1990), 'Suburban Redevelopment: An Appraisal of Recent Pressures and Policy Responses in an Outer London Borough', *The Planner*, 10 August.

Crook, A.D.H. and Whitehead, C. (2002), 'Social Housing and Planning Gain: Is this an Appropriate Way of Providing Affordable Housing?', *Environment and Planning A* 34:7, 1259–79.

Crouch, S., Shaftoe, H. and Fleming, R. (1999), *Design for Secure Residential Environments*, London, Longman, Chartered Institute of Building.

CTF – Construction Task Force (1998), *Rethinking Construction* (The Egan Report), London, DETR.

Cullingworth, J.B. (1980), *Land Values, Compensation and Betterment, Peacetime History, Environmental Planning, Vol. IV*, London, HMSO.

CUS – Centre for Urban Studies (collective author) (ed.) (1964), *London: Aspects of Change*, London, MacGibbon and Kee.

Damer, S. and Madigan, R. (1974), 'The Housing Investigator', *New Society* 29, 226, 25 July.

Daunton, M.J. (1983), *House and Home in the Victorian city*, London, Edward Arnold.

Davidson, J. (1988), *How Green is Your City*, London, Bedford Square Press.

Davidson, M. (2000), 'Local Authority Housing in England: Physical Condition and Need for Repair and Improvement', paper presented at the European Network of Housing Research Conference, Gävle.

Davies, J.G. (1972), *The Evangelistic Bureaucrat*, London, Tavistock.

Davies, L. (1992), 'The Plan – a European Comparison', *Journal of Planning and Environment Law*, Occasional Paper 19, 55–65.

Davis, M. (1998), *City of Quartz*, London, Pimlico (original by Verson, 1990).

DCLG – see Department for Communities and Local Government.

Deleuze, G. and Guattari, F. (1995), 'La production des différences', in Roman, J. (ed.) *Chronique des Idées Contemporaines*, Paris, Bréal, 238–40 (original 1991).

Denman, D.R. (1975), *Prospects of Cooperative Planning*, Berkhamsted, Geographical Publications.

Department for Communities and Local Government (collective author) (2006a), *Building a Greener Future, Towards Zero Carbon Development*, London, DCLG.

—— (2006b), *English House Condition Survey 2004: Annual Report, Decent Homes and Decent Places*, London, DCLG.

—— (2006c), *Planning Policy Guidance 13 (PPG13):Transport*, London. DCLG (original 2001).

—— (2006d), *Planning Policy Statement 3 (PPS3): Housing*, London. DCLG.

—— (2007a), *Eco-towns Prospectus*, London, DCLG.

—— (2007b), *English House Condition Survey 2005: Annual Report*, London, DCLG.

—— (2007c), *Homes for the Future*, London, DCLG, Cm 7191.

—— (2007d), *Land Use Change in England: Residential Development to 2006 (LUCS 22)*, London, DCLG and National Statistics.

—— (2007e), *Planning Together Local Strategic Partnerships (LSPs) and Spatial Planning: A Practical Guide*, London, DCLG.

Department of Environment (1972), *The Estate Outside the Dwelling*, Design Bulletin 25, London, HMSO.

—— (1975), *Housing Act, 1974: Renewal Strategies*, Circular 13/75, London, HMSO.

—— (1979), *English House Condition Survey, 1976, Part 2: Report of the Social Survey*, London, HMSO.

—— (1981), *A Survey of Tenants' Attitudes to Recently Completed Estates*, Housing Development Directorate Occasional Paper 2/81, HMSO.

—— (1983), *English House Condition Survey 1981. Part 2: Report of the Interview and Local Authority Survey*, London, HMSO.

—— (1993), *English House Condition Survey 1991*, London, HMSO.

—— (1996), *English House Condition Survey 1991, Energy Report*, London, The Stationery Office.

Department of Environment/Department of Transport (1992), *Residential Roads and Footpaths: Layout Considerations*, Design Bulletin 32, London, HMSO (original 1977).

DETR – Department of the Environment, Transport and the Regions (1998), *Planning and Affordable Housing*, Circular 6/98, London: The Stationery Office.

—— (1999), *Approved Document Part M: Access and Facilities for Disabled People*, HMSO, London.

—— (2000a), *By Design, Urban Design in the Planning System: Towards Better Practice*, London, The Stationery Office/DETR.

—— (2000b), *Our Towns and Cities: The Future*, London, The Stationery Office/DETR.

—— (2000c), *Planning Policy Guidance 3 Housing*, London, The Stationery Office/DETR.

—— (undated), *English House Condition Survey 1996: Summary*, London, DETR.

DH-ODPM – Department of Health and Office of the Deputy Prime Minister (collective authors) (2003), *Preparing Older People's Strategies: Linking Housing to Health, Social Care and Other Local Strategies*, London, Department of Health.

Diamond, J. (1976), 'Residential Density and Housing Form', *Journal of Architectural Education*, 29:3, 15–17.

DoE – see Department of the Environment.

Donzelot, J. (2003), *Faire Société*, Paris, Editions du Seuil.

Dorling, D., Rigby, J., Wheeler, B., Ballas, D., Thomas, B., Fahmy, E. Gordon, D. and Lupton, R. (2007), *Poverty, Wealth and Place in Britain, 1968 to 2005*, Bristol, Policy Press.

DPM – Deputy Prime Minister (2005), *The Government's Response to the ODPM: Housing, Planning, Local Government and the Regions Select Committee's Eighth Report on Empty Homes and Low Demand Pathfinders*, London, The Stationery Office, Cm 6651.

Drover, G. (1973), *Urban Residential Denrities: A Comparison of Policies with Particular Reference to London and New York, 1945–1970*, submitted for the degree of Doctor of Philosophy, University of London.

—— (1975), 'London and New York', *The Town Planning Review*, 46:2 165–82.

DTLR – Department for Transport, Local Government and the Regions (Corporate Author) (2002), *Open Spaces, Better Places*, DTLR, London.

DTZ Pieda Consulting (2004), *Housing Market Assessment Manual: A Manual Produced for the Office of the Deputy Prime Minister*, London, ODPM, HMSO.

Duany, A. (2002), 'Introduction to the Special Issue: The Transect', *Journal of Urban Design* 7:3, 251–60.

Duany, A. and Plater-Zyberk, E. (2003), 'The Neighbourhood, the District and the Corridor', in LeGates, R.T. and Stout, F. (eds) *The City Reader*, London, Routledge, third edition, 207–11 (extract orginally published in 1993).

Duffy, F. (2002), 'Changing Lifestyles and Aspirations: Designing for Contemporary Customers', in Bartlett, K. et al. (eds) *Consumer Choice in Housing: The Beginnings of a House Buyer Revolt*, York, The Joseph Rowntree Foundation, 21–44.

Dugmore, K. (1976), 'Social Pattern in GLC Housing', *Greater London Intelligence Quarterly* 35, 26–33.

—— (1977), 'A Note on "Social Pattern in GLC Housing"', *Greater London Intelligence Quarterly* 38, 25–27.

Duncan, P. and Thomas, S. (2000), *Neighbourhood Regeneration: Resourcing Community Involvement*, Bristol, The Policy Press.

Dunleavy, P. (1981), *The Politics of Mass Housing in Britain, 1945–1975*, London, Clarendon Press.

Echenique, M. and Homewood, R. (2003), *The Future of Suburbs and Exurbs, Report for the Independent Transport Commission*, Cambridge, The Martin Centre for Architectural and Urban Studies, University of Cambridge.

Edwards, A.M. (1981), *The Design of Suburbia: A Critical Study in Environmental History*, London, Pembridge Publications.

Edwards, A.T. (1913), 'A Criticism of the Town Planning Movement', *The Town Planning Review* IV:2, 150–57.

Edwards, S. (1981), 'Briefed for Variety', *Building Design*, 27 March.

English, J., Madigan, R. and Norman, P. (1976), *Slum Clearance*, London, Croom Helm.

Entec UK (main authors) (2005), *A Sustainability Impact Study of Additional Housing Scenarios in England*, London, ODPM.

Evans, R, (1998), 'Policy Review: Tackling Deprivation on Social Housing Estates in England: An Assessment of the Housing Plus Approach', *Housing Studies* 13:5, 713–26.

Fainstein, S. (2001), 'Competitiveness, Cohesion, and Governance: Their Implications for Social Justice', *International Journal of Urban and Regional Research* 25:4, 884–8.

Faludi, A.(1973), 'What is Planning Theory?', Introduction to Faludi, A. (ed.) *Planning Theory*, Oxford, Pergamon Press.

Feindt, P. and Oels, A. (2005), 'Introduction to the Special Issue: Does Discourse Matter? Discourse Analysis in Environmental Policy Making', *Journal of Environmental Policy and Planning* 7:3, 161–73.

Fitzpatrick, S. (2005), *The Poverty of Place*, Working paper, Centre for Housing Policy, York, University of York and the Joseph Rowntree Foundation.

Flyvbjerg, B. et al. (2002), 'Underestimating Costs in Public Works Projects: Error or Lie?', *Journal of the American Planning Association* 68:3, 279–5.

Fogarty, M.P. (1948), *Town and Country Planning*, London, Hutchinson's University Library.

Foley, D. (1973), 'British Town Planning: One Ideology or Three?', in Faludi, A. (ed.) *A Reader in Planning Theory*, Oxford, Pergamon Press, 69–93 (original 1960).

Foot, M. (1973), *Aneurin Bevan, a Biography, Vol. Two: 1945–1969*, London, Davis-Poynter.

Forester, J. (1993), *Critical Theory, Public Policy and Planning Practice*, Albany, NY, SUNY Press.

Forrest, R. and Kearns, A. (1999), *Joined-up Places?*, York, York Publishing Services.

Forshaw, J.H. and Abercrombie, P. (1943), *County of London Plan*, London, Macmillan and Co.

Forty, A. and Moss, H. (1980), 'A Housing Style for Troubled Consumers: The Success of the Neo-vernacular', *Architectural Review* 167:996, 73–8.

Fotel, T. (2006), 'Space, Power, and Mobility: Car Traffic as a Controversial Issue in Neighbourhood Regeneration', *Environment and Planning A* 38:4, 733–48.

Fouchier, V. (1997), *Les Densités Urbaines et le Développement Durable*, Paris, Edition du SGVN, La Documentation Française.

FPDSavills Research with Davis Langdon & Everest (2003), *The Value of Housing Design and Layout*, London, CABE.

Frank, S. (on behalf the Humboldt study team) (2006), *The European URBAN Experience – Seen from the Academic Perspective Study Report*, Berlin, Humboldt University.

Franklin, B. (2006), *Housing Transformations*, London, Routledge.

Franklin, B. and Tait, M. (2002), 'Constructing an Image: The Urban Village Concept in the UK', *Planning Theory* 1:3, 250–72.

Friedmann, J. (1987), *Planning in the Public Domain*, Princenton, NJ. Princeton University Press.

Friedmann, J. and Hudson, B. (1974), 'Knowledge and Action: A Guide to Planning Theory', *American Institute of Planners' Journal* 40, 2–16, January.

Furbey, R. and Goodchild, B. (1986), *Housing in Use: A Study of Design and Standards in the Public Sector*, Sheffield, Pavic Publication, Sheffield City Polytechnic.

Gallent, N. and Tewdr-Jones, M. (2007), *Decent Homes for All*, London, Routledge.

Geddes, P. (1968), *Cities in Evolution*, London, Ernest Benn (original 1915).

Gee, D. (1974), *Slum Clearance*, London, Shelter.

Gershuny, J. (1983), *Social Innovation and the Division of Labour*, Oxford, Oxford University Press.

—— (2002), 'Social Leisure and Home IT: A Panel Time-Diary Approach', *IT and Society* 1:1, 54–72.

Ghékiere, L. (1991), *Marchés et Politiques du Logement dans la CEE*, Paris, La Documentation Française.

Gibb, K. and Kearns, A. (2001), *Low Demand in the Owner-occupied Sector: Issues for Lenders*, London, Council of Mortgage Lenders.

Gibson, M. (1994), 'The Greening of Housing Policy', in Bhatti et al., op. cit., 34–59.

Giddens, A. (1991), *The Consequences of Modernity*, Cambridge and Oxford, Polity Press and Blackwell Publishers.

Gittus, E.E. (1976), *Flats, Families and Under Fives*, London, Routledge and Kegan Paul.

GLA – see Greater London Authority.

Glass, R. (1948), *The Social Background of a Plan. A Study of Middlesbrough*, London, Roudledge and Kegan Paul.

—— (1964), 'Aspects of Change', in CUS (ed.) op. cit.

—— (1973), 'The Evaluation of Planning', in Faludi (ed.), op. cit., 45–67 (original 1959).

Glasser, H. (1998), 'On the Evaluation of Wicked Problems', in Lichfield, N. (ed.) *Evaluation in Planning*, Dordrecht, Kluwer Academic Publishers, 229–49.

Glendinning, M. and Muthesius, G. (1994), *Tower Block: Modern Public Housing in England, Scotland, Wales, and Northern Ireland*, New Haven, NJ, Yale University Press.

Goffman, E. (1971), *Relations in Public: Micro Studies of the Public Order*, New York, Harper and Row.

Golland, A. and Blake, R. (eds) (2004), *Housing Development: Theory, Process and Practice*, London, Routledge.

Golland, A. and Oxley, M. (2004), 'Housing Development in Europe', in Golland and Blake, op. cit., 295–321.

Goodchild, B. (1981), *The Application of Self-Help to Housing*, Sheffield City Polytechnic Working Papers in Urban and Regional Studies.

—— (1984), 'Housing Layout, Housing Quality and Residential Density', *The Housing Review*, July/August.

—— (1985), 'Local Authority Flats: A Study in Area Management and Design', *Town Planning Review* 58:3, 293–316.

—— (1992), 'Land Allocation for Housing: A Review of Practice and Possibilities in England', *Housing Studies* 7:1, 45–55.

—— (1997), *Housing and the Urban Environment*, Oxford, Blackwell Science.

—— (1998), 'Learning the Lessons of Housing Over Shops Schemes', *Journal of Urban Design* 3:1, 73–92.

—— (2005), *Housing Design: A Survey and Literature Review*, prepared for the Royal Institution of Chartered Surveyors (unpublished).

Goodchild, B. and Cole, I. (2001), 'Social Balance and Mixed Neighbourhoods; A Review of Discourse and Practice in British Social Housing', *Environment and Planning D: Society and Space* 19:1, 103–22.

Goodchild, B. and Henneberry, J. (1994), *Impact Fees for Planning*, London, The Royal Institution of Chartered Surveyors.

Goodchild, B. and Hickman, P. (2006), 'Towards a Regional Strategy for the North of England? An Assessment of "The Northern Way"', *Regional Studies* 40:1, 121–33.

Goodchild, B. et al. (1996a), 'Impact Fees: A Review of Alternatives and their Implications for Planning Practice in Britain', *The Town Planning Review* 67:2, 161–81 (Barry Goodchild, John Henneberry, Christine Booth).

—— (1996b), *Volume Procurement: 'Operation Breakthrough' Evaluated*, London, The Housing Corporation, Research Report 18 (Barry Goodchild, Oliver Chamberlain and Christina Beatty).

—— (2002), 'Unpopular Housing in England in Conditions of Low Demand: Coping with a Diversity of Problems and Policy Measures', *The Town Planning Review* 73:4, 373–94 (Barry Goodchild, Paul Hickman, David Robinson).

Goodlad, R. (1994), presentation made at the University of Glasgow, cited by Forrest, R. and Williams, P. (997) 'Future Directions', in Williams, P. (ed.) *Directions in Housing Policy*, London, Paul Chapman Publishing, 209.

Graham, S. and Marvin, S. (2001), *Splintering Urbanism: Networked Infrastructures, Technological Mobilities and the Urban Condition*, London, Routledge.

Grant, L. and Buckner, L. (2007), *Connecting Women with the Labour Market: Synthesis Report*, Centre for Social Inclusion, Sheffield Hallam University.

Greater London Authority (collective author) (2002a), *A City of Villages: Promoting a Sustainable Future for London Suburbs*, SDS Technical Report 11, London, GLA.

—— (2002b), *Spatial Development Strategy Scenario Testing*, SDS Technical Report Seventeen, London, GLA.

—— (2003), *Housing for a Compact City*, London, GLA.

Grebler, L. (1956), *Europe's Reborn Cities*, Washington DC, The Urban Land Institute.

Grieve, R. (1954), 'The Clyde Valley – A Review', *Town and Country Planning Summer School*, Report of Proceedings.

Grimsley, M., Hickman, P. Lawless, P. Manning, J. and Wilson, I. (2005), *Community Involvement and Social Capital*, New Deal for Communities National Evaluation Data Analysis Paper 30: Centre for Regional Economic and Social Research, Sheffield Hallam University.

Groat, L. and Canter, D. (1979), 'Does Post-Modernism Communicate?', *Progressive Architecture* 12, 84–7.

Groves, R., Middleton, A., Murie, A. and Broughton, K. (2003), 'Neighbourhoods that Work', *Findings* 733 Joseph Rowntree Foundation.

Gunder, M. (2005), 'The Production of Desirous Space: Mere Fantasies of the Utopian City?', *Planning Theory* 4:2, 173–99.

Gunder, M. and Hillier, J.(2004), 'Conforming to the Expectations of the Profession: A Lacanian Perspective on Planning Practice, Norms and Values', *Planning Theory and Practice* 5:2, 217–35.

Gurney, C.(1999), 'Pride and Prejudice: Discourses of Normalisation in Public and Private Accounts of Home Ownership', *Housing Studies* 14:2, 163–83.

Habermas, J. (1971), *Towards a Rational Society*, London, Heinemann (relevant section originally published in 1968).

Habraken, N.J. (1972), *Supports: An Alternative to Mass Housing*, London: Architectural Press (Dutch original 1962).

Hajer, M.A. (1995), *The Politics of Environmental Discourse: Ecological Modernization and the Policy Process*, Oxford, Oxford University Press.

Hall, P. (1997), 'Regeneration Policies for Peripheral Housing Estates: Inward- and Outward-looking Approaches', *Urban Studies* 34:5–6, 873–90.

Hall, P. (2002), *Cities of Tomorrow: An Intellectual History of Urban Planning and Design in the Twentieth Century*, Oxford, Blackwell (original 1988).

Hall, P., Gracey, H., Drewett, R. and Thomas, R. (1973), *The Containment of Urban England, Vol. 2: The Planning System*, London, George Allen and Unwin.

Hamnett, C. (2003), 'Gentrification and the Middle-class Remaking of Inner London, 1961–2001', *Urban Studies* 40:12, 2401–26.

Hardy, D. (1991), *From New Towns to Green Politics*, London, E&FN Spon.

Hardy, D. and Ward, C. (1984), *Arcadia for All: The Legacy of a Makeshift Landscape*, London, Mansell.

Hare, P. (1983), 'The Preconditions for Effective Planning in the UK', in Sawyer, M. and Scott, K. (eds) *Socialist Economic Review, 1983*, London, The Merlin Press.

Harmon, M.M. and Mayer, R.T. (1986), *Organization Theory for Public Administration*, Boston, Little, Brown.

Harrison, P. (1983), *Inside the Inner City*, Harmondsworth, Penguin Books.

Harvey, D. (1989), *The Condition of Postmodernity*, Oxford, Basil Blackwell.

Hassan, I. (1985), 'The Culture of Postmodernism', *Theory, Culture and Society* 2:3, 119–33.

Hastings, A. (2000), 'Discourse Analysis: What Does it Offer Housing Studies?', *Housing, Theory and Society* 17:3, 131–9.

Hayek, F.A. (1944), *The Road to Serfdom*, London, George Routledge and Sons, (page numbers and quotations are taken from the 1962 Routledge paperback edition).

—— (1960), *The Constitution of Liberty*, London, Routledge and Kegan Paul.

Healey, P. (1992), 'Planning through Debate: The Communicative Turn in Planning Theory', *Town Planning Review* 63:2, 143–62.

—— (1998a), 'Building institutional Capacity Through Collaborative Approaches to Urban Planning', *Environment and Planning A* 30:9, 1531–46.

—— (1998b), 'Collaborative Planning in a Stakeholder Society', *Town Planning Review* 69:1, 1–21.

—— (2003), '"Collaborative Planning" in Perspective', *Planning Theory* 2:2, 101–23.

Hebbert, M. (1983), 'The Daring Experiment: Social Scientists and Land Use Planning in 1940s Britain', *Environment and Planning B: Planning and Design* 10:1, 3–17.

Henney, A. (1973), 'Managing Older Housing Areas', *Journal of the Town Planning Institute* February, 73–7.

Heywood, F. et al, (2002), *Housing and Home in Later Life*, Buckingham, Open University Press.

Hickman, P., Robinson, D., Casey, R., Green, S. and Powell, R. (2007), *Understanding Housing Demand: Learning from Rising Markets in Yorkshire and the Humber*, Coventry, Chartered Institute of Housing.

Hildebrand W., Ferguson, N., Bagaeen, S. and Woods, L. (2006), 'Suburbs Reconsidered: Form, Mobility and Sustainability', *Built Environment* 32:3, 250–66.

Hillier, J. (2003), 'Agonizing over Consensus: Why Habermasian Ideals cannot be "Real"', *Planning Theory* 2:1, 37–59.

Hillier, W. and Hanson, J. (1984), *The Social Logic of Space*, Cambridge, Cambridge University Press.

Hillier, W. and Sahbaz, O. (2005), 'High Resolution Analysis of Crime Patterns in Urban Street Networks: An Initial Statistical Sketch from an Ongoing Study of a London Borough', *5th International Space Syntax Symposium*, Delft, 15 June.

Hillier, W., Burdett, R., Peponis, J. and Penn, A. (1987), 'Creating Life: Or, Does Architecture Create Anything?', *Architecture and Behaviour* 3:3.

Hills, J. (2007), *Ends and Means: The Future Roles of Social Housing in England*, CASE report 34, London, London School of Economics.

Hinchcliffe, S. (1997), 'Locating Risk: Energy Use, the "Ideal" Home and the Non-ideal World', *Transactions Institute British Geographers* NS 22, 197–209.

Hirsch, F. (1977), *The Social Limits to Growth*, London, Routledge and Kegan Paul.

HMG – HM Government (1977), *Policy for the Inner Cities*, London, Department of Environment, HMSO.

—— (1997), *Standards in Public Life: Standards of Conduct in Local Government in England, Scotland and Wales*, (Third Report of Lord Nolan's Committee on Standards in Public Life) HMSO, Cm 3702–I.

HM Treasury (with the Department of Trade and Industry) (2001), *Productivity in the UK: 3 – The Regional Dimension*, HM Treasury, London.

HM Treasury-ODPM (collective authors) (2005), *Housing Policy: An Overview*, London, HMSO.

HM Treasury, HM Customs and Excise and the Office of the Deputy Prime Minister (collective authors) (2005), *Planning Gain Supplement: A Consultation*, London, HMSO.

Ho, S.Y. (1999), 'Evaluating Urban Regeneration Programmes in Britain: Exploring the Potential of the Realist Approach', *Evaluation* 5:4, 422–38.

Hobsbawm, E. (1994), *The Age of Extremes: The Short Twentieth Century, 1914–1991*, London, Michael Joseph.

Hole, W.V. and Pountney, M.T. (1971), *Trends in Population, Housing and Occupancy Rates 1861–1961*, London, HMSO.

Holmes, C. (2003), *Housing, Equality and Choice*, London, Institute for Public Policy Research (IPPR).

Hooper, A. and Nicol, C. (2000), 'Design Practice and Volume Production in Speculative Housebuilding', *Construction Management and Economics* 18, 295–310.

Hooper, B. (1995), 'The Poem of Male Desire: Female Bodies, Modernity and Paris, Capital of Nineteenth Century', *Planning Theory* 13, 105–29.

Hopkins, B. (2000), 'The Food Producing Neighbourhood', in Barton, H. (ed.) *Sustainable Communities: The Potential for Neighbourhoods*, London, Earthscan, 199–215.

Horsfall, T.C. (1905), *The Improvement of the Dwellings and Surroundings of the People*, Manchester: Manchester University Press.

House of Commons (2005a), *Housing: Building a Sustainable Future*, Environmental Audit Committee First Report of Session 2004–05 Volume I, HC 135–I.

—— (2005b), *Housing Market Renewal Initiative*, Eighth Report of the Select Committee on Office of the Deputy Prime Minister: Housing, Planning, Local Government and the Regions, Session 2004–2005.

Housing Corporation (collective author) (2003), *Strategy for Housing Older People in England*, London, The Housing Corporation.

—— *Annual Report and Accounts 2004/05*, London The Housing Corporation.

Housing Forum, The (corporate author) (2002a), *Homing in on Excellence: A Commentary on the Use of Offsite Fabrication Methods for the UK Housebuilding Industry*, London, The Housing Forum.

—— (2002b), *The Housing Forum Demonstration Projects Report: The Challenges Ahead*, London, The Housing Forum.

Howard, E. (1898), *To-morrow: A Peaceful Path to Real Reform* (the publication consulted is by Attic Books of Eastbourne, 1995) (first published in 1898, republished in 1902 as 'Garden Cities of To-morrow').

Hunter, A.J. and Suttles, G.D. (1972), 'The Expanding Community of Limited Liability', in Suttles, G.D. (ed.) *The Social Construction of Communities*, Chicago, University of Chicago Press.

Hutton, W (1996), *The State We're In*, London, Vintage.

Hutton, W. and Massey, A. (2006), 'Professional Ethics and Public Service', *Public Service and Management*, January, 23–30.

Huyssen, A. (1984), 'Mapping the Postmodern', *New German Critique* 33, Fall.

Huxley, A. (1994), *Brave New World*, London, Flamingo (originally published 1932).

ICC – Institute of Community Cohesion (2007), *Promoting Sustainable Communities and Community Cohesion*, Leeds, Academy of Sustainable Communities.

Imrie, R. (2003), *The Impact of Part M on the Design of New Housing*, York, The Joseph Rowntree Foundation.

Independent Review Team (2001), *Community Cohesion* (The Cantle Report), London, The Home Office.

Innes, M. and Jones, V. (2006) *Neighbourhood Security and Urban Change: Risk, Resilience and Recovery*, York, The Joseph Rowntree Foundation.

ITC – Independent Transport Commission (collective author) (2004) *Suburban Future*, London, ITC.

Jacobs, J. (1964), *The Death and Life of Great American Cities*, Harmondsworth, Pelican Books.

Jaillet, M.-C. (1999), 'Peut-on parler de sécession à propos des villes européennes', *Esprit* Novembre, 145–67.

Jain, J. and Guiver, J. (2001), 'Turning the Car Inside Out: Transport, Equity and Environment', *Social Policy and Administration* 35:5, 569–86.

Jameson, F. (1984a), 'Foreword' in Lyotard, op. cit.

—— (1984b), 'Postmodernism or the Cultural Logic of Late Capitalism', *New Left Review* 146, 53–92.

Jarmain, J.R. (1948), *Housing Subsidies and Rents*, London, Stevens and Sons.

Jeannot. G. (2005), *Les métiers flous*, Toulouse, Octarès Éditions.

Jencks, C. (1969), 'Pop-Nonpop (2)', *Architectural Association Quarterly* 1:20, 56–4.

—— (1977), *The Language of Post-Modern Architecture*, London, Academy Editions.

Jephcott, P. (1971), *Homes in High Flats*, Occasional Paper No. 13, University of Glasgow Social and Economic Studies, Oliver and Boyd.

Jones, P. (2005), 'The Suburban High Flat in the Post-War Reconstruction of Birmingham, 1945–71', *Urban History* 32:2, 308–26.

Julien, P. (1994), *Jacques Lacan's Return to Freud: The Real, the Symbolic and the Imaginary*, New York and London, New York University Press (from an undated French original).

Jupp, B. (1999), *Living Together: Community Life on Mixed Tenure Estates*, London, Demos.

Kagan, C. (20007), 'Interpersonal Skills and Reflection in Regeneration Practice', *Public Money and Management* 27:3, 169–74.

Kambites, C. and Owen, S. (2006), 'Renewed Prospects for Green Infrastructure Planning in the UK' *Planning Practice and Research* 21:4, 483–96.

Karn, V. and Sheridan, L. (1994), *New Homes in the 1990s*, York, The Joseph Rowntree Foundation.

Keeble, L. (1969), *Principles and Practice of Town and Country Planning*, London, The Estates Gazette (fourth edition) (first published 1952).

Kemeny, J. (1992), *Housing and Social Theory*, London, Routledge.

King, A. (1984), *The Bungalow: The Production of a Global Culture*, Routledge and Kegan Paul.

Kintrea, K. and Morgan, J. (2005), *Evaluation of English Housing Policy 1975–2000: Theme 3: Housing Quality and Neighbourhood Quality*, London, ODPM.

Kirby, D.A. (1971), 'The Inter-War Council Dwelling', *Town Planning Review* 42, 250–68.

Kitchen, T. (2002), 'The Balance between Certainty, Speed, Public Involvement and the Achievement of Sustainable Development in the Planning System: The Impact of the Planning Green Paper', in *Certainty, Quality, Consistency and the Planning Green Paper: Can Planning Deliver the Goods?*, Report of the Proceedings of a Conference held at Leeds Civic Hall on 13 February 2002, available from Sheffield Hallam University.

—— (2007), *Skills for Planning Practice*, Basingstoke, Palgrave.

Kitchin, R. and Tate, N.J. (2000), *Conducting Research in human Geography: Theory, Methodology and Practice*, Harlow, Prentice Hall.

Kleinman, M. (1996), *Housing, Welfare and the State in Europe*, Edward Elgar, Cheltenham.

Knowles, P. (2003), *Defensible Space and the Distribution of Crime and Disorder in Residential Areas*, Bedfordshire Police (unpublished).

Konttinen, S.-L. (1983), *Byker*, London, Cape.

Kornai, J. (1971), *Anti-equilibrium*, Amsterdam, North Holland Publishing.

Krier, L. (1984), 'The City within the City', *Architectural Design* 54:7/8.

Kuper, L. (1953), 'Blueprint for Living Together', in Kuper, L. (ed.) *Living in Towns*, London, The Cresset Press.

Lai, L. W.-C. (2002), 'Libertarians on the Road to Town Planning', *Town Planning Review* 73:3, 289–310.

Land Enquiry Committee (1914), *Report, The Land*, Vol. II. London, Hodder and Stoughton.

Landman, K (2003), 'Alley-Gating and Neighbourhood Gating: Are They Two Sides of the Same Face?', paper delivered at the conference *Gated Communities: Building Social Division or Safer Communities?*, Glasgow.

Lawless, P. (2006), 'New Deal for Communities 2001– 2005: Some Emerging Lessons', presentation at Sheffield Hallam University.

Le Corbusier (1931), *Towards a New Architecture*, London, John Rodker (the text used is the 1986 reprint by Dover Publications, Mineola, NY) (French original 1923).

Leather, P., Cole, I. and Ferrari, E. (2007), *National Evaluation of the HMR Pathfinder Programme, Baseline Report*, London, Department for Communities and Local Government.

Lee, P. and Murie, A. (1999), 'Spatial and Social Divisions within British cities: Beyond Residualisation', *Housing Studies* 14:4, 625–40.

Lefèbvre. H. (1991), *The Production of Space*, Oxford, Blackwell (French original 1974).

Ley, D. (1996), *The New Middle Class and the Remaking of the Central City*, Oxford, Oxford University Press.

—— (2003), 'Artists, Aestheticisation and the Field of Gentrification', *Urban Studies* 40:12, 2527–44.

Liscombe, R.W. (2006), 'The Ideal City', World Urban Forum Vancouver Working Group, Discussion Paper, Vancouver, University of British Columbia.

Littlewood J. and Tinker, A. (1981), *Families in Flats*, London, Department of the Environment, HMSO.

Llewelyn Davies (2004), *Safer Places; The Planning System and Crime Prevention*, London, ODPM.

Local Government Board and Secretary of State for Scotland, Housing (Building Construction) Committee (1918), *Questions of Building Construction in Connection with the Provision of Dwellings for the Working Classes* (The Tudor Walters Report) Cd. 9191 London, HMSO.

London Housing (collective author) (2004), *Overcrowding in London*, London, London Housing.

Longley, P., Batty, M., Shepherds, J. and Sadlers, G. (1992), 'Do Green Belts Change the Shape of Urban Areas? A Preliminary Analysis of the Settlement Geography of South East England', *Regional Studies* 26:5, 437–52.

Louvot-Runavot, C. (2001), 'Le logement dans l'Union européenne: la propriété prend le pas sur la location', *Economie et Statistique* 343, 29–50.

Lovell, H. (2004), 'Framing Sustainable Housing as a Solution to Climate Change', *Journal of Environmental Policy and Planning* 6:1, 35–55.

Lucy, W.H. and Phillips, D.L. (2000), *Confronting Suburban Decline*, Washington DC, Island Press.

Luhmann, N. (1986), 'The Self-reproduction of Law and its Limits', in Teubner, G. (ed.) *Dilemmas of Law in the Welfare State*, Berlin, Walter de Gruyter, 111–27.

Lynch, K. (1972), *What Time is this Place?*, Cambridge, MA, MIT Press.

Lynch, K. and Hack, G. (1984), *Site Planning*, Cambridge, MA, MIT Press.

Lyotard, J.-F. (1984), *The Postmodern Condition. A Report on Knowledge*, Manchester. Manchester University (French original 1979).

M'Gonigle, G.C.M. (1933), 'Poverty, Nutrition and the Public Health', *Proceedings of the Royal Society of Medicine* 26, 677–87.

McCarthy, J. (2007), *Partnership, Collaborative Planning and Urban Regeneration*, Aldershot, Ashgate.

McConnell, S. (1969), 'Residential Density', *Official Architecture and Planning*, April, 410–16.

McCulloch, A. (2004), 'Localism and its Neo-liberal Application: A Case Study of the Westgate New Deal for Communities in Newcastle', *Capital and Class* 83, 133–65.

McCutcheon, R. (1975), 'High Flats in Britain, 1945–1971', in *Political Economy and the Housing Question*, London, Political Economy of Housing Workshop.

McKean, C. (1999), 'Between the Wars', in Reed, P. (ed.) *Glasgow: The Forming of the City*, Edinburgh, Edinburgh University Press.

McKenzie, E. (2003), 'Common-interest Housing in the Communities of Tomorrow', *Housing Policy Debate* 14:1+2, 203–34.

McKie, R. (1971), *Housing and the Whitehall Bulldozer*, Hobart Paper No. 52, London, The Institute of Economic Affairs.

McKie, R. (1974), 'Cellular Renewal', *The Town Planning Review*, 45:3, 274–90.

Maclennan, D. (1983), 'Housing Rehabilitation in Glasgow', *Housing Review* November/December.

McLoughlin, J.B. (1969), *Urban and Regional Planning: A Systems Approach*, London, Faber and Faber.

Malpass, P. (2000a), 'Public Utility Societies and the Housing and Town Planning Act, 1919', *Planning Perspectives* 15:4, 377–92.

—— (2000b), 'The Discontinuous History of Housing Associations in England', *Housing Studies* 15:2, 195–212.

—— (2003a), 'Private Enterprise in Eclipse? A Reassessment of British Housing Policy in the 1940s', *Housing Studies* 18:5, 645–59.

—— (2003b), 'The Wobbly Pillar? Housing and the British Postwar Welfare State', *Journal of Social Policy* 32:4, 589–606.

Malpass, P. and Murie, A. (1982), *Housing Policy and Practice*, London, Macmillan (first edition).

Manchester City Council (collective author and publisher) (2003), *Manchester City Centre Strategic Plan, 2004–2007*, The Town Hall, Manchester.

Mann, P.H. (1965), *An Approach to Urban Sociology*, London, Routledge and Kegan Paul.

Mannheim, K. (1971), *Man and Society in Age of Reconstruction*, London, Routledge and Kegan Paul (first published in English in 1940, partly based on a German original of 1935).

Manzi; T, and Smith-Bowers, B. (2005), 'Gated Communities as Club Goods: Segregation or Social Cohesion?', *Housing Studies* 20:2, 345–59.

Marcuse, H. (1964), *One-dimensional Man: Studies in the Ideology of Advanced Industrial Society*, London, Routledge and Kegan Paul.

Marcuse, P. (1980), 'Housing Policy and City Planning: The Puzzling Split in the United States, 1893–1931', in Cherry, G.E. (ed.) *Shaping an Urban World*, London, Mansell, 23–58.

—— (1995), 'Not Chaos but Walls: Postmodernism and the Partitioned City', in Watson, S. and Gibson, K. (eds) *Post-modern Cities and Spaces*, Oxford, Blackwell Publishing, 243–53.

Marwick, A. (1964), 'Middle Opinion in the Thirties: Planning, Progress and Political 'Agreement', *The English Historical Review* 79:311, 285–98.

Mason, T. (1977), *Inner City Housing and Urban Renewal Policy: A Housing Profile of Cheetham Hill, Manchester and Salford*, CES Research Series 23, London, Centre for Environmental Studies.

Mass-Observation (1943), *An Enquiry into People's Homes*, London, John Murray.

Maurin, E. (2004), *Le ghetto français*, Paris, La République des Idées, Le Seuil.

Mboumoua, I. (2007), 'L'Union Européenne et les Villes: Du développement des instruments d'action publique Urban et Urbact à leur traduction localisée', PhD thesis, University of Paris VIII.

Mercier, S. (2006), *L'avenir des grands ensembles: leurs habitants ont-ils pris la parole? Marseille et Sheffield*, Thèse pour obtenir le grade de Docteur, Université Paul Cézanne-Marseille III.

Merrett, S. (1979), *State Housing in Britain*, London, Routledge and Kegan Paul.

MH – Ministry of Health (1944), Central Housing Advisory Committee, *The Design of Dwellings* (The Dudley Report), London, HMSO.

MHLG – see Ministry of Housing and Local Government.

Miller Lane, B. (1968), *Architecture and Politics in Germany, 1918–1945*, Cambridge, MA, Harvard University Press.

Ministry of Housing and Local Government (1952), *The Density of Residential Areas*, London, HMSO.

—— (1953), *Houses 1953*, London, HMSO.

—— (1958), *Flats and Houses 1958, Design and Economy*, London, HMSO.

—— (1961), *Homes for Today and Tomorrow* (The Parker Morris Report) London, HMSO.

Ministry of Reconstruction, Advisory Council, Women's Housing Sub-committee, (1918), *First Interim Report*, Cd. 9166, London: HMSO.

—— (1919), *Final Report*, Cd. 9232. London: HMSO.

Ministry of Works and Planning Expert Committee on Compensation and Betterment (1942), *Final Report* (The Uthwatt Report), London, HMSO.

Mirrlees-Black, C. and Allen, J. (1998), *Concern about Crime: Findings from the 1998 British Crime Survey*, Home Office Research, Development and Statistics Directorate, Research Findings, No. 83.

Monbiot, G. (2006), 'Small-scale Renewable Power – Low-wattage Thinking?', *New Scientist* 2571, 3 September.

Mooney, G. and Danson, M. (1997), 'Beyond "Culture City": Glasgow as a "Dual City"', in Jewson, N. and MacGregor, S. (eds) op. cit., 73–86.

Morley, D. (2005), 'What's Home Got to do With It?', *European Journal of Cultural Studies* 6:4, 435–58.

Mort, F. (2004), 'Fantasies of Metropolitan Life: Planning London in the 1940s', *Journal of British Studies* 43:1, 120–51.

Muggeridge, M. (1940), *The Thirties*, London, Hamish Hamilton.

Mulholland Research and Consulting (2003), *Perceptions of Privacy and Density in Housing Report on Research Findings prepared for the Popular Housing Group*, London, Mulholland Research & Consulting.

—— (2004), *Understanding Attitudes towards Social Housing*, a presentation made at a social housing event organised by Bellwether Forums, London, 9 December.

Munro, W. and Lane, R., (1990), 'An Environmental Assessment of the Residential Areas of Harrow', *The Planner*, 12 January.

Murie, A. and Rowlands, R. (2007), 'The New Politics of Urban Housing', *Environment and Planning C: Government and Policy*, advance online publication.

Murphy, J.W. (1988), 'Making Sense of Postmodern Sociology', *The British Journal of Sociology*, XXXIX:4.

Muthesius. S. (1982), *The English Terraced House*, New Haven, NJ and London, Yale University Press.

Muthesius, W. (1979, 1st English edition), *The English House*, London, Crosby Lockwood (originally published in German in 1904).

Næss, P. (2006), 'Accessibility, Activity Participation and Location of Activities: Exploring the Links between Residential Location and Travel Behaviour', *Urban Studies* 43:3, 627–52.

Nairn, I. (1956), *Counter Attack against Subtopia*, London, The Architectural Press.

—— (1961), 'Spec-built', *Architectural Review* 129(769), March.

NAO – National Audit Office (collective author) (2005), *Using Modern Methods of Construction to Build Homes more Quickly and Efficiently*, London, NAO.

Nathan, M. and Urwin, C. (2005), *City People: City Centre Living in the UK*, London, Centre for Cities.

National Building Agency (collective author) (1981), *Residential Renewal in Scottish Cities: A Report to the Scottish Development Department*, Edinburgh, NBA.

National Centre for Social Research (2006), *Housing in England 2004/05 A Report Principally from the 2004/05 Survey of English Housing*, London, Department for Communities and Local Government.

National Community Development Project (1976), *Whatever Happened to Council Housing*, CDP Information and Intelligence Unit.

Navez-Bouchanine, F. (2002), 'Emergence d'une notion: quelques repères historique', in Navez-Bouchanine, F. (ed.) *La fragmentation en question*, Paris, L'Harmattan.

NCSR – National Centre for Social Research.

Nettlefold, J. (1908), *Practical Housing*, Letchworth, Garden City Press.

Newman, O. (1973), *Defensible Space People and Design in the Violent City*, Architectural Press, London.

—— (1980), *Community of Interest*, New York, Anchor Press-Doubleday.

Newman, P. and Kenworthy, J. (1989), *Cities and Automobile Dependence: A Sourcebook*, Aldershot and Brookfield, VT, Gower.

Nicholas, S., Kershaw, C. and Walker, A. (eds) (2007), *Crime in England and Wales 2006/07*, Home Office Statistical Bulletin, London, Home Office.

Nicol, C. and Golland, A. (2004), 'Innovation and Emerging Trends in Housebuilding', in Golland, A. and Blake, R. op. cit., 321–40.

Nicol, C. and Hooper, A. (1999), 'Contemporary Change and the Housebuilding Industry: Concentration and Qtandardisation in Production', *Housing Studies* 14:1, 57–76.

Niner, P. and Forrest, R. (1982), *Housing Action Area Policy and Progress: The Residents' Perspective*, University of Birmingham, Centre for Urban and Regional Studies, Research Memorandum 91.

North, P. (2000), 'Is there Space for Organisation from Below within the UK Governmelt's Action Zone? A Test of "Collaborative Planning"', *Urban Studies* 37:8, 1261–78.

NRU – Neighbourhood Renewal Unit (2002), *The Learning Curve: Developing Skills and Knowledge for Neighbourhood Renewal*, London, ODPM.

Nubani, L. and Wineman, J. (2005), 'The Role of Space Syntax in Identifying the Relationship Between Space and Crime', *5th International Space Syntax Symposium*, Delft.

NWSP – Northern Way Steering Group (collective author) (2004), *Moving Forward: The Northern Way*, Newcastle-upon-Tyne, The Northern Way.

Oakes, C. and McKee, E. (1997), *City-centre Apartments for Single People at Affordable Rents (CASPAR)*, York, York Publishing Services for the Joseph Rowntree Foundation.

ODPM – see Office of the Deputy Prime Minister.

OECD – Organisation for Economic Cooperation and Development (collective author) (1995), *Women in the City*, Paris, OECD.

Office for National Statistics (collective author) (2001), *Social Capital: A Review of the Literature*, HMSO, National Statistics.

—— (2003), *Census 2001, National Report for England and Wales*, London, TSO.

Office of the Deputy Prime Minister (2000), *Housing Quality Indicators: Live Piloting*, London, The Stationery Office.

—— (2002), *Living Places Cleaner, Safer, Greener*, London, HMSO.

—— (2003a), *English House Condition Survey 2001*, London, HMSO.

—— (2003b), *Sustainable Communities: Building for the Future*, London, ODPM.

—— (2003c), *Sustainable Communities: Delivering through Planning*, London, ODPM.

—— (2004a), *Skills for Sustainable Communities* (The Egan Review), London, ODPM.

—— (2004b), *Housing Market Assessment Manual*, Sustainable Communities Research Summary No. 1, London, ODPM.

—— (2004c), *Planning Policy Statement 22, Renewable Energy*, London, ODPM.

Oldenburg, R. (2007), 'The Character of Third Places', in Carmona, M. and Tiesdell, S. (eds) *Urban Design Reader*, Oxford, Architectural Press, 170–76 (US original 1989).

ONS – Office for National Statistics.

Orbach, L. F. (1977), *Homes for Heroes. A Study of the Evolution of British Public Housing, 1915–1921*, London, Seeley.

Oreopoulis, P. (2003), 'The Long-run Consequences of Living in a Poor Neighbourhood', *Quarterly Journal of Economics* 118:4.

Osborn, F.J. (1945), 'The Garden City Movement: A Revaluation', *Journal of the Town Planning Institute* XXXI:6, 193–207.

Osborn, S., (1993), *Crime Prevention on Council Estates*, London, The Department of the Environment, HMSO.

Ove Arup & Partners Ltd, Regional Forecasts Ltd, Oxford Economic Forecasting Ltd (2005), *Regional Futures: England's Regions in 2030: Final Report*, London, English Regions Network RDA Planning Leads Group, Office of the Deputy Prime Minister, Department for Transport.

Owens, S. and Driffill, L. (2006), *How to Change Attitudes and Behaviours in the Context of Energy*, London, Office of Science and Innovation.

Page, D. (1993), *Building for Communities: A Study of New Housing Association Estates*, York: Joseph Rowntree Foundation.

—— (2006), *Respect and Renewal: A Study of Neighbourhood Social Regeneration*, York: Joseph Rowntree Foundation.

Palmer, J. et al. (2006), *Reducing the Environmental Impact of Housing: Final Report, Consultancy Study in Support of the Royal Commission on Environmental Pollution's 26th Report on the Urban Environment*, Oxford, Environmental Change Institute, University of Oxford.

Paris, C. (2007), 'International Perspectives on Planning and Affordable Housing', *Housing Studies* 22:1, 120–39.

Parkes, A. et al. (2002), 'What Makes People Dissatisfied with their Neighbourhoods', *Urban Studies* 39:13, 2413–38.

Parkinson, M. (2004), *Competitive European Cities: Where do the Core Cities Stand?*, London, ODPM Research Report.

Parkinson, M., Champion, T. and Evans, R. (2006), *State of the English Cities A Research Study*, Vols 1 and 2, London, ODPM.

PAT5– Policy Action Team 5 (1999), *Housing Management*, London, Department of the Environment, Transport and the Regions, HMSO.

PAT7– Policy Action Team 7 (2000), *Unpopular Housing*, London, Department of the Environment, Transport and the Regions, HMSO.

Pauleit, S. and Golding, Y. (2005), 'The Spatial Impact of Compaction: A Fine-scaled Investigation based on Merseyside', *Town Planning Review* 76:2, 143–66.

Peach, C. (1996), 'The Meaning of Segregation', *Planning Practice and Research* 11:2, 137–50.

Pennington, M. (2003), 'To What Extent and in What Ways Should Governmental Bodies Regulate Urban Planning? A Response to Charles C. Bohl', *Journal of Markets and Morality* 6:1, 213–26.

Perrault, D. (2003), 'La ville rêvée doit être permanence en projet', in de Moncan, P. (ed.) *Villes utopiques, villes rêvées,* Paris, Les Éditions du Mécène.

Pevsner, N. (1952), *The Buildings of England: London, except the Cities of London and Westminster*, Harmondsworth, Penguin Books.

—— (1969), *The Buildings of England: South Lancashire*, London, Penguin Books (the quotation and page number comes from the 1993 edition).

Phillips, M. (2002), 'The Production, Symbolization and Socialization of Gentrification: Impressions from Two Berkshire Villages', *Transactions of the Institute of British Geographers* 27:3, 282–308.

Phillipson, C., Bernard, M., Phillips, J. and Ogg, J. (1999), 'Older People's Experiences of Community Life: Patterns of Neighbouring in Three Urban Areas', *Sociological Review* 47:4, 715–39.

Popkin, S., Katz, B., Cunningham, M., Brown, K., Gustafson, J. and Turner, M. (2004), *A Decade of Hope VI: Research Findings and Policy Challenges*, Washington DC, The Urban Institute.

POS-RHG: Planning Officers Society and the Retirement Housing Group (2003), *Planning For Retirement Housing*, London, The House Builders Federation.

Pouyanne, G. (2004), 'Des avantages comparatifs de la ville compacte à l'interaction forme urbaine-mobilité. Méthodologie et premiers résultats', *les Cahiers Scientifiques du Transport* 45, 49–82.

Power, A. (1984), 'Rescuing Unpopular Council Estates through Local Management', *The Geographical Journal* 150:3, 359–62.

Power, A. and Tunstall, R. (1995), *Swimming Against the Tide: Polarisation or Progress on 20 Unpopular Council Estates, 1980–1995,* York, Joseph Rowntree Foundation.

Poyner, B. (2006), *Crime-free Housing in the 21st Century*, London, Jill Dando Institute of Crime Science, University College London.

Pragnell, M. et al. (on behalf of the Consumers' Association) (2000), 'The market potential for Smart Homes', *Findings* 40, York, The Joseph Rowntree Foundation.

Price, T. (2006), 'The Effects of Brownfield Development Constraints on Housing Supply', thesis submitted towards a BA(Hons) Planning Studies, Sheffield Hallam University.

PRI-CUDEM PRI – Policy Research Institute and the Centre for Urban Development and Environmental Management (collective authors) (2007), *Skills for the Future 2006 European Skills Symposium Evaluation Report*, Leeds, Leeds Metropolitan University.

Priestley, J.B. (1934), *English Journey. Being a Rambling but Truthful Account of What One Man Saw and Heard and Felt and Thought during a Journey through England during the Autumn of the Year 1933*, London, William Heinemann and Victor Gollancz.

Pryce, G. (1999), 'Construction Elasticities and Land Availability: A Two Stage Squares Model of Housing Supply using the Variable Elasticity Approach', *Urban Studies* 36:13, 2283–304.

Purdom, C.B. (1913), *The Garden City*, London: J.M. Dent.

—— (1921), *Town Theory and Practice*, London, Benn Bros.

—— (1922), 'Public Utility Societies', *Garden Cities and Town Planning* XII:7, July/August.

Purdue et al. (2000), 'Strengthening Community Leaders in Area Regeneration', *Findings* 720, York The Joseph Rowntree Foundation.

Putnam, R. (2000), *Bowling Alone: The Collapse and Revival of American Community*, New York: Simon and Schuster, 2000.

Ramsey, S.C. (1939), 'The Ready Built House', in Abercrombie, P. (ed.) *The Book of the Modern House*, London: Hodder and Stoughton, 130–40.

Ramwell, R. and Saltburn, H. (1998), *Trick or Treat? City Challenge and the Regeneration of Hulme*, Preston, North British Housing Association: High Wycombe, The Guinness Trust.

Rapoport, A. (1982), *The Meaning of the Built Environment*, Beverly Hills, CA, Sage.

Rasmussen, S.E. (1947), *London: The Unique City*, London: Jonathan Cape.

—— (1969), *Towns and Buildings* Cambridge, MA, MIT Press (orginal 1951).

Raulet, G, (1984), 'From Modernity as a One-Way Street to Postmodernity as a Dead End', *New German Critique* 33, 155–79.

Ravetz, A. (1974), 'From Working Class Tenement to Modern Flat', in Sutcliffe, A. (ed.) op. cit., 122–50.

—— (1976), *The Housing Poor*, The Catholic Housing Aid Society.

Ravetz, A. with Turkington, R. (1995), *The Place of Home English Domestic Environments, 1914–2000*, London, E&FN Spon.

RCEP – Royal Commission on Environmental Pollution.

RCHS – Royal Commission on Housing in Scotland.

Reade, C.R.A. (1913), 'A Defence of the Garden City Movement', *Town Planning Review* IV:3.

Reade, E. (1987), *British Town and Country Planning*, Milton Keynes, The Open University.

Reed, P. (ed.) (1999), *Glasgow: The Forming of the City*, Edinburgh, Edinburgh University Press.

Richards, J.M. (1973), *The Castles on the Ground*, London, John Murray (original 1946).

Richards, J.M. and Cullen, G. (1953), 'The Failure of the New Towns', *Architectural Review* 114, July.

RIBA/IoH – Royal Institute of British Architects/Institute of Housing (1983), *Homes for the Future: Standards for New Housing Development*, London, Institute of Housing.

Rittel, H.W.J. and Webber, M.M. (1973), 'Dilemmas in a General Theory of Planning', *Policy Sciences* 4, 155–69.

Robertson, D. and Bailey, N. (1996), *Review of the Impact of Housing Action Areas*, Research Report 47, Edinburgh, Scottish Homes.

Robinson, C., Humphrey, A., Kafka, E., Oliver, R. and Bose, S. (2004), *Housing in England 2002/3 A Report Principally from the 2002/2003 Survey of English Housing Carried Out by the National Centre for Social Research on Behalf of the Office of the Deputy Prime Minister*, London, Office of the Deputy Prime Minister.

Robinson, D. (2005), 'The Search for Community Cohesion: Key Themes and Dominant Concepts of the Public Policy Agenda', *Urban Studies* 42:8, 1411–27.

Robson, W.A. (1926), *Socialism and the Standardised Life*, Fabian Tract No. 219, London, The Fabian Society.

Rodger, R., (1989), *Housing in Urban Britain, 1780–1914*, Basingstoke, Macmillan Educational.

Roger Tym & Partners (Corporate author) (2005), *The Costs and Funding of Growth in South East England*, Final Report, London, Roger Tym and Partners.

Rogers, R. and Power, A. (2000), *Cities for a Small Country*, London, Faber.

Ross, K. (on behalf of the Building Research Establishment) (2002), *Non-traditional Housing in the UK – A Brief Review*, London, The Council of Mortgage Lenders.

Roy, R., Brown, J. and Gaze, C. (2003), 'Re-engineering the Construction Process in the Speculative House-building Sector', *Construction Management and Economics* 21:2, 137–46.

Royal Commission on Environmental Pollution (2007), *Twenty-sixth Report, The Urban Environment*, Cm 7009, London, Crown Copyright.

Royal Commission on Housing in Scotland, (1917), *Report of the Royal Commission on the Housing of the Industrial Population of Scotland, Rural and Urban*, Edinburgh, HMSO, Cd. 8731.

Royal Commission on the Distribution of the Industrial Population (1940), *Report*, London: HMSO, Cd. 6153.

RTPI – Royal Town Planning Institute (collective author) (2007), *Shaping and Delivering Tomorrow's Places: Effective Practice in Spatial Planning*, London, RTPI.

Rudlin, D. and Falk, N. (1995), *21st Century Homes: Building to Last*, London, URBED, Joseph Rowntree Foundation.

—— (1999), *Building the 21st Century Home*, London, Architectural Press.

Sabatino, R.A. (1956), *Housing in Great Britain, 1945–49*, Dallas, Southern Methodist University Press.

Sadler, S. (2000), 'Open Ends', in Hughes, J. and Sadler, S. (eds) *Non-Plan: Essays on Freedom, Participation and Change in Modern Architecture and Urbanism*, Oxford: Architectural Press., 138–55.

Sandercock, L. (1998), *Towards Cosmopolis*, Chichester, John Wiley.

—— (2003), *Mongrel Cities*, London, Continuum Press.

Sanderson Furniss, A.D. and Phillips, M. (1919), *The Working Woman's House*, London, The Swarthmore Press.

Savitch, H.V. (1988), *Post-Industrial Cities, Politics and Planning in New York, Paris and London*, Princeton, NJ, Princeton University Press.

Sayle, A. (1924), *The Houses of the Workers*, London, T. Fisher Unwin.

Schiralli, M. (1999), *Constructive Postmodernism: Toward Renewal in Cultural and Literary Studies*, Westport, CN, Bergin Garvey/Greenwood.

Schoon, N. (2001), *The Chosen City*, London, Spon Press.

Scottish Executive (2003), *Scottish Planning Policy SPP 3 Planning for Housing*, Edinburgh, Crown Copyright.

SDC – Sustainable Development Commission.

Self, P. (1960), *Cities in Flood*, London, Faber and Faber (original 1957).

Sennett, R. (1990), *The Conscience of the Eye. The Design and Social life of Cities*, London, Faber (the page number refers to the 1993 paperback edition).

SEU – Social Exclusion Unit.

Shankland et al. (1977), *Inner London: Policies for Dispersal and Balance*, Shankland Cox Partnership and the Institute of Community Studies, for the Department of the Environment, London, HMSO.

Shonfield, K. (1998), *At Home with Strangers: Public Space and the New Urbanity*, Working Paper 8: The Richness of Cities, Comedia and Demos, London.

Shove, E. (2003), 'Converging Conventions of Comfort, Cleanliness and Convenience', *Journal of Consumer Policy* 26:4, 395–418.

SHU – Sheffield Hallam University (2006), 'Addressing Housing Affordability, Clearance and Relocation Issues in the Housing Market Renewal Pathfinders', *Findings*, York, Joseph Rowntree Foundation.

Sim, D. (1993), *British Housing Design*, London, Longman/Institute of Housing.

Simon, H. (1957), *Models of Man*, New York, Wiley.

Simonson, P. (1996), 'Dreams of Democratic Togetherness: Communication Hope from Colley to Katz', *Critical Studies in Mass Communication* 13:4, 324–42.

Smith, D.P. and Holt, L. (2007), 'Studentification and "Apprentice" Gentrifiers within Britain's Provincial Towns and Cities: Extending the Meaning of Gentrification', *Environment and Planning A* 39:1, 142–61.

Smith, N. (1979), 'Toward a Theory of Gentrification; A Back to the City Movement by Capital not People', *Journal of the American Planning Association* 45, 538–48.

—— (1982), 'Gentrification and Uneven Development', *Economic Geography* 58, 139–55.

—— (1996), *The New Urban Frontier: Gentrification and the Revanchist City*, Routledge, London and New York.

Smith, N. and Williams, P. (eds) (1986), *Gentrification of the City*, London: Unwin and Hyman.

Smith, R. and Burbidge, M., (1973), *Density and Residents' Satisfaction*, London, Sociological Research Branch of the Department of the Environment (unpublished).

Social Exclusion Unit (1998), *Bringing Britain Together: A National Strategy for Neighbourhood Renewal*, Cm 4045.

—— (2004), *Jobs and Enterprise in Deprived Areas*, London, HMSO, Office of the Deputy Prime Minister.

Sokal, A. and Bricmont, J. (1999), *Intellectual Impostures: Postmodern Philosophers' Abuse of Science*, London: Profile.

Sorensen, A.D. and Day, R.A. (1981), 'Libertarian Planning', *Town Planning Review* 52:4, 390–402.

Stamp, L.D. (1950), 'Planning and Agriculture', *Journal of the Town Planning Institute* XXXVI:4, March–April.

Stead, D. and Marshall, S. (2001), 'The Relationships between Urban Form and Travel Patterns: An International Review and Evaluation', *European Journal of Transport and Infrastructure, Research* 1:2, 113–41.

Steemers, K. (2003), 'Energy and the City: Density, Buildings and Transport', *Energy and Buildings* 35, 3–14.

Stewart, M. (1999), 'Local Action to Counter Exclusion', in Policy Action Team 17 (2000) *Joining it up Locally The Evidence Base*, 13–78, London, DETR.

Stubbs, M. (2002), 'Car Parking and Residential Development: Sustainability, Design and Planning Policy, and Public Perceptions of Parking Provision', *Journal of Urban Design* 7:2, 213–37.

Sustainable Development Commission (collective author) (2006), *Stock Take*, London, SDC.

—— (2007), *Building Houses or Creating Communities?*, London, SDC.

Sutcliffe, A. (ed.) (1974), *Multi-storey Living – the British Working Class Experience*, London, Croom Helm.

Suttles, G. D. (1972), 'The Defended Neighborhood', in Suttles, G. D. (1972) *The Social Construction of Communities,* Chicago, University of Chicago Press.

Swenarton, M. (1981), *Homes fit for Heroes*, London, Heinemann Educational.

Swyngedouw, E., Moulaert, F. and Rodriguez, A. (2002), 'Neoliberal Urbanization in Europe: Large-scale Urban Development Projects and the New Urban Policy', *Antipode* 34:3, 542–77.

Syms, P. (1997), *Contaminated Land : The Practice and Economics of Redevelopment*, Oxford, Blackwell Science.

—— (2002), *Land, Development and Design*, Oxford, Blackwell.

Tafuri, M. (1976), *Architecture and Utopia*, Cambridge and London, MIT Press.

Taylor, C. (1979), *Hegel and Modern Society*, Cambridge, Cambridge University Press.

Taylor, N. (Nicholas) (1973), *The Village in the City*, London, Maurice Temple Smith.

Taylor, N. (Nigel) (1998), *Urban Planning Theory since 1945*, London, Sage.

Tetlow, J. and Goss, A. (1965), *Homes, Towns and Traffic*, London, Faber and Faber.

Teubner, G. (1987), 'Juridification Concepts, Aspects, Limits, Solutions', in Teubner, G. (ed.) *Juridification of Social Spheres: A Comparative Analysis in the Areas of Labor Corporate, Antitrust and Social Welfare Law*, Berlin/New York, Walter de Gruyter, 3–48.

—— (1993), *Law as an Autopoietic System*, Oxford and Cambriudge, MA, Blackwell.

Thomas, A.D. (1986), *Housing and Urban Renewal*, London, George Allen and Unwin.

Thomas, H. (2007), 'From Radicalism to Reformism', *Planning Theory* 6:3, 332–5.

Thompson, W. (1903), *The Housing Handbook*, London, The National Housing Reform Council.

Thrift, N. (2005), 'Panicsville: Paul Virilio and the Esthetic of Disaster', *Cultural Politics* 1:3, 337–48.

Timmer, V. and Seymoar, N.-K. (2006), *The Livable City*, The World Urban Forum Vancouver Working Group, Discussion Paper, Vancouver, University of British Columbia.

Tinker A. (1984), *Staying at Home: Helping Elderly People*, London, Department of the Environment.

Titmus, R.M. (1958), *Essays in the Welfare State*, London, Unwin University Books.

Toennies, F. (1971), *On Sociology; Pure, Applied and Empirical*, translated and edited by Cahnman, W.J. and Heberle, R., Chicago, University of Chicago Press (original published in 1925).

Town and Country Planning Association (1979), *A Third Garden City Outline Prospectus*, London, T&CPA.

—— (2000), *Housing Policy Statement*, London, T&CPA.

Triggs, I.H. (1909), *Town Planning, Past, Present and Possible*, London, Methuen & Co.

Troni, L. and Kornblatt, T. (2006), *City Markets Business Location in Deprived Areas*, London, IPPR, Centre for Cities.

Tunstall, R. (2002), *Housing Density: What Do Residents Think?*, London, The East Thames Housing Group and The National Housing Federation London Branch.

Tunstall, R. and Coulter, A. (2006), *Twenty-five Years On: Twenty Estates: Turning the Tide?*, Bristol, The Policy Press.

Turner, J.F.C. (1976), *Housing by People*, London, Marion Boyars.

Turok, I. and Edge, N. (1999), 'The Jobs Gap in Britain's Cities', *Findings* 569, York, Joseph Rowntree Foundation.

Turok, I., Kearns, A., Fitch, D., Flint, J., McKenzie, C. and Abbotts, J. (2006), *State of the English Cities – Social Cohesion*, London, Department for Communities and Local Government.

UNECE – United Nations Economic Commission for Europe (1969), *Proceedings of the Seminar on the Management, Maintenance and Modernisation of Housing*, organised by the Committee on Housing, Building and Planning of UNECE and held in Warsaw, Poland (report ST/ECE/HOU/38: Vol. 1), New York, United Nations.

Unwin, R. (1902), *Cottage Plans and Commonsense*, Fabian Tract No. 109, London, The Fabian Society.

—— (1909), *Town Planning in Practice*, London, T. Fisher Unwin.

—— (1912), *Nothing Gained from Overcrowding!*, London: Garden Cities and Town Planning Association.

URBED (collective author) (2004a), *Neighbourhood Revival: Towards more Sustainable Suburbs in the South East*, Report for the South East of England Regional Assembly.

—— (2004b), *Tomorrow's Suburbs: Tools for Making London's Suburbs more Sustainable*, Report for for the Greater London Authority, the London Development Agency, the Association of London Government and Transport for London.

—— (2005), *Spreading the Benefits of Town and City Centre Renewal: Literature and Trends Review*, London, URBED.

UTC – Urban Task Force (Collective author) (1999), *Final Report towards an Urban Renaissance, London*, Department of the Environment, Transport and the Regions, E&FN Spon.

Venturi, R. (1976), 'A House is more than a Home', *Progressive Architecture*, August, 62–7.

Virilio, P. (2000), 'The Overexposed City', in Hays, M. (ed.) *Architectural Theory since 1968*, Cambridge, MA, MIT Press, 542–550) (French original 1984).

—— (2005), *City of Panic*, Oxford, Berg.

Vivian, H. (1912), 'Garden Cities, Housing and Town Planning', *The Quarterly Review* CCX:VI.

Wallace, A. (2004), *Understanding Local Housing Markets? The Need for a Complementary Institutional Approach*, York, Centre for Housing Policy, University of York.

Walters, D. (2007), *Designing Community: Charrettes, Masterplans and Form-based Codes*, Oxford, Elsevier/Architectural Press.

Ward, C. (1976), *Housing: An Anarchist Approach*, London, Freedom Press.

Ward, S. (2004), *Planning and Urban Change* (second edition) London, Sage. (first edition 1994).

Warr, M. (1990), 'Dangerous Situations: Social Context and Fear of Victimization', *Social Forces* 68, 891–907.

Webster, C. (2001a), 'Gated Cities of Tomorrow', *Town Planning Review* 72:2, 149–70.

—— (2001b), 'Contractual Agreements and Neighbourhood Evolution', *Planning and Markets* 4:1.

—— (2002), 'Property Rights and the Public Realm: Gates, Green Belts and Gemeinschaft', *Environment and Planning B* 29:3, 397–412.

—— (2005), 'The New Institutional Economics and the Evolution of Modern Planning: Insights, Issues and Lessons', *Town Planning Review* 76:4, 455–84.

Werner, K. (1991), 'Fragmentation and Juncture', *Architecture et Comportement/ Architecture and Behaviour* 7:4, 407–14.

Westminster City Council (1980), *Living at Higher Densities*, London, Westminster City Council Planning Department.

While, A. (2003), 'Locating Art Worlds: London and the Making of Young British art', *Area* 35:3, 251–63.

White, L.E. (1950), *Community or Chaos, Housing Estates and their Social Problems*, London, The National Council of Social Service.

Whitehand, J.W.R. and Carr, C.M.H. (1999), 'England's Interwar Suburban Landscape: Myth and Reality', *Journal of Historical Geography* 24:4, 483–501.

Whitehead, C. (2007), 'Planning Policies and Affordable Housing: England as a Successful Case Study?', *Housing Studies* 22:1, 25–44.

Whitelegg, J. and Williams, J.N. (2003), Memorandum to The United Kingdom Parliament, Select Committee on Office of the Deputy Prime Minister, Session 2002/03, *Planning for Sustainable Housing and Communities*, London House of Commons.

Wildavsky, A. (1973), 'If Planning is Everything, Maybe it's Nothing', *Policy Sciences* 4:2, 127–53.

Wilding, P. (1972), 'Towards Exchequer Subsidies for Housing 1906–1914', *Social and Economic Administration* 6:1, 3–18.

Williams, P. (2002), 'The Competent Boundary Spanner', *Public Administration* 80:1, 103–24.

Williams-Ellis, C. (1928), *England and the Octopus*, London, Geoffrey Bles.

Wilson, S. (1980), 'Vandalism and Defensible Space on London Housing Estates', in Clarke, R.G.V. and Mayhew, P. (eds) *Designing Out Crime*, Home Office Research Unit, London, HMSO.

Wolfe, de, I. (ed.) (1971), 'Civilia: The End of Sub Urban Man', *Architectural Review* 149:892, 326–408.

Wood, R. and Ravetz, J. (2000), 'Recasting the Urban Fringe', *Landscape Design* 294, 13–16.

Woodford, G., Williams, K. and Hill, N. (1974), *The Value of Standards for the External Residential Environment*, London, the Department of the Environment, Research Report No. 6.

Wootton, B. (1934), *Plan or no Plan*, London, Victor Gollancz.

—— (1945), *Freedom under Planning*, London, G. Allen & Unwin.

World Commission on Environment and Development (1987), *Our Common Future*, Oxford, Oxford University Press.

Worsdall, F. (1979), *The Tenement: A Way of Life*, Edinburgh, Chambers.

Wren et al. (2001), *Space Standards in Dwellings*, Edinburgh, Scottish Executive Central Research Unit.

Yelling, T. (2000), 'The Incidence of Slum Clearance in England and Wales, 1955–85', *Urban History* 27:2, 234–54.

Yiftachel, O. (2001), 'Introduction: Outlining the Power of Planning', in Yiftachel, O., Little, J. Hedgcock, D. and Alexander, I. (eds) *The Power of Planning*, London: Kluwer Academic Publishers, 1–20.

Young, C. (1999), *The Smithdown Road Pilot 'Alleygating' Project. Evaluated on Behalf of the Safer Merseyside Partnership*, University of Liverpool: Department of Civic Design report.

Young, M. and Lemos, G., (1997), *The Communities we have Lost and can Regain*, London, Lemos and Crane.

Young, R. (1997), 'A House is a Machine for Living in?', in Bazlington, C. and Bartlett, K. (eds) *Rethinking Housebuilding*, York, The Joseph Rowntree Foundation.

Žižek, S (1999), *The Ticklish Subject: Absent Centre of Political Ontology*, London, Verso.

—— (2003), 'General Introduction', in Žižek, S. (ed.) *Jacques Lacan: Critical Evaluations in Cultural Theory*, London, Routledge, 1–3.

Zukin, S. (1989), *Loft Living Culture and Capital in Urban Change*, New Brunswick, NJ, Rutgers University Press.

Index